# Behavioral Operational Research

Martin Kunc • Jonathan Malpass • Leroy White
Editors

# Behavioral Operational Research

## Theory, Methodology and Practice

*Editors*
Martin Kunc
Warwick Business School
University of Warwick
Coventry, United Kingdom

Leroy White
Warwick Business School
University of Warwick
Coventry, United Kingdom

Jonathan Malpass
BT Technology, Service & Operations
Martlesham Heath, United Kingdom

ISBN 978-1-137-53549-8      ISBN 978-1-137-53551-1   (eBook)
DOI 10.1057/978-1-137-53551-1

Library of Congress Control Number: 2016936719

Printed on acid-free paper

This Palgrave Macmillan imprint is published by Springer Nature
The registered company is Macmillan Publishers Ltd. London

# Introduction to the Book

Students in university courses on management often find disciplinary silos as tall and impregnable as the silos in many corporations. Most operational research and management science (OR/MS) courses focus on the 'physics' of factories and other systems and teach how to find optimal policies; people play little role in these models, and where they appear they are usually assumed to be the perfectly rational, self-interested maximizers central to economics. At the same time, courses in organizational behavior, human resources, and leadership focus on the foibles and failings of humans in social settings, where decisions are imperfect and biased; learning is slow or absent; people are swayed by social pressures; and values, norms and emotions play a central role. In these courses, however, there is little role for the physics of complex operations. The result is contradiction, confusion, and a self-reinforcing pathology: How often have you been told, 'That's a marketing problem,' 'That's an operations problem,' 'That's a human resources problem,' and 'Whatever you do, don't bring your personal problems to work'? But we don't have marketing problems, operations problems, financial problems and people problems; we don't have workplace issues, personal problems and family problems. We just have problems. We create these boundaries and impose these categories on the world to simplify its overwhelming complexity. Some boundaries are necessary and inevitable. But all too often, the invisible boundaries in our minds cut off critical feedbacks, deny us the insights of people with different experience and perspectives, and breed arrogance about our ability to control nature and other people—and then our problems grow worse.

Fortunately, over the past few decades, scholars in fields including operations management, economics, organizations psychology and others have engaged in fruitful and often intense debate over core assumptions "such as rationality" and have begun to collaborate fruitfully. New fields integrating these disciplines, such as behavioral economics, behavioral finance and behavioral operations, have emerged, and their insights are being applied by firms and governments at the highest levels. Interest in understanding both human behavior in practice and how to capture it in models and analysis is growing. Experiments and theory increasingly recognize aspects of individual behavior such as decision-making heuristics and biases, bounded rationality and misperceptions of feedback, as well as the ways in which these attributes of human behavior both shape and are shaped by the physical and institutional systems in which we are embedded.

Behavioral issues in operations management and OR are especially relevant today. The global economic crisis that began in 2007–8 revealed important interactions among organizational failure, weak policy and strategy, and our lack of understanding of the ways our organizational processes and operational systems, from financial markets to global supply chains, actually operate. Behaviorally realistic models have never been more important.

Students and practitioners of OR need to understand the implications of behavioral OR. How can organizations incorporate behavioral factors to model the impact of an intervention? What are the implications for models and management if the all-too-human people in organizations use decision-making shortcuts and heuristics and suffer from biases? What are the implications of behavioral issues for the OR toolkit and training?

This book, *Behavioral Operational Research,* is a timely look at behavioral matters in organizational life. The book does not promote behavioral OR as a magic potion for today's organizational ills. Instead, the book surveys critical current issues that researchers, students and practitioners are tackling as they break down the silos across disciplines and integrate models of processes and systems with realistic assumptions about the behavior of the people who work in, manage and design those systems.

John Sterman
Jay W. Forrester Professor of Management,
MIT Sloan School of Management,
Massachusetts Institute of Technology,
Cambridge, MA, USA

# Preface

This book is a collection of articles on Behavioral Operational Research. It arose from a number of events and conferences highlighting a resurgence of interest in Operational Research (OR) and the behavioral sciences. It was clear from these events that behavior, its representation in models and its effects on how users respond to models, is attracting the attention of OR researchers and practitioners. This current growth in interest, in our view, also stems from the long observed gap in *behavioral issues* in a wide sense, coupled with the emergence of a set of methods that promise the potential of being able to address behavioral concerns. While the field of OR has been aware of the relevance of behavioral issues for a long time now, it might be said to have danced around them. So, the interest in behavior is not new, nor does the resurgence of interest represent a "revolution". What may be novel is the emergence of a set of ideas and methods from other areas, such as economics and psychology, that may allow a more rigorous approach to addressing behavioral issues *within* the OR field, perhaps with more focus on the use of laboratory and field experiments of individual and team decision-making. In particular, based on related concerns in economics and psychology, we are witnessing developments in the field as being shaped through the integration of insights from psychological research into OR theory and methods, especially concerning human judgment and decision-making under uncertainty and establishing more experimental approaches as a tool in empirical OR analysis, especially in the study of group behavior. Equally, we think that advances in computing as applied to the social sciences, particularly the increasing ability to model assemblies of interacting intelligent *agents* is opening up new avenues for research that Behavioral OR can exploit.

Our aim for the book is to bring coherence to the range of existing activities in this important area and help to identify and encourage further research projects and endeavours. The book is designed to make access to the latest research on behavioral OR reachable to a wide range of interested readers. In so doing, we have attempted to organize the materials in such a way as to appeal to both researchers and practitioners. Thus, the book is organized to cover broadly "Theory", "Methods" and "Practice" perspectives. Within each of these sections the articles presented aim to cover themes relating to a simple logic: "behavior *with* models", "behavior *in* models" and "behavior *beyond* models". These refer to models of human activity systems that incorporate behavioral factors, models of human decision-making, cognitive factors, and accounts of organizational and social norms and control, with an orientation around the effects of behavioral and cognitive factors on the activity of analysis and modeling itself and on the communication of results that affect its impact. The means by which the book is organized should therefore make it possible for the reader to establish an informed view of the current state of the art in this important area. It is worth pointing out that the choice of material is not meant to be comprehensive and exhaustive. There are many theories and methods that are not covered by the materials presented. However, one of the great advantages of the book, from our point of view, is that readers will be drawn to some of the ideas and concepts presented and will be able to pursue lines of reasoning from the extensive list of readings that each of the contributors have drawn on. We also feel that readers may be able to establish an informed view of what each of the ideas and methods claim or do. It will not convert the reader into a skilled expert in a particular idea or method. But, it should enable her or him to follow up on their interest through appropriate means or otherwise.

The book is organized in four parts. Part I: Theory begins with Engaging with Behavioral OR: On Methods, Actors and Praxis, which provides an introduction to Behavioral OR. The next three chapters, Behavior with Models: The Role of Psychological Heuristics in OR, Behavior in Models: A Framework for Representing Human Behavior and Behavior Beyond the Model are mostly theoretical and intend to provide frameworks to embed behavior with, in and beyond models.

Part II: Methods aims to show some of the diverse methods used to address behavioral issues in OR. The six chapters are organized from "hard", mathematical and experimental, approaches depicting behavior to more "soft" approaches. The section begins with a study of queuing and cellular automata in Simulation and Laboratory Experiments: Exploring Self-Organizing Behavior in a Collective Choice Model. Chapter 6, Misperception of Behavioral Operations and Bodies of Knowledge looks at System Dynamics presents a study on supply chain dynamics using System Dynamics and experimentation and Chap. 7 introduces agent-based models—Agent-based Models and Behavioral OR. The next chapter in the section, Modeling Behavioral Decision Making: Creation and Representation of Judgment, continues to move along the hard-soft spectrum and Chap. 9, Big Data and Behavior in OR: Towards a "Smart OR", examines how analytical techniques can be used to extract behavioral insight from Big Data. The final two chapters in this section introduce two "soft OR" techniques; in Chap. 10, the role of facilitation on reducing biases in scenarios is discussed in Behavioral Issues in the Practical Application of Scenario Thinking: Cognitive Biases, Effective Group Facilitation and Overcoming Business-as-Usual Thinking, and group model building is the subject of Chap. 12, Group Model Building and Behavior: Case Study.

Part III: Practice offers five relevant examples from OR practice in which behavior has a key role in the performance of the models and the future use of the insights from the models. The first chapter in this section, Overview: Behavioral Operational Research in Practice, provides a brief literature review of the subject and highlights the breadth of studies that have been undertaken. The next chapters describe examples drawn from a wide variety of industries and organizations and discuss many different methods. Chapter 13, Healthcare: Human Behavior in Simulation Models, demonstrates how simulation methods can be used in practice. A framework for carrying out behavioral studies is described in Chap. 14,

Service Operations: Behavioral Operational Research in BT, and Chap. 15 provides an example of Big Data analytics, Smart Cities: Big Data and Behavioral OR. The last two examples of behavioral OR in practice cover two soft OR approaches. Chapter 16, Mergers and Acquisitions: Modeling Decision Making in Integration Projects, discusses how to model behavior and how models behave dealing with strategic issues and Chap. 17, Supporting Strategy: Behavioral Influences on Resource Conceptualization Processes, examines the impact of behavioral factors in the development of strategies.

The final chapter of the book, The Past, Present and Futures of Behavioral Operational Research, offers a review of behavioral OR and presents a view of the future, arguing that incorporating behavior into OR projects is the most important aspect of the development of the subject.

We have endeavoured to ensure that the book appeals to both academics and practitioners. We are aware it could also appeal to a number of other audiences, in that it could be a resource for those already immersed in the discipline, and it could also be an invaluable source to those who don't yet know much about the subject. As such, there is no requirement for any particular level of mathematical preparation, but there are some mathematical treatments of some of the material.

Leroy White
Jonathan Malpass
Martin Kunc

# Acknowledgements

First, we want to thank all of the contributors to this book, which would not have been possible without the support and encouragement of all the authors. Through this joint effort, our enormous admiration for them and their work has grown even greater, and it has been a tremendous pleasure to work with them.

Second, we are indebted to several institutions for their support as this book grew from an idea into a reality. In particular, we thank the Operational Research Society, UK, for their continuing support and their wide set of actions aimed at raising the profile of behavioral sciences in OR in recent years. We are also grateful for the support from our own institutions, which were flexible in allowing us to pursue this project.

Last, but certainly not least, we are indebted to Palgrave, and in particular to Josephine Taylor for her patience in dealing with our many inquiries, as well as their anonymous expert reviewers for their encouragement, insights and feedback in refining this book. Finally, any errors are, of course, our own.

# Contents

# About the Editors

**Martin Kunc** is Associate Professor of Management Science at Warwick Business School, University of Warwick. He has a PhD in Decision Science from the University of London. His research interests are in the area of strategic planning, systems modeling and managerial decision-making, having published articles in diverse journals such as *Journal of the Operational Research Society, Strategic Management Journal, Management Decision,* and *Systemic Practice and Action Research.* He was previously a consultant at Arthur Andersen and an independent consultant with projects in the media, pharmaceuticals, financial services, consumer goods, and the cement and wine industries. He is a member of the Operational Research Society, Strategic Management Society, System Dynamics Society, and Arthur Andersen Alumni. He is a System Dynamics expert modeller, a member of the board and co-organiser of conferences for the Operational Research Society (UK), and a co-organiser of streams at conferences such as EURAM, IFORS, OR, ISDC.

**Jonathan Malpass** is a Principal Researcher at British Telecommunications. He has a PhD in Multivariate Statistics from the University of Portsmouth. His primary research area is Business Transformation and he has extensive experience in understanding employee behavior, how employees interact with systems, incentivisation, Lean and Six Sigma philosophies, and employee engagement and morale, working primarily with field-based engineering teams. He has supervised Operational Research students for both PhD and Masters degrees and has published his work in several edited books. He is a member of the Operational Research Society (UK).

**Leroy White** is Professor of Operational Research and Management Science at Warwick Business School, University of Warwick. His main research interests are management science/operational research, problem structuring methods, social network analysis, strategic partnerships, large group decision-making. He has worked with a range of clients including the Department of Health, local health authorities, health trusts, the BBC and the voluntary sector in both the UK and abroad. He has published over 100 papers in journals such as *The Leadership Quarterly, Organization Studies,* and the *European Journal of OR,* on the process of operational research, statistical social networks, systems thinking, and large group processes. He has also had a book published jointly with Ann Taket called *Partnerships and Participation: Decision-making in the Multiagency setting.* His current funded research work includes ESRC KTP with Barclays Bank, a British Academy award for a field experiment with the BBC, and ESRC Capacity Building Cluster work on the impact of the third sector.

# Notes on Contributors

**Ann van Ackere** is Professor of Decision Sciences at HEC, University of Lausanne, where she has been academic director of the PhD, MBA and EMBA programmes. Her research focuses on quantitative modeling, with a special interest in queueing, energy policy and healthcare. She has published in *Management Science, Operational Research, Health Care Management Science, Energy Policy* and *Interfaces*.

**Santiago Arango-Aramburo** is Full Professor and Director of the Decision Science group at the Universidad Nacional de Colombia. His research focuses on energy markets and dynamic complex systems through simulation and experimental economics. His papers have appeared in *Energy Economics, Energy Policy, Utilities Policy,* the *Journal of Economic Behavior & Organization,* and *Socio-Economic Planning,* among others.

**Shanie Atkinson** is a PhD candidate at UNSW Australia Business School where her research focuses on mergers and acquisitions integration. She also has considerable M&A industry experience from roles in investment banking, private equity and strategy consulting. Shanie has a Bachelor of Commerce, MBA, and a Masters of Philosophy.

**Sally C. Brailsford** is Professor of Management Science at the University of Southampton with over 25 years' experience of Health OR. She is chair of the EURO Working Group on OR Applied to Health Services, co-chair of the OR Society's Special Interest Group on Behavioral OR, and an Editor-in-Chief of the OR Society's new journal *Health Systems*.

**Stephanie Bryson** is an independent management consultant operating in Financial Services and the Public Sector. Her background includes roles in strategy and project management. Stephanie is currently undertaking a DBA, specializing in scenario planning.

**Katharina Burger** is Lecturer in Project Management at Portsmouth Business School, which she joined after completing her PhD at the University of Bristol. Her research interests lie in the area of behavioral and soft operational research, especially in understanding problem structuring methods interventions.

**L. Alberto Franco** is Professor of Management Sciences at Loughborough University. His research focuses on the use of facilitated modeling to support group decision-making. Together with Raimo Hämäläinen, he has been at the forefront of the behavioral OR movement in Europe; they recently co-edited a special issue of *European Journal of Operational Research* in this area.

**Michael Shayne Gary** is associate professor at UNSW Australia Business School where he teaches Strategic Management across MBA and Executive Programs. His research in behavioral strategy focuses on the dynamics of firm growth and includes corporate diversification and mergers and acquisitions. Shayne received his PhD at London Business School.

**Paulo Gonçalves** is Associate Professor of Management and Director of the Master in Humanitarian Logistics and Management (MASHLM) at the University of Lugano, Switzerland; and Research Affiliate at the MIT Sloan School of Management. He obtained his PhD in System Dynamics from MIT Sloan and his MSc in Technology and Policy from MIT.

**Andrew Greasley** lectures in Operations Management and Simulation Modeling at Aston University. His research area is simulation modeling. He has over 15 years' experience of building simulation models for industrial clients in the private and public sectors, and he is the author of the books *Building a Simulation Capability in the Organisation* and *Simulation Modeling for Business*.

**Megan Grime** is a PhD student in the Strategy and Organisation Department of the Strathclyde Business School. She holds an MSc in Behavioral and Economic Sciences as well as a BA in both Psychology and Philosophy. Her research is mainly focussed on biases in the decision-making process and risky behavior.

**Raimo P. Hämäläinen** is Director of the Systems Analysis Laboratory, Aalto University, Finland. His research covers game and decision theory, multicriteria optimization, environmental decision-making and systems intelligence. He co-authored the paper which introduced the term Behavioral Operational Research in 2013. He is recipient of the Edgeworth-Pareto Award of the MCDM Society.

**Kenneth Kyunghyun Huh** is currently a consultant in IMS Consulting Group, where he provides strategic advice to the healthcare industry. He was awarded his PhD in Warwick Business School, where he researched resource-based strategy processes. His research interest is in group-based strategizing, resource conceptualisation, and strategic reaction to environmental shifts.

**Konstantinos V. Katsikopoulos** is Deputy Director of the Center for Adaptive Behavior and Cognition at the Max Planck Institute for Human Development. He works on the intersection of behavioral science and operational research, with emphasis on decision-making. He has worked with government and businesses on complex problems in economics, management and health.

**Erik R. Larsen** is Professor of Management at Universita della Svizzera Italia in Lugano, Switzerland. He previously held appointments at Cass Business School, University of Bologna and London Business School. His main areas of interest include operations management, organizational theory and energy policy.

**Adarsh Murthy** currently works in the industry as a strategy consultant, leading change initiatives and strategy projects. After completing his full-time MBA from the London Business School, his interest in the psychology of decision-making processes and the implications for day-to-day business decisions led him to pursue his DBA in scenario thinking.

**Chris Owen** leads the Systems Modeling and Simulation Team at Aston Business School. His research is in the area of supply chain performance improvement using modeling and simulation, and he has a particular interest in the challenges of modeling complex systems and representing human behavior in simulation models.

**Duncan A. Robertson** is a lecturer in management sciences at Loughborough University. He is a Fellow of St Catherine's College, Oxford. Before undertaking his DPhil at Saïd Business School, he qualified as a Chartered Accountant with KPMG. He originally trained as a physicist at Imperial College London.

**Etiënne A. J. A. Rouwette** is Chair for Research and Intervention Methodology at the Nijmegen School of Management. His research focuses on interventions such as facilitated modeling and its effect on behavior. He is the 2016 President of the System Dynamics Society and a reviewer for amongst others the *European Journal of Operational Research*.

**Geoff Royston** is a recent President of the OR Society and a former chair of the UK Government Operational Research Service. He was head of strategic analysis and operational research in the Department of Health for England, where for almost two decades he was the professional lead for a large group of health analysts.

**Sebastian Villa** is a PhD candidate in Operations Management at the University of Lugano, Switzerland and a Visiting Researcher at the University of Texas at Dallas. He is currently focusing on inventory and capacity models for understanding behavioral aspects in supply chain operations.

**George Wright** is a professor at Strathclyde Business School. He has published widely on scenario thinking in a range of journals. His most recent book is *Scenario Thinking: Practical Approaches to the Future* (published by Palgrave Macmillan in 2011), which he co-authored with George Cairns.

**Mike Yearworth** is Reader in Systems Engineering in the Faculty of Engineering at the University of Bristol. His research focuses on the methodological issues of problem structuring in engineering organizations. He is currently investigating the non-codified use of problem structuring methods and the ethical questions arising from problematizing the role of engineering in society.

# List of Figures

# List of Tables

# Part I

## Theory

# 1

# Engaging with Behavioral Operational Research: On Methods, Actors and Praxis

## L. Alberto Franco and Raimo P. Hämäläinen

## 1.1 Introduction

In many other disciplines, attention to the study of behavioral issues becomes prominent when their theoretical core has reached maturity. This has happened in economics (Camerer and Lowenstein 2003), finance (Bruce 2010), accounting (Birnberg et al. 2007) and strategic management (Powell et al. 2011), as well as in cognate disciplines such as operations management (Bendoly et al. 2015), decision and Game Theory (Camerer 2003; Von Winterfeldt and Edwards 1986) and environmental modeling (Hämäläinen 2015). The development of the discipline of

L.A. Franco (✉)
School of Business and Economics, Loughborough University, Loughborough, Leicestershire LE11 3TU, UK

R.P. Hämäläinen
Systems Analysis Laboratory, Aalto University, P.O. Box 11100, 00076 Aalto, Finland

© The Editor(s) (if applicable) and The Author(s) 2016    **3**
M. Kunc et al. (eds.), *Behavioral Operational Research*,
DOI 10.1057/978-1-137-53551-1_1

Operational Research (OR) is similar, and thus the current resurgence of interest in the behavioral perspective (Franco and Hämäläinen 2016) is not surprising. We use the term *resurgence* deliberately: attention to the non-mathematical and behavioral aspects of the OR profession can be traced back to past debates in the 1960s and 1970s within mainstream OR (e.g. Ackoff 1977; Churchman 1970; Dutton and Walton 1964; Lawrence 1966) and in the 1980s and 1990s within systems thinking (e.g. Senge and Sterman 1992) and in the specialized domain of soft OR (e.g. Jackson et al. 1989). Behavioral issues received less attention in subsequent years. For example, they are hardly mentioned in the 50th anniversary issues of *Operational Research* (Wein 2002) and the *Journal of the Operational Research Society* (Brailsford et al. 2009). However, as the OR discipline attends to the improvement of *human* problem solving and decision making in practice, a return to behavioral concerns within the discipline was in some ways foreseeable. What motivates this renewed attention to behavioral issues in OR is the recognition that developing technically correct and valid models is not enough; we also need to design model-supported interventions by taking into account behavioral factors that could enhance or hinder their effectiveness.

The latest evidence of the revival of what is now known as *behavioral OR* (Hämäläinen et al. 2013), or BOR for short, can be found in the special issue of the *European Journal of Operational Research* that focused on BOR (Franco and Hämäläinen 2016). In addition, high levels of participation in BOR streams at international conferences, the creation of a BOR national interest group sponsored by the UK OR Society[1] and the launch of a BOR website portal hosted by Aalto University[2] are all clear testimony to the closer attention that the OR community is increasingly showing to the behavioral perspective. Noticeable in this return to BOR is a commitment to *empirically* examine what people actually do within a system or when engaged in OR-supported processes, for not doing so would limit the development of relevant theories that could help advance explanations linking the key behavioral dimensions that shape the conduct of OR in practice. Such behavioral-based explanations would go

---

[1] https://www.theorsociety.com/Pages/SpecialInterest/Behaviouralor.aspx.
[2] bor.aalto.fi.

beyond pure description and have a prescriptive orientation concerned with improving the use of OR in practice (Franco and Hämäläinen 2016), including the responsible and ethical use of OR-supported processes (Le Menestrel and Van Wassenhove 2004, 2009; Ormerod and Ulrich 2013).

Two main streams of work that have generated attention within BOR can be identified. The first stream has a long history within academic OR and concentrates on the use of the OR approach to model human behavior in complex settings. For example, there is long standing tradition of modeling behavior in decision analysis (e.g. French et al. 2009) and System Dynamics (e.g. Sterman 2000). The second stream investigates how behavior affects or is affected by OR model–supported processes in individual, group and organizational contexts. Although still relatively under researched, this stream is receiving increasing attention from both OR academics and practitioners, particularly in Europe (e.g. Ackermann and Eden 2011; Amini et al. 2012; Brailsford and Schmidt 2003; Franco 2013; Hämäläinen et al. 2013; Morton and Fasolo 2009; Ormerod 2014a; Rouwette et al. 2011; White 2009). While different in focus, the two streams share the common goal of designing and deploying OR-supported interventions to improve organizational systems and operations.

Against the above background, we propose in this introductory chapter an agenda for driving the development of BOR as a legitimate subdiscipline within OR, by means of an integrative framework based on the three interdependent concepts of OR methods, OR actors and OR praxis. The framework is intended as an organizing device for the conduct of empirical BOR studies, highlighting different analytical foci and points of entry into the study of behavioral issues in the practice of OR.

The chapter is structured as follows. In the next section we draw on practice theories within the social and organizational sciences to introduce the three central concepts of OR methods, OR actors and OR praxis. Next, we link these three concepts together within an integrative framework intended to organize and guide the conduct of empirical BOR studies. The framework is illustrated with exemplars from the developing BOR literature that increase or challenge our current understandings of OR practice and its impacts. We end the chapter with a discussion of the implications of the behavioral perspective for advancing the OR discipline.

## 1.2   OR Methods, OR Actors, OR Praxis

In this section we draw upon the practice traditions within the social and organization sciences (Feldman and Orlikowski 2011; Jarzabkowski et al. 2007; Nicolini 2012; Reckwitz 2002; Schatzki et al. 2001; Turner 1994; Whittington 2006) and in particular the work of Richard Whittington within strategy research (e.g. Whittington 2003; Whittington 2006, 2011), with a view to offering an integrative framework that highlights different analytic foci and entry points for the conduct of empirical BOR studies. Three important questions derived from practice theories are particularly relevant to the BOR perspective, and they underpin the central elements in our framework. Specifically, when examining an OR-supported process using a behavioral lens, we need to address the following questions: (*i*) What guides behavior in the process? (*ii*) Whose behavior counts in the process? and (*iii*) How behavior is enacted in the process? Importantly, answers to these questions can explain the impacts that are achieved (or not) from the application of OR. We turn to each of these questions below.

What guides behavior in an OR-supported process are the *methods* used by those engaged with that process. OR methods provide the resources through which people are able to interact in order to accomplish OR-supported work. At a basic level, then, methods include the range of OR techniques and tools available to support interactions in an OR-supported process. However, our conceptualization of OR methods goes beyond techniques and tools; it also includes standardized routines for building and using models; approaches to communicating with and about models; and norms and procedures for intervention design, data collection, training and teaching and embedding OR-supported processes in organizational routines. These are important but often over-looked aspects of the methods of OR, and they too provide a source of guidance for actual problem solving and decision making interactions.

From a BOR perspective, the role or identity of those participating in an OR-supported process also matters. Here we adopt the general category of *actors* to refer to those individuals who—acting in isolation or as part of a team—design, implement, or engage with OR-supported processes. Thus, OR actors include not just mainstream OR practitioners (e.g. modellers, analysts, facilitators, consultants) who are at the center of any OR-supported work but also others who participate in OR-related activity as clients, sponsors, experts or simply users. All these can be seen as OR actors whose behavior is critical to the success or failure of OR-supported processes. Indeed, actors' behaviors matter because their effects and those of the OR methods used are intertwined in practice.

How behavior is enacted in an OR-supported process is also important from a BOR perspective, because it has to do with what OR actors actually *do* with OR methods in situ. We adopt the term *praxis* to conceptualize this process, namely, all the various streams of actual OR activity carried out by OR actors. Although actual OR praxis involves dynamic flows of activity taking place at different organizational levels (Mitchell 1993), behavioral aspects of OR praxis are most visible within specific episodes (cf. Luhmann 1995) of OR-related activity, such as modeling sessions, meetings, presentations and workshops of varying duration, frequency and sequence. Examining actual behavior in OR praxis has the benefit of highlighting potential gaps between espoused or *textbook* OR practice and what actually happens on the ground.

Answers to the above questions can provide a more holistic picture of the role and impact of behavior-related issues in OR-supported processes. To find possible answers, we need to investigate a wider range of OR methods in context, attend to who engages in them and closely examine how they are actually used in practice. In the next section we build on our preceding discussion to introduce an integrative framework that links the three central concepts of OR methods, OR actors and OR praxis to the context and outcomes of OR practice.

## 1.3    An Integrative Framework to Study Behavior in OR

Figure 1.1 shows an integrative framework for the study of behavioral issues in OR-supported processes. The framework highlights three key interrelated concepts of OR methods, OR actors and OR praxis (cf.

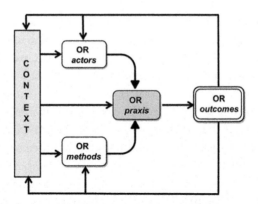

**Fig. 1.1**   An integrative framework for the study of behavior in OR

Whittington 2006) already introduced above. Our framework also makes clear that OR methods are available for use by OR actors when they engage in OR praxis. Although shown in separate boxes, methods, actors and praxis are not discrete entities operating in a vacuum but highly intertwined within their organizational context. Thus, OR methods cannot be separated from the actors who use them, and OR methods can have material existence only within OR praxis. Furthermore, the framework shows that the impact of OR methods on outcomes cannot be understood without taking into account the behavior of OR actors and that this will be particularly salient within given episodes of OR praxis. Finally, the framework underlines the potential feedback effects of OR outcomes on the actors and how they carry out their praxis, on the OR methods themselves and on the organizational context within which actors, methods and praxis are all embedded.

Our framework contrasts with that proposed recently by White (2016), which is offered as a device for thinking about behavior across a three-dimensional typology of OR interventions. This typology is theoretically derived from alternative configurations of the values taken by the dimensions of *OR user* (individual/group), *issue divergence* (high/low) and *model use* (instrumental/symbolic). Thus, behavioral issues pertaining to individual–low divergence–instrumental interventions will be different to those pertaining to group–high issue divergence–symbolic interventions. While useful as a heuristic device, the dimensions in White's framework would be difficult to use to guide practical BOR studies. For example, whilst there may be instances where models are indeed used in purely instrumental or symbolic terms, model use can vary considerably across OR interventions and it has been shown that models can in fact show both uses within the same type of intervention (e.g. Franco and Lord 2011). The elements in our proposed framework do not represent binary conceptualizations, as in White's framework but, instead, allow a range of empirical possibilities intended to facilitate the conduct of empirical BOR studies in both the field and the lab.

From a behavioral perspective, any BOR study will inevitably link all three intertwined concepts, methods, actors and praxis, to OR outcomes. Empirically, however, this can be challenging due to the complex nature of the relationship among these elements. One way to get round this issue is to choose one dominant area of empirical focus by foregrounding only one of the three central concepts while backgrounding the others, and then to examine the link between the chosen focus and OR outcomes. It is to a wider consideration of such an empirical approach that we now turn.

### 1.3.1 Focus on OR Methods

Perhaps unsurprisingly, in most OR studies the focus is on OR methods and the outcomes achieved from using them. Typically, the methods of interest are modeling techniques and models. From a BOR perspective, however, a major concern is to examine the extent to which OR methods produce *behavior-related* outcomes, such as changes in cognition (e.g. learning), attitudes or interactions. Current empirical evidence of the methods–outcomes link is relatively strong only for some OR methods, such as group model building (e.g. Rouwette et al. 2002; Schilling et al. 2007; Scott et al. 2016), and thus more BOR studies with this choice of focus are needed.

It is important to clarify that a focus on OR methods does not necessarily imply that the methods must capture behavior explicitly. Hence, for example, an optimization model that does not take into account any behavioral considerations would still be of interest from a BOR perspective, as long as the study connects the model to behavior-related outcomes. Likewise, OR methods that capture behavior explicitly by drawing on experience or formal theory (e.g. Brailsford et al. 2012) are not in themselves of interest to BOR unless they are linked to behavior-related outcomes.

Methods other than modeling techniques and models should also be studied in relation to OR outcomes. As discussed in the previous section, OR methods also include norms and standardized procedures for designing interventions, eliciting data, training and teaching and communicating with and about models and even for selling or embedding OR in organizations. For example, scripts for running modeling workshops have been developed (e.g. Ackermann et al. 2011; Hovmand et al. 2012) and their link to behavioral outcomes examined (e.g. Scott et al. 2013; Tavella and Papadopoulos 2015b). With respect to methods for eliciting data, there is a long tradition in decision analysis and risk analysis of using of standard protocols to produce unbiased expert judgments of probabilities and preferences (for a recent review, see Montibeller and Von Winterfeldt 2015). The impact of training methods using structured procedures (e.g. Carlson and Bond 2006; Ellspermann et al. 2007) and games (Graham et al. 1992; Lane 1995; Morecroft 1988) has a long history too (e.g. Hartley et al. 1979) and is typically analyzed via experimentation (Bakken et al. 1992; Capelo and Dias 2009). By contrast, the behavioral impacts of OR teaching methods have not been the focus of empirical research, although shared experiences and reflections about different teaching methods used in the classroom are available (e.g. Kunc 2012; Mingers and Rosenhead 2012; O'Brien 2004; Pierre Brans and Macharis 1997; Wright et al. 2009). Finally, the impact of approaches to communicating with and about models, selling or embedding OR are perhaps the areas that have received the least empirical attention to date, with some exceptions (e.g. Brailsford et al. 2013; Franco et al. 2004; Hämäläinen et al. 2013).

Other under researched areas with a focus on the methods–outcomes dimensions include the multiple interdependencies that OR methods can have in practice. The effect of a particular method (e.g. a model) in practice can vary according to the presence or absence of other methods (e.g. modeling script, communication protocol). In addition, the introduction of new OR methods and their behavioral effects offers further research possibilities. For example, Internet technologies are generating new methods of expert judgment elicitation (e.g. Hämäläinen et al. 2010). Overall, the adoption of a methods analytic focus prompts us to investigate the wider range of OR methods actually used in practice (e.g. Ahmed and Robinson 2013; O'Brien 2011; Ranyard et al. 2015); how method use changes over time (e.g. Fortuin and Zijlstra 2000); and, crucially for BOR, what the behavioral consequences of different use patterns are (e.g. Chung et al. 2000; O'Keefe 2016).

## 1.3.2 Focus on OR Actors

Foregrounding OR actors and their impact on outcomes offers a different choice of analytical focus that makes the behavioral dimension particularly salient. Indeed, if we were to adopt a more holistic BOR perspective then we should move beyond just OR methods to include the individuals and teams that engage with them. There is a long but sparse tradition of BOR studies that focus on particular types of OR actors and the outcomes of methods used. For example, there is a stream of research that examines the work of expert modellers (Tako 2014; Tako and Robinson 2010; Waisel et al. 2008; Willemain 1994, 1995), novice modellers (S. G. Powell and Willemain 2007; Tavella and Papadopoulos 2015b; Willemain and Powell 2007) or both (Tavella and Papadopoulos 2015a). Research focusing on other types of actors is also beginning to appear, such as studies of forecasting experts (Petropoulos et al. 2016; Syntetos et al. 2016), decision analysts (Papamichail et al. 2007), and OR consultants providing strategy support (O'Brien 2015).

Consequently, from a BOR perspective, claims about the link between OR methods and OR outcomes should be taken with caution if they do not account for the role and impact that the different OR actors involved can have, for OR actors may be more or less successful in their use of particular OR methods, depending on their level of competence and expertise (Huxham and Cropper 1994; Keys 2006; Ormerod 2008, 2014b; Wright and Bolger 1992), their cognitive style (Fasolo and Bana e Costa 2014; Franco and Meadows 2007; Franco et al. 2016) or their preferred consulting approach (Cropper 1990; Eden and Ackermann 2004; Franco and Montibeller 2010). Thus, the same OR method may lead to different outcomes when deployed, used or even sponsored by a competent and experienced actor who enjoys analysis carried out in participative fashion than by a novice actor who relies highly on intuition and prefers expert advice.

As in the case of methods, OR actors can also exhibit interdependencies that can affect outcomes. For example, the effectiveness of a modeling workshop facilitator will be contingent on who participates in the workshop: the presence or absence of a powerful and skillful actor can undercut the work of the facilitator and increase or decrease the participation of other actors, hence affecting the quality of the model. A similar argument can be made for the case of larger OR interventions. Therefore, this is an area that is worth exploring empirically, as most published accounts of OR practice tend to be positive about or downplay the impact of OR actors (Connell 2001). An empirical focus on OR actors and their impact on outcomes also can begin to unravel the feedback effects of outcomes on actors. For example, a few BOR studies have shown enduring changes in actors' mental models (Scott et al. 2013). Other long term effects on actors can be subject to empirical examination within this focus, including effects on actors' competences, status and professional relationships.

### 1.3.3   Focus on OR Praxis

At the core of the BOR perspective lies the assumption that to improve OR methods we must pay attention to *how* they are actually used by those who engage in them. As most OR practitioners will already know, the actual use of OR methods is influenced by the needs of the users and the specific contexts of use. Thus, a focus on OR praxis reminds us of the complex and *situated* dynamics of method use, which must be taken into account to avoid superficial understandings of what OR actors actually do in practice and of the critical role of these doings on generating OR outcomes. This is an area that is still relatively under explored, particularly in the field. Nevertheless, some relevant work is beginning to appear following calls to conduct fine-grained studies of the use of OR methods (e.g. Franco and Rouwette 2011; Horlick-Jones and Rosenhead 2007).

For example, Shaw et al. (2003) show how management teams using the same OR method within a workshop context develop knowledge about issues with different degrees of complexity, which affects their ability to develop in-depth understanding about those issues. Also within a workshop context, White et al. (2016) use activity theory to show how participants use mediating artifacts to wrestle with the object of a *zero carbon zone*, and they demonstrate how a shared activity system is developed to accommodate contradictions between participants' motives. On a larger scale, Ormerod (2014a) reflects on the development of the National Coal Board UK Energy model in the 1970s and 1980s and discusses how the *mangled* (Pickering 1995) intersection of OR actors and methods affected the intervention's design, deployment and outcomes.

Despite their standardization, OR methods can be used in diverse and variable ways and adapted to the uses to which they are put by those engaged with OR-supported processes, and this has particular effects on outcomes . This is a salient feature of the three works mentioned above and is also evident in the recent review of mixed-methods interventions by Howick and Ackermann (2011). However, deviations from expectations of method use do not necessarily imply bad praxis. There might be cases where skillful adaptations and improvizations in the use of OR methods can take place in specific contexts (e.g. Montibeller et al. 2009; Robinson et al. 2013), which may reveal potential OR method innovations. Therefore, the adoption of OR praxis as the analytic focus means attention is paid to the situated nature of OR method use: by examining how OR methods are enacted locally in practice, in ways that perhaps are not recognizable to the methods' originators, BOR studies can develop theories about the role of method adaptations in generating OR outcomes.

Of course, not all method adaptations or even transformations may be positive, and in this case empirical research that examines uses of methods that deviate from their standard forms can highlight areas for improvements in method use. For example, Lahtinen and Hämäläinen (2016) conducted a controlled experiment to show the emergence of path dependence in the use of the Even Swaps method[3], which they explain is

---

[3] Even Swaps method helps decision makers to find the most preferred alternative out of a set of multi-attribute alternatives (Lahtinen and Hämäläinen 2016).

the result of the accumulated effect of successive biased even swap tasks. Their findings led them to develop a strategy for carrying out the even swaps process so that the accumulation of the effects of biases is reduced.

## 1.4    Implications of a Behavioral Perspective for OR

In this section we build on our preceding discussion to develop four broader implications of adopting the behavioral perspective for advancing the OR discipline: foregrounding OR praxis in academic papers, attending to a wide diversity of OR actors, developing OR competences and grounding BOR studies on relevant theories. We briefly discuss these implications next.

### 1.4.1    Foregrounding OR Praxis in Academic Papers

The first implication is the recognition that the practice of OR will remain a "black box" unless we examine how methods are actually used by OR actors. That is, a focus on OR praxis is central to advancing the BOR agenda. Therefore, it is proposed here that the kind of micro-level examinations of praxis that are common in practice and decision making studies within the behavioral, social and organization sciences and which are beginning to appear in the OR literature (e.g. Horlick-Jones and Rosenhead 2007; Lahtinen and Hämäläinen 2016; Velez-Castiblanco et al. 2016) be used. The goal here is to demonstrate how OR methods are actually used by conducting empirical and close interrogations of their claimed effects in the field or the lab.

### 1.4.2    Evaluating Impact of Diverse OR Actors

A second implication is the consideration of the wide variety of OR actors that participate in the practice of OR. The research agenda here concerns the study of different types of practitioners and their role and influence in the use of OR methods. Traditionally, published accounts of OR practice are written from the perspective of the OR practitioner (e.g. modeller, analyst, consultant). This focus is natural, as OR practitioners are central in designing, deploying and adapting OR methods. However, actors such as sponsors, clients and users also play a key role in OR-supported processes and ultimately determine what OR can practically accomplish. Considering a wider range of actors will extend our understanding of OR practice beyond that provided by the OR-practitioner view. Empirical studies in the field and the lab should undertake fine-grained analyses that can illuminate how the characteristics of different types of OR actors (e.g. roles, motivations, cognitive styles, emotional states) and the dynamics in which they engage contribute to shaping outcomes of OR-supported processes.

### 1.4.3  Developing Different Competences in OR

The third implication is that effective OR praxis relies heavily on OR actors' competence in applying and engaging with OR methods. Lack of adequate skills for the deployment, use or interpretation of OR methods can profoundly affect OR outcomes, and this requires managing effectively the technical as well as the behavioral and social aspects of OR-supported processes. From a BOR perspective, how OR actors become competent in the application, use and interpretation of OR methods in praxis is a crucial research question. Here, empirical research that focuses on the teaching and training of *doers* (practitioners) and *users* of OR is highly relevant. BOR studies might thus track how OR actors learn, master or embrace different methods within the classroom or during actual praxis. Such research can help to produce empirically grounded theories of what it takes to become a competent OR actor in different settings.

### 1.4.4  Grounding BOR Studies on Relevant Theories?

The final implication is the need to ground empirical BOR studies in relevant theories drawn from outside the OR field. Attention to theory might seem at odds with the applied nature of the OR discipline.

However, as Brocklesby (2016) notes, the practice of OR involves a complex array of dimensions that need to be better understood, and thus the use of a relevant theory can bring into view those dimensions that otherwise would remain hidden in the background, which can help generate new levels of awareness to inform OR practice. This does not imply a preference for a particular theory, nor the adoption of a specific research method to empirically test it. Thus, for example, the adoption of a theory of heuristics and biases to conduct empirical research via experimental methods (e.g. Tversky and Kahneman 1974), a common approach that has produced many useful insights in economics, finance and operations management, would represent in our view just one possible way of studying behavioral issues in OR.

Consequently, the concern here is less with what theories or research methods are adopted than by what behavioral issue related to OR practice is examined. In this respect, our proposed framework should be seen as an organizing device that could help inform empirical BOR studies grounded on a wide range of theories and research methodologies, as illustrated by the collection of works published in the 2016 special issue of the *European Journal of Operational Research* (Franco and Hämäläinen 2016). It is worth noting that besides the use of experiments, research methods that can track behavioral factors in OR-supported processes as they arise are also needed (e.g. Franco and Rouwette 2011). In this respect the use of data generated from process-type research (e.g. Poole 2004), both macro and micro, has the potential to offer additional valuable insights into the practice of OR from a BOR perspective.

## 1.5   Conclusions

The "science of better", as the OR discipline is commonly referred to, is never just about modeling and models, but also about people. Thus, *empirically grounded* explanations of how actors use OR methods in their praxis can help to develop a theory of effective OR practice. Such a theory can highlight the generative mechanisms that are responsible for the success or failure of OR interventions.

We have argued elsewhere that the current concern with the behavioral aspects of OR practice represents a return to the roots of the OR profession (Franco and Hämäläinen 2016), as evidenced by the growing number of empirical studies being published in this area. These studies represent an eclectic collection of works examining behavioral issues in OR practice from different theoretical perspectives, at different levels of analysis (individual, group, organizational) and with different research methodologies. We embrace this eclectic approach to conducting BOR studies, and in this chapter we have proposed an integrative framework to organize extant studies and also guide future research according to specific analytic lines. Specifically, the framework helps define different emphases for conducting empirical BOR studies. Furthermore, the framework suggests a wider approach to OR outcomes that considers not just improved organizational performance but also the performance of the individuals and groups involved in an actual episode of OR praxis.

The behavioral perspective in OR offers a distinctive lens that highlights the interdependencies among OR methods, OR actors and OR praxis and the ways they affect and are affected by OR outcomes. By adopting this perspective, OR academics would be more likely to produce robust and empirically grounded advice for improving the science of better. Ultimately, the central promise of the behavioral perspective is to enable the production of better OR methods, the conduct of improved OR praxis and the development of increasingly competent OR actors.

# References

Ackermann, F., and C. Eden. 2011. Negotiation in strategy making teams: Group support systems and the process of cognitive change. *Group Decision and Negotiation* 20: 293–314.

Ackermann, F., D.F. Andersen, C. Eden, and G.P. Richardson. 2011. ScriptsMap: A tool for designing multi-method policy-making workshops. *Omega* 39: 427–434.

Ackoff, R. 1977. Optimization + objectivity = opt out. *European Journal of Operational Research* 1: 1–7.

Ahmed, R., and S. Robinson. 2013. Modeling and simulation in business and industry: Insights into the processes and practices of expert modellers. *Journal of the Operational Research Society* 65: 660–672.

Amini, M., T. Wakolbinger, M. Racer, and M.G. Nejad. 2012. Alternative supply chain production-sales policies for new product diffusion: An agent-based modeling and simulation approach. *European Journal of Operational Research* 216: 301–311.

Bakken, B., J. Gould, and D. Kim. 1992. Experimentation in learning organizations: A management flight simulator approach. *European Journal of Operational Research* 59: 167–182.

Bendoly, E., W. Van Wezel, and D.G. Bachrach (eds.). 2015. *The handbook of behavioral operations management: Social and psychological dynamics in production and service settings*. New York: Oxford University Press.

Birnberg, J.G., J. Luft, and M.D. Shields. 2007. Psychology theory in management accounting research. In *Handbook of management accounting research*, ed. C.S. Chapman and A.G. Hopwood, 113–135. Oxford: Elsevier.

Brailsford, S.C., and B. Schmidt. 2003. Towards incorporating human behaviour in models of health care systems: An approach using discrete event eimulation. *European Journal of Operational Research* 150: 19–31.

Brailsford, S.C., P. Harper, and D. Shaw. 2009. Milestones in OR. *Journal of the Operational Research Society* 60: S1–S4.

Brailsford, S.C., P.R. Harper, and J. Sykes. 2012. Incorporating human behaviour in simulation models of screening for breast cancer. *European Journal of Operational Research* 219: 491–507.

Brailsford, S.C., T.B. Bolt, G. Bucci, T.M. Chaussalet, N.A. Connell, P.R. Harper, J.H. Klein, M. Pitt, and M. Taylor. 2013. Overcoming the barriers: A qualitative study of simulation adoption in the NHS. *Journal of the Operational Research Society* 64: 157–168.

Brocklesby, J. 2016. The what, the why and the how of behavioural operational research: An invitation to potential sceptics. *European Journal of Operational Research* 249: 796–805.

Bruce, B. (ed.). 2010. *Handbook of behavioral finance*. Northampton: Edward Elgar Publishing.

Camerer, C.F. 2003. *Behavioral game theory: Experiments in strategic interaction*. Princeton: Princeton University Press.

Camerer, C.F., and G. Lowenstein (eds.). 2003. *Advances in behavioral economics*. Princeton: Princeton University Press.

Capelo, C., and J.F. Dias. 2009. A system dynamics-based simulation experiment for testing mental model and performance effects of using the balanced scorecard. *System Dynamics Review* 25: 1–34.

Carlson, K.A., and S.D. Bond. 2006. Improving preference assessment: Limiting the effect of context through pre-exposure to attribute levels. *Management Science* 52: 410–421.

Chung, Q., T. Willemain, and R. O'Keefe. 2000. Influence of model management systems on decision making: Empirical evidence and implications. *Journal of the Operational Research Society* 51: 936–948.

Churchman, C.W. 1970. Operations research as a profession. *Management Science* 17: 37–53.

Connell, N. 2001. Evaluating soft OR: Some reflections on an apparently 'unsuccessful' implementation using a soft systems methodology (SSM) based approach. *Journal of Operational Research Society* 52: 150–160.

Cropper, S. 1990. Variety, formality and style: Choosing amongst decision-support methods. In *Tackling strategic problems: The role of group decision support*, ed. C. Eden and J. Radford, 92–98. London: Sage.

Dutton, J.M., and R.E. Walton. 1964. Operational research and the behavioural sciences. *Operational Research Quarterly* 15: 207–217.

Eden, C., and F. Ackermann. 2004. Use of 'soft OR' methods by clients, what do they want from them? In *Systems modeling: Theory and practice*, ed. M. Pidd, 146–163. Chichester: Wiley.

Ellspermann, S.J., G.W. Evans, and M. Basadur. 2007. The impact of training on the formulation of ill-structured problems. *Omega* 35: 221–236.

Fasolo, B., and C.A. Bana e Costa. 2014. Tailoring value elicitation to decision makers' numeracy and fluency: Expressing value judgments in numbers or words. *Omega* 44: 83–90.

Feldman, M.S., and W.J. Orlikowski. 2011. Theorizing practice and practicing theory. *Organization Science* 22(5): 1240–1253.

Fortuin, L., and M. Zijlstra. 2000. Operational research in practice: Consultancy in industry revisited. *European Journal of Operational Research* 120: 1–13.

Franco, L.A. 2013. Rethinking soft OR interventions: Models as boundary objects. *European Journal of Operational Research* 231: 720–733.

Franco, L.A., and R.P. Hämäläinen. 2016. Behavioural operational research: Returning to the roots of the OR profession. *European Journal of Operational Research* 249: 791–795.

Franco, L.A., and E. Lord. 2011. Understanding multi-methodology: Evaluating the perceived impact of mixing methods for group budgetary decisions. *Omega* 39: 362–372.

Franco, L.A., and M. Meadows. 2007. Exploring new directions in problem structuring methods research: On the role of cognitive style. *Journal of the Operational Research Society* 58: 1621–1629.

Franco, L.A., and G. Montibeller. 2010. Facilitated modeling in operational research. *European Journal of Operational Research* 205: 489–500.

Franco, L.A., and E.A. Rouwette. 2011. Decision development in facilitated modeling workshops. *European Journal of Operational Research* 212: 164–178.

Franco, L.A., M. Cushman, and J. Rosenhead. 2004. Project review and learning in the UK construction industry: Embedding a problem structuring method within a partnership context. *European Journal of Operational Research* 152: 586–601.

Franco, L.A., E.A. Rouwette, and H. Korzilius. 2016. Different paths to consensus? The impact of need for closure on model-supported group conflict management. *European Journal of Operational Research* 249: 878–889.

French, S., J. Maule, and N. Papamichail. 2009. *Decision behaviour, analysis and support*. Cambridge: Cambridge University Press.

Graham, A.K., J.D.W. Morecroft, P.M. Senge, and J.D. Sterman. 1992. Model-supported case studies for management education. *European Journal of Operational Research* 59: 151–166.

Hämäläinen, R.P. 2015. Behavioural issues in environmental modeling: The missing perspective. *Environmental Modeling and Software* 73: 244–253.

Hämäläinen, R.P., J. Mustajoki, and M. Marttunen. 2010. Web-based decision support: Creating a culture of applying multi-criteria decision analysis and web supported participation in environmental decision making. In *e-Democracy: A group decision and negotiation perspective*, ed. D. Rios-Insua and S. French, 201–221. Dordrecht: Springer Science and Business Media B.V.

Hämäläinen, R.P., J. Luoma, and E. Saarinen. 2013. On the importance of behavioral operational research: The case of understanding and communicating about dynamic systems. *European Journal of Operational Research* 228: 623–634.

Hartley, D.A., P.V. Johnson, A. Fitzsimons, J. Lovell, B. Chippendale, and J.K. Clayton. 1979. A case study on the development of the home defence training game HOT SEAT. *Journal of the Operational Research Society* 30: 861–871.

Horlick-Jones, T., and J. Rosenhead. 2007. The uses of observation: Combining problem structuring methods and ethnography. *Journal of the Operational Research Society* 58: 588–601.

Hovmand, P.S., D.F. Andersen, E. Rouwette, G.P. Richardson, K. Rux, and A. Calhoun. 2012. Group model-building 'scripts' as a collaborative planning tool. *Systems Research and Behavioral Science* 29: 179–193.

Howick, S., and F. Ackermann. 2011. Mixing OR methods in practice: Past, present and future directions. *European Journal of Operational Research* 215: 503–511.

Huxham, C., and S. Cropper. 1994. From many to one—And back. An exploration of some components of facilitation. *Omega* 22: 1–11.

Jackson, M.C., P. Keys, and S.A. Cropper (eds.). 1989. *OR and the social sciences.* New York: Plenum Press.

Jarzabkowski, P., J. Balogun, and D. Seidl. 2007. Strategizing: The challenges of a practice perspective. *Human Relations* 60: 5–27.

Keys, P. 2006. On becoming expert in the use of problem structuring methods. *Journal of the Operational Research Society* 57: 822–829.

Kunc, M. 2012. Teaching strategic thinking using system dynamics: Lessons from a strategic development course. *System Dynamics Review* 28: 28–45.

Lahtinen, T.J., and R.P. Hämäläinen. 2016. Path dependence and biases in the even swaps decision analysis method. *European Journal of Operational Research* 249: 890–898.

Lane, D.C. 1995. On a resurgence of management simulations and games. *Journal of the Operational Research Society* 46: 604–625.

Lawrence, J.E. (ed.). 1966. *Operational research and the social sciences.* London: Tavistock Publications.

Le Menestrel, M., and L.N. Van Wassenhove. 2004. Ethics outside, within or beyond OR models? *European Journal of Operational Research* 153: 477–484.

Le Menestrel, M., and L.N. Van Wassenhove. 2009. Ethics in operations research and management sciences: A never-ending effort to combine rigor and passion. *Omega* 37: 1039–1043.

Luhmann, N. 1995. *Social systems.* Stanford: Stanford University Press.

Mingers, J., and J. Rosenhead. 2012. Introduction to the special issue: Teaching soft O.R., problem structuring methods, and multimethodology. *INFORMS Transactions on Education* 12: 1–3.

Mitchell, G. 1993. *The practice of operational research.* Chichester: Wiley.

Montibeller, G., and D. Von Winterfeldt. 2015. Cognitive and motivational biases in decision and risk analysis. *Risk Analysis* 35: 1230–1251.

Montibeller, G., L.A. Franco, E. Lord, and A. Iglesias. 2009. Structuring resource allocation decisions: A framework for building multi-criteria portfolio models with area-grouped projects. *European Journal of Operational Research* 199: 846–856.

Morecroft, J.D. 1988. System dynamics and microworlds for policymakers. *European Journal of Operational Research* 35: 301–320.

Morton, A., and B. Fasolo. 2009. Behavioural decision theory for multi-criteria decision analysis: A guided tour. *Journal of the Operational Research Society* 60: 268–275.

Nicolini, D. 2012. *Practice theory, work and organization: An introduction.* Oxford: Oxford University Press.

O'Brien, F.A. 2004. Scenario planning: Lessons for practice from teaching and learning. *European Journal of Operational Research* 154: 709–722.

O'Brien, F.A. 2011. Supporting the strategy process: A survey of UK OR/MS practitioners. *Journal of the Operational Research Society* 62: 900–920.

O'Brien, F.A. 2015. On the roles of OR/MS practitioners in supporting strategy. *Journal of the Operational Research Society* 66: 202–218.

O'Keefe, R.M. 2016. Experimental behavioural research in operational research: What we know and what we might come to know. *European Journal of Operational Research* 249: 899–907.

Ormerod, R.J. 2008. The transformation competence perspective. *Journal of the Operational Research Society* 59: 1435–1448.

Ormerod, R.J. 2014a. The mangle of OR practice: Towards more informative case studies of 'technical' projects. *Journal of the Operational Research Society* 65: 1245–1260.

Ormerod, R.J. 2014b. OR competences: The demands of problem structuring methods. *EURO Journal on Decision Processes* 2: 313–340.

Ormerod, R.J., and W. Ulrich. 2013. Operational research and ethics: A literature review. *European Journal of Operational Research* 228: 291–307.

Papamichail, K.N., G. Alves, S. French, J.B. Yang, and R. Snowdon. 2007. Facilitation practices in decision workshops. *Journal of the Operational Research Society* 58: 614–632.

Petropoulos, F., R. Fildes, and P. Goodwin. 2016. Do 'big losses' in judgmental adjustments to statistical forecasts affect experts' behaviour? *European Journal of Operational Research* 249: 842–852.

Pickering, A. 1995. *The mangle of practice: Time, agency and science.* Chicago: University of Chicago Press.

Pierre Brans, J., and C. Macharis. 1997. Play theatre a new way to teach O.R. *European Journal of Operational Research* 99: 241–247.

Poole, M.S. 2004. Generalization in process theories of communication. *Communication Methods and Measures* 1: 181–190.

Powell, S.G., and T.R. Willemain. 2007. How novices formulate models. Part I: Qualitative insights and implications for teaching. *Journal of the Operational Research Society* 58: 983–995.

Powell, T.C., D. Lovallo, and C.R. Fox. 2011. Behavioral strategy. *Strategic Management Journal* 32: 1369–1386.

Ranyard, J.C., R. Fildes, and T.-I. Hu. 2015. Reassessing the scope of OR practice: The influences of problem structuring methods and the analytics movement. *European Journal of Operational Research* 245: 1–13.

Reckwitz, A. 2002. Towards a theory of social practices: A development in cultural theorizing. *European Journal of Social Theory* 5: 243–263.

Robinson, S., C. Worthington, N. Burgess, and Z.J. Radnor. 2013. Facilitated modeling with discrete-event simulation: Reality or myth? *European Journal of Operational Research* 234: 231–240.

Rouwette, E.A.J.A., J.A.M. Vennix, and T. Van Mullekom. 2002. Group model building effectiveness. A review of assessment studies. *System Dynamics Review* 18: 5–45.

Rouwette, E.A.J.A., H. Korzilius, J.A.M. Vennix, and E. Jacobs. 2011. Modeling as persuasion: The impact of group model building on attitudes and behavior. *System Dynamics Review* 27: 1–21.

Schatzki, T.R., K. Knorr-Cetina, and E. Von Savigny (eds.). 2001. *The practice turn in contermporary theory*. London: Routledge.

Schilling, M.S., N. Oeser, and C. Schaub. 2007. How effective are decision analyses? Assessing decision process and group alignment effects. *Decision Analysis* 4: 227–242.

Scott, R.J., R.Y. Cavana, and D. Cameron. 2013. Evaluating immediate and long-term impacts of qualitative group model building workshops on participants' mental models. *System Dynamics Review* 29: 216–236.

Scott, R.J., R.Y. Cavana, and D. Cameron. 2016. Recent evidence on the effectiveness of group model building. *European Journal of Operational Research* 249: 908–918.

Senge, P.M., and J.D. Sterman. 1992. Systems thinking and organizational learning: Acting locally and thinking globally in the organization of the future. *European Journal of Operational Research* 59: 137–150.

Shaw, D., F. Ackermann, and C. Eden. 2003. Approaches to sharing knowledge in group problem structuring. *Journal of the Operational Research Society* 54: 936–948.

Sterman, J.D. 2000. *Business dynamics: Systems thinking and modeling for a complex world*. Boston: Irwin McGraw-Hill.

Syntetos, A.A., I. Kholidasari, and M.M. Naim. 2016. The effects of integrating management judgement into OUT levels: In or out of context? *European Journal of Operational Research* 249: 853–863.

Tako, A.A. 2014. Exploring the model development process in discrete-event simulation: Insights from six expert modellers. *Journal of the Operational Research Society* 66: 747–760.

Tako, A.A., and S. Robinson. 2010. Model development in discrete-event simulation and system dynamics: An empirical study of expert modellers. *European Journal of Operational Research* 207: 784–794.

Tavella, E., and T. Papadopoulos. 2015a. Expert and novice facilitated modeling: A case of a viable system model workshop in a local food network. *Journal of the Operational Research Society* 66: 247–264.

Tavella, E., and T. Papadopoulos. 2015b. Novice facilitators and the use of scripts for managing facilitated modeling workshops. *Journal of the Operational Research Society* 66: 1967–1988.

Turner, S. 1994. *The social theory of practices*. Cambridge: Polity Press.

Tversky, A., and D. Kahneman. 1974. Judgment under uncertainty. Heuristics and biases. *Science* 185: 1124–1131.

Velez-Castiblanco, J., J. Brocklesby, and G. Midgley. 2016. Boundary games: How teams of OR practitioners explore the boundaries of intervention. *European Journal of Operational Research* 249: 968–982.

Von Winterfeldt, D., and W. Edwards. 1986. *Decision analysis and behavioral research*. Cambridge: Cambridge University Press.

Waisel, L., W. Wallace, and T. Willemain. 2008. Visualization and model formulation: An analysis of the sketches of expert modellers. *Journal of the Operational Research Society* 59: 353–361.

Wein, L.M. 2002. Introduction to the 50th anniversary issue of operations research. *Operations Research* 50: iii-iii.

White, L. 2009. Understanding problem structuring methods interventions. *European Journal of Operational Research* 99: 823–833.

White, L. 2016. Behavioural operational research: Towards a framework for understanding behaviour in OR interventions. *European Journal of Operational Research* 249: 827–841.

White, L., K. Burger, and M. Yearworth. 2016. Understanding behaviour in problem structuring methods interventions with activity theory. *European Journal of Operational Research* 249: 983–1004.

Whittington, R. 2003. The work of strategizing and organizing: For a practice perspective. *Strategic Organization* 1: 117–125.

Whittington, R. 2006. Completing the practice turn in strategy research. *Organization Studies* 27: 613–634.

Whittington, R. 2011. The practice turn in organization research: Towards a disciplined transdisciplinarity. *Accounting, Organizations and Society* 36: 183–186.

Willemain, T.R. 1994. Insights on modeling from a dozen experts. *Operations Research* 42: 213–222.

Willemain, T.R. 1995. Model formulation: What experts think about and when. *Operations Research* 43: 916–932.

Willemain, T.R., and S.G. Powell. 2007. How novices formulate models. Part II: A quantitative description of behaviour. *Journal of the Operational Research Society* 58: 1271–1283.

Wright, G and Bolger, F. 1992. *Expertise and decision support.* New York: Springer Science and Business Media.

Wright, G., G. Cairns, and P. Goodwin. 2009. Teaching scenario planning: Lessons from practice in academe and business. *European Journal of Operational Research* 194: 323–335.

# 2

# Behavior with Models: The Role of Psychological Heuristics in Operational Research

Konstantinos V. Katsikopoulos

## 2.1 Introduction

Are you as rational as a clever philosopher or a professor of economics? Well, you answer, it depends on what "rational" means. In the traditional view of rationality, the decision maker possesses all information that can possibly be gathered and based on it makes all logically correct deductions, which she uses to make an optimal decision. For example, when choosing among probabilistic options, this decision maker knows all possible outcomes of each option, knows the probability that each outcome will occur, is able to assign a numerical utility to each outcome and finally calculates the expected utility of each option and picks an option which maximizes it.

K.V. Katsikopoulos (✉)
Center for Adaptive Behavior and Cognition (ABC), Max Planck Institute for Human Development, Lentzeallee 94, 14195 Berlin, Germany

© The Editor(s) (if applicable) and The Author(s) 2016                    **27**
M. Kunc et al. (eds.), *Behavioral Operational Research*,
DOI 10.1057/978-1-137-53551-1_2

This traditional kind of rationality is called *unbounded rationality*. In contrast, *bounded rationality* refers to problems for which there is not adequate time or computational resources to obtain all information and find an optimal solution but nevertheless a good solution must be identified. In other words, bounded rationality is the realistic kind of rationality that laypeople and experts need to exhibit in their lives and work, save for decisions for which all possible values and probabilities of all options can be known, such as in casinos.

Herbert Simon (1955– ), one of the great twentieth-century polymaths—who sometimes also wore the hat of an Operational Researcher—is credited as the father of bounded rationality, but he refrained from giving a precise definition. Thus, there are multiple views of bounded rationality (Rubinstein 1998; Gigerenzer and Selten 2001; Lee 2011; Katsikopoulos 2014).

This chapter presents one view of bounded rationality, which I see as particularly relevant to Operational Research (OR). This view has a very strong behavioral component: it consists of prescriptive models of decision making, which have also been used to describe people's actual behavior. The models include the few pieces of information that people use and also specify the simple ways in which people process this information. These models go under labels such as "fast and frugal heuristics" (Gigerenzer et al. 1999), "simple models" (Hogarth and Karelaia 2005), "psychological heuristics" (Katsikopoulos 2011) and "simple rules" (Sull and Eisenhardt 2012). This chapter uses the label *psychological heuristics* for all of these.

The contribution of the chapter is fourfold: The conceptual foundation of the psychological heuristics research program, along with a discussion of its relationship to soft and hard OR, is provided in Sect. 2.2. Then, Sect. 2.3 presents an introduction to models of psychological heuristics. In Sect. 2.4, conditions are reviewed under which models of psychological heuristics perform better or worse than more complex models of optimization in problems of multi-attribute choice, classification and forecasting; based on these conditions, a guide is provided for deciding which of the two approaches to use for which types of problems. Finally, Sect. 2.5 concludes by providing the main take-home messages and briefly discusses the role that psychological heuristics can play in OR theory and practice.

## 2.2    The Conceptual Foundation of Psychological Heuristics

There are at least three interpretations of heuristics which are relevant to this chapter. First, in hard OR, *heuristics* refers to computationally simple models which allow one to "quickly [find] good feasible solutions" (Hillier and Lieberman 2001, p. 624). The other two interpretations of heuristics come from the behavioral sciences, such as psychology and economics. Kahneman et al. (1982) focused on the experimental study of psychological processes that "in general…are quite useful, but sometimes lead to severe and systematic errors" (Tversky and Kahneman 1974, p. 1124) and proposed informal models (i.e. models that do not make precise quantitative predictions) of heuristics. Gigerenzer et al. (1999) developed and tested formal models of heuristics that, they argued, "… when compared to standard benchmark strategies…, can be faster, more frugal and more accurate at the same time" (Gigerenzer and Todd 1999, p. 22).

Katsikopoulos (2011) proposed a definition which is a hybrid of these interpretations, i.e. psychological heuristics are formal models for making decisions that:

> *(i)* rely heavily on core psychological capacities (e.g. recognizing patterns or recalling information from memory);
>
> *(ii)* do not necessarily use all available information and process the information they use by simple computations (e.g. ordinal comparisons or un-weighted sums);
>
> *(iii)* are easy to understand, apply and explain.

Requirements *(i)*, *(ii)* and *(iii)* are partly underspecified, but the following discussion should clarify their meaning. Consider the problem of choosing one out of many apartments to rent based on attributes such as price, duration of contract, distance from the center of town and so on. The standard approach of hard OR, decision analysis (Keeney and Raiffa 1976), includes eliciting attribute weights, single attribute functions, interactions among attributes, and so on. Then these different pieces of information are integrated by using additive or multi-linear functions. On the other hand, a psychological heuristic for solving the problem could be to decide based on one attribute (e.g. price) or order attributes by subjective importance and decide based on the first attribute in the order which sufficiently discriminates among the alternatives (Hogarth and Karelaia 2005).

For example, price could be ranked first and contract duration second, and prices could differ only by 50 pounds per month while contract durations could differ by a year, in which case the apartment with the longest contract would be chosen (assuming that you prefer longer to shorter contracts). In a review of 45 studies, Ford et al. (1989) found that people very often use such heuristics for choosing items as diverse as apartments, microwaves and birth control methods.

As a second example, consider the problem of forecasting which one of two companies will have higher stock value five years from now. Assuming that you recognize only one of the two companies, a psychological heuristic for making such decisions is to pick the recognized company (Goldstein and Gigerenzer 2009). This is in stark contrast with doing the computations of mean-variance portfolio optimization (Markowitz 1952).

Psychological heuristics differ from the heuristics of the "heuristics-and-biases" research program of (Kahneman et al. (1982)) mainly in that they are models which make precise quantitative predictions. For further discussion, see Kelman (2011) and Katsikopoulos and Gigerenzer (2013). Formal modeling also differentiates psychological heuristics from the "naturalistic decision making" research program (Zsambok and Klein 1997). For a discussion of how the two programs are related and can learn from each other, see Keller et al. (2010). For a discussion of how psychological heuristics can be integrated with systems approaches (Sage 1992), see Clausing and Katsikopoulos (2008).

Psychological heuristics target problems which have been tackled by hard OR models as well. In these problems, there is a clear objective (e.g. choose the company with the higher stock value five years from now), and the success of a method may be evaluated by using standards such as agreement with the ground truth (e.g. company stock values). Like hard OR methods, heuristics are models of people's behavior and thus differ from a mere restatement or reuse of managerial intuition. In particular, they are formalized so that they conform to (*i*), (*ii*) and (*iii*).

Psychological heuristics differ from the heuristics of hard OR in that they are not mere computational shortcuts but have an identifiable psychological basis. This psychological basis can be due to expertise (Zsambok and Klein 1997). For example, some experienced managers are aware of the fact that customers who have not bought anything from an apparel company in the last nine months are very unlikely to buy something in the future, and use this single attribute to make more accurate decisions about targeted advertising than they could using a standard forecasting model (83% vs. 75%; Wuebben and von Wangenheim 2008). Furthermore, the psychological basis of heuristics can be available to laypeople as well. For example, a human child can recognize faces better than currently available software (with the possible exception of new anti-terrorist technologies).

Of course, some heuristics of hard OR may formally look like the heuristics a person would spontaneously use, as in solving the traveling salesman problem by always going to the closest unvisited town. But the process of arriving at the heuristics is different. Unlike hard OR models, psychological heuristics are not derived by solving or approximating the solution of an optimization model. Rather, psychological heuristics are based on the observation and analysis of human behavior, and in particular of how people make good decisions with little data.

Psychological heuristics have a nuanced relationship with methods of soft OR (Rosenhead and Mingers 2001). The main point is that psychological heuristics and soft OR methods target different problems. Unlike soft OR, the heuristics discussed in this chapter do not apply to wicked problems (Churchman 1967) with unclear objectives or multiple disagreeing stakeholders. The sSuccess of soft OR methods may mean that communication among stakeholders was enhanced or that consensus was achieved (Mingers 2011), whereas the success of psychological heuristics may be measured quantitatively.

On the other hand, there is a crucial point of convergence of psychological heuristics and soft OR. Both approaches acknowledge the possibility that high-quality data—say, on utilities or probabilities—is missing, and tailor their methods appropriately.

Table 2.1 summarizes these conceptual connections among soft OR, psychological heuristics and hard OR. It can be argued that psychological heuristics lie between hard and soft OR.

**Table 2.1** A summary of conceptual connections among soft OR, psychological heuristics and hard OR

|  | Soft OR | Psychological heuristics | Hard OR |
|---|---|---|---|
| Target problems | Unclear objectives, multiple disagreeing stakeholders, success may mean enhancing communication or achieving consensus | Clear objectives, individual decision makers, success may be measured by agreement with ground truth | Clear objectives, success may be measured by agreement with ground truth |
| Process of deriving solutions | Observe and analyze people's purposeful behavior, aiming at counteracting behavioral biases | Observe and analyze people's behavior, in particular when they made good decisions with little data | Solve or approximate the solution of an optimization model, not using knowledge of people's behavior |
| Characteristics of solutions | Qualitative principles which allow objectives to be clarified and stakeholders to work together | Models of people's behavior, formalized so that they conform to (*i*), (*ii*) and (*iii*) (in the definition of heuristics) | Models, not descriptive of people's behavior, meant to improve on unaided intuition |

# 2.3    Models of Psychological Heuristics

A main family of psychological heuristics is *lexicographic* models (Fishburn 1974). Consider the problem of choosing one out of many apartments to rent based on attributes such as price, duration of contract, and distance from the center of town. Lexicographic models decide based on one attribute—say, price—or order attributes by subjective importance and decide based on the first attribute in the order which sufficiently discriminates among the alternatives (Hogarth and Karelaia 2005). For example, price could be ranked first and contract duration second, and prices could differ only by 50 pounds per month while contract durations could differ by a year, in which case the apartment with the longest contract would be chosen (assuming that you prefer longer to shorter contracts).

Lexicographic models have been applied to problems of multi-attribute choice, classification and forecasting. In *multi-attribute choice*, the objective is to choose one out of many alternatives, an approach which obtains the maximum true multi-attribute utility to the decision maker, such as, for example, overall satisfaction from renting an apartment.

In *classification*, the objective is to classify an object into one out of many possible categories, again based on its attribute values. For example, one classification problem is to decide if a patient with some known symptoms, such as intense chest pain, is at a high risk of a heart attack and needs to be in the emergency room or should just be monitored in a regular nursing bed.

*Forecasting* refers to any type of problem where the ground truth is not known now but will be available in the future (e.g. company stock values in five years). It does not necessarily refer to making point estimates (e.g. predicting the stock value of a company in five years). Rather, forecasting here could mean making multi-attribute choices (e.g. which one of two companies will have a higher stock value in five years?) or classifications (e.g. will this company be bankrupt within five years?) into the future.

It is a mathematical fact that lexicographic models for multi-attribute choice, classification and forecasting can be formally represented by a simple graphical structure, called *fast and frugal trees* (Martignon et al. 2008). An example fast and frugal tree is provided in Fig. 2.1. It was developed for classifying vehicles approaching a military checkpoint as hostile or nonhostile (Keller and Katsikopoulos 2016). Fast and frugal trees use a small number of attributes, which are first ordered and then inspected one at a time. Every time an attribute is inspected, a yes-or-no question on the value of the attribute is asked. Typically, the question refers to an ordinal comparison; for example, in the first attribute of the tree in Fig. 2.1, the number of occupants in the vehicle is compared to 1. For each attribute, for one of the two possible answers a classification is made immediately (e.g. in the tree of Fig. 2.1, the vehicle is immediately classified as non-hostile if there are more than one occupant), whereas for the other possible answer the next attribute is inspected. Of course, a classification is made for each answer on the last attribute in the order.

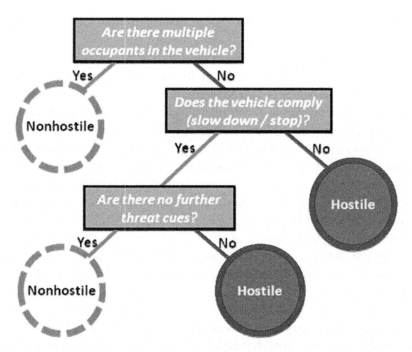

**Fig. 2.1** A fast and frugal tree for classifying vehicles approaching a military checkpoint as hostile or non-hostile (Keller and Katsikopoulos, 2016)

Typically, attributes are ordered by a measure of the statistical correlation between each attribute of the object and the utility or category of the object (Martignon et al. 2008). This means that data on attributes and utilities or categories of objects is required. This data comprises the *training set*. It has been found that when people are given a training set of adequate size and enough time to learn from it, they can order attributes by their correlation (Broeder and Newell 2008).

It is important to note that fast and frugal trees do not necessarily require statistical data. An alternative possibility is expert knowledge, combined with a task analysis (Vicente 1999). Indeed, the tree of Fig. 2.1 could not be built based on statistics, because the available database, 1,060 incident reports of situations involving motor vehicles approaching a NATO military checkpoint in Afghanistan between January 2004 and December 2009, included only seven successful suicide attacks, and on those only one attribute was available.

Because of this, methods of statistics and computer science, such as classification and regression trees (Breiman et al. 1984) and support vector machines (Vapnik 1999), also cannot be applied to this problem in an obvious way. The tree of Fig. 2.1 was built based on semi-structured interviews with German armed forces training instructors and combat-experienced personnel, and a literature review. Had it been applied in Afghanistan, the tree would have reduced civilian casualties by 60% (from 204 to 78) (Keller and Katsikopoulos 2016).

Financial and medical practitioners have been positive toward fast and frugal trees. Economists from the Bank of England developed a fast and frugal tree for forecasting whether a bank is at risk of bankruptcy or not (Aikman et al. 2014), anticipating that it will be a useful aid to regulators. The tree used four economic indicators: leverage ratio in the balance sheet, market-based capital ratio, total amount of wholesale funding and loan to deposit ratio. In the dataset of 116 banks which had more than 100 billion USD in assets at the end of 2006, the tree correctly identified 82% of the banks which subsequently failed and 50% of the banks which did not fail. The fast and frugal tree was not outperformed by any of 20 versions of the usual tool of financial economics, logistic regression, which used the same economic indicators as the tree while being much easier to understand and use.

Louis Cook and his team at the Emergency Medical Services Division of the New York City Fire Department used a fast and frugal tree for deciding which of the victims of the September 11 terrorist attack needed urgent care (Cook 2001). Based on their own medical experience, Green and Mehr (1997) developed a fast and frugal tree for the heart attack problem discussed earlier, which improved upon the unaided performance of doctors in a Michigan hospital. Overall, it has been argued that fast and frugal trees make the medical decision process more transparent and easier to understand and to communicate to patients (Elwyn et al. 2001).

There are many other models of psychological heuristics beyond lexicographic ones (Gigerenzer et al. 2011). Another main type of heuristics is *tallying* (or *unit-weights*) models (Dawes and Corrigan 1974). Tallying models are linear models for multi-attribute choice, classification and forecasting in which the weights of all attributes are set to 1.

Surprisingly, it has been found in applications in psychometrics and personnel selection that tallying could sometimes forecast better than linear regression with unconstrained attribute weights (Bobko et al. 2007). Tallying also could not be outperformed by 13 versions of Markowitz's mean-variance optimization model in allocating wealth across assets in seven real financial portfolios (DeMiguel et al. 2009).

Finally, note that tallying and lexicographic models occupy the two extremes of a continuum: in tallying models, each attribute can compensate for any other attribute, whereas in lexicographic models, the first discriminating attribute cannot be compensated for by all other attributes put together.

The few applications discussed in this section suggest that psychological heuristics compete well with more complex models used in statistics, computer science and hard OR. But are these isolated incidents? The next section provides a systematic review.

## 2.4    When to Use Psychological Heuristics and When Not To

In 1979, Herbert Simon wrote: "decision makers can [find] optimal solutions for a simplified world, or satisfactory solutions for a more realistic world. Neither approach, in general, dominates the other and both have continued to co-exist in the world of management science" (Simon 1979, p. 498).

Almost 40 years later, this point can be elaborated on: a fair amount of research has focused on the comparison between one approach to finding satisfactory solutions, psychological heuristics, and the more standard approach of using models of *optimization*, where an optimum of a mathematical function that models a simplified but supposedly sufficient version of the problem is computed (this definition of optimization is inspired by Kimball 1958). Here, optimization models include regressions (linear, logistic and regularized), Bayesian networks (such as naïve Bayes), neural networks, classification and regression trees, and support vector machines.

Some empirical evidence from this research was provided in Sects. 2.2 and 2.3, with the examples on targeted advertisement, identification of hostiles at checkpoints and flagging banks at a high risk of bankruptcy. For a systematic review of the empirical evidence, which comes from such diverse domains as economics, management, health, transportation and engineering, see Katsikopoulos (2011).

In this section, I focus on the theoretical analyses. A general framework for understanding the comparative performance of psychological heuristics and more complex models is provided by the statistical theory of prediction, and in particular by the *bias-variance* decomposition-of-prediction error (Geman et al. 1992; Gigerenzer and Brighton 2009).

This decomposition is a mathematical fact which says that the prediction error of any model is the sum of two terms. The first term is called bias, and it measures how well, on the average, the model agrees with the ground truth. Complex models—which usually have many parameters—tend to have less bias than simple models—which usually have fewer parameters—because when parameters can be tweaked, the agreement between model prediction and ground truth can increase as well. For example, Markowitz's multi-parameter optimization model achieves low bias, whereas tallying attribute values has zero parameters and has relatively high bias.

But this is not the whole story. There is a second term, called *variance,* which contributes to a model's total prediction error. Variance measures the variation of model predictions around the model's average prediction. Unlike the bias term, when it comes to the variance term, model complexity is less of a blessing and more of a curse. Complex multi-parameter models tend to have higher variance than simple models with fewer parameters, because more parameters can combine in more ways and generate more distinct predictions.

For example, one can intuit why simple models tend to have lower variance than more complex models for small training set sizes. The smaller the training set, the more likely it is that sampling error and natural variations in the instances which are included in the training set will lead to variation in the parameter estimates of a given model. This variation can be expected to have an influence on the more heavily parameterized models to a greater degree than on the simpler rules. In an extreme case, Markowitz's multi-parameter optimization model has relatively high variance, whereas tallying has zero variance because it has zero parameters.

Because a model's total prediction error is the sum of its bias and variance, one can see that the result can go either way: a simple or a more complex model can have higher predictive accuracy in a particular dataset, depending on whether an advantage in bias is larger than an advantage in variance in this dataset.

It has been argued that in practice variance may be more critical than bias (Brighton and Gigerenzer 2015). This claim is consistent with a recent review of the forecasting literature which concluded that all valid evidence-based forecasting methods are simple and urged decision makers to accept forecasts only from simple methods (Green and Armstrong 2015).

Surprisingly, it has been recently discovered that simple rules may also achieve competitive bias in practice. This happens when there exists an attribute or an alternative option which dominates the others.

An attribute dominates other attributes when it is subjectively much more important to the decision maker than the other attributes. For example, the distance of an apartment to the city center may be much more important to a particular renter than other apartment attributes. A second meaning of attribute dominance is when an attribute is statistically much more informative of the utility of options than other attributes. For instance, time since last purchase predicts future sales much more accurately than customer age does (Wuebben and von Wangenheim 2008). It has been analytically shown that lexicographic models which decide based on a dominant attribute incur zero bias (Martignon and Hoffrage 2002; Katsikopoulos 2011).

An alternative option dominates other options when its attribute values are better than or equal to the attribute values of the other options. In this case, most psychological heuristics incur zero bias. Furthermore, less restrictive definitions of dominance exist, which also have been shown to lead to zero bias for lexicographic models and tallying (Baucells et al. 2008). These results hold when utility is an additive or multi-linear function of the attributes (Katsikopoulos et al. 2014).

One may think that dominant attributes and alternatives are rare in the real world. In fact, the opposite seems to be the case (Şimşek 2013). Across 51 real datasets, it was found that dominant attributes exist in 93% of binary datasets (i.e. attributes that had values of 1 or 0) and in 83% of the numeric datasets and that dominant alternatives exist in 87% and 58% of binary and numeric datasets, respectively.

In sum, the conclusion of the theoretical work is that psychological heuristics tend to perform better than more complex models of optimization when (*i*) the information available is not of high quality or not ample enough to estimate the parameters of models reliably or (*ii*) there exists one attribute or one alternative option which dominates the others. On the other hand, when neither condition (*i*) or condition (*ii*) holds, more complex models tend to perform better than psychological heuristics.

Condition (*i*) essentially says that a problem is difficult. Such difficulties may arise when a problem is dynamic or future developments are unpredictable. If (*i*) holds, an advantage in the variance component of the prediction error is much larger than the bias component and simpler models have a very good chance of outperforming more complex models.

An interesting interpretation of condition (*ii*) is that it says that the problem is easy, in the following sense: either there exists one alternative option which is better than all other options and the decision maker needs only to identify it, or there exists one attribute which is so important or informative that it suffices to consult only this attribute and again the decision maker needs only to identify it. If (*ii*) holds, as empirical research has shown that it often does in practice, several simple models achieve zero bias and thus can indeed outperform more complex models.

Based on the empirical and theoretical results, shown in Table 2.2, a guide is provided for deciding which of the two approaches to use for which types of problems.

Table 2.2 A guide for deciding which of the two approaches to decision making to use for which types of problems

| Approach to decision making | Types of problems for which each approach tends to perform better |
| --- | --- |
| *Psychological heuristics* (e.g. lexicographic models, fast and frugal trees, and tallying) | *Difficult problems* (e.g. low-quality or scant information, dynamic or unpredictable situations) *Easy problems* (i.e. problems with dominant attributes or dominant alternative options) |
| *More complex models of optimization* (e.g. linear and logistic regression, Bayesian networks, neural networks, classification and regression trees) | *Other problems* (e.g. ample high-quality information, static or predictable situations problems without dominant attributes or dominant alternative options) |

## 2.5    Conclusions

This chapter presented one view of bounded rationality, which I see as particularly relevant to OR. Psychological heuristics, which have been used to describe people's actual behavior, were proposed as prescriptive methods for how people should make multi-attribute choices, classify objects into categories and make forecasts. Psychological heuristics specify the few pieces of information that people—experts as well as laypeople—use and the simple ways in which people process this information. A few relevant examples were provided, including targeted advertisement, identification of hostiles at checkpoints (Fig. 2.1) and flagging of banks at a high risk of bankruptcy.

Why should one consider psychological heuristics as prescriptive models when so much effort has already been put into developing models of optimization? In one of his fables, Russell Ackoff (1979) complained about pronouncing optimization models optimal without checking if their assumptions held: a very large intrasystem distribution problem was modeled as a linear programming problem, and its optimal solution was derived; the argument offered for implementing this solution was that its performance was superior, according to the linear programming model, to that of another solution!

Ultimately, choosing a method for making decisions should be based on facts. This chapter contrasted the empirical evidence and theoretical analyses on the relative performance of psychological heuristics and optimization models, in problems of multi-attribute choice, classification and forecasting (Sect. 2.3). On the basis of these facts, a guide was provided for deciding which of the two approaches to use for which types of problems (Table 2.2). Perhaps the main message is that, so far as we know, psychological heuristics should be chosen for problems that are either easy or difficult and more complex models should be used for problems in between.

Of course, more work needs to be done. For example, most psychological heuristics research has ignored the case of more than two alternatives or categories (for exceptions, see Hogarth and Karelaia 2005 and Katsikopoulos 2013), which may be more representative of real problems.

But in any case, the study of psychological heuristics can serve as a conceptual bridge between soft and hard OR. This point was also made in Sect. 2.1 (Table 2.1).

But can psychological heuristics scale up to more complex problems, as for example strategic problems with unclear objectives and multiple disagreeing stakeholders? French et al. (2009) seem to believe they cannot, when they say that psychological heuristics can be applied to "simple decision tasks with known correct solutions" (p. 169) and to "some tactical and operational decisions" (p. 419).

I basically agree with French et al. (2009) that it is not yet possible to scale up the formal models of psychological heuristics presented in this chapter. But there are two caveats: The first is that psychological heuristics require only that there exist a correct solution, not that it be given to them. In fact, as was shown, psychological heuristics perform especially well when the correct solution will be available in the future. This is a point where psychological heuristics exhibit the kind of robust power of human intuition and expertise (Klein 1999) that is often lost in hard OR and that soft OR tries to capture. The second caveat is that a heuristics approach has in fact been applied to problems of understanding information about health conditions and making informed decisions about treatments; these are problems where patients, doctors, pharmaceutical companies, health administrators and policy makers often have unclear or conflicting objectives (Gigerenzer and Gray 2011). These heuristics are based on knowledge from the psychology of thinking, perception and emotion and from social psychology. Integrating this approach with the one presented in this chapter and with soft and hard OR is a key task for the future.

# References

Ackoff, R.L. 1979. The future of operational research is past. *Journal of Operational Research Society* 30: 93–104.

Aikman, D., M. Galesic, G. Gigerenzer, S. Kapadia, K.V. Katsikopoulos, A. Kothiyal, E. Murphy, and T. Neumann. 2014. *Taking uncertainty seriously: Simplicity versus complexity in financial regulation*. Bank of England, Financial Stability Working Paper No. 28, UK.

Baucells, M., J.A. Carrasco, and R.M. Hogarth. 2008. Cumulative dominance and heuristic performance in binary multi-attribute choice. *Operations Research* 56: 1289–1304.

Bobko, P., P.L. Roth, and M.A. Buster. 2007. The usefulness of unit weights in creating composite scores: A literature review, application to content validity and meta-analysis. *Organizational Research Methods* 10: 689–709.

Breiman, L., J.H. Friedman, R.A. Olshen, and C.J. Stone. 1984. *Classification and regression trees*. New York: Chapman and Hall.

Brighton, H., and G. Gigerenzer. 2015. The bias bias. *Journal of Business Research* 68: 1772–1784.

Broeder, A., and B.R. Newell. 2008. Challenging some common beliefs: Empirical work within the adaptive toolbox metaphor. *Judgment and Decision Making* 3: 205–214.

Churchman, C.W. 1967. Wicked problems. *Management Science* 14: 141–142.

Clausing, D.P., and K.V. Katsikopoulos. 2008. Rationality in systems engineering: Beyond calculation or political action. *Systems Engineering* 11: 309–328.

Cook, L. 2001. The World Trade Center attack—The paramedic response: An insider's view. *Critical Care* 5: 301–303.

Dawes, R.M., and B. Corrigan. 1974. Linear models in decision making. *Psychological Bulletin* 81: 95–106.

DeMiguel, V., L. Garlappi, and R. Uppal. 2009. Optimal *versus* naïve diversification: How inefficient is the 1/N portfolio strategy? *Review of Financial Studies* 22: 1915–1953.

Elwyn, G., A. Edwards, M. Eccles, and D. Rovner. 2001. Decision analysis in patient care. *The Lancet* 358: 571–574.

Fishburn, P.C. 1974. Lexicographic orders, decisions and utilities: A survey. *Management Science* 20: 1442–1471.

Ford, J.K., N. Schmitt, S.L. Schechtman, B.H. Hults, and M.L. Doherty. 1989. Process tracing methods: Contributions, problems and neglected research questions. *Organizational Behavior and Human Decision Processes* 43: 75–117.

French, S., J. Maule, and N. Papamichail. 2009. *Decision behaviour, analysis and support*. Cambridge: Cambridge University Press.

Geman, S., E. Bienenstock, and E. Doursat. 1992. Neural networks and the bias/variance dilemma. *Neural Computation* 4: 1–58.

Gigerenzer, G., and H. Brighton. 2009. Homo heuristicus: Why biased minds make better inferences. *Topics in Cognitive Science* 1: 107–143.

Gigerenzer, G., and J.A.M. Gray (eds.). 2011. *Better doctors, better patients, better decisions: Envisioning health care 2020.* Cambridge, MA: MIT Press.

Gigerenzer, G., and R. Selten (eds.). 2001. *Bounded rationality: The adaptive toolbox.* Cambridge, MA: MIT Press.

Gigerenzer, G., and P.M. Todd.1999. Fast and frugal heuristics: The adaptive toolbox. In *Simple heuristics that make us smart,* ed. G. Gigerenzer, P.M. Todd and The ABC Research Group. New York: Oxford University Press.

Gigerenzer, G., P.M. Todd, and The ABC Research Group. 1999. *Simple heuristics that make us smart.* New York: Oxford University Press.

Gigerenzer, G., R. Hertwig, and T. Pachur (eds.). 2011. *Heuristics: The foundations of adaptive behavior.* New York: Oxford University Press.

Goldstein, D.G., and G. Gigerenzer. 2009. Fast and frugal forecasting. *International Journal of Forecasting* 5: 760–772.

Green, K.C., and J.S. Armstrong. 2015. Simple *versus* complex forecasting: The evidence. *Journal of Business Research* 68: 1678–1685.

Green, L., and D.R. Mehr. 1997. What alters physicians' decisions to admit to the coronary care unit? *The Journal of Family Practice* 45: 219–226.

Hillier, F.S., and G.J. Lieberman. 2001. *Introduction to operations research.* New York: McGraw Hill.

Hogarth, R.M., and N. Karelaia. 2005. Simple models for multiattribute choice with many alternatives: When it does and does not pay to face tradeoffs with binary attributes? *Management Science* 51: 1860–1872.

Kahneman, D., P. Slovic, and A. Tversky (eds.). 1982. *Judgment under uncertainty: Heuristics and biases.* Cambridge: Cambridge University Press.

Katsikopoulos, K.V. 2011. Psychological heuristics for making inferences: Definition, performance and the emerging theory and practice. *Decision Analysis* 8: 10–29.

Katsikopoulos, K.V. 2013. Why do simple heuristics perform well in choices with binary attributes? *Decision Analysis* 10: 327–340.

Katsikopoulos, K.V. 2014. Bounded rationality: The two cultures. *Journal of Economic Methodology* 21: 361–374.

Katsikopoulos, K.V., and G. Gigerenzer. 2013. Behavioral operations management: A blind spot and a research program. *Journal of Supply Chain Management* 49: 3–7.

Katsikopoulos, K.V., M. Egozcue, and L.F. Garcia. 2014. Cumulative dominance in multi-attribute choice: Benefits and limits. *EURO Journal on Decision Processes* 2: 153–163.

Keeney, R.L., and H. Raiffa. 1976. *Decision-making with multiple objectives: Preferences and value tradeoffs*. New York: Wiley.

Keller, N., and K.V. Katsikopoulos. 2016. On the role of psychological heuristics in operational research; and a demonstration in military stability operations. *European Journal of Operational Research* 249(3), 1063–1073.

Keller, N., E.T. Cokely, K.V. Katsikopoulos, and O. Wegwarth. 2010. Naturalistic heuristics for decision making. *Journal of Cognitive Engineering and Decision Making* 4: 256–274.

Kelman, M.G. 2011. *The heuristics debate*. New York: Oxford University Press.

Kimball, G.E. 1958. A critique of operations research. *Journal of the Washington Academy of Sciences* 48: 33–37.

Klein, G.A. 1999. *Sources of power: How people make decisions*. Cambridge, MA: MIT press.

Lee, C. 2011. Bounded rationality and the emergence of simplicity amidst complexity. *Journal of Economic Surveys* 25: 507–526.

Markowitz, H.M. 1952. Portfolio selection. *Journal of Finance* 7: 77–91.

Martignon, L., and U. Hoffrage. 2002. Fast, frugal and fit: Simple heuristics for paired comparison. *Theory and Decision* 52: 29–71.

Martignon, L., K.V. Katsikopoulos, and J.K. Woike. 2008. Categorization with limited resources: A family of simple heuristics. *Journal of Mathematical Psychology* 52: 352–361.

Mingers, J. 2011. Soft OR comes of age—But not everywhere! *Omega* 39: 729–741.

Rosenhead, J., and J. Mingers (eds.). 2001. *Rational analysis for a problematic world revisited: Problem structuring methods for complexity, uncertainty and conflict*. New York: Wiley.

Rubinstein, A.S. 1998. *Modeling bounded rationality*. Cambridge, MA: MIT Press.

Sage, A.P. 1992. *Systems engineering*. New York: Wiley.

Simon, H.A. 1955. A behavioral model of rational choice. *Quarterly Journal of Economics* 69: 99–118.

Simon, H.A. 1979. Rational decision making in business organizations. *American Economic Review* 69: 493–513.

Şimşek, Ö. 2013. Linear decision rule as aspiration for simple decision heuristics. *Advances in Neural Information Processing Systems* 26: 2904–2912.

Sull, D. N., & Eisenhardt, K. M. (September, 2012). Simple rules for a complex world. *Harvard Business Review*, 90(9), 68–74.

Tversky, A., and D. Kahneman. 1974. Heuristics and biases: Judgment under uncertainty. *Science* 185: 1124–1130.

Vapnik, V.N. 1999. *The nature of statistical learning theory*. New York: Springer.

Vicente, K.J. 1999. *Cognitive work analysis: Toward safe, productive, and healthy computer-based work*. Boca Raton: CRC Press.

Wuebben, M., and F. von Wagenheim. 2008. Instant customer base analysis: Managerial heuristics often "get it right". *Journal of Marketing* 72: 82–93.

Zsambok, C.E., and G.E. Klein (eds.).1997. *Naturalistic decision making*. New York, USA: Psychology Press.

# 3

# Behavior in Models: A Framework for Representing Human Behavior

Andrew Greasley and Chris Owen

## 3.1  Introduction

The modeling of people is becoming increasingly important in the design of industrial and business support systems. Despite the increasing dependency on technology in many such systems, the importance of humans is expected to increase, and in order to provide a realistic basis for decision support, both technical and organizational practices must be included in simulation models (Ilar 2008) if they are to be effective tools. The need to incorporate people when modeling systems is demonstrated by Baines et al. (2004), who found that the results from a simulation study that incorporated human factors could vary by 35% compared to a traditional study, in which no human factors were con-

A. Greasley (✉) • C. Owen
Aston Business School, Aston University, Aston Triangle,
Birmingham B4 7ET, UK

sidered. In the context of operations management, Croson et al. (2013) suggest that the scope of behavioral Operational Research is expanding significantly away from a historically narrow focus on inventory and supply chain issues and into wider areas of customer satisfaction, motivation, decision making and knowledge management, amongst many. The authors suggest that any behavior that deviates from the *hyper-rational*, i.e. behavior that is dictated purely by logic and physical evidence, is a candidate for research. They suggest that this opens up a wide range of domain areas of interest. This means that the potential scope of the modeling and simulation of human behavior is significant. Recent events such as the global financial crisis illustrate the risks and consequences of human behavior in today's hyper connected world. Many of the systems that we would like to understand or improve involve human actors, either as customers of the system or as people performing various roles within the system. There is a strong tradition within Operational Research of model building and simulation, where a model of the system is constructed in order to understand, to change or to improve the system (Pidd 2003). Modeling passive, predictable objects in a factory or a warehouse, however, is very different from trying to model people. Modeling people can be challenging, because people exhibit many traits to do with being conscious, sentient beings with free will. Human beings can be awkward and unpredictable in their behavior, and they may not conform to our ideas about how they should behave in a given situation. This presents a practical challenge to model builders, i.e. when and how to represent human behavior in our simulation models. In some situations, the role of human behavior in the model may be small and may be simplified or even left out of the model. In other cases, human behavior may be central to the understanding of the system under study, and then it becomes important that the modeller represent this in an appropriate way. These practical challenges also extend to the choice of modeling approach. In this chapter, we will argue that different modeling approaches are more or less suited to the modeling of human behavior and thus that the challenge extends beyond when and how to model human behavior, to what approach to use in which situation.

## 3.2    A Framework for Modeling Human Behavior

A framework will be presented based on a literature review of potential methods of modeling people which were identified and classified by the level of detail (termed *abstraction*) required to model human behavior. Each approach is given a *method name* and *method description*, listed in order of the level of abstraction used to model human behavior. The framework recognizes that the incorporation of human behavior in a simulation study does not necessarily involve the coding of human behavior in the simulation model itself. This relates to the point that a simulation model is used in conjunction with the user of that model to form a system (Pidd 2003). It is the combination of these two elements that will provide the analysis of human behavior required, and thus the framework recognizes that this may be achieved by an analysis ranging from being done solely by the user to the detailed modeling of individual human behavior in the simulation model itself. Thus, the methods are classified into those that are undertaken *outside the model* (i.e. elements of human behavior are considered in the simulation study but not incorporated in the simulation model) and those that incorporate human behavior within the simulation model, termed *inside the model*. Methods inside the model are classified in terms of a *world view*. Pegden et al. (1995) describe a world view as giving a framework for defining the components of the system in sufficient detail to allow the model to execute and simulate the system. *Model abstraction* is categorized as micro, meso or macro in order to clarify the different levels of abstraction for methods inside the model.

The framework then provides a suggested *simulation approach* for each of the levels of abstraction identified from the literature. The simulation approaches identified are *continuous simulation,* which may be in the form of a *System Dynamics model, Discrete-Event Simulation* and *agent-based simulation.* Continuous simulation describes a situation when the state of the system changes continuously over time and systems are described by differential equations. The implementation of the continuous world view is usually associated with the use of the System Dynamics technique (Forrester 1961). For a Discrete-Event Simulation, a system consists of a number of objects (*entities*) which flow from point to point in a system while competing with each other for the use of scarce resources (*resources*). The attributes of one entity may be used to determine future actions taken by the other entities. Agent-based simulation is an increasingly popular tool for modeling human behavior (Macal and North 2006). An *agent* can be defined as an entity with autonomy (it can undertake a set of local operations) and interactivity (it can interact with other agents to accomplish its own tasks and goals) (Hayes 1999). A particular class of agent-based systems, termed *multi-agent simulations*, are concerned with modeling both individual agents (with autonomy and interactivity) and also the emergent system behavior that is a consequence of the agents' collective actions and interactions.

The methods of modeling human behavior shown in Fig. 3.1 are now described in more detail.

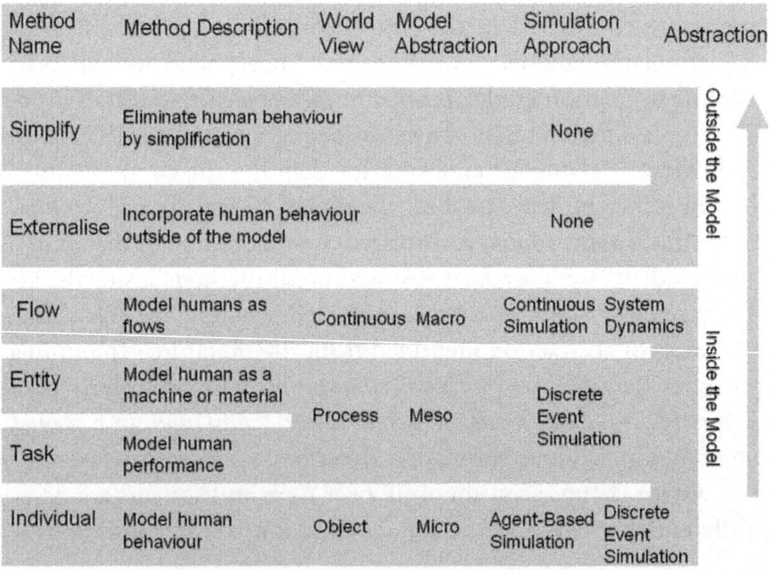

| Method Name | Method Description | World View | Model Abstraction | Simulation Approach | Abstraction |
|---|---|---|---|---|---|
| Simplify | Eliminate human behaviour by simplification | | | None | Outside the Model |
| Externalise | Incorporate human behaviour outside of the model | | | None | Outside the Model |
| Flow | Model humans as flows | Continuous | Macro | Continuous Simulation | System Dynamics | Inside the Model |
| Entity | Model human as a machine or material | Process | Meso | Discrete Event Simulation | Inside the Model |
| Task | Model human performance | Process | Meso | Discrete Event Simulation | Inside the Model |
| Individual | Model human behaviour | Object | Micro | Agent-Based Simulation | Discrete Event Simulation | Inside the Model |

**Fig. 3.1** Methods of modeling human behavior in a simulation study

## 3.2.1 Simplify (Eliminate Human Behavior by Simplification)

This involves the simplification of the simulation model in order to eliminate any requirement to codify human behavior. This strategy is relevant because a simulation model is not a copy of reality and should include only those elements necessary to meet the study objectives. This may make the incorporation of human behavior unnecessary. It may also be the case that the simulation user can utilize their knowledge of human behavior in conjunction with the model results to provide a suitable analysis. Actual mechanisms for the simplification of reality in a simulation model can be classified into (i) omission, (ii) aggregation and (iii) substitution (Pegden et al. 1995). In terms of modeling human behavior this can be elaborated as follows:

(i) *Omission:* Omitting human behavior from the model, such as unexpected absences through sickness. It may be assumed in the model that alternative staffing is allocated by managers. Often machine-based processes are modelled without reference to the human operator they employ.

(ii) *Aggregation:* Processes or the work of whole departments may be aggregated if their internal working is not the focus of the simulation study.

(iii) *Substitution:* For example, human processes may be substituted by a *delay* element with a constant process time in a simulation model, thus removing any complicating factors of human behavior.

An example of the use of the simplification technique is described in Johnson et al. (2005).

## 3.2.2 Externalize (Incorporate Human Behavior Outside of the Model)

This approach involves incorporating aspects of human behavior in the simulation study but externalizing them from the simulation model itself. The *externalize* approach to representing human decision making is to elicit the decision rules from the people involved in the relevant decisions and so avoid the simplification inherent when codifying complex behavior. Three approaches to externalizing human behavior are:

- Convert decision points and other aspects of the model into parameters which require human input. Most likely in this context the model will operate in a gaming mode in order to combine the benefits of real performance while retaining experimenter control and keeping costs low (Warren et al. 2005).
- Represent decisions in an expert system linked to the simulation model (Robinson et al. 2003).
- Use the simulation model as a recording tool to build up a set of examples of human behavior at a decision point. This data set is then used by a neural network to represent human behavior (Robinson et al. 2005).

### 3.2.3   Flow (Model Humans as Flows)

At the highest level of abstraction inside the model, humans can be modelled as a group which behaves like a flow in a pipe. In the case of the flow method of modeling human behavior, the world view is termed continuous and the model abstraction is termed macro. The type of simulation used for implementation of the *flow* method is either a continuous simulation approach or the System Dynamics technique. Hanisch et al. (2003) present a continuous model of the behavior of pedestrian flows in public buildings. Cavana et al. (1999) provide a System Dynamics analysis of the drivers of quality in health services. Sterman et al. (1997) developed a System Dynamics model to analyze the behavioral responses of people to the introduction of a Total Quality Management (TQM) initiative. Khanna et al. (2003) use System Dynamics to identify the various dynamic interactions among the subsystems of TQM.

### 3.2.4   Entity (Model Human as a Machine or Material)

This relates to a mesoscopic (meso) simulation in which elements are modelled as a number of discrete particles whose behavior is governed by predefined rules. One way of modeling human behavior in this way would mean that a human would be treated as a resource, such as a piece of equipment that is either *busy* or *idle*. Alternatively, modeling a human as an entity would mean that they would undertake a number of predetermined steps, like the flow of material in a manufacturing plant. This approach can be related to the process world view, which models the flow of entities through a series of *process* steps. Greasley and Barlow (1998) present a Discrete-Event Simulation of the arrest process in the UK Police service. Here the arrested person is the *customer* and is represented by an entity object. The police personnel, for example a police constable, is represented by a resource object in the simulation. The police personnel are either busy—engaged in an activity (for example interviewing an arrested person)—or are idle. This method permits people modelled as resource objects to be monitored for factors such as utilization in the same way a machine might be.

## 3.2.5  Task (Model Human Performance)

This method models the action of humans in response to a pre-defined sequence of tasks and is often associated with the term *human performance modeling*. Human performance modeling relates to the simulation of purposeful actions of a human as generated by well-understood psychological phenomena, rather than modeling in detail all aspects of human behavior not driven by purpose (Shaw and Prichett ). The *task* approach can be related to the process world view and mesoscopic (meso) modeling abstraction level, which models the flow of entities, in this case people, through a series of process steps. The task approach is implemented using a Discrete-Event Simulation which incorporates attributes of human behavior into the rules governing the behavior of the simulation. These attributes may relate to factors such as skill level, task attributes such as length of task and organizational factors such as perceived value of the task to the organization. Bernhard and Schilling (1997) outline a technique for dynamically allocating people to processes depending on their qualification to undertake the task. When material is ready to be processed at a work station, the model checks for and allocates the requisite number of qualified workers necessary for the task. The approach is particularly suitable for modeling group work, and the paper investigates the relative overall throughput time for a manufacturing process with different worker skill sets.

Elliman et al. (2005) present a case study of the use of simulation to model knowledge workers carrying out a series of tasks. Two assumptions of simulation models are seen as particular barriers to modeling knowledge workers. The first is that all resources are assumed to belong to pools where any worker within the pool has the ability to carry out the task. Secondly, there is an assumption that once a task is initiated it will be completed. The paper outlines a mechanism for representing people as entities, rather than resource pools, and enabling work on a task to be segmented into sessions. At the end of each session work priorities are reassessed and work continues either on the same tasks, if priorities have not changed, or on an alternative task. The paper then discusses how knowledge workers prioritize which task they will initiate next. Tasks are classified into *scheduled, on-demand and at-will*. The first two types of tasks are routinely modelled in simulation models. Future scheduled tasks whose start time is known can be triggered by a time delay, and on-demand tasks can be handled by a queuing mechanism. At-will tasks are more difficult to model, because the choice of task is made on an individual basis. Acknowledging individual behavior, the paper identifies four common factors used to prioritize work derived from observation of knowledge workers. Two factors—deadline and length of task—are properties of the task itself, whilst the other two—importance of the customer of the task and value of the task to the organization—are considered environmental properties.

Baines et al. (2004) show how the inclusion of human performance factors has an impact on the performance of a simulated production system. The factors incorporated in the model are performance reduction due to ageing and performance variation caused by biorhythms. In order to develop a modeling tool that enables the assessment of key human factors, Baines et al. (2005) provide a theoretical framework which aims to enable a prediction of individual human performance derived from 30 input factors arranged in the domains of the individual (e.g. age, gender, job satisfaction), physical working environment (e.g. noise, light) and organizational working environment (e.g. training, communications). A transformation function converts these factors into three critical human performance indicators: activity time, dependability and error rate. Three further indicators, absenteeism rate, accident rate and staff turnover rate, are computed for long-run simulations.

Neumann and Medbo (2009) demonstrate an approach to integrating human factors into a Discrete-Event Simulation study of production strategies. Human factors such as operator autonomy are operationalized as the percentage of break time taken when scheduled for each operator. The authors conclude that it is possible to operationalize and embed both simple (capability) and complex (autonomy) human factors into Discrete-Event Simulation and test their impact on system design alternatives. The approach studies the interaction effect among the multiple human factors using a factorial approach to the simulation experimental design.

## 3.2.6  Individual (Model Human Behavior)

This method involves modeling how humans actually behave based on individual attributes such as perception and attention. The approach is associated with an object world view where objects are self-contained units combining data and functions but are also able to interact with one another. The modeling approach can be termed microscopic (micro) and utilizes either the discrete-event or the agent-based simulation types.

Brailsford and Schmidt (2003) provide a case study of using discrete event simulation to model the attendance of patients for screening of a sight-threatening complication of diabetes. The model takes into account the physical state, emotions, cognition and social status of the persons involved. This approach is intended to provide a more accurate method of modeling patients' attendance behavior than the standard approach used in simulation studies using a simple random sampling of patients. The approach uses Physis, Emotion, Cognition and Status (PECS) (Schmidt 2005) architecture for modeling human behavior at an individual level. This was implemented by assigning numerical attributes, representing various psychological characteristics, to the patient entities. These characteristics included anxiety, perceived susceptibility, knowledge of disease, belief about disease prevention, health motivation and educational level. Each characteristic was rated as low, medium or high. These characteristics are then used to calculate the four PECS components. These in turn were used to calculate compliance, or likelihood that the patient would attend. The form of these calculations and the parameters within them were derived from trial and error in finding a plausible range of values for compliance compared with known estimates of population compliance derived from the literature.

Another example of the use of Discrete-Event Simulation to model individual human behavior is the development of a Micro Saint model by Keller (2002) which uses the Visual, Cognitive, Auditory, Psychomotor (VCAP) resource components (Wickens 1984) to estimate the total workload on a person driving a car while talking on a mobile phone. In terms of using agent-based simulation at the micro level, Prichett et al. (2001) use Agent-Based Modeling to investigate the behavior of air traffic controllers. Siebers et al. (2007) use an agent-based approach to simulate management approaches such as training and empowerment. The simulation has three different types of agents: customers, sales staff and managers. Lam (2007) demonstrates the use of an agent-based simulation to explore decision-making policies for service policy decisions.

## 3.3    Evaluating the Framework

The framework options are now discussed and the limitations of the framework are presented.

The *Simplify* approach ignores the role of humans in the process and is appropriate when it is not necessary to model the role of human behavior to meet the study objectives. Also, in practical terms it may take too long to model every aspect of a system even if it were feasible, which it may not be in most cases due to a lack of data, for example. The potential problem with the strategy of simplification is that the resulting model may be too far removed from reality for the client to have confidence in the model's results. The job of validation is to ensure the *right* model has been built, and a *social* role of the simulation developer is to ensure that the simulation clients are assured about simulation validity if they are to have confidence in the simulation's results.

The *Externalize* approach attempts to incorporate human behavior in the study, but not within the simulation model itself. The area of gaming simulation represents a specialized area of simulation when the model is being used in effect to collect data from a human in real time and react to this information. Alternative techniques such as expert systems and neural networks can be interfaced with the simulation and used to provide a suitable repository for human behavior. There will, however, most likely be a large overhead in terms of integrating these systems with simulation software.

The *Flow* approach models humans at the highest level of abstraction using differential equations. The level of abstraction, however, means that this approach does not possess the ability to carry information about each entity (person) through the system being modelled and is not able to show queuing behavior of people derived from demand and supply (Stahl 1995). Thus, the simulation of human behavior in customer processing applications for example may not be feasible using this approach.

The *Entity* approach models human behavior using the process world view to represent people by simulated machines (resources) and/or simulated materials (entities). This allows the availability of staff to be monitored in the case of resources and the flow characteristics of people, such as customers, to be monitored in the case of entities. Staff may be categorized with different skill sets, and variability in process durations can be estimated using sampling techniques. This will provide useful information in many instances but does not reflect the way people actually work. For instance in this approach staff may have different priorities, particularly in a service context where their day-to-day schedule may be a matter of personal preference.

The *Task* approach attempts to model how humans act without the complexity of modeling the cognitive and other variables that lead to that behavior. Elliman et al. (2005) use task and environmental variables rather than individual characteristics to model individual behavior. Bernhard and Schilling (1997) model people using the entity method but separate material flow from people flow. No individual differences are taken into account, and the approach uses a centralized mechanism/ database to control workers. The approach by Baines et al. (2005) was hindered by he difficulty in practice of collecting data on 30 input variables and six performance indicators in order to derive the transformation function required (Benedettini et al. 2006). Also, the variables were derived from literature, and when they were tried in practice other variables affecting human performance were found. For instance human performance differed due to the type of task undertaken. Related to this, an issue regarding the approach by Neumann and Medbo (2009), who operationalized human factors such as autonomy into variables that could be integrated in a Discrete-Event Simulation, is obtaining empirical evidence to validate the operationalization. This approach did, however, allow the interaction effect among multiple human factors to be studied using a factorial approach to the simulation experimental design.

The *Individual* approach attempts to model the internal cognitive processes that lead to human behavior. A number of architectures that model human cognition, such as Physis Emotion Cognition Status (PECS) (Schmidt 2000), Adaptive Control of Thought-Rational (ACT-R) (Anderson and Lebiere 1998), Soar(Newell 1990) and Theory of Planned Behavior (TPB) (Ajzen 1991) have been developed. These have the aim of being able to handle a range of situations in which the person has discretion on what to do next and are more realistic with respect to internal perceptual and cognitive processes for which the external environment constraint is less useful (Pew 2008). However, the difficulty of implementation of the results of studies on human behavior by behavioral and cognitive researchers into a simulation remains a significant barrier. Silverman (2004, p. 472) states, "There are well over one million pages of peer-reviewed, published studies on human behavior and performance as a function of demographics, personality differences, cognitive style, situational and emotive variables, task elements, group and organizational dynamics and culture" but goes on to state "unfortunately, almost none of the existing literature addresses how to interpret and translate reported findings as principles and methods suitable for implementation or synthetic agent development." Another barrier is the issue of the context of the behavior represented in the simulation. Silverman (1991) states,

"Many first principle models from the behavioral science literature have been derived within a particular setting, whereas simulation developers may wish to deploy these models in different contexts." Further issues are the difficulty of use of these architectures (Pew 2008) and the difficulty of validation of multiple factors of human behavior when the research literature is largely limited to the study of the independent rather than the interactive effects of these factors. In terms of the choice of simulation method at the micro level, the agent-based approach has been put forward as a more appropriate method for modeling people than Discrete-Event Simulation (Siebers et al. 2010), but it is also argued that it is not currently clear whether agent-based models do offer new capabilities over and above what Discrete-Event Simulation can provide (Brailsford 2014).

There are limitations with the framework that need to be considered.

- The framework presents the options and provides guidance on the choice of option by relating each option to the level of abstraction required to meet the simulation study objectives. Here the principle of modeling to the highest level of abstraction to meet the study objectives should apply. However, it may be in practical terms that there is a need to rationalize the modeling task further to make it workable (Baines et al. 2005).
- The level of abstraction does not take into account other variables, such as the nature of the complexity of the modeling task. For example the framework does not distinguish between the different complexities of modeling individual behavior and of modeling interactions between people (Joo et al. 2013).
- There is a debate about the suitability of Discrete-Event Simulation to model human behavior. For example, Elkosantini (2015) states that Discrete-Event Simulation software is not appropriate for modeling individual human behavior. One solution could be the use of Discrete-Event Simulation software to implement agent-based models (Greasley and Owen 2015) and Robinson (2015).
- There are other simulation methods available that are used for modeling human behavior not included in the framework, including petri-nets (a graphical modeling technique) and social networks.

- Further work is required to identify the literature on cognitive models and to provide guidance on their use in modeling human behavior in simulation models.
- The need to be aware of what human performance and cognitive models are appropriate and how they can be deployed for a particular simulation application adds another skill to the already wide skillset of the simulation practitioner. This implies a team approach to simulation development when modeling human behavior applications.

## 3.4   Conclusion

In summary, to assist in modeling human behavior, a framework has been presented outlining approaches available when considering incorporating an analysis of human behavior in a simulation study. The approaches are categorized by the level of abstraction of human behavior required in order to meet the simulation study objectives. Examples are provided of studies that have taken place using each of the methods described. A distinction is drawn between methods used in the simulation study, such as simplification and externalization, and methods which incorporate human behavior in the simulation model itself. In terms of the latter, the use of human performance factors and application of models of human cognition represent significant challenges to simulation practitioners. In conclusion, the framework provides a view of the options available when modeling human behavior but further work is needed to provide guidance on how and when human behavior should be incorporated into a simulation model.

## References

Ajzen, A. 1991. The theory of planned behavior. *Organizational Behavior and Human Decision Processes* 50: 179–211.

Anderson, J.R., and C. Lebiere. 1998. *The atomic components of thought.* Mahwah: Erlbaum.

Baines, T., S. Mason, P. Siebers, and J. Ladbrook. 2004. Humans: The missing link in manufacturing simulation? *Simulation Modeling Practice and Theory* 12: 515–526.

Baines, T., R. Asch, L. Hadfield, J.P. Mason, S. Fletcher, and J.M. Kay. 2005. Towards a theoretical framework for human performance modelling within manufacturing systems design. *Simulation Modelling Practice and Theory* 13: 486–504.

Benedettini, O., T. Baines, and J. Ladbrook. 2006. Human performance modelling within manufacturing systems design: From theory to practice. *Proceedings of the 2006 OR Society Simulation Workshop.*

Bernhard, W., and A. Schilling. 1997. Simulation of group work processes in manufacturing. *Proceedings of the 1997 Winter Simulation Conference*, IEEE Computer Society.

Brailsford, S.C. 2014. Discrete-event simulation is alive and kicking! *Journal of Simulation* 8(1): 1–8.

Brailsford, S., and B. Schmidt. 2003. Towards incorporating human behavior in models of health care systems: An approach using discrete-event simulation. *European Journal of Operational Research* 150: 19–31.

Cavana, R.Y., P.K. Davies, R.M. Robson, and K.J. Wilson. 1999. Drivers of quality in health services: Different worldviews of clinicians and policy managers revealed. *System Dynamics Review* 15: 331–340.

Croson, R., K. Schultz, E. Siemsen, and M.L. Yeo. 2013. Behavioural operations: The state of the field. *Journal of Operations Management* 31: 1–5.

Elkosantini, S. 2015. Towards a new generic behavior model for human centered system simulation. *Simulation Modelling Practice and Theory* 52: 108–122.

Elliman, T., J. Eatock, and N. Spencer. 2005. Modelling knowledge worker behavior in business process studies. *The Journal of Enterprise Information Management* 18: 79–94.

Forrester, J. 1961. *Industrial dynamics.* Cambridge, MA: Productivity Press.

Greasley, A., and S. Barlow. 1998. Using simulation modelling for BPR: Resource allocation in a police custody process. *International Journal of Operations and Production Management* 18: 978–988.

Greasley, A., and C. Owen. 2015. Implementing an agent-based model with a spatial visual display in discrete-event simulation software. *Proceedings of the 5th International Conference on Simulation and Modeling Methodologies, Technologies and Applications (SIMULTECH 2015)*, Colmar.

Hanisch, A., J. Tolujew, K. Richter, and T. Schulze. 2003. Online simulation of pedestrian flow in public buildings. *Proceedings of the 2003 Winter Simulation Conference*, SCS, New Orleans, pp. 1635–1641.

Hayes, C.C. 1999. Agents in a nutshell—A very brief introduction. *IEEE Transactions on Knowledge and Data Engineering* 11: 127–132.

Ilar, T.B.E. 2008. *Proceedings of the 40th Conference on Winter Simulation.* Winter Simulation Conference, pp. 903–908.

Johnson, R.T., J.W. Fowler, and G.T. Mackulak. 2005. A discrete event simulation model simplification technique. *Proceedings of the 2005 Winter Simulation Conference*, SCS, pp. 2172–2176.

Joo, J., N. Kim, R.A. Wysk, L. Rothrock, Y.-J. Son, Y. Oh, and S. Lee. 2013. Agent-based simulation of affordance-based human behaviors in emergency evacuation. *Simulation Modelling Practice and Theory* 32: 99–115.

Keller, J. 2002. Human performance modelling for discrete-event simulation: Workload. *Proceedings of the 2002 Winter Simulation Conference*, pp. 157–162.

Khanna, V.K., P. Vat, R. Shanker, B.S. Sahay, and A. Gautam. 2003. TQM modeling of the automobile manufacturing sector: A system dynamics approach. *Work Study* 52: 94–101.

Lam, R.B. 2007. Agent-based simulations of service policy decisions. *Proceedings of the 2007 Winter Simulation Conference*, SCS, pp. 2241–2246.

Macal, C.M., and M.J. North. 2006. Tutorial on agent-based modeling and simulation part 2: How to model with agents. *Proceedings of the 2006 Winter Simulation Conference*, SCS, pp. 73–83.

Neuman, W.P., and P. Medbo. 2009. Integrating human factors into discrete event simulations of parallel flow strategies. *Production Planning and Control* 20: 3–16.

Newell, A. 1990. *Unified theories of cognition.* Cambridge, MA: Harvard University Press.

Pegden, C.D., R.E. Shannon, and R.P. Sadowski. 1995. *Introduction to simulation using SIMAN*, 2nd ed. New York: McGraw-Hill.

Pew, R.W. 2008. More than 50 years of history and accomplishments in human performance model development. *Human Factors* 50: 489–496.

Pidd, M. 2003. *Tools for thinking: Modelling in management science*, 2nd ed. Hoboken: Wiley.

Prichett, A.R., S.M. Lee, and D. Goldsman. 2001. Hybrid-system simulation for national airspace safety systems analysis. *AIAA Journal of Aircraft* 38: 835–840.

Robinson, S. 2015. Modelling without queues: Adapting discrete-event simulation for service operations. *Journal of Simulation* 9: 195–205.

Robinson, S., J.S. Edwards, and W. Yongfa. 2003. Linking the witness simulation software to an expert system to represent a decision-making process. *Journal of Computing and Information Technology* 11: 123–133.

Robinson, S., T. Alifantis, J.S. Edwards, J. Ladbrook, and T. Waller. 2005. Knowledge based improvement: Simulation and artificial intelligence for identifying and improving human decision-making in an operations system. *Journal of the Operational Research Society* 56: 912–921.

Schmidt, B. 2000. *The modelling of human behavior*. Erlangen: SCS Publications.

Schmidt, B. 2005. Human factors in complex systems: The modeling of human behavior. *Proceedings 19th European Conference of Modelling and Simulation*, ECMS.

Siebers, P., U. Aickelin, H. Celia, and C.W. Clegg. 2007. Using intelligent agents to understand management practices and retail productivity. *Proceedings of the 2007 Winter Simulation Conference*, SCS, pp. 2212–2220.

Siebers, P.O., C.M. Macal, J. Garnett, D. Buxton, and M. Pidd. 2010. Discrete-event simulation is dead, long live agent-based simulation! *Journal of Simulation* 4: 204–210.

Silverman, B.G. 1991. Expert critics: Operationalising the judgement/decision making literature as a theory of "bugs" and repair strategies. *Knowledge Acquisition* 3: 175–214.

Silverman, B.G. 2004. Toward realism in human performance simulation. In *The science and simulation of human performance*, ed. J.W. Ness, V. Tepe, and D.R. Rizer. Oxford: Elsevier.

Stahl, I. 1995. New product development: When discrete simulation is preferable to system dynamics. *Proceedings of the 1995 EUROSIM Conference*, Elsevier Science B.V.

Sterman, J.D., N.P. Repenning, and F. Kofman. 1997. Unanticipated side effects of successful quality programs: Exploring a paradox of organizational improvement. *Management Science* 43: 503–521.

Warren, R., D.E. Diller, A. Leung, and W. Ferguson. 2005. Simulating scenarios for research on culture and cognition using a commercial role-play game. *Proceedings of the 2005 Winter Simulation Conference*, SCS, pp. 1109–1117.

Wickens, C.D. 1984. *Engineering psychology and human performance*. New York: HarperCollins Publishers.

# 4

# Behavior Beyond the Model

## Leroy White

## 4.1 Introduction

Without doubt, understanding the relationship among knowledge, behavior and action has been an academic preoccupation in OR since the beginning of the discipline (Ackoff 1977, 1978; Dutton and Walton 1964). Moreover, it is found in some older studies that psychological or behavioral ideas were invoked, if somewhat casually, particularly from disciplines such as group and social psychology (Phillips and Phillips 1993; Friend et al. 1998). Yet it is claimed that these ideas have not penetrated OR theory or practice in any significant way (Bendoly et al. 2006; Hämäläinen et al. 2013). This may be due to the fact that these earlier studies tend to make some fairly basic behavioral assumptions (see Eden 1989, 1992 for a similar argument). Whatever the reasons, there is a clear sense that

L. White (✉)
Warwick Business School, University of Warwick,
Coventry CV4 7AL, UK

behavioral concerns are under-developed, particularly in the area of the process of OR, termed here *OR Beyond the Model*.

Given the recent interest in "Behavior" and "Operational Research" (OR) (Royston 2013), in this chapter it will be argued that if OR scholars and practitioners are to benefit meaningfully from behavioral research, they must establish a viable means of engaging with the theoretical and empirical developments in this field, without losing sight of the *socially situated nature* of OR practice (Midgley et al. 2013; Franco 2013; White 2006, 2009). To address the above issue and to explore behavior for OR beyond the model, the chapter introduces three propositions which together form a framework that should enable more productive and robust exchanges between behavioral research and the process of OR.

## 4.2    A Philosophical and Theoretical Basis for Behavior in the Process of OR

Recently, it was suggested that inferences about OR practice require the working out of more middle range theories (and models) (White 2006; Yearworth and White 2014). This aligns with a general movement in the social sciences based on the idea that middle range theorizing makes more sense for avoiding the pitfalls of agency or structure explanations of social phenomena (Merton 1967; Bourgeois 1979). In relation to the process of OR, it is suggested that adopting a stance with a modest scope helps to explain a specific set of phenomena, as opposed to taking a stance based on a grand theory that seeks to explain phenomena at a broader level (White 2006). Thus, the position for this chapter is in favor of middle range theorizing (Bourgeois 1979), and in particular it will draw on the work of Hacking as perhaps providing a more compelling basis for understanding behavioral OR beyond the model.

### 4.2.1    Representing and Intervening

The work of Hacking (1983, 1999) sees epistemological common ground for the physical and social sciences, even while maintaining a unique ontology for the transitive objects of social scientific study (Hacking

1983). A notable feature of Hacking's idea is that scholars are encouraged to move from puzzles of rationality to problems of reality, and to consider practice as concerning *representing* and *intervening*.

*We represent and we intervene. We represent in order to intervene, and we intervene in the light of representations.* (Hacking 1983, p. 31)

What is relevant is, first, his argument on representation. Hacking criticizes the positivist philosophy of science for its single-minded obsession with representation, thinking and theory, at the expense of intervention, action and experiment.

Hacking suggested reversing this trend to focus on intervening in our case, the process of OR). He illustrates how interventions often have a life independent of theory. He also argued that although the philosophical problems of scientific realism cannot be resolved when put in terms of theory alone, a sound philosophy of intervention provides compelling grounds for a realistic attitude. He thus claims that the theoretical entities that feature in (scientific) theories can be regarded as real if and only if they refer to phenomena that can be routinely used to create effects in domains that can be investigated independently. He refers to this as *manipulative success*, which becomes the criterion by which to judge the reality of (typically unobservable) *scientific* entities.

*When we use tools as instruments of inquiry, we are entitled to regard them as real.* (Hacking 1983, p. 23)

In this way, forms of representing may be merely theoretical entities within an OR intervention. But once they can be used to manipulate an intervention in a systematic way, they cease to be something hypothetical or something inferred.

But what is the role of Hacking's idea of representing and intervening, and of behavior in OR? First, central to the process of OR is that it captures, through representing, models of viewpoints and beliefs to enhance an understanding of a problematic situation and to help resolve the situation (Eden 1992). Overall, it is claimed that through representing it is possible to fashion an improvement in problematic situations at the individual level (i.e. the representation through models improves the mental models of the participants and therefore the understanding of the issues), and also that these models bring forth a change in the attitude towards mental model alignment, consensus and agreement. This implies an emergent organization- or system-level change, in that members of the organization can move towards a set of improvements and decisions to resolve a problematic situation (Mingers 2011).

Second, mapping the underlying problem into a simple representation which, in turn, is amenable to mediating behavior within a process (intervening) is an important aspect of understanding the process of OR. Thus, while under the allure of the style and power of the OR process or intervention, the fact that the basis for this process is an act of representation is often under-theorized or under-reflected. This relative neglect deprives scholars of the opportunity to think more carefully about the relationship between representing and intervening, as there is an implicit notion that the representation is, in fact, a characterization of the true problem setting and not simply one out of a vast sea of possible options (Taket and White 2000; Mingers 2011). Also, a failure to recognize the inherent connection between models of the world and the actual situations is likely to lead to misinformed readings of the process of OR as intervening on the part of decision-makers (Neale and Bazerman 1985).

*Proposition 1* The philosophical basis for considering behavior for OR beyond the model should be the relationship between representing and intervening and should focus on emergence and the mediating role of the model

## 4.3    Behavior and OR Beyond the Model

In this section we draw on the relationship among knowledge, behavior and action that has been ever present in OR theory and practice since the beginning of the discipline (Ackoff 1977; Keys 1997). While there is a large literature both within and outside OR, these studies rarely if ever focus on biases or on behavior directly. By loosely aligning themselves with behavior, these studies located themselves in hotly contested philosophical territory (Miser 1991, 1993; Dando et al. 1977), where several theoretical strands have sprung up that have implications for behavioral issues in OR (Ormerod 2012). Some of these are now considered.

## 4.3.1 Internalization and Externalization

Ackoff's work (1978, 1983) is drawn on as some of the first to introduce a formal approach to behavior and OR. He criticized OR for its failure to incorporate "psychological and social variables" (Kirby and Rosenhead 2005). He suggested an approach to understanding OR processes that involved two dichotomies (Ackoff 1989)—subjective versus objective—and two behavioral aspects—one representing internalization (an inclination to act on oneself, to adapt oneself and to modify one's own behavior to solve problems) and the other representing externalization (an inclination to act on and modify the environment in problem-solving efforts). Thus, for Ackoff (1978, 1989), OR has relied on the debate concerning what may be called the *internalization* versus the *externalization* of behavioral processes, namely whether such processes occur uniquely within individual minds or whether they can occur outside of individuals.

To lay out this territory, Ackoff's two conceptual (and hypothetical) extreme positions are built upon. Between these extreme positions can be found a plethora of intermediate and hybrid positions, to be understood based on how they integrate internalist and externalist positions (Theiner et al. 2010).

With regard to internalization, there is vast literature on individual judgment, behavior and decision-making, drawing on Tverksy and Kahneman's (1981) classic work on choice under uncertainty, which are all now commonplace. The rational choice solutions to these problems (that is, choices that are mutually consistent and obey the axioms of expected utility theory) are known, and individuals can readily contrast those solutions with actual behavior. This has been and continues to be a tremendously important and vibrant line of inquiry for behavioral decision-making (for an overview see Maule and Hodgkinson 2003). This body of work began to address cognitive biases in decision-making.

In particular, studies focusing on why managers make poor decisions when planning find that observed psychological biases are deep-seated and play an important role in influencing the decisions of OR managers. So, according to this perspective, even if through the model people know and understand the facts, they may still make poor or different decisions due to personality/individual characteristics.

With regard to externalization, the case for behavior beyond the individual is made, in order to explore making some general claims about the plausibility of collective behavior. For this, a different reading is drawn on and adopted. At a rather mundane level, the institutional and social positions of actors in OR interventions shape their views of their roles in these systems, which in turn interact with their cognitive processes, which do not resemble the simple rational models suggested by traditional behavioralists (Kahneman 2003; Kahneman and Tversky 2000). Instead, running across these perspectives is the question of how individual information-processing behavior, through OR interventions, coalesces into collective behavior; when this is framed in terms of internalization/externalization, different theoretical scenarios emerge, from which behavioral insights can be made.

*Proposition 2* To understand behavioral OR beyond the model, the theoretical basis should be externalization

## 4.3.2   The Individual or the Group: Procedural Rationality and Satisficing

Scholars have been particularly interested in the idea that it may be useful to view rationality for the practice of OR as a process (Best et al. 1986; Rosenhead 1986; Pidd 2004). This implicitly drew on the work of Simon (see Simon 1976), which has played a key role in the decision-making literature (see Eisenhardt and Zbaracki 1992; Maule and Hodgkinson 2003) and the process of OR literature (see Pidd 2004). For Simon, adapting to an outer environment (substantive rationality) is the main goal of individuals in a decision-making situation, and if they were perfectly rational and adaptable, we would need to study only their environments (as in much of classical economics). However, in reality, the problem for individuals is often to calculate what the appropriate, let alone the optimal, options are. For such reasons, Simon introduced the theory of *bounded rationality*. This is the notion that individuals are limited by the information and skills they have access to, the finite time they have to make a decision, and the cognitive limitations they have in their minds. Here, Simon suggests that the way forward is to view rationality as a process, or *procedural rationality*, which concerns the choice or development of procedures for making decisions when the decision-maker effectively has limited access to information in the first place (bounded rationality). Procedural rationality refers generally to a reliance on processes that reflect a problem-solving approach and involve the gathering and analysis of relevant information for making choices (Simon 1976). Central to the idea of procedural rationality is *satisficing*, or accepting a "good enough" solution for a problem (Simon 1991).

According to Simon, actors attempting to make good decisions are not capable of an objectively rational approach and therefore do not conform to the requirements of a normative model. They do nonetheless engage on a form of analytic problem-solving that reflects attention to process. From this perspective, rationality is seen as a particular way to approach action in a complex, intractable problem setting. As Pidd argued (2004), OR approaches aim to provide decision support that is procedurally rational, although how they do this varies. Thus, even if it can be shown that there is an optimal solution or decision based on the model of the real world, the process by which the real world is simplified into a model is subject to other, sometimes behavioral, effects (Simon 1976).

What would this mean for behavioral OR, beyond the model? Phillips (1984) was perhaps one of the first to conceive of a behavioral orientation for OR beyond the model. He introduced the term "requisite models" to distinguish a form of representation from descriptive, normative, optimal or even satisficing modeling. He claims that a model is requisite when "it is a representation of the problem deemed sufficiently adequate by the decision makers to provide them with a useful guide to thinking about the problem" (Phillips 1984, p. 19). In this way, requisite models do not prescribe action—they are a guide to action, where "action" is a collective activity aiming at system-level improvement. This idea has been important in a number of OR studies.

Phillips's (1984) argument for requisite models (and for a focus on collective behavior) countered the research on judgment and decision-making that draws on the classic work of behavioral economics (Simon 1976; Kahneman and Tversky 2000). As stated earlier, the basis of the classic work is not that people have no idea how to make decisions but that they think they know but are *wrong* by the conventional standards of rationality. The usual response is: if they are to do better, they first have to see the error of their ways. Indeed, many behavioral scholars think that the appropriate thing to do is to nudge people in the direction they would want to find themselves after taking expert advice. Thus, equipped with an understanding of the behavioral findings of bounded rationality and bounded self-control, experts should attempt to nudge people's choices in certain directions without eliminating freedom of choice.

Phillips also claimed not only that the work of classic behavioral economics sees people as limited and biased in their judgments but that the research itself is limited and biased in its presumption that what people do is all that they can do. He argues that in the processes that search for requisite models, it is assumed that people are capable of constructing futures that deal adequately with uncertainty, risk and the complexity they face. Phillips's approach is that behavioral research needs to focus on a more positive interpretation of behavior that aims to meet the challenge of finding the conditions in which people can be "intellectual athletes rather than intellectual cripples", i.e. to create a notion of behavior in OR based on what people can do.

*Proposition 3* OR beyond the model is a form of social practice that should be understood as model-mediated activity, which has the potential to be both generative and emergent

## 4.4    Collective Behavior: Emergent Property for Behavior Beyond the Model

Proposition 3 is relevant to OR beyond the model, research has shown that sharing of arguments often allows a group to converge on the best answers, even if these are defended only by a minority (Moshman and Geil 1998). This is exemplified by the work of Eden and Ackermann (1998), where, through modeling in groups with cognitive maps, participants are able to estimate each other's confidence as well as to exchange their position on issues arguments in order to reach consensus. It is claimed that the group can reach a collective decision that is beyond and better than the range of individual responses held by the participants before the intervention. Thus, through models mediating the group's activities, participants can reach a deep understanding of the issues, and in some cases this is transferable to new situations (Laughin et al. 2002; Eden and Ackermann 2006). The work of scholars also seems to imply that through the mediating role of the model, the authority of the more self-assured individuals can be superseded by the quality of the collective (or convincing) argumentation. More importantly, the OR interventions have a number of other salutary effects, including increasing the degree of group acceptance of and satisfaction with the eventual choice (Priem et al. 1995). Overall, group-oriented OR interventions could claim group-level behaviors. However, the *meaningful* nature of collective behavior would not be evidenced by such output, in that collective behavior would have to have a higher burden of proof than it has in aggregating information-processing views. This remains under-researched. To move forward there is a need to take seriously the generative nature of OR interventions (Franco 2013; White 2006) and to emphasize the role of models as representations, integrating and coordinating the practice of stakeholder engagement.

For the rest of this chapter, the focus is on behavior beyond the model. We introduce here a simple map of the different types and domains of behavior for OR beyond the model that can be characterized by our propositions above. We focus mainly on externalization. We chose externalization as an explanatory vehicle because it is related to many other theories of behavioral decision-making, both individually and in groups.

In the simplest of terms, the map (Fig. 4.1) graphs two analytical dimensions: (i) the extent to which the OR process focuses on representing or on intervening and (ii) whether the focus is on individuals or on groups. The northern edge of the map represents a situation where individual decision-making is the focus, and the southern edge represents group decision-making, where behaviors are based on group behavior or a similar social process. The east–west dimension of the map represents a continuum from representing to intervening, or—more formally—the extent to which there is mediation between the model and the consequences of the OR process, i.e. OR beyond the model. The farther east we go on the map, the more attuned the intervention will be with the landscape of models as representation. As we move west, the interventions will be more complex and models will be less and less

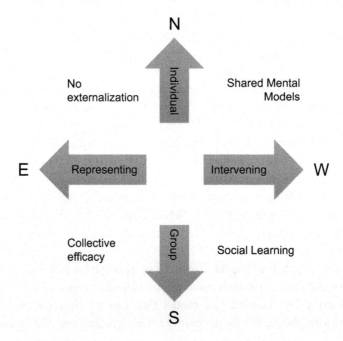

**Fig. 4.1** A map for understanding behavior beyond the model

able to discern differences in potential benefits among the choices available to the participants and may lead to emergent social behavior.

The map is considerably more than a qualitative description, as it is grounded in the established propositions above. The map is divided into quadrants for ease of discussion. Importantly, the characterizations are based on extreme positions of actors within each quadrant. As actors move away from extremes, the characterizations can be relaxed.

The northeast quadrant contains individuals who make decisions independently and who know the impact their decisions will have on them. The extreme northeast corner is where rational-actor approaches and economic assumptions are dominant. For example, individuals in this corner will always choose the option that provides the best benefit/cost ratio—most obviously and directly. Bounded-rationality theories (e.g. Simon 1991; Kahneman 2003) are placed in the northeast, because of their emphasis on actual cognitive costs of information processing, which a rational response to economizing on information-processing and other types of costs in dealing with decision-making in a complex world. Here we expect no externalization.

## 4.5    Further Understanding of the Map

### 4.5.1    Southeast Quadrant: Collective Efficacy

Some scholars of group decision-making research claim that because the information-sharing or informational output processes among group members would be observable, they could be used to infer collective behavior in terms of outputs such as efficacy (Bandura 1991).

This seems to relate to the map in that it provides some insights on situations that refer to group perspective and instrumental use of models as representation (Fig. 4.1). Here it is suggested that in attempting to understand collective behavior, less attention should be given to the insights from groupthink and instead the focus should be on the notion of collective efficacy (CE). This is defined as a group's belief in their conjoint capabilities to organize and execute the course of action required to produce given levels of attainment (Bandura 2000). CE refers to a group's shared perception of its ability to successfully perform a task. It is a prospective rather than a retrospective assessment of a group's capability. The task-specific performance perceptions in turn can influence what type of future the group members seek to achieve, how they manage the plans and strategies they construct, how much effort they put into their group behavior and how much staying power they have when the collective efforts fail to produce quick results or encounter forcible opposition (Gully et al. 2002). Bandura described four sources of efficacy: (i) past performance, (ii) vicarious experience, (iii) verbal persuasion and (iv) physiological and affective states. CE also arises through group interaction and forms as group members acquire, store, manipulate and exchange information about each other and about their task, context, process, and prior performance (Gibson 1999). Thus, efficacy perceptions are dynamic and so may change as experience changes (Lindsley et al. 1995).

Interestingly, other studies imply that defective decision-making practices are mainly associated with highly cohesive groups through groupthink, but this might also be explained by an excess or deficit of CE (Whyte 1998). Thus, such groups would be well advised to assess, or be conscious of, and to take into account, or be systematic about, the processes by which they make decisions. These groups are likely to display the types of behavior that produces unsatisfactory results, or they may miss seeing the advantages of OR interventions.

## 4.5.2 Northwest Quadrant: Shared Mental Models

There is a large literature on shared mental models. This focuses on shared content as evidence for collective behavior (see Mohammed et al. 2010). This is similar to studies on organizational approaches stressing thinking *with* objects. The exemplar here is the use of cognitive maps and of System Dynamics modeling and group model building (Eden 2004; Sterman 1989; Vennix 1997). Here, individuals are able to access common meanings and to partake in a common present through which they pass together, thus creating a shared world; yet even in this *collective sharedness*, individuals must interpret and infer the intentionality of others, and thus it might be possible for no collective-level behavioral domain to emerge at all from the shared referential objects of individuals (see Joldersma and Roelofs 2004).

Early views (e.g. Eden et al. 1979; Eden 2004) focused on the aggregation of individual cognitive maps in collective-level phenomena (e.g. Eden 1992). The concern of this early literature was to explain how organization-level stability in culture and values can persist in the face of individual member attrition while maintaining a focus on individuals (Eden et al. 1979). These mental states are structured around representations of cognition that instantiate thought through systems of representation (e.g. Eden 2004). However, it is also claimed that these shared mental models, while placing cognition at the individual level, also open the possibility that group processes will emerge through coordination, i.e. *thinking at the group level*. In the main, however, this is metaphorical, creating a vivid image of *thinking groups* yet remaining rooted at the individual level.

## 4.5.3   Southwest Quadrant: Social Learning

With regard to this perspective, it was shown recently that the notion of cognitive affordances (Gibson 1977) is useful for understanding the role of models in facilitated OR interventions (see Franco 2013). The notion of cognitive affordances (Gibson 1977) is useful for understanding the role of models as representation (for applications of the affordance notion in organizational settings see Zammuto et al. (2007) and in OR see Franco (2013)). "Affordances" refers to the environmental configurations given by material properties of the environment, which shape the behavioral possibilities in a given situation. To the extent that affordances act as environmental constraints on behavior (see Zammuto et al. 2007), they form the context for behavior. These arguments link with the earlier point about people thinking *with* models as objects. It can be inferred from studies that models have affordances that shape the way that people frame problems but can also enable people to advance their own interests in those problems. However, when affordances allow individuals to think *with* objects, these objects seem more deeply integrated into the cognitive apparatus itself, as models for cognition. To the extent that they are, the case for externalism could be bolstered by pointing to model affordances provided by diverse means, whether via a model or via the social interaction (Franco 2013). Franco discusses model affordances (Franco 2013) as a source of behavioral consideration. However, there are some limitations. First, the study could not adequately address the issues of power and contradiction (see Nicolini et al. 2012). Second, Franco's study (2013), while it connected the idea of boundary objects to learning, did not explore this at the collective level. When in fact Gibson sought to extend his ecological theory of affordances to the societal realm, he emphasized the need to reflect on learning: "Social learning is inevitably moral, in an elementary sense of the term, and it is probably a mistake first to construct a behavior theory without reference to social interaction, and then attach it only at the end" (Gibson 1950, p. 155). This is why we suggest that the concept of affordances in OR interventions requires embedding in a theory that enables active, reflexive and social construction (White 2006) and deconstruction and reconstruction of hegemonic discourses which artifacts may serve.

## 4.6   Discussion and Conclusion

It is suggested from the research above that the most significant convergence of behavioral research and OR beyond the model is to see and relate (collective) behavior to the core of OR interventions and theories. It seems reasonable to identify some themes emerging from the above that indicate potential areas for future research.

First, the focus on collective behavior: it could be argued that collective behavior is not yet a coherent field, particularly compared to one dominated by the work of Kahneman and others. Much of the work on OR does not yet suggest that there is a unity in the set of conditions that are engendered through collective OR interventions but refer to the fascinating characteristics of the interventions themselves. Collective behavior, despite its loose formulation, is concerned with crucial problems and is pre-occupied with relating social psychological phenomena to (social) change. These considerations alone ensure that there could be a fruitful and active agenda for OR beyond the model. It is also contended that collective behavior will be of vital interest to those concerned with OR theory development.

Second, a focus on the level of proof: many scholars of OR will agree that the nature of the link between OR processes and outcomes has yet to be definitively proven. Operationally, since a great deal of OR interventions are one-off and temporary, it becomes necessary to devise systematic techniques to ensure an adequate test of the efficacy of the approaches. An example of an approach that we think could be fruitful for exploring behavior for OR beyond the model are the ideas of the *Collaboratory* (Wulf 1989).

A Collaboratory is defined by Wulf (1989) as "a centre without walls, in which researchers can perform their research without regard to physical location—interacting with colleagues, accessing instrumentation, sharing data and computational resources, and accessing information in digital libraries." The Collaboratory can be used as a mechanism for building shared understandings and knowledge among the network participants and for activities such as building, acquiring and analyzing together. In this sense a Collaboratory can be seen as a Living Lab—as a gathering of stakeholders in which organizations, researchers, authorities and citizens work together for the creation, validation and testing of new services, ideas and technologies in real-life contexts. This concept could potentially allow shared experiments to be carried out, drawing on the experience of workshops in the creation of spaces enabling dialogue among stakeholders, using models as representations, games, simulations and visualizations—tools based on research at the intersection of social sciences, art and technology.

The Collaboratory is focused on multi-agency brokerage and development of shared understanding and on experimentation, exchange and translation. In this regard, the Collaboratory will enable a move to a more collective level of analysis, to examine interdependencies and interactions at the group level rather than examining behavior at the individual level of analysis.

In sum, collective behavior can have significant and beneficial implications for soft OR beyond the model. There are a variety of components to these highly complex interventions and a multitude of factors that may influence the emergence of collective behavior. However, teams and organizations can create conditions to foster and facilitate the process. In developing the proposed framework of behavioral OR, this study has taken a highly pragmatic approach to understanding how the collective behavioral process emerges.

# References

Ackoff, R.L. 1977. Optimization + objectivity = Opt out. *European Journal of Operational Research* 1: 17.

Ackoff, R.L. 1978. *The art of problem solving: Accompanied by Ackoffs Fables.* New York: Wiley.

Ackoff, R.L. 1983. An interactive view of rationality. *Journal of the Operational Research Society* 34: 719–722.

Ackoff, R.L. 1989. Dangerous dichotomies. *Systems Practice* 2: 155–157.

Bandura, A. 1991. Social cognitive theory of self-regulation. *Organizational Behavior and Human Decision Processes* 50: 248–287.

Bandura, A. 2000. Exercise of human agency through collective efficacy. *Current Directions in Psychological Science* 9: 75–78.

Bendoly, E., K. Donohue, and K.L. Schultz. 2006. Behavior in operations management: Assessing recent findings and revisiting old assumptions. *Journal of Operations Management* 24: 737–752.

Best, G., G. Parston, and J. Rosenhead. 1986. Robustness in practice—The regional planning of health services. *Journal of the Operational Research Society* 37: 463–478.

Bourgeois, L.J. 1979. Toward a method of middle-range theorizing. *Academy of Management Review* 4: 443–447.

Dando, M., A. Defrenne, and R. Sharp. 1977. Could OR be a science? *Omega* 5: 89–92.

Dutton, J.M., and R.E. Walton. 1964. Operational research and the behavioral sciences. *OR* 15: 207–217.

Eden, C. 1989. Operational research as negotiation. In *Operational research and the social sciences*, ed. M. Jackson, P. Keys, and S. Cropper, 43–50. London: Plenum.

Eden, C. 1992. On the nature of cognitive maps. *Journal of Management Studies* 29: 261–266.

Eden, C. 2004. Analyzing cognitive maps to help structure issues or problems. *European Journal of Operational Research* 159: 673–686.

Eden, C., and F. Ackermann. 1998. *Making strategy: The journey of strategic management.* London: Sage.

Eden, C., and F. Ackermann. 2006. Where next for problem structuring methods. *Journal of the Operational Research Society* 57: 766–768.

Eden, C., D. Sims, and S. Jones. 1979. *Thinking in organisations.* London: Sage.

Eisenhardt, K., and M. Zbaracki. 1992. Strategic decision making. *Strategic Management Journal* 13: 17–37.

Franco, L.A. 2013. Rethinking soft OR interventions: Models as boundary objects. *European Journal of Operational Research* 231: 720–733.

Friend, J., D. Bryant, B. Cunningham, and J. Luckman. 1998. Negotiated project engagements: Learning from experience. *Human Relations* 51: 1509–1542.

Gibson, J. 1950. The implications of learning theory for social psychology. In *Experiments in social process*, ed. J.G. Miller. New York: McGraw-Hill.

Gibson, J. 1977. The theory of affordances. In *Perceiving, acting, and knowing: Toward an ecological psychology*, ed. R. Shaw and J. Bransford. Hillsdale, NJ: Erlbaum.

Gibson, C.B. 1999. Do they do what they believe they can? Group efficacy beliefs and group performance across tasks and cultures. *Academy of Management Journal* 42: 138–152.

Gully, S.M., A. Joshi, K.A. Incalcaterra, and J.M. Beaubien. 2002. A meta-analysis of team-efficacy, potency and performance. *Journal of Applied Psychology* 87: 819–832.

Hacking, I. 1983. *Representing and intervening.* Cambridge, MA: Cambridge University Press, Harvard University Press.

Hacking, I. 1999. *The social construction of what?* Cambridge, MA: Cambridge University Press, Harvard University Press.

Hämäläinen, R.P., J. Luoma, and E. Saarinen. 2013. On the importance of behavioral operational research: The case of understanding and communicating about dynamic systems. *European Journal of Operational Research* 228: 623–634.

Joldersma, C., and E. Roelofs. 2004. The impact of soft OR methods on problem structuring. *European Journal of Operational Research* 152: 696–708.

Kahneman, D. 2003. A perspective on judgement and choice: Mapping bounded rationality. *American Psychologist* 58: 697–720.

Kahneman, D., and A. Tversky (eds.). 2000. *Choices, values and frames.* New York: Cambridge University Press.

Keys, P. 1997. Approaches to understanding the process of OR: Review, critique and extension. *Omega* 25: 1–13.

Kirby, M., and J. Rosenhead. 2005. IFORS operational research hall of fame: Russell L. Ackoff. *International Transactions in Operational Research* 12: 129–134.

Laughin, P.R., B.L. Bonner, and A.G. Miner. 2002. Groups perform better than the best individuals on letters-to-numbers problems. *Organizational Behavior and Human Decision Processes* 88: 605–620.

Lindsley, D.H., D.J. Brass, and J.B. Thomas. 1995. Efficacy-performance spirals: A multilevel perspective. *Academy of Management Review* 20: 645–678.

Maule, A., and G. Hodgkinson. 2003. Re-appraising managers perceptual errors: A behavioral decision making perspective. *British Journal of Management* 14: 33–37.

Merton, R. 1967. On sociological theories of the middle-range. In *On theoretical sociology: Five essays old and new*, ed. R. Merton. New York: Free Press.

Midgley, G., R.Y. Cavana, J. Brocklesby, J.L. Foote, D.R. Wood, and A. Ahuriri-Driscoll. 2013. Towards a new framework for evaluating systemic problem structuring methods. *European Journal of Operational Research* 229: 143–154.

Mingers, J. 2011. Soft OR comes of age—But not everywhere! *Omega* 39: 729–741.

Miser, H.J. 1991. Toward a philosophy of operational research. *INFOR* 29: 4–13.

Miser, H.J. 1993. A foundational concept of science appropriate for validation in operational research. *European Journal of Operational Research* 66: 204–215.

Mohammed, S., L. Ferzandi, and K. Hamilton. 2010. Metaphor no more: A 15-year review of the team mental model construct. *Journal of Management* 36: 876–910.

Moshman, D., and M. Geil. 1998. Collaborative reasoning: Evidence for collective rationality. *Thinking and Reasoning* 4: 231–248.

Neale, M., and M. Bazerman. 1985. The effects of framing and negotiator overconfidence on bargaining behaviors and outcomes. *Academy of Management Journal* 28: 34–49.

Nicolini, D., J. Mengis, and J. Swan. 2012. Understanding the role of objects in cross-disciplinary collaboration. *Organization Science* 23: 612–629.

Ormerod, R.J. 2012. Logic and rationality in OR interventions: An examination in the light of the 'Critical rationalist' approach. *Journal of the Operational Research Society* 64: 469–487.

Phillips, L. 1984. A theory of requisite decision models. *Acta Psychologica* 56: 29–48.

Phillips, L., and M. Phillips. 1993. Facilitated work groups: Theory and practice. *Journal of the Operational Research Society* 44: 533–549.

Pidd, M. 2004. Contemporary OR/MS in strategy development and policymaking: Some reflections. *Journal of the Operational Research Society* 55: 791–800.

Priem, R.L., D.A. Harrison, and N.K. Muir. 1995. Structured conflict and consensus outcomes in group decision making. *Journal of Management* 21: 691–710.

Rosenhead, J. 1986. Custom and practice. *Journal of the Operational Research Society* 33: 335–343.

Royston, G. 2013. Operational research for the real world: Big questions from a small island. *Journal of the Operational Research Society* 64: 793–804.

Simon, H.A. 1976. From substantive to procedural rationality. In *Models of bounded rationality: Behavioral economics and business organization*, ed. H.A. Simon (1982). Cambridge, MA: MIT Press.

Simon, H.A. 1991. Bounded rationality and organisational learning. *Organisation Science* 2: 125–134.

Sterman, J.D. 1989. Modeling managerial behavior: Misperceptions of feedback in a dynamic decision making experiment. *Management Science* 35: 321–339.

Taket, A., and L. White. 2000. *Partnerships and participation*. Chichester: Wiley.

Theiner, G., C. Allen, and R.L. Goldstone. 2010. Recognizing group cognition. *Cognitive Systems Research* 11: 378–395.

Tversky, A., and D. Kahneman. 1981. The framing of decisions and the psychology of choice. *Science* 185: 453–458.

Vennix, J. 1997. *Group model building: Facilitating team learning using system dynamics*. Chichester: Wiley.

White, L. 2006. Evaluating problem-structuring methods: Developing an approach to show the value and effectiveness of PSMs. *Journal of the Operational Research Society* 57: 842–855.

White, L. 2009. Understanding problem structuring methods interventions. *European Journal of Operational Research* 199: 823–833.

Whyte, G. 1998. Recasting Janis's groupthink model: The key role of collective efficacy in decision fiascoes. *Organizational Behavior and Human Decision Processes* 73: 163–184.

Wulf, W.A. 1989. *The national collaboratory—A white paper, in towards a national collaboratory*. Unpublished report of a workshop held at Rockefeller University.

Yearworth, M., and L. White. 2014. The non-codified use of problem structuring methods and the need for a generic constitutive definition. *European Journal of Operational Research* 237: 932–945.

Zammuto, R.F., T.L. Griffith, A. Majchrzak, D.J. Dougherty, and S. Faraj. 2007. Information technology and the changing fabric of organization. *Organization Science* 18: 749–762.

# Part II

## Methodology

# 5

# Simulation and Laboratory Experiments: Exploring Self-Organizing Behavior in a Collective Choice Model

Santiago Arango-Aramburo, Ann van Ackere
and Erik R. Larsen

## 5.1 Introduction

Traditionally, work in the queuing area has focused on the design, running and performance of a facility, with relatively little emphasis on the customers, i.e. the facility's users. While this has been useful in helping to understand capacity requirements and the impact of different configurations of production and service facilities, it has in many cases also been a built-in constraint, limiting our ability to explain the behavior observed in many

S. Arango-Aramburo (✉)
Decision Science Department, Universidad Nacional de Colombia,
Carrera 80 N. 65-223, bloque M8-211, Medellín, Colombia

A. van Ackere
Faculty of Business and Economics, University of Lausanne,
Quartier UNIL-Dorigny, Bâtiment Internef, 1015 Lausanne, Switzerland

E.R. Larsen
Institute of Management, Università della Svizzera italiana, Via Buffi 13, 6900
Lugano, Switzerland

© The Editor(s) (if applicable) and The Author(s) 2016          **87**
M. Kunc et al. (eds.), *Behavioral Operational Research*,
DOI 10.1057/978-1-137-53551-1_5

real queues. This chapter continues research that tries to shift the focus to the information structure and the behavior of the customer, and illustrates how simulation and laboratory experiments are used for this research.

We are interested in what happens to queues when customers become more *intelligent*, i.e. they are not assumed to arrive at the facility according to some random process. In other words, we attempt to move from the optimal design of facilities to the understanding of the behavior of customers and their influence on the facility. However, in order to do this we need to extend traditional queuing models in several ways: (*i*) we must provide some information about the performance of the facility to the customer, (*ii*) we need to endow the customer with enough computational capability to enable him to react to this information and (*iii*) we introduce the idea of the repeat customer, i.e. a customer who uses the same set of facilities more than once. Given these elements, the customers can decide which facility to use next based on their previous experience and their information.

There are different methods that could be used to create more behavioral queuing models, including System Dynamics, agent-based models and discrete-event models. In this chapter we use a micro approach, i.e. we focus on the behavior of the individual and study the system-level (or aggregated) consequences of these individual decisions. We focus on two methods: agent simulations and laboratory experiments.

Using agent-based models, we can create individual experiences for the customers, i.e. each customer bases his decisions on his own experiences and information, not on system-wide averages. This allows us to model heterogeneous customers who may have different sensitivities regarding the cost of waiting on queue as well as different perceptions of the efficiency of a facility. Agent-Based Modeling enables us to characterize not only the facility but also the population of users of the facility, thus creating a much better understanding of how customers might co-evolve with the facility that serves them, something which cannot be done within the traditional queuing framework.

The experimental approach has been used extensively in behavioral research, in situations where empirical data is difficult, if not impossible, to obtain. Furthermore, experiments allow testing of specific aspects of a problem while controlling for different factors, e.g. for information; this is almost impossible in real-life settings. The use of experiments complements simulation, as it allows (*i*) validation of the simulation results and (*ii*) discovery of new behaviors both at the individual and at the aggregated level.

This chapter is part of a broader attempt to understand the behavioral aspects of queuing theory, with a focus on methodologies appropriate for such an analysis.

## 5.2    Behavioral Models of Queues

The literature on queuing models can be categorized depending on whether (*i*) the arrival and service rates are exogenous or endogenous (i.e. the model includes a feedback mechanism) and (*ii*) the arrival and service processes are stochastic or deterministic. We distinguish three forms of feedback for the arrival rate: state-dependent (i.e. a system whose current state is known to the customer and/or service provider, e.g. Naor 1969), steady-state (i.e. an equilibrium analysis where customer behavior depends on system averages, e.g. Dewan and Mendelson 1990) and dynamic (i.e. an analysis based either on a sequence of independent, discrete time-periods, with steady-state being achieved in each period (stochastic approach, e.g. Rump and Stidham 1998), or on a continuous time analysis (deterministic approach, e.g. Haxholdt et al. 2003). A variation of state-dependent arrival rates is to consider impatient customers: some customers balk if they find all servers busy upon arrival; some new customers renege after a certain time if they are kept waiting too long, resulting in the effective arrival rate's being state-dependent, e.g. Whitt (1999), Boots and Tijms (1999) and Zohar et al. (2002).

Historically, the emphasis has been on stochastic models, aiming to understand the impact of variability on the day-to-day management of service systems. Many of these papers focus on controlling access to the system via pricing and compare Pareto-optima to individual optima- and profit-maximizing behavior. The effective arrival rate thus depends on the current state of the system; the feedback is immediate. The seminal papers in this area include Naor (1969) and Yechiali (1971), who analyze, respectively, the basic M/M/1 and the GI/M/1 system.

Dewan and Mendelson (1990) consider the problem from a cost-allocation point of view: what price should a service department charge to its users? The analysis is fundamentally different in that customers base their decision to join or not to join on their expected waiting time, which is determined by the steady-state average waiting time. The arrival rate is thus independent of the current state of the system. Having determined the optimal price (and the corresponding arrival rate) for a given capacity, service provider then optimize the capacity of the service facility. This steady-state-based approach allows a deterministic analysis of the underlying stochastic model. Their work has been generalized by Stidham (1992). Ha (1998, 2001) also analyses steady-state stochastic models with an endogenous service rate, but this rate is selected by a cost-minimizing customer rather than by the service provider.

Rump and Stidham (1998) and Zohar et al. (2002) introduce the concept of repeat customers who decide based on past system performance. The former consider a sequence of discrete time periods, with steady-state being reached in each time period; customers view each period as a separate experience and form expectations about waiting time using exponential smoothing. The model is analyzed as a deterministic dynamic system. The latter use a discrete event simulation approach to model impatient customers, with adaptive expectations regarding expected waiting times; each customer forms his own expectation based on his individual prior experiences.

The interest in deterministic queuing models is more recent. One exception is Edelson (1971), who analyses the issue of externalities in road congestion and determines the toll level that will optimally allocate customers between a congestion-prone road and a railway which is not subject to congestion. The main difference between Edelson (1971) and the work in the line of Dewan and Mendelson (1990) is that the former does not assume an underlying stochastic model.

Haxholdt et al. (2003) builds on Rump and Stidham (1998). They incorporate adaptive customer expectations in a continuous, deterministic System Dynamics–based simulation model (Morecroft 2007). The assumption that the system attains steady-state between successive adjustments of the arrival rate is relaxed; both the arrival and service rates are assumed to be endogenous, the latter being modeled as a non-linear function of the queue length.

Over the years, customer behavior has received increasing attention, creating the field known as the *psychology of queues*. Early papers include Maister (1985) and Larson (1987), most of this work can be found in the marketing literature, e.g. Taylor (1994), Carmon et al. (1995), Hui and Tse (1996), Kumar et al. (1997), Zhou and Soman (2003) and Whiting and Donthu (2006). These authors focus on evaluating how waiting affects customer satisfaction and how the waiting process could be managed to minimize the resulting dissatisfaction. Few papers go a step further, asking the question: how will waiting time (dis)satisfaction affect customer loyalty (i.e. the likelihood of repeat business) and word of mouth (the impact on potential future customers).

Building on Edelson (1971), Zohar et al. (2002), and the *psychology of queues* literature, van Ackere and Larsen (2004) use a cellular automata approach (Wolfram 1994) to explore repeat behavior of commuters forced to choose repeatedly among three alternative roads. The commuters estimate the different travel times based on their past experience (adaptive expectations) and make their choice based on these estimates and information received from their neighbors. One of the advantages of this approach is the ability to make the link between (individual-level) micro-behavior and (system-level) macro-behavior. Sankaranarayanan et al. (2014) apply a similar approach to a context where captive customers repeatedly choose among different service facilities. They allow customers to update their expectations of the sojourn times at these facilities based on both their own experiences and those of their best-performing neighbor, and also consider heterogeneous customers.

Law et al. (2004) and Bielen and Dumoulin (2007) have approached this issue from an empirical point of view. Law et al. (2004) study the return frequency of a student population to various fast-food outlets. They conclude that while waiting time impacts customer satisfaction in all periods, it has a significant impact on return frequency only during the busy lunch period. Bielen and Dumoulin (2007) find empirical support for their hypothesis that waiting-time satisfaction moderates the effect of service satisfaction on loyalty. In particular, when waiting-time satisfaction is high, loyalty will be high, whatever the overall service satisfaction level.

Empirical work in this area is very limited. Additionally, it is hard to draw definite conclusions from empirical observations due to the large number of confounding factors and the current lack of theoretical hypotheses. Experimental research in this area thus looks like a promising avenue and could lay the foundations for further empirical work. Critics of experiments argue that real markets are inherently more complex than the markets analyzed in laboratories. Behavior in a very complex system may indeed be governed by laws different from those of simple systems (Plott 1982).

Whereas experiments in dynamic environments improve the external validity of more traditional (static) experiments, most experimental markets do not include dynamic structures and are reset each period (e.g. Plott 1982; Smith 1982; Plott and Smith 2008). Frequently, there are no elements carrying over to future periods, such as capacities, size of customer groups, and so on. Arango et al. (2015) address this aspect by using an experimental approach in an attempt to validate some insights from the multi-period cellular automata models developed by van Ackere and Larsen (2004) and Sankaranarayanan et al. (2014). They focus on how information and system complexity impact both individual performance and overall system performance.

## 5.3    An Agent-Based Approach

We use a class of agent-based models known as *cellular automata*. This category of models have the desirable characteristic that they provide a very structured environment in which to model information diffusion among agents which can easily be replicated in experiments. We provide only a short description of the model, generalizing the context from a choice among three commuting roads to a choice among service facilities. For a more detailed discussion, see van Ackere and Larsen (2004).

We consider a system consisting of three facilities, $i = 1, 2, 3$, each with a different service capacity given by:

$$ST_t^i = C^i + \text{Max}\left(CR_t^i - \beta_{\text{low}}^i, 0\right) \times x_i + \left(\text{Max}\left(CR_t^i - \beta_{\text{high}}^i, 0\right)\right)^{1.5} \quad (5.1)$$

where $ST_t^i$ is the sojourn time for facility $i$ at time $t$ and $CR_t^i$ the number of agents choosing to use facility $i$ at time $t$. The parameters $C^i$, $\beta_{\text{low}}^i$, $x_i$, and $\beta_{\text{high}}^i$ characterize the different facilities. We initialize the three facilities with $C^i$ = 20, 40 and 60; $\beta_{\text{low}}^i$ = 15, 30 and 60; $\beta_{\text{high}}^i$ = 30, 60 and 120; and $x_i$ = 3, 2 and 1. This implies that facility 1 is a small congestion-prone facility, facility 3 has a large capacity, and facility 2 is of intermediate size. We use 120 agents who, each period, decide which facility to use. Agents are placed next to each other on a circle so that each agent has two neighbors, one on each side. Each agent selects the facility it believes will have the shortest sojourn time in the current period based on its past experience and the most recent experience of its best-performing neighbor.

Each agent has a memory that represents its expectation of the sojourn time for each facility. This memory is updated for the chosen facility after each period based on the agent's experience. This is done using adaptive expectations:

$$\overline{E}_{i,t}^j = \lambda AT_{i,t-1}^j + (1 - \lambda)\overline{E}_{i,t-1}^j \quad 0 \leq \lambda \leq 1 \quad (5.2)$$

where $\overline{E}_{i,t}^j$ represents the expectation of agent $j$ for facility $i$ at time $t$, $AT_{i,t-1}^j$ the actual sojourn time agent $j$ experienced at facility $i$ at time $t-1$, $\lambda$ the weight given to the actual sojourn time and $(1-\lambda)$ the weight given to the expected sojourn time at time $t-1$. We initialize the memory of the agents using a uniform random distribution around the Nash equilibrium (i.e. a customer allocation resulting in identical sojourn times for the three facilities).

We first discuss results at the micro-level, i.e. the individual agents, before moving on to the macro-level, i.e. the system performance. Figure 5.1 shows a run for the case $\lambda = 0.5$, i.e. the agents give equal weight to their new experience and to the expected sojourn time. Figure 5.1a shows the evolution of each agent's choice over a period of 100 time units. Each color (white, grey and black) represents a facility. We can observe how during the first periods the agents try out different facilities

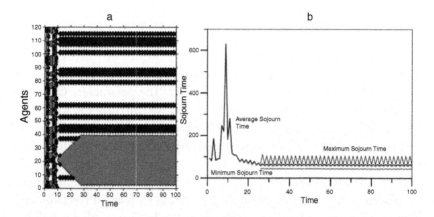

**Fig. 5.1** (*a*) shows the temporal—spatial evolution of choices made by the 120 agents for one model run (*black*: facility 1; *white*; facility 2; *grey*: facility 3). (*b*) shows the system average sojourn time as well as the minimum and maximum travel time faced by an agent in steady-state for the same model run

to learn about the system. After time 28, a more stable pattern emerges, as the majority of the agents stay at the same facility throughout the remainder of the simulation. A minority of agents, located on the edge between two stable areas, keep switching between two facilities. Their presence increases the sojourn time at the chosen facility and reduces the sojourn time at the facility they used in the previous period. Consequently, the information received from their neighbor induces them to return to the previous facility.

Figure 5.1b shows the average sojourn time for the first 100 periods as well as the minimum and maximum sojourn times after time 20. During the transition period, as the agents learn about the system, the sojourn times are highly variable. Eventually the average sojourn time settles down at a value around 73, with a relatively low variability; even the agent with the highest value experiences only slightly higher sojourn times.

Figure 5.2 consists of two sets of aggregate steady-state results (i.e. after the transition period). Figure 5.2a shows the mean sojourn time as a function of $\lambda$; a value of $\lambda$ equal to zero indicates that agents never update their expectations and a $\lambda$ of 0.99 implies that agents update their expectations very quickly, giving a weight of 99 % to the sojourn time

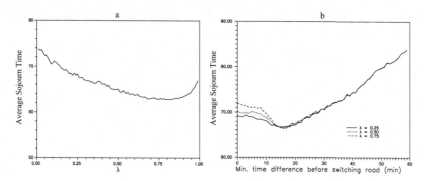

**Fig. 5.2** (*a*) shows the mean sojourn time (averaged over 1,000 runs) as a function of λ. (*b*) shows the mean sojourn time (averaged over 1,000 runs) for three values of λ as a function of the minimum time difference required for agents to switch facilities

they experienced most recently. The figure shows the system's weighted average sojourn time for each value of λ, averaged over 1,000 runs with different initial conditions. We observe that, as λ increases from 0 to 0.75, the average sojourn time decreases slowly, i.e. as the agents pay increasing attention to their most recent experience, the average sojourn time decreases almost linearly. As λ increases beyond 0.75, the average sojourn time starts to increase. In other words, the system achieves the best overall performance when agents give a weight of about 75 % to their new experience and 25 % to their previous expectations.

In Fig. 5.2b we investigate the consequence of inertia among agents, i.e. we assume that an agent changes facilities only if the gain is sufficient to justify the effort. Indeed, in many situations, due to the existence of switching costs, customers will turn to a new product or supplier only if they expect a significant benefit. In our example, we could argue that an agent will consider switching to another facility only if he expects a reasonable reduction of sojourn time. We consider thresholds ranging from 0 to 60 minutes. Figure 5.2b shows the results for 3 different values of λ (0.25, 0.50 and 0.75). We observe that for these three examples system performance improves if the agents exhibit a reasonable amount of inertia, i.e. the optimal threshold is about 15 minutes (25 % of the Nash sojourn time). As the threshold increases from 0 to 15 minutes, system performance improves and the impact of λ on the performance decreases.

When the threshold increases above 15 minutes, performance deteriorates and is no longer affected by the value of $\lambda$.

The simulation results show that, at the aggregate level, a distributed system without any coordination is able to converge towards an equilibrium close to the optimum. However, the exact spatial distribution of which agent uses which facility is not predictable. The time agents take to update their expectations is critical for the system performance: updating too slowly or too quickly worsens the performance.

## 5.4    An Experimental Approach

While the previous section illustrated how simulation is used in the analysis of behavioral queues, this section introduces how laboratory experiments enable investigation of queuing systems from another angle. Using simulation requires making assumptions about the rationality of the agents, in particular about their expectation formation and the heuristics they use to select a service facility. In laboratory experiments, participants make decisions based on their own logic and the information they are presented with. Therefore, this method allows testing of theory-based hypotheses, as well as conjectures derived from simulation results; in particular, this approach enables us to verify the decision rules used in the simulation model.

There are only a limited number of experimental studies of queuing systems. Rapoport et al. (2004) study the conditions for reaching equilibrium in a queuing system with endogenously determined arrival rates and state-dependent ones, representing a situation where subjects must decide on the timing to join the queue for their car's emission control test. Seale et al. (2005) extend this approach to non-cooperative $n$-person games with complete information, by including information about the other group members (Seale et al. 2005). Stein et al. (2007) and Rapoport et al. (2010) consider endogenous arrival rates and batch service, in order to analyze how customers decide whether to join a queue and, if they do, with what timing. Finally, Delgado et al. (2014) present an experiment based on a single-facility queuing system: participants, playing the role of manager, must adjust the facility's service capacity to maximize profits while the artificial agents decide whether or not to patronize the facility based on their experienced sojourn times.

We performed a laboratory experiment based on the simulation model discussed in Sect. 5.3, what we might call a *human cellular automaton*. The *artificial* agents are replaced by *cash-motivated human* subjects. They are in the same *cellular automata structure*, have the same information about their own sojourn time and their best-performing neighbor's decision and sojourn time and have a record of their own expected sojourn time for the three facilities. For practical reasons the size of this human cellular automaton is limited to 18 subjects. Each participant receives the relevant information and records his decisions using a computer interface. Subjects must choose one of three facilities; reneging and balking are both prohibited. The subjects are cash-motivated based on performance: the shorter the sojourn time, the higher the payoff. This context represents a repeated-choice model with externalities, where the facility could for instance be the choice of a road for daily commute. We follow the standardized protocol for laboratory experiments for decision making (Smith 1982; Friedman and Cassar 2004). Further details about the set-up can be found in Arango et al. (2015).

The sojourn time of a facility $j$ on a given day $t$ equals:

$$F_{j,t} = \beta_j \left( n_{j,t} \right)^2 \tag{5.3}$$

where the parameter $\beta_j$ (known to the participants) characterizes the facility and $n_{j,t}$ represents the number of subjects who selected this facility. All subjects selecting the same facility experience the same sojourn time. Customers receive a reward $R$ to complete the service, but they incur a waiting cost equal to $C$ per time unit (minute) of sojourn time. Thus, the net payoff of customer $i$ choosing facility $j$ at time $t$ equals:

$$P_{i,j,t} = R - C \times F_{j,t} \tag{5.4}$$

The experimental set-up (treatments) consists of two factors: the capacity of the facilities (equal or different) and the information flow between subjects (none or partial). This provides a classic $2 \times 2$ experimental design with four treatments: (i) equal facilities, no information; (ii) equal facilities, partial information; (iii) unequal facilities, no information; and (iv) unequal facilities, partial information. In treatments without information, subjects were given only their own sojourn time at the end of each period, while in the treatments with partial information subjects were informed about their own sojourn time as well as the decision and sojourn time of one neighbor on each side, mimicking the neighborhood structure of the simulation model discussed in Sect. 5.3. The characteristics of the three facilities were known to the subjects in all treatments. For equal facilities we use $\beta = 1$ and in the unequal case $\beta = 1$, 2.25 and 9, respectively, for the service facilities 1, 2 and 3.

As our performance benchmark we again use the Nash equilibrium, which results in a sojourn time of 36 minutes for the equal-treatment cases and 81 minutes for the unequal-treatment cases.

The full experiment consists of 12 independent groups of 18 subjects, i.e. three groups for each treatment. The experiment was conducted with students from the Faculty of Mines, Universidad Nacional de Colombia, Medellín. Each subject participated in one 90-minute session representing 35 time periods. In each period, subjects were asked to decide on a facility to join and to record their expected sojourn time for each of the three facilities. At the end of the session, participants were rewarded in cash based on their cumulative sojourn times.

We provide a brief summary of the main results at the system and individual levels, before discussing in more detail the subjects' expectation formation. A detailed analysis can be found in Arango et al. (2015).

For the equal treatments (i.e. all facilities have the same capacity), the average number of subjects per facility is independent of the amount of information available to the subjects and the average sojourn times are not statistically different from the equilibrium values. For the unequal treatments, the results are similar, with one exception: the sojourn time of the smallest facility differs statistically from the Nash equilibrium; it is larger. Thus, an increase in the availability of information does not lead to a better performance, and we might conclude that providing this extra information is not worth its cost.

At the individual level, the picture is quite different: few subjects come close to the Nash equilibrium values; the average sojourn is often 30% above the Nash equilibrium. These poor performances are the consequence of occasional very high sojourn times, particularly at the smallest facility, which are not visible when one focusses solely on average system performance.

Subjects were asked to record their expectations about the sojourn time for each facility every period. Table 5.1 presents the average cumulative sojourn time (ACST), the average cumulative error of expectations (CEE), and the coefficient of correlation (Corr) between the individual subjects' cumulative sojourn times and their cumulative expectations. The table also shows the number of times that subjects expect the system to achieve the Nash equilibrium, i.e. equal expected sojourn times for all facilities (EE).

The CEE always significantly exceeds the ACST. The ratio CEE/ACT is larger when the facilities are unequal and/or no information is available; the highest ratio occurs for the case with unequal facilities and no information.

The correlation (Corr) in Table 5.1 can be interpreted as an indication of the consistency of the mental models of the subjects. More specifically, we expect that a better performance is the result of a better expectation formation, given that subjects with a proper understanding of the problem and a good strategy should also form consistent expectations and make better choices. In this sense, there should be positive correlation between ACST and CEE. According to the table, the empirical evidence shows a lack of systematic observation. Correlations range from −0.30 to 0.53, and all treatments exhibit at least one positive and one negative value. One way to interpret this result is that subjects may be using different (and independent) mental models for the two parts of the decision-making problem: one to form the expectations and another one to pick a queue. Such division of mental models has also been reported in previous experimental work (e.g. Moxnes 1998; Arango and Moxnes 2012).

Moreover, the number of times that subjects expect equilibrium during the 35 rounds of the experiment (EE) is at most 5.67, i.e. around 16% of the cases, with a minimum of around 3% and an average across the

**Table 5.1** Different indicators for average values of individual results for all groups (G1, G2, and G3) and all treatments

| | Equal facilities and no information | | | Unequal facilities and no information | | |
|---|---|---|---|---|---|---|
| | G1 | G2 | G3 | G1 | G2 | G3 |
| ACST | 1,640 | 1,598 | 1,667 | 4,219 | 3,633 | 3,763 |
| CEE | 3,218 | 2,903 | 2,997 | 12,970 | 7,730 | 8,678 |
| Corr | −0.13 | −0.05 | 0.31 | 0.14 | −0.30 | −0.15 |
| EE | 5.67 | 4.78 | 3.56 | 4.33 | 5.17 | 2.94 |
| | Equal facilities and partial information | | | Unequal facilities and partial information | | |
| | G1 | G2 | G3 | G1 | G2 | G3 |
| ACST | 1,730 | 1,694 | 1,658 | 3,811 | 4,114 | 3,903 |
| CEE | 3,168 | 2,954 | 2,936 | 7,354 | 7,666 | 9,749 |
| Corr | −0.22 | −0.02 | 0.53 | −0.05 | 0.07 | 0.16 |
| EE | 2.72 | 4.67 | 0.89 | 4.06 | 3.39 | 1.17 |

*ACST* average cumulative sojourn time, *CEE* cumulative error of expectations, *Corr* coefficient of correlation between the individual CEE and ACST, *EE* number of times that subjects expect equilibrium, i.e. equal expected sojourn times for all facilities

whole sample of about 10 %. Thus, while behavior seems close to equilibrium at the aggregate level, individuals neither experience nor expect to experience equilibrium. This observation reinforces the conclusion mentioned above, that while system-level behavior seems close to the Nash equilibrium, individual subjects experience a much worse performance.

The experimental results reveal several important insights. In particular, analyzing the performance at different levels is critical to the understanding of queuing systems. What at the system level looks like a good performance can be far from optimal when considering the individual participants' results. Furthermore, the amount of information available has surprisingly little influence on performance, except in the case of very small facilities. We also conclude that the subjects are aware of their suboptimal performance: they rarely expect the system to reach equilibrium.

# 5.5    Discussion and Conclusions

Our analysis confirms that providing more information does not necessarily lead to improved system performance; in certain cases performance even worsened. This is in line with previous research on information overload (Hwang and Lin 1999). We have also observed both in the simulations and in the experiments that subjects or agents distribute themselves reasonably well among the facilities, i.e. we observed an example of self-organization. However, while in the simulations the majority of the agents stayed with the same facility after the initial transition period, this was not the case in the experiments. The analysis of the subjects' expectations goes in the same direction: the participants do not expect the system to stabilize. This is a form of self-fulfilling prophecy, as it is their continuous switching behavior that prevents the system from reaching a steady state.

Queuing as an area of study has been around for more than 100 years; very sophisticated models provide solutions for many situations. However, only over the last two decades have questions arisen concerning about the impact of incorporating bounded rationality and human behavior on the applicability and optimality of the proposed solutions. The introduction of repeat business, where customers might choose to return to the same facility or not, based on past experience, raises a new set of challenges for the queuing research area. Phenomena such as customer arrivals' resulting from a conscious decision-making process are influenced by how the facility is managed; such queuing processes require new methods. We have discussed two such methods in this chapter: simulations and experiments. Both these methods can be seen as lying between traditional stylized models with closed-form solutions and empirical studies. The former are limited by the strong simplifying assumptions they require, the latter by the dearth of available data.

This chapter has illustrated how the two methods complement each other. We developed a spatial simulation model where individual agents make decisions based on locally available information and observed how these agents chose between different facilities. While this is an intuitively reasonable way to model agents, one should query whether this is an acceptable representation of reality or just one more theoretical model with limited applicability to real systems. Combining this approach with laboratory experiments allows validation of the simulation results and further insight into what happens when humans make these decisions.

The combination of simulations and experiments can in many situations help researchers. On the one hand, experiments enable validation of theoretical models and propositions in situations where empirical data is too time-consuming, too costly or simply impossible to collect. On the other hand, simulation can be used to generalize experimental results, as conditions can more easily be varied, thus helping to establish boundaries for the validity of experimental results.

# References

Arango, S., and E. Moxnes. 2012. Commodity cycles, a function of market complexity? Extending the cobweb experiment. *Journal of Economic Behavior and Organization* 84: 321–334.

Arango, S., E.R. Larsen, and A. van Ackere. 2015. *Self-organizing behavior in collective choice models: Laboratory experiments.* Working paper, University of Lugnao.

Bielen, F., and N. Dumoulin. 2007. Waiting time influence on the satisfaction-loyalty relationship in services. *Managing Service Quality* 17: 174–193.

Boots, N.K., and H. Tijms. 1999. A multi-server queuing system with impatient customers. *Management Science* 45: 444–448.

Carmon, Z., J.G. Shanthikumar, and T.F. Carmon. 1995. A psychological perspective on service segmentation models: The significance of accounting for consumers' perceptions of waiting and service. *Management Science* 41: 1806–1815.

Delgado, C.A., A. van Ackere, E.R. Larsen, and S. Arango. (2014). *Managing capacity at a service facility: An experimental approach.* Working paper, University of Lugano.

Dewan, S., and H. Mendelson. 1990. User delay costs and internal pricing for a service facility. *Management Science* 36(12): 1502–1517.

Edelson, N.M. 1971. Congestion tolls under monopoly. *American Economic Review* 61: 873–882.

Friedman, D., and A. Cassar. 2004. *Economics lab.* Oxon: Routledge.

Ha, A.Y. 1998. Incentive-compatible pricing for a service facility with joint production and congestion externalities. *Management Science* 44: 1623–1636.

Ha, A.Y. 2001. Optimal pricing that coordinates queues with customer chosen service requirements. *Management Science* 47: 915–930.

Haxholdt, C., E.R. Larsen, and A. van Ackere. 2003. Mode locking and chaos in a deterministic queueing model with feedback. *Management Science* 49: 816–830.

Hui, M.K., and D.K. Tse. 1996. What to tell consumers in waits of different lengths: An integrative model of service evaluation. *Journal of Marketing* 60: 81–90.

Hwang, M.I., and J.W. Lin. 1999. Information dimensions, information overload and decision quality. *Journal of Information Science* 25: 213–218.

Kumar, P., M.U. Kalwani, and M. Dada. 1997. The impact of waiting time guarantees on customers' waiting experiences. *Marketing Science* 16: 295–314.

Larson, R.C. 1987. Perspectives on queues: Social justice and the psychology of queueing. *Operations Research* 35: 895–905.

Law, A.K.Y., Y.V. Hui, and X. Zhao. 2004. Modeling repurchase frequency and customer satisfaction for fast food outlets. *International Journal of Quality & Reliability Management* 21: 545–563.

Maister, D. 1985. The psychology of waiting lines. In *The service encounter*, ed. J. Czepiel, M. Solomon, and M. Surprenant. Lexington: Lexington Book.

Morecroft, J. 2007. *Strategic modelling and business dynamics*. Chichester: Wiley.

Moxnes, E. 1998. Overexploitation of renewable resources: The role of misperceptions. *Journal of Economic Behavior and Organization* 37: 107–127.

Naor, P. 1969. On the regulation of queue size by levying tolls. *Econometrica* 36: 15–24.

Plott, C.R. 1982. Industrial organization theory and experimental economics. *Journal of Economic Literature* 20: 1485–1587.

Plott, C.R., and V.L. Smith (eds.). 2008. *Handbook of experimental economics results. Handbook in economics*. North-Holland: Elsevier.

Rapoport, A., W.E. Stein, J.E. Parco, and D.A. Seale. 2004. Equilibrium play in single-server queues with endogenously determined arrival times. *Journal of Economic Behavior & Organization* 55: 67–91.

Rapoport, A., E. William, W.E. Stein, V. Mak, R. Zwick, and D.A. Seale. 2010. Endogenous arrivals in batch queues with constant or variable capacity. *Transportation Research Part B: Methodological* 44: 1166–1185.

Rump, C.M., and S. Stidham Jr. 1998. Stability and chaos in input pricing for a service facility with adaptive customer response to congestion. *Management Science* 44: 246–261.

Sankaranarayanan, K., C. Delgado, A. van Ackere, and E.R. Larsen. 2014. The micro-dynamics of queuing: Understanding the formation of queues. *Journal of Simulation* 8: 304–313.

Seale, D.A., J.E. Parco, W.E. Stein, and A. Rapoport. 2005. Joining a queue or staying out: Effects of information structure and service time on arrival and staying out decisions. *Experimental Economics* 8: 117–144.

Smith, V.L. 1982. Microeconomics systems as an experimental science. *American Economic Review* 72: 923–955.

Stein, W.E., A. Rapoport, D.A. Seale, H. Zhang, and R. Zwick. 2007. Batch queues with choice of arrivals: Equilibrium analysis and experimental study. *Games and Economic Behavior* 59: 345–363.

Stidham, S. 1992. Pricing capacity decisions for a service facility: Stability and multiple local optima. *Management Science* 38: 1121–1139.

Taylor, S. 1994. Waiting for service: The relationship between delays and evaluations of service. *Journal of Marketing* 58: 56–69.

van Ackere, A., and E.R. Larsen. 2004. Self-organising behaviour in the presence of negative externalities: A conceptual model of commuter choice. *European Journal of Operational Research* 157: 501–513.

Whiting, A., and N. Donthu. 2006. Managing voice-to-voice encounters: Reducing the agony of being put on hold. *Journal of Service Research* 8: 234–244.

Whitt, W. 1999. Improving service by informing customers about anticipated delays. *Management Science* 45(2): 192–207.

Wolfram, S. 1994. *Cellular automata and complexity*. Reading: Addison-Wesley.

Yechiali, U. 1971. On optimal balking rules and toll charges in the GI/M/1 queuing process. *Operations Research* 19: 349–370.

Zhou, R., and D. Soman. 2003. Looking back: Exploring the psychology of queueing and the effect of the number of people behind. *Journal of Consumer Research* 29: 517–530.

Zohar, E., A. Mandelbaum, and N. Shimkin. 2002. Adaptive behaviour of impatient customers in tele-queues: Theory and empirical support. *Management Science* 48: 566–583.

# 6

# Misperception of Behavioral Operations and Bodies of Knowledge

Paulo Gonçalves and Sebastian Villa

## 6.1 Introduction

In the last decades, controlled human experiments have been used to better understand the behavioral factors that affect performance in operations and supply chain management (Croson and Donohue 2002). These behavioral experiments provide insight at both the practical and the theoretical level and focus on (i) understanding the effect and robustness of human decisions on operations, (ii) analyzing the effect of different operational factors and (iii) incorporating human behavioral factors into operations management models (Croson and Donohue 2002; Bendoly et al. 2010). Studies in behavioral operational research show that humans display poor performance even in systems with low dynamic complexity. In a lab experiment, where subjects play the Beer Distribution Game, Sterman (1989a) finds that subjects' ordering behavior follows an anchoring and adjust-

P. Gonçalves (✉) • S. Villa
Faculty of Economics, Universita della Svizza italia, Via Buffi 13, 6900 Lugano, Switzerland

© The Editor(s) (if applicable) and The Author(s) 2016
M. Kunc et al. (eds.), *Behavioral Operational Research*,
DOI 10.1057/978-1-137-53551-1_6

ment heuristic, as proposed by Tversky and Kahneman (1974). In a different lab experiment, where subjects make capital investment decisions to satisfy the demand of an entire capital-producing sector, Sterman (1989b) also finds subjects' capital investment decisions following an anchoring and adjustment heuristic. In both experiments, Sterman (1989a, b) finds that subjects display poor performance relative to optimum. In addition, he reports that the systematic deviations presented in subjects' decisions and subsequent underperformance can be understood to be due to a pervasive misperception of the delays involved in the experimental systems.

Another System Dynamics research suggests that other factors contribute to subjects' poor performance in complex systems. In particular, decision makers perform poorly in environments with significant feedback delays (Sterman 1987, 1989a), feedback complexity (Diehl and Sterman 1995; Sterman (1989a, b)) and changing conditions (Kleinmuntz and Thomas 1987). Research also suggests that behavior in dynamic environments remains sub-optimal, even when the decision maker has the opportunity to identify and correct errors (Hogarth 1981). Beyond analyzing the relationship between system structure and system behavior, System Dynamics captures how people make decisions and how they affect system level behavior. Hence, to design ways to improve overall system performance, System Dynamics models incorporate decisions that are boundedly rational (Simon 1982) and can follow simple heuristics or/ and contain biases (Tversky and Kahneman 1974).

Follow on research has focused on improving subjects' dynamic understanding of the system while modifying its dynamic complexity. For instance, Kampmann (1992) created an economic setting with three price institutions and two market complexity conditions. He concluded that market complexity reduces subjects' performance and that while subjects perform better in a simpler market condition, their performance remains sub-optimal. In an experiment studying the effect of feedback strength on boom-and-bust dynamics of new product introductions, Paich and Sterman (1993) explored the effectiveness of different heuristics for subjects' decisions.[1] They found that while subjects' performance

---

[1] Feedback strength refers to the speed and intensity of the feedback processes existing in a system. In System Dynamics models, the strength relates to the change to the variables.

improves from trial to trial, subjects fail to gain insights into the System Dynamics (misperception of feedback). In a lab experiment testing the effect cognitive feedback or feedforward information on subjects' performance, Sengupta and Abdel-Hamid (1993) showed that subjects provided with cognitive feedback perform better than those provided with outcome feedback. In an experiment in a management setting, Diehl and Sterman (1995) systematically varied the complexity of the system by changing the time delays and the strength of the feedback loops. They found that in dynamically complex systems there is little evidence of learning and that a do-nothing policy outperforms most subjects, even if the latter have perfect knowledge of system structure and parameters.

More recently, several behavioral experiments using System Dynamics have focused on reducing dynamic complexity and evaluating subjects' understanding of basic systems thinking concepts and their dynamics (Arango Aramburo et al. 2012). For instance, Booth Sweeney and Sterman (2000) created a test with a basic stock and flow structure to assess fundamental systems thinking concepts. Their findings show that subjects have a poor understanding of stock and flow relationships, as well as time delays. In a related study, Kainz and Ossimitz (2002) experimentally evaluated whether subjects' underperformance was due to failures in reading and interpreting graphs and not in understanding the stock and flow relationships. Results show that regardless of the task's simplicity, the systematic errors were independent of calculation errors and of the ability to draw and interpret graphs (Kainz and Ossimitz 2002). In another experiment, Barlas and Özevin (2004) evaluated the effects of different patterns of final customer demand, minimum possible order decision interval and type of receiving delay on subjects' behavior within a stock management problem. They show that subjects' decisions display oscillatory and unstable behavior that deviates from optimal patterns and that subjects' ordering decisions can be modeled either by a linear heuristic (such as anchoring and adjustment) or by a non-linear heuristic (such as an (s, S) policy). Thereafter, Moxnes (2004) and Moxnes and Saysel (2009) developed behavioral experiments to evaluate the misperceptions of basic dynamics associated with renewable resource management and $CO_2$ accumulation. They used a simplified System Dynamics model and provided subjects with sufficient information to create perfect mental models to help them understand the structure of the system. Results show that (i) providing subjects with accurate mental models helps them improve their performance and (ii) subjects still present both misperception of the causal structure of the systems and low performance compared with analytical benchmarks.

More recently, Sterman and Dogan (2015) created an experimental study with the Beer Distribution Game where all participants had complete knowledge of the system structure and the final customer demand was constant. They explored the role of behavioral phenomena in hoarding and phantom ordering, and their results show that subjects do not behave rationally. Subjects tried to adapt to the perceived scarce resources by inflating their orders. In addition, econometric analyses showed that a simple anchoring and adjustment heuristic accounted for the desired inventory coverage. Finally, Villa et al. (2015) and Gonçalves and Arango (2010) built on the System Dynamics model proposed by Gonçalves (2003) to explore subjects' behavior in a single-supplier, single-retailer supply chain with deterministic and known final customer demand. Despite the simple structure of the system and the full information about the evolution of the main variables, Villa et al. (2015) and Gonçalves and Arango (2010) showed that subjects assuming the role of a retailer (placing orders to a supplier) or a supplier (defining changes in production capacity to satisfy retailers' orders) performed poorly compared to optimal benchmarks. In particular, they showed that longer time delays and higher customer aggressiveness lead to poorer subject performance and that anchoring and adjustment heuristics are a good representation of subjects' behavior in each setting.

These studies highlight that the mental models people use to guide their decisions are dynamically deficient (Sterman 2000). People generally do not understand stock and flow or the associated delays between action and response. In fact, the experiments above suggest that subjects use a reactive and erroneous heuristic based on an event-based, open-loop view of causality, ignoring system structure and feedback processes (Arango et al. 2012). These experimental results show that system complexity and information availability limit our knowledge of the real world. In particular, the higher the system complexity, the worse the subjects' performance with respect to desired benchmarks (Sterman 1989b, 2000;

Paich and Sterman 1993), and the poorer the available information, the lower the potential for learning.

The strong bounds observed in human rationality, evidenced by poor understanding of feedback and its effects, are due to two basic and related deficiencies in our mental maps (Sterman 2000; Bendoly et al. 2010). First, our mental maps often capture a simplified and flawed representation of the actual causal structure of systems—which we name *misperception of feedback structure*. Second, even when we perfectly understand the structure of a system, we are unable to infer how it behaves over time, which we name *misperception of feedback dynamics*.

The chapter proceeds as follows: In the next section, we present some theoretical concepts that explain how bounded rationality arises from flawed representations of system structure. The section that follows it discusses and exemplifies how misperception of the dynamics of the system can lead to biases and the use of poor heuristics. We conclude with a discussion of main findings and lessons learned.

## 6.2    Misperceptions of Feedback Structure

Different studies conclude that people present dysfunctional behaviors in dynamically complex systems even with the inclusion of feedback (Kleinmuntz 1993) or external incentives (Diehl and Sterman 1995; Kampmann and Sterman 1998). In addition, Sterman (1989b) explains that individuals tend to have an event-focused approach in their understanding of the world, centering on events instead of the structures that caused them. Under such conditions, focus on events may lead to decisions to improve short-term results without separating the cause from the effect of the real problem, which may lead to low long-term performance. Failing to have a closed-loop view of causality leads to misperceptions of delays, accumulations and non-linearities, which are key elements to the comprehension of the structure and behavior of the system. For example, understanding delays and accumulations helps decision makers to separate causes from effects and helps individuals to learn from their experiences. In addition, identifying the non-linearities of the system improves the understanding of the strength of feedback processes over time, again allowing accurate attribution of outcomes to decisions.

Therefore, if a person does not identify the real feedback structure of a system, his mental models will exclude important interconnections that in fact exist, and this will cause the person to be reactive (Sterman 2000; Bendoly et al. 2010). These errors in the understanding of System Dynamics are frequent in operations management contexts. For instance, in a supply chain setting, a manufacturer's poor mental model can cause systematic errors in inventory decisions by leading to an assumption that the on-hand inventory has no effect on final customer demand, whereas long delivery delays actually reduce customer satisfaction and future demand (Bendoly et al. 2010).

Even if we know that failure to capture feedback processes lead a person to be reactive, research on cognitive psychology concludes that people often adopt this open-loop perspective and that they unconsciously use different mechanisms that worsen their understanding of system structure (Axelrod 1976; Dörner 1980). We now describe four important mechanisms that involve misperception of the feedback structure of a system: heuristics, cognitive biases, motivations and the Fundamental Attribution Error.

## 6.2.1 Heuristics

Heuristics are mental shortcuts or rule-of-thumb strategies that shorten decision-making time and allow people to come up with decisions quickly and efficiently without regularly stopping to evaluate different alternatives of action (Kahneman and Tversky 1972; Haselton et al. 2005). Although heuristics can speed up our problem-solving and decision-making process, in many situations, they can also lead to cognitive biases that make it difficult to see alternative solutions or come up with better ideas.

One of the most used heuristics within the behavioral operational research literature is the anchoring and adjustment heuristic. This heuristic is a mechanism individuals use to estimate values that they do not really know (Tversky and Kahneman 1974). Many behavioral studies suggest that subjects anchor their decisions on the first piece of available information (environmental, operational or situational factors) and then they do some (typically insufficient) adjustment away from the anchor to get to their final decision. However, the insufficient adjustment presented in the final decision is closer to the anchor than it would be otherwise (Kahneman and Tversky 1974). These environmental, operational or situational available factors (anchors) have direct influence in subjects' decision-making process, and these decisions lead to systematic biases that generate instabilities in the System Dynamics. For example, Sterman (1989b) proposes an anchoring and adjustment heuristic for capturing subjects' behavior during the Beer Distribution Game. This heuristic captures participants' ordering behavior. However, typical results show that this heuristic leads to orders that do not completely account for operational variables in the supply chain, which may generate inflated orders and supply chain instability.

## 6.2.2 Cognitive Biases

Cognitive biases are limitations on human thinking that lead to deviations from full rationality (Tversky and Kahneman 1974). This kind of error in thinking arises when subjects process and interpret information in the world around them. Cognitive biases are often a result of our attempt to simplify information processing using simple heuristics, but in other cases, they are the result of either judgmental factors, such as overconfidence (Healy and Moore 2007), or situational factors, such as framing (Kahneman and Tversky 1972).

Overconfidence is a judgmental bias in which subjects think that they understand how the system works more than their current knowledge. People do not follow simple statistical theorems, and their mental models about feedback structure are biased by perception, the availability of examples and the desirability of outcomes (Sterman 2000). For instance, subjects think that the available information they have is enough and accurate (tight confidence level) to make optimal decisions (Healy and Moore 2007) when they are not. Therefore, in an operations management setting, overconfidence can create errors in demand forecasting, which may lead to the formulation of inaccurate safety stock policies.

Framing has its roots in Prospect Theory (Kahneman and Tversky 1979), which explains the regular tendency for individuals to treat losses asymmetrically from gains (Tversky and Kahneman 1992). That is, framing is an important situational factor that affects the way subjects perceive the system; different ways of perceiving a situation influence the way subjects understand the system structure and therefore the decisions they make (Bendoly et al. 2010).

## 6.2.3 Motivation

While heuristics and biases have effects on subjects' decisions, motivation is a psychological factor that may affect our mental models in a conscious and unconscious manner, through the effort we make to understand the systems and the persistence we have in reducing the discrepancies between model predictions and outcomes. In addition, the information we receive from the system about how work is organized also affects motivation, which in turn affects our willingness to improve our mental models about feedback structure and our decisions. One of the main factors that affect individual motivation is goal setting (Bendoly et al. 2010). Effective goals lead to better decision making. This is because when people have clear goals, they show higher levels of effort as well as higher levels of strategic thinking (Latham and Locke 1991). Better strategic thinking processes increase the likelihood of learning from the system and therefore the likelihood of formulating better heuristics that reduce use of inappropriate short-term strategies and increase long-term improvement.

## 6.2.4 Fundamental Attribution Error

Another factor affecting the identification of accurate feedback structures is blame. People usually attribute the cause of unexpected outcomes to external factors. For example, in the Beer Distribution Game, subjects argue that the cause of their poor performance is the decisions of the other players or the poor coordination of the game administrator rather than their own decisions or the internal structure of the supply chain (Sterman

1989a; Sterman and Dogan 2015). Misunderstanding of the causes generating the perceived effects stops people from getting better information about the system structure and from creating policies that may lead to better performance. The propensity to blame others rather than the system structure is so frequent in the human behavior that psychologists call this phenomenon the "fundamental attribution error" (Ross 1977). People usually use their mental models to generate decision-making rules that allow them to infer causal relationships. Nevertheless, our cognitive maps judge causality assuming temporal and spatial proximity of cause and effect and ignoring feedbacks, non-linearities and other elements of dynamic complexity. The lack of interconnectedness of our mental models leads us to confound the causes of perceived behaviors and to attribute behavior to others or to special circumstances rather to than system structure. Evidence shows that attribution error has a negative effect on the redesigning of policies created to improve system performance (Forrester 1969).

Attribution error also involves misperception of causality within group dynamics. Poor performance results in external or internal blame. External blame in groups leads to defensive routines and groupthink dynamics (Janis 1982; Sterman 2000). In this scenario, members of a cohesive group engage in a mode of thinking that mutually reinforces their current beliefs, causing the group to defend their (sometimes irrational) decisions and to attribute poor outcomes to external pressures. In contrast, the Abilene paradox (Harvey 1974) explains internal blame. In this case, poor decisions are explained by situations in which no one in a group is prepared to take control of the system (Kim 2001). Therefore, the group continues on a course of action that (almost) no one within the group wants but no one is willing to express objections to (Harvey 1974). Thus, low performance is more likely to be attributed to individuals within the group rather than themselves (their own responsibility).

Blame tends to be subject to errors in perceived causation (attribution errors), which create operational and organizational difficulties. Both groupthink and Abilene Paradox dynamics involve misperception of causality and lead to sub-optimal decisions. Therefore, the best-performing individuals or teams are those who have a better understanding of the complexity of the system (Kunc and Morecroft 2010).

# 6.3    Misperception of Feedback Dynamics

The second common error in System Dynamics is that even if our mental maps of the causal relations of the system structure were perfect, our bounded rationality would constrain our mental model and our ability to identify the extent to which the System Dynamics will affect future situations (Sterman 2000). Therefore, appropriate mental models based on an understanding of the sources of complexity of a system still fail to create accurate mental simulations that provide useful insights for understanding the dynamics of the system (Simon 1982). In fact, many experimental studies conclude that this misperception of feedback dynamics persists even when subjects are facing a system with an extremely simple structure (Diehl and Sterman 1995; Sweeney and Sterman 2000).

As examples of the misperception of feedback in an operational setting, we build on the behavioral experiments explored by Gonçalves and Arango (2010) and Villa et al. (2015) in which they used a System Dynamics model with a simple structure to understand subjects' misperception of feedback.

## 6.3.1  Study Context

A frequent and costly problem in supply chains is caused by retailers' order amplification (Armony and Plambeck 2005). These amplifications have been captured in the literature since as early as 1924, when Mitchell described the case of retailers' inflating their orders to manufacturers when competing with other retailers for scarce supply (Mitchell 1924, p. 645). When faced with limited capacity, suppliers typically allocate available supply among retailers. In turn, a retailer receiving only a fraction of previous orders amplifies future ones in an attempt to secure more units (Lee et al. 1997a, b). This phenomenon can propagate through the supply chain, causing orders (and subsequently inventories) to chronically overshoot and undershoot desired levels. These fluctuations can lead retailers and suppliers alike to overreact, leading to problems such as excessive supplier capital investment, inventory gluts, low capacity utilization and poor service (Lee et al. 1997a; Anderson and Fine 1999; Sterman 2000;

Gonçalves 2003; Armony and Plambeck 2005). Academic interest in the subject has its roots in real and frequent problems faced by businesses in diverse industries. For example, a post-shortage demand surge for Hewlett-Packard's LaserJet printers led to unnecessary capacity and excess inventory (Lee et al. 1997b). Increased orders and part shortages for Pentium III processors in November 1999 motivated Intel to introduce a new Fab (Semiconductor Fabrication plant) the following year (Foremski 1999), but a large number of order cancellations and flat sales caused it to revise it soon after (Gaither 2001). Part shortages followed by a strong inventory build-up and a drastic decrease in retailer orders caused Cisco Systems to post a $2.7 billion inventory write-off and lay off 8,500 people.

This chapter builds on the behavioral experiments explored by Villa et al. (2015) and Gonçalves and Arango (2010), which present a formal model to capture the impact of the rationing game in an arborescent (tree-like) supply chain, where a single supplier sells a unique product to a single retailer. The emphasis of this chapter is (i) on the ordering behavior of a single retailer trying to match products received from its supplier with final customer demand (Villa et al. 2015) and (ii) on the supplier's ability to adjust its capacity to meet retailers' orders (Gonçalves and Arango 2010). Figure 6.1 displays the structure of the supply chain.

## 6.3.2  Model Description

Gonçalves (2003) offers a parsimonious model (see Fig. 6.2) for representing the main dynamics and feedbacks of a single-supplier single-retailer supply chain, which offers a unique, non-substitutable product with a deterministic final customer demand ($d$). Our examples analyze the decision-making processes in two operational settings: (i) retailers' orders

**Fig. 6.1**  Supply chain structure (*Source*: Villa et al. 2015)

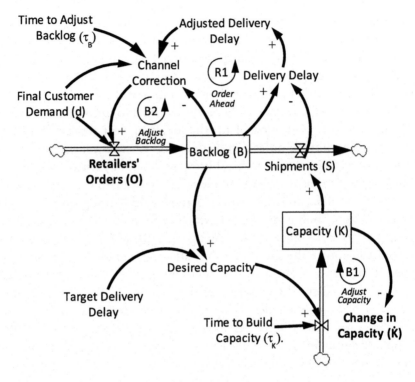

**Fig. 6.2** System Dynamics model for a single-supplier single-retailer supply chain (*Source*: adapted from Gonçalves 2003)

(*O*), as previously explored by Villa et al. (2015), and (ii) capacity management ($\dot{K}$), as previously explored by Gonçalves and Arango (2010).

The supplier's backlog of orders (*B*) increases with retailers' orders (*O*) and decreases with supplier shipments (*S*).

$$\dot{B} = R_D - S \qquad (6.1)$$

Retailers' orders are modeled with an anchoring and adjustment heuristic. Retailers anchor their orders on a forecast of final customer demand and adjust the anchor to maintain orders with the supplier at a desired level. Hence, the anchor term captures retailers' intention to place sufficient orders to meet their customers' orders.

The adjustment term closes the gap between a desired backlog ($B^*$) of orders from retailers and actual the backlog of retailers' orders. In addition, a retailer closes the gap between desired and actual backlog of orders within a specific adjustment time ($\tau_B$). In addition, the total retailers' orders are non-negative.

$$O = \mathrm{Max}\left( 0, d + \frac{B^* - B}{\tau_B} \right) \tag{6.2}$$

Actual shipments are normally determined by the minimum of desired shipments and available capacity, and shipments are modeled as determined by available capacity ($K$). The supplier's capacity ($K$) is given by a first-order exponential smooth of desired shipments, with a time constant given by the time to build capacity ($\tau_K$). Desired shipments are given by the ratio of Backlog ($B$) to Target Delivery Delay ($\tau_D$).

$$\dot{K} = \frac{B / \tau_D - K}{\tau_K} \tag{6.3}$$

The System Dynamics model presented in Fig. 6.2 is used as a basis for a management flight simulator to experimentally analyze subjects' behavior when assuming the role of a retailer (placing orders to the supplier) or that of a supplier (changing its capacity) (Sterman 1989b). $O$ represents a decision variable for the subjects in the retailer's orders experiment, and ($\dot{K}$) is a decision for the subjects in the supplier's capacity management experiment.

### 6.3.3 Experimental Protocol

The experiment starts in dynamic equilibrium, where the supplier has sufficient production capacity (100 units/week) to meet final customer orders (100 units/week). In period 4, the retailer faces a 20% step-up in final customer orders. In addition, to simplify the task's complexity during the experiment, subjects had complete information about the system structure. The experiments followed the standard experimental economics protocol (see Friedman and Sunder 1994; Friedman and Cassar 2004). Subjects were Management Engineering students at the Universidad Nacional de Colombia, and we paid them between $5 and $20 for their participation in the experiment. Subjects made their decisions trying to minimize the total accumulated cost at the end of the simulation horizon.

## 6.3.4 Retailers' Orders Experiment

In this experiment, subjects play the role of a retailer placing orders to the supplier. Their task was to match products received from their supplier with final customer demand at minimum cost. Retailers faced two quadratic cost components: (i) supply gap cost ($C_{\text{gap}}$), which represents the difference between customer demand and shipments, and (ii) ordering cost ($C_o$), which represents subjects' decisions in each simulated period. Equation 6.1 presents the structure of the Total Cost function ($TC_R$):

$$TC_R = \sum_{t=1}^{35} \left( \theta \cdot C_{\text{gap}}^2 + \gamma \cdot C_o^2 \right) \tag{6.4}$$

This experiment explores two characteristics affecting the performance of the retailer's decisions. The first one is related to the retailer's ability to get its orders in place: retailer-ordering delays, either because of its own internal process or because of possible delays on the part of the supplier in processing the orders that its receives: ($\Delta_O$). The second characteristic is related to the ability of the supplier to adjust to the orders that it is receiving: supplier capacity acquisition delays ($\tau_K$). The experiment explores the impact of short ($\Delta_O = 2$) and long ($\Delta_O = 3$) delays on retailer ordering behavior. In addition, the experiment explores the impact of a short ($\tau_K = 1$) and a long ($\tau_K = 3$) time required to build capacity. Therefore, this experiment is a full experimental design, with four experimental treatments. The first treatment (T1) presents an agile system. This is the system with less dynamics in the experiments. It considers the lowest value in the experimental variables. The fourth treatment (T4) is a slow system, because it is the most dynamically complex; both experimental variables

**Table 6.1** Retailer experimental treatments

| | | Supplier's capacity investment delay $(\tau_K)$ | |
|---|---|---|---|
| | | 1 | 3 |
| Retailer's order decision | 2 | Agile system $(n=20)$-T1 | Agile retailer $(n=20)$-T2 |
| delay $(\Delta_O)$ | 3 | Agile supplier $(n=20)$-T3 | Slow system $(n=20)$-T4 |

take the highest possible value. Treatment 2 (T2) presents an agile retailer with a slow supplier, combining a short retailer ordering delay and a long supplier capacity acquisition delay. Finally, treatment 3 (T3) presents an agile supplier with a slow retailer, combining a short supplier capacity acquisition delay with a long retailer ordering delay. Table 6.1 characterizes each treatment conducted and the number of participants ($n$) in each treatment.

## 6.3.5 Suppliers' Capacity Experiment

In this experiment, subjects play the role of a supplier deciding its capacity investment strategy to satisfy final customer demand at minimum cost. The supplier faces three quadratic cost components: (i) capacity cost ($C_K$), (ii) backlog cost ($C_B$) and (iii) change in capacity cost ($C_{\Delta K}$), which represents subjects' decisions in each simulated period. Equation 6.5 presents the structure of the Total Cost function ($TC_S$):

$$TC_S = \sum_{t=1}^{35} \left( \varepsilon \cdot C_K^2 + \varphi \cdot C_B^2 + \delta \cdot C_{\Delta K}^2 \right) \tag{6.5}$$

This experiment explores two characteristics influencing a supplier's change in its capacity decisions: retailer competition for scarce supply and supplier capacity acquisition delays. It builds on a full experimental design with four experimental treatments: two different delays in changing capacity (short =2, long =3) and two levels of retailer order aggressiveness ($\alpha$); a 10% increase in orders is expressed by $\alpha =1.1$ and a 50% increase in orders by $\alpha =1.5$%). Table 6.2 specifies all treatments conducted in the experiment. The first treatment (T1) again presents an agile system. This

**Table 6.2** Supplier experimental treatments

|  |  | Supplier's capacity investment delay ($\tau_K$) | |
|---|---|---|---|
|  |  | 2 | 3 |
| Retailer order | 2 | Agile system ($n = 19$)-T1 | Calm retailer ($n = 19$)-T2 |
| Aggressiveness ($\alpha$) | 3 | Agile supplier ($n = 19$)-T3 | Aggressive system ($n = 18$)-T4 |

is the system with longer supplier capacity investment delay and lower retailer aggressiveness. The fourth treatment (T4) is an aggressive system), because it is the most complex system, where our experimental variables take the highest possible value. Treatment 2 (T2) presents an agile supplier with a retailer of low aggressiveness. Finally, Treatment 3 (T3) presents a passive retailer with a slow supplier. Table 6.2 characterizes each treatment conducted and the number of participants ($n$) in each treatment.

## 6.3.6 Results

To properly assess subjects' performance, we numerically estimated the optimal decision trajectory for each experimental treatment. These optimal trajectories provide the sequence of decisions that subjects should make during the experiment to minimize the total cumulative cost at the end of the simulation. Tables 6.3 and 6.4 provide the total cumulative costs seen after using these optimal decisions in each experimental treatment. The lowest optimal costs are observed in the agile-system treatments ($610 for the retailer experiment T1 - Table 6.1 and $2,798 for the supplier experiment T1 - Table 6.2) and the highest are observed in the slow-system ($712 for the retailer experiment T4 - Table 6.1) and aggressive system ($6,499 for the supplier experiment T4 - Table 6.2) treatments. These results highlight the increasing system difficulty when longer delays are

**Table 6.3** Average and optimal costs across treatments for the retailer experiment

| Subject | Agile system ($) | Agile retailer ($) | Agile supplier ($) | Slow system ($) |
|---|---|---|---|---|
| Average | 7,891 | 4,428 | 2,157 | 10,076 |
| Minimum | 805 | 781 | 885 | 1,388 |
| Optimal | 610 | 654 | 647 | 712 |
| Minimum/optimal | 1.32 | 1.20 | 1.37 | 1.95 |

**Table 6.4** Average and optimal costs across treatments for the supplier experiment

| Subject | Agile system ($) | Calm retailer ($) | Agile supplier ($) | Aggressive system ($) |
|---|---|---|---|---|
| Average | 25,621 | 84,056 | 4,538,038 | 1,787,030 |
| Minimum | 3,506 | 4,591 | 7,365 | 22,265 |
| Optimal | 2,798 | 3,015 | 4,470 | 6,499 |
| Minimum/optimal | 1.25 | 1.52 | 1.65 | 3.43 |

introduced in a system. In addition, Tables 6.3 and 6.4 present average and minimum costs achieved by the subjects in all treatments. General results show that despite the simple structure of our experimental setting and the full information given about the variables involved in the system, subjects in both experiments perform far from optimally. However, consistent with our expectations, subjects' total cumulative costs are higher in the experimental treatments with higher complexity (the slow system in the retailer treatment and the aggressive system in the supplier experiment).

On the one hand, for the retailer experiment, the lowest total cost achieved by a subject varied between 20% (agile-retailer treatment) and 95% (slow-system treatment) higher than the optimal cost of the specific treatment (P12 in the agile-retailer treatment). In addition, subjects' average performances vary from 333% to 1,414%higher than the optimal performance.

On the other hand, for the supplier experiment, the lowest total cost achieved by a subject is 25% higher than the optimal value for that treatment (agile system, T1 - Tables 6.1 and 6.2). Similarly, best performances in other treatments were also significantly above optimal costs: 52% above optimal in the calm retailer treatment (T2 - Table 6.2), 65% above optimal in the agile supplier treatment (T3 - Table 6.2) and 343% above optimal in the aggressive system treatment (T4 - Table 6.2). In addition, the average costs ranged from nine to over 1,000 times higher than optimal performance.

Tables 6.5 and 6.6 show how cost components contribute to optimal and average subjects' total cost in each experimental treatment. For the retailer experiment, optimal trajectories propose solutions that avoid the high costs produced by the supply gap. However, subjects have difficulties balancing supply and demand, and they place orders that fail to minimize the supply gap cost component. This underperformance is worse as the complexity of

**Table 6.5** Costs distribution for retailer experiment

|  | Ordering cost | Supply gap cost | Ordering cost | Supply gap cost |
|---|---|---|---|---|
|  | **Agile system** | | **Agile supplier** | |
| Average | 26.9% | **73.1%** | 32.2% | **67.7%** |
| Optimal | **95.7%** | 4.3% | 91.1% | 8.9% |
|  | **Agile supplier** | | **Slow system** | |
| Average | 41.5% | **58.5%** | 19.6% | **80.4%** |
| Optimal | **92.5%** | 7.5% | 86.6% | 13.4% |

the system increases; therefore, in the slow-system treatment, subjects present the highest proportion of costs due to the supply gap (80.4%).

For the supplier experiment, Table 6.6 highlights the difference in component costs for all four treatments. For treatments with low retailer order aggressiveness (the agile system and calm retailer treatments), the fraction of the optimal cost due to changes in capacity is the cost component with the lowest percentage (15.1% and 17.1% for the agile system and calm retailer treatments, respectively). The remaining percentage of the optimal costs components are divided between capacity cost and backlog cost. On the other hand, for treatments with high retailer order aggressiveness (gile supplier and aggressive system treatments), the cost given by the changes in capacity are now the cost component displaying the highest percentage of the total costs, while the backlog cost component presents the lowest percentage of the total costs.

Opposite to optimal trajectory cost distributions, subjects facing the treatments with low retailer order aggressiveness incur the largest fraction of costs through changes in capacity (78.6% and 92.0% of total costs) and the backlog cost represents the majority of the total costs (93.8% and

**Table 6.6** Costs distribution for supplier experiment

|  | Change in capacity cost | Capacity cost | Backlog cost | Change in capacity cost | Capacity cost | Backlog cost |
|---|---|---|---|---|---|---|
|  | **Agile system** | | | **Calm retailer** | | |
| Average | **78.6%** | 13.5% | 7.9% | **92.0%** | 6.1% | 1.9% |
| Optimal | 15.1% | 42.7% | **42.3%** | 17.1% | **40.9%** | 27.8% |
|  | **Agile retailer** | | | **Aggressive system** | | |
| Average | 6.0% | 0.2% | **93.8%** | 25.7% | 4.4% | **69.9%** |
| Optimal | **42.3%** | 41.9% | 25.8% | **50.5%** | 26.6% | 22.8% |

69.9% of total costs) for subjects facing the treatments with high retailer order aggressiveness. These switches in the proportion of costs incurred by the subjects for each cost component provide clues about the sources of subjects' underperformance. The inherent complexity of the task in treatments with mild retailer aggressiveness makes subjects implement costly decisions associated with changes in capacity. For high retailer order aggressiveness, the inherent complexity of managing the positive feedback loop makes subjects incur excessive costs associated with the management of the backlog. As subjects struggle to control backlog early on, the positive feedback loop takes off, destabilizing the system and producing high costs.

To identify systematic differences across treatments, we computed the average retailer supply gap and the average supplier capacity for all players for the retailer and the supplier approach, respectively (see Figs. 6.3 and 6.4), and we compared these results with the solutions obtained using the optimal solution in each experimental condition. For the retailer experiment, Fig. 6.3 shows the evolution of the retailers' supply gap. The average evolution of subjects' decisions leads to supply gaps that are far from optimal in all treatments, especially for the most complex condition (slow system). Both subjects' average decisions and their optimal trajectories lead

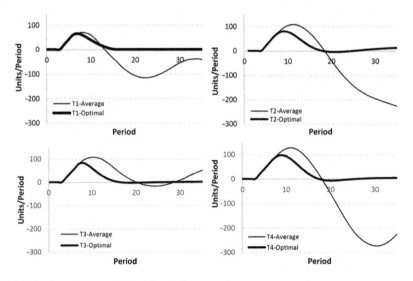

**Fig. 6.3**  Average vs. optimal retailer supply gap

to an initial increase in the supply gap, which is due to the increase in the final customer demand and the lack of in-hand inventory from the retailer to satisfy that increased final customer demand. After this initial increase in the supply gap, the optimal ordering trajectory is able to quickly reduce this gap until it settles around an equilibrium close to zero (desired supply gap). However, subjects' ordering decisions lead to longer and higher increases in the supply gap than the optimal solution yields. These initial deviations in the supply gap are due to the retailers' overordering during the first periods, which makes the supply gap negative later on and makes it difficult to settle close to the equilibrium value. Failing to get the supply gap to settle close to the equilibrium value can lead either to excessive and costly inventory or to deficits; in many cases this affects goodwill toward the organization.

For the supplier experiment, Fig. 6.4 presents the evolution of supplier capacity over time. The average evolution of subjects' decisions lead to capacity trajectories that are dominated by the optimal capacity trajectory. As in the retailers' experiment, optimal decisions lead to overall behavior that settles (easily) the capacity of the supplier close to the equilibrium value (final customer demand). For the subjects' decisions, the level of underperformance (overinvestment in capacity) increases as

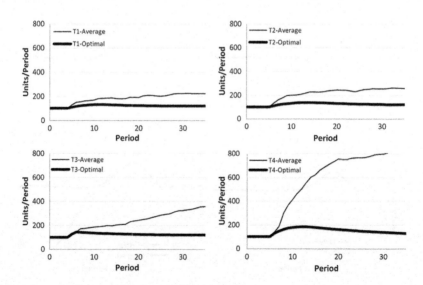

**Fig. 6.4** Average vs. optimal supplier capacity

the system becomes more complex (higher loop gain and longer supplier capacity investment delay). Excessive investments building supplier capacity lead to high investment and operational costs and to low capacity utilization, which affects supplier profits.

In the next section, we propose and econometrically analyze the anchoring and adjustment heuristic presented in Sect. 6.3.2 as a way to explain subjects' decisions in each experimental treatment and as a way to understand how the main state variables of the system could be influencing subjects' behavior.

### 6.3.6.1  Heuristics

To get insight into the nature of the subjects' decisions, we consider the heuristics that subjects may use. A possible heuristic that they might use can be obtained from the mathematical model presented in Sect. 6.4.1. We characterized subjects' decisions by the first-order Taylor series approximation of the non-linear Eqs. 6.2 and 6.3.[2] Deductions from these linear approximations can be found in Villa et al. (2015) and Gonçalves and Arango 2010). Therefore, the decision rules followed by subjects during the experiments can be expressed as a linear combination of supplier capacity and retailer backlog, as explained in the following section.

### 6.3.6.2  Heuristic Estimations

Based on the equations proposed in Table 6.7, we could estimate the parameters for each subject's decision using ordinary least squares (OLS). Figure 6.5 shows the estimation of the heuristic, the actual orders and the simulated heuristic for one subject in each of the four treatments in the retailer experiment. Subjects' actual decisions initially overshoot and then undershoot, eventually settling around an equilibrium. This pattern of behavior is amplified in treatments with higher dynamic complexity.

---

[2] The first-order Taylor series is an approximation of a non-linear function using a linear function. The components of the polynomial are calculated from the non-linear function's derivatives (Note from the editors).

**Table 6.7** Linearized heuristics for each experimental design

| | Linearized heuristic | Generic form |
|---|---|---|
| Retailer orders | $O = \text{Max}\begin{pmatrix} 0, \left( d + \dfrac{\alpha d\tau_D}{\tau_B} \right) - \left( \dfrac{\alpha d\tau_D}{\tau_B K_0} \right)K \\ + \left( \dfrac{\alpha d - K_0}{\tau_B K_0} \right)B \end{pmatrix}$ | $O_t = \beta_{0ij} + \beta_{1ij}K_t + \beta_{2ij}B_t + \varepsilon_{tij}$ |
| Supplier change in capacity | $\dot{K} = \left( \dfrac{d}{\tau_K} + \dfrac{d\alpha\tau_D}{\tau_K\tau_B} \right) - \left( \dfrac{d\alpha\tau_D}{K_0\tau_K\tau_B} - \dfrac{1}{\tau_K} \right)K$ $+ \left( \dfrac{d\alpha}{K_0\tau_K\tau_B} - \dfrac{1}{\tau_K\tau_B} \right)B$ | $\dot{K}_t = \beta_{0ij} + \beta_{1ij}K_t + \beta_{2ij}B_t + \varepsilon_{tij}$ |

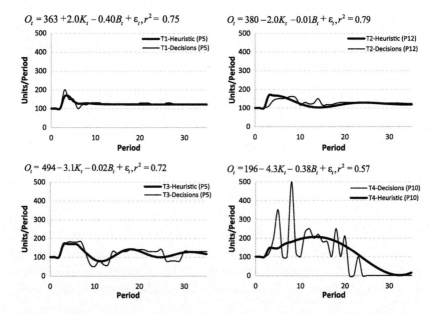

$O_t = 363 + 2.0K_t - 0.40B_t + \varepsilon_t, r^2 = 0.75$

$O_t = 380 - 2.0K_t - 0.01B_t + \varepsilon_t, r^2 = 0.79$

$O_t = 494 - 3.1K_t - 0.02B_t + \varepsilon_t, r^2 = 0.72$

$O_t = 196 - 4.3K_t - 0.38B_t + \varepsilon_t, r^2 = 0.57$

**Fig. 6.5** Simulation of the proposed heuristic and actual decisions for selected subjects in each treatment for the retailer experiment (subject ID in parenthesis)

Therefore, predicting subjects' behavior becomes more complicated as longer delays are introduced into the system. Figure 6.5 also shows that the pattern of subjects' ordering decisions can be, on average, represented by the evolution of the proposed linearized heuristic. This result is also supported by the high $r^2$ values obtained by the econometrical estimation provided for each subject. As expected, the slow system treatment leads to the lower $r^2$ value, which also reflect the difficulty of determining subjects' behavior under highly reinforcing systems.

Figure 6.6 shows the estimation of the heuristic, the actual orders and the simulated heuristic for one subject in each of the four treatments for the supplier experiment. In general, subjects' decisions show a similar pattern of behavior for all experimental treatments. Initially, the supplier increases its capacity as a response to the perceived increase in retailers' orders. Then the supplier decreases its capacity, trying to get rid of the excess capacity obtained during the investment periods. This

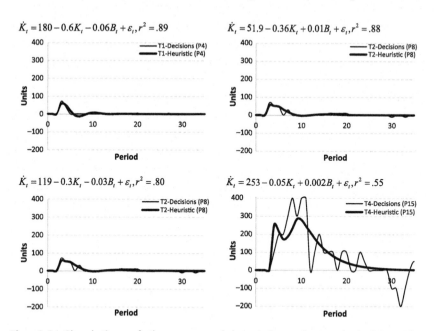

**Fig. 6.6** Simulation of the proposed heuristic and actual decisions for selected subjects in each treatment for the supplier experiment (subject ID in parenthesis)

overinvestment and divestment cycle is attenuated over time but can take place in subsequent weeks. Once the proper size for the capacity is obtained, suppliers stop making changes in their capacity and anchor their decisions close to the equilibrium. The peak in capacity and investment decision tends to occur earlier in treatments with shorter delays, while treatments with longer delays lead to higher volatility in subjects' decisions. On the other hand, the proposed heuristic is able to represent subjects' behavior with a high level of accuracy ($r^2 > 0.5$), especially in treatments with low dynamics.

Finally, we analyzed subjects' decisions using a panel data approach. The panel accounts for individual heterogeneity and controls for omitted variables that vary over time but are constant among subjects in each treatment; therefore, we will be able to provide general conclusions about the way subjects could be making their decisions based on the proposed heuristic. Given the random assignment used in experiments, there is no expectation to have time-invariant omitted variables among subjects and thus fixed effects are not necessary. Consequently, and to allow for variation among subjects, we use a random effects intercept for the model. Results are shown in Tables 6.8 and 6.9 for the different experimental designs.

For the retailer experiment, estimations of parameter $\beta_1$ are significantly lower than zero in all treatments ($p < 0.1$ in all cases). The negative coefficient for $\beta_1$ is intuitive, since a higher value of supplier capacity induces lower orders by the retailer. In addition, estimations of parameter $\beta_2$ are significantly higher than zero in all treatments ($p < 0.1$ in all cases). These results are also consistent with our expectations, since a retailer will order more in an attempt to receive what it needs, when it is faced with a

**Table 6.8** Coefficient estimates of retailers' decision rules for each treatment

| Regressors | Agile system | Agile retailer | Agile supplier | Slow system |
|---|---|---|---|---|
| $\beta_0$ (Intercept) | 141.97[a] | 186.30[a] | 187.11[a] | 183.13[a] |
| $\beta_1$ (Capacity) | −3.40[a] | −2.59[a] | −3.28[a] | −1.94[a] |
| $\beta_2$ (Backlog) | 0.35[a] | 0.21[a] | 0.29[a] | 0.15[a] |
| $R^2$ (within) | 0.25 | 0.32 | 0.15 | 0.26 |
| No. observations | 495 | 561 | 462 | 495 |

[a]Significant at 10%

**Table 6.9** Coefficient estimates of suppliers' decision rules for each treatment

| Regressors | Agile system | Passive retailer | Agile supplier | Aggressive system |
|---|---|---|---|---|
| $\beta_0$ (Intercept) | 22.98[a] | 26.04[a] | 5.78[a] | 50.45[a] |
| $\beta_1$ (Capacity) | −0.111[a] | −0.101[a] | 0.007 | −0.051[a] |
| $\beta_2$ (Backlog) | 0.002[a] | −0.001 | 2.5e−5[a] | 0.000 |
| -LL | 5,998 | 6,667 | 6,891 | 7,523 |
| No observations | 722 | 722 | 722 | 684 |

[a]Significant at 10%

large backlog. Additional insight can be obtained now from the parameter estimates. As an example, $\beta_1$ estimations in the agile system treatment (−3.40) and the agile retailer treatment (−2.59) are lower than those in the agile supplier treatment (−3.28) and the slow system treatment (−1.94), respectively. This result shows that subjects increase their orders when their orders take longer to be received by the supplier, which means that subjects are taking into account the effect of their ordering decision delays in their decision process. A similar analysis can be done for the effect of the parameter $\beta_2$.

Finally, for the supplier experiment, estimations of parameter $\beta_1$ are significantly lower than zero in three out of four of the experimental treatments (with $p < 0.1$ in all cases). A negative coefficient for $\beta_1$ means that a higher value of supplier capacity induces a change in capacity in the opposite direction. This result is probably associated with the frequent overinvestments in capacity that suppliers make when they perceive an increase in retailers' orders; later on, this overinvestment leads to a reduction of capacity. Estimations of parameter $\beta_2$ are significantly higher than zero in treatments with low supplier capacity investment delay (in the agile system and calm retailer treatments), which means that subjects increase their investment in capacity when they perceive that the number of outstanding orders is increasing. However, in the presence of longer supplier capacity investment delays, subjects reduce their dependence on the number of outstanding orders, and they base their decisions the current capacity.

## 6.4    Behavioral Implications

In the previous sections, we have shown that subjects make decisions that exhibit both misperception of feedback structure and misperception of feedback dynamics. However, these misperceptions and inefficiencies also exist in multiple supply chain systems that exhibit a similar structure. In Table 6.10, we identify a similar structure of flows, stocks and delays that

**Table 6.10** Behavioral implications in different kinds of systems

| System | Stock | Flows | Delays | Behavioral implications |
|---|---|---|---|---|
| Inventory management | Inventory | Production (+) Shipments (−) | Goods on order | Inventory gluts Shortages Over/under forecast Unsatisfied customers |
| Capacity management | Capacity | Capacity investment (+) Capacity depreciation (−) Capacity divestment (−) | Capacity under construction | Excess capacity Tight capacity Loss of good will |
| Human resources | Employees | Hiring (+) Firing (−) Quits (−) | Training Hiring Firing Worker overloading policies | Over/under hiring High attrition Low morale Fatigue Inadequate training |
| Cash management | Cash balance | Income (+) Expenditure (−) | Loans approval Debt amortization | Cash constraints Bankruptcy Excess available credit |
| Marketing | Customer base | New customers (+) Customer attrition (−) | Time to attract potential customers Time to awareness | Low marketing prospects Low awareness Product failure |

play a major role in proper operations of different managerial systems. The presence and mismanagement of delays in each of these systems lead to different behavioral implications that reduce system performance. For example, in the capacity management system, the general structure is formed by the actual capacity (stock), which is dynamically modified by the three main flows: capacity ivestment, capacity depreciation and capacity divestment. Capacity investment increase the production capacity (indicated by + in Table 6.10), while capacity depreciation and capacity divestment (−) reduce it (− in Table 6.10). The most common type of delay in a capacity management system is the frequent long periods required for the capacity under construction to become available. In the presence of tight capacity and failure to satisfy customer demand, customers duplicate their orders and manufacturers use a strong capacity expansion strategy. Due to the initial unsatisfied customers and the inability of the manufacturers to respond properly to its customers, it will face a *loss of good will*. Once capacity under construction finally becomes available and deliveries go back to normal, customers cancel duplicated orders and the manufacturer ends up with significant Excess Capacity and a remarkable amount of inventory.

## 6.5 Conclusions

In this chapter, we have reviewed how the misperception of feedback structure and dynamics affects people's decisions and can lead to poor performance. In our laboratory experiments, participants were given complete knowledge of all structural relationships and parameters along with perfect, comprehensive and immediate knowledge of all variables. In addition, the systems were simple and the number of variables under consideration small. Yet performance was poor and subject learning slow. Poor performance in these tasks reflects subjects' inability to make proper dynamic inferences about the system, despite complete knowledge of the system structure. Our description highlights the important difference between the misperception of feedback structure (associated with the awareness of specific feedback processes) and of feedback dynamics (associated with the ability to predict the behavior of such feedback processes). While participants were aware of specific feedback processes and expected a particular behavior, they significantly underestimated the strength of their impact and they made decisions that led to poor distribution of the costs' components.

Understanding the actual feedback processes and properly incorporating their strength can increase the usefulness and performance of the current supply chain models and processes. We believe, in particular, that incorporating human behavioral factors into the key supply chain management processes, as suggested in Sect. 6.4, will provide gains not only to the practical nature of existing theoretical models but also to the field's general understanding of what it means to have effective operations. A wider inclusion of human behavior in future supply chain management work will be diverse. The next steps in the evolution of this literature should clearly be focused on explaining the causes of perceived gaps (theory vs. behavior), measuring their impacts and attempting to redesign systems, processes and organizations to either counteract or at least provide adjustability for behavioral causes. We believe that an increased understanding of human behavior and practice-oriented models can be more constructive for designing systems and improving supply chain processes that are robust to subjects' biases, unanticipated feedback loops and unexpected dynamics.

# References

Anderson, E., and C. Fine. 1999. Business cycles and productivity in capital equipment supply chains. In *Quantitative models for supply chain management*, ed. S. Tayur, R. Ganshan, and M. Magazine, 381–415. Norwell: Kluwer Academic Publishers.

Arango Aramburo, S., J.A. Castañeda Acevedo, and Y. Olaya Morales. 2012. Laboratory experiments in the system dynamics field. *System Dynamics Review* 28: 94–106.

Armony, M., and E. Plambeck. 2005. The impact of duplicate orders on demand estimation and capacity investment. *Management Science* 51: 1505–1518.

Axelrod, R. 1976. *Structure of decision: The cognitive maps of political elites.* Princeton: Princeton University Press.

Barlas, Y., and M.G. Özevin. 2004. Analysis of stock management gaming experiments and alternative ordering formulations. *System Research and Behavioral Science* 21: 439–470.

Bendoly, E., R. Croson, P. Goncalves, and K. Schultz. 2010. Bodies of knowledge for research in behavioral operations. *Production and Operations Management* 19: 434–452.

Croson, R., and K. Donohue. 2002. The impact of POS data sharing on supply chain management: An experimental study. *Production and Operations Management* 12: 1–11.

Diehl, E., and J.D. Sterman. 1995. Effects of feedback complexity on dynamic decision making. *Organizational Behavior and Human Decision Processes* 62: 198–215.

Dörner, D. 1980. On the difficulties people have in dealing with complexity. *Simulations and Games* 11(1): 87–106.

Foremski, T. (1999). Intel struggles to meet strong demand for chips. *Financial Times* (London), November 18, p. 42.

Forrester, J.W. 1969. *Urban dynamics.* Waltham: Pegasus Communications.

Friedman, D., and A. Cassar. 2004. *Economics lab: An intensive course in experimental economics.* London: Routledge.

Friedman, D., and S. Sunder. 1994. *Experimental methods: A primer for economists.* Cambridge, MA: Cambridge University Press.

Gaither, C. 2001. Intel beats forecast; Warns of revenue shortfall. *The New York Times*, January 17, C1.

Gonçalves, P. 2003. Phantom orders and demand bubbles in supply chains. *Ph.D. Dissertation, Sloan School of Management, MIT*, Cambridge, MA.

Gonçalves, P., and S. Arango. 2010. Supplier capacity decisions under retailer competition and delays: Theoretical and experimental results. *28th international conference of the System Dynamics Society*, Seoul-Korea.

Harvey, J.B. 1974. The Abilene paradox: The management of agreement. *Organizational Dynamics* 17: 16–34.

Haselton, M.G., D. Nettle, and P.W. Andrews. 2005. The evolution of cognitive bias. In *The handbook of evolutionary psychology*, ed. D.M. Buss, 724–746. Hoboken: Wiley.

Healy, P.J., and D.A. Moore. 2007. *The trouble with overconfidence.* Working Paper. Carnegie-Mellon University.

Hogarth, R.M. 1981. Beyond discrete biases: Functional and dysfunctional aspects of judgmental heuristics. *Psychological Bulletin* 90: 197–217.

Janis, I.L. 1982. *Groupthink: Psychological studies of policy decisions and fiascoes*, 2nd ed. Boston: Houghton Mifflin.

Kahneman, D., and A. Tversky. 1972. Subjective probability: A judgment of representativeness. *Cognitive Psychology* 3: 430–454.

Kahneman, D., and A. Tversky. 1979. Prospect theory: An analysis of decision under risk. *Econometrica: Journal of the Econometric Society* 47: 263–291.

Kainz, D., and G. Ossimitz. 2002. Can students learn stock-flow-thinking? An empirical investigation. In *Proceedings of the 20th international conference of the System Dynamics Society.*

Kampmann, C.P.E. 1992. Feedback complexity and market adjustment: An experimental approach. Ph.D. thesis, *Massachusetts Institute of Technology, Sloan School of Management*, Cambridge MA.

Kampmann, C., and J.D. Sterman. 1998. Feedback complexity, bounded rationality, and market dynamics. Memo D-4802, *System Dynamics Group. Massachusetts Institute of Technology.*

Kim, Y. 2001. A comparative study of the "Abilene paradox" and "Groupthink". *Public Administration Quarterly* 25: 168–191.

Kleinmuntz, D.N. 1993. Information processing and misperceptions of the implications of feedback in dynamic decision making. *System Dynamics Review* 9: 223–237.

Kleinmuntz, D.N., and J.B. Thomas. 1987. The value of action and inference in dynamic decision making. *Organizational Behavior and Human Decision Processes* 39: 341–364.

Kunc, M., and J. Morecroft. 2010. Managerial decision-making and firm performance under a resource-based paradigm. *Strategic Management Journal* 31: 1164–1182.

Latham, G.P., and E.A. Locke. 1991. Self-regulation through goal setting. *Organizational Behavior and Human Decision Processes* 50: 212–247.

Lee, H., V. Padmanabhan, and W. Seungjin. 1997a. Information distortion in a supply chain: The bullwhip effect. *Management Science* 43: 546–558.

Lee, H., V. Padmanabhan, and W. Seungjin. 1997b. The bullwhip effect in supply chains. *Sloan Management Review* 38: 93–102.

Mitchell, T.W. 1924. Competitive illusion as a cause of business cycles. *Quarterly Journal of Economics* 38: 631–652.

Moxnes, E. 2004. Misperceptions of basic dynamics: The case of renewable resource management. *System Dynamics Review* 20: 139–162.

Moxnes, E., and A.K. Saysel. 2009. Misperceptions of global climate change: Information policies. *Climatic Change* 93: 15–37.

Paich, M., and J. Sterman. 1993. Boom, bust and learn in experimental markets. *Management Science* 39: 1439–1458.

Ross, L. 1977. The intuitive psychologist and his shortcomings: Distortions in the attribution process. *Advances in Experimental Social Psychology* 10: 173–220.

Sengupta, K., and T.K. Abdel-Hamid. 1993. Alternative conceptions of feedback in dynamic decision environments: An experimental investigation. *Management Science* 39: 411–428.

Simon, H.A. 1982. *Models of bounded rationality: Empirically grounded economic reason*. Cambridge, MA: MIT Press.

Sterman, J.D., 1987. Testing behavioral simulation models by direct experiment. *Management Science* 33: 1572–1592.

Sterman, J.D. 1989a. Modeling managerial behavior: Misperceptions of feedback in a dynamic decision making experiment. *Management Science* 35: 321–339.

Sterman, J.D. 1989b. Misperceptions of feedback in dynamic decision making. *Organizational Behavior and Human Decision Sciences* 43: 301–335.

Sterman, J.D. 2000. *Business dynamics: Systems thinking and modeling for a complex world*. Boston: McGraw-Hill/Irwin.

Sterman, J.D., and G. Dogan. 2015. "I'm not hoarding, I'm just stocking up before the hoarders get here".: Behavioral causes of phantom ordering in supply chains. *Journal of Operations Management* 39: 6–22.

Sweeney, L.B., and J.D. Sterman. 2000. Bathtub dynamics: initial results of a systems thinking inventory. *System Dynamics Review* 16: 249–286.

Tversky, A., and D. Kahneman. 1974. Judgment under uncertainty: Heuristics and biases. *Science* 185: 1124–1131.

Tversky, A., and D. Kahneman. 1992. Advances in prospect theory: Cumulative representation of uncertainty. *Journal of Risk and Uncertainty* 5: 297–323.

Villa, S., P. Gonçalves, and S. Arango. 2015. Exploring retailers' ordering decisions under delays. *System Dynamics Review* 31: 1–27.

# 7

# Agent-Based Models and Behavioral Operational Research

## 7.1   Introduction

Agent-Based Modeling is a form of computational modeling where individual constituent components of a system—such as individuals, firms, cells, or atoms—are modelled. In behavioral operational research, these constituent *agents* can be people within a group of interest and the model can also include interactions with members in other groups or interactions with the wider environment in which agents reside. Agents within the system may act according to simple rules, or *heuristics,* which gives rise to the interactions between these agents. These interactions can combine in such a way that emergent properties are seen—properties that are not imposed on the model in a top-down fashion but are generated by the interactions of agents themselves. Agent-Based Modeling is not, however, confined to systems that exhibit equilibrium but can be used to

D. A. Robertson
School of Business and Economics, University of Loughborough,
Loughborough, Leicestershire, LE11 3TU, UK

© The Editor(s) (if applicable) and The Author(s) 2016                    **137**
M. Kunc et al. (eds.), *Behavioral Operational Research*,
DOI 10.1057/978-1-137-53551-1_7

model the dynamics of a system (System Dynamics modeling) over time. As such, Agent-Based Modeling provides a rich simulation methodology to augment and potentially extend more traditional modeling techniques, where behavior and interactions of individuals are at the forefront of the modeller's mind.

Sterman (1989) highlights, in the context of System Dynamics models such as the Beer Distribution Game (Forrester 1961), how the microbehavior of actors within the system generates dynamics, such as the bullwhip effect, where boundedly rational (Simon 1957) behavior by the individuals, particularly their "misperceptions of feedback", generate dynamics that are unpredictable and are contrary to purely rational behavior. Sterman states that merely understanding the behavior of individuals and carrying out observations of individuals is not sufficient: what is needed is to "understand how micro-level behaviors link to the behavior of the system" (Coleman 1987).

We follow and extend Sterman's (1989) approach to models. Due to the complexity of the behavioral interactions among individuals within the system, the situation cannot successfully be modelled using System Dynamics or systems-level modeling, whose interactions at the micro level *form* the system—behavior that is *emergent* (Goldstein 1999). Without understanding and modeling the behavioral characteristics of the agents, we are very much restricted in what we can understand from the model if we intend to model the system purely from a systems perspective.

Hämäläinen et al. (2013) extend this to a call for the development of a holistic field of behavioral operational research, extending Cronin et al.'s (2009) work showing that system-level constructs such as the concept of *accumulation* are not well understood by otherwise intelligent, rational individuals. Hämäläinen and Saarinen (2006) and Saarinen and Hämäläinen (2007) advocate educating individuals in "systems intelligence", allowing users to sense the "feeling of the system" (Hämäläinen and Saarinen 2008) to overcome Ackoff's (2006) assertion that relatively few organizations adopt systems thinking.

We will discuss some of the reasons for this: the systems that we profess to understand are *complex systems* of interacting individuals, and therefore it is not truly possible to understand the emergent, system-level properties that we tend to interpret if we do not understandthe micro-level interactions that make up that emergent system. For example, this applies to interactions of the actors that make up the accumulation in Cronin et al.'s (2009) and Hämäläinen et al.'s (2013) work: in system-level models, we cannot visualize 'the individuals and the system is therefore too abstract for "well educated adults" (Cronin et al. 2009) to comprehend. We will advocate the use of agent-based models to explore these micro-level interactions whose behavioral interactions, either between actors or between individual actors and the system itself, contribute to or indeed *are* the behavior of the system itself.

## 7.2    Complex Systems of Interacting Individuals

### 7.2.1  Complex Systems

Complexity science is engaged with the understanding of systems comprising interacting agents, for example the interactions between individuals in a social system. Johnson (2009) acknowledges that many of the systems that we currently analyze may be thought of as complex systems without being studied explicitly as such: "...however, the *way* in which scientists have traditionally looked at these systems does not use any of the insights of complexity science". The same is true of behavioral operational research: we are so used to studying the system as a whole that we have neglected individual behavior. One definition of complexity science is "the study of the phenomena which emerge from a collection of interacting objects" (Johnson 2009). In our case, these interacting objects are individual people and the phenomena are the socially constructed behavior of the system itself.

We shall concentrate on one insight from complexity science, that of studying the interactions of agents that comprise a system. That is to say interactions between agents within a system, interactions between agents and the environment, and interactions between participants studying the system behavior, for example in a workshop environment.

We agree wholeheartedly with Luoma et al. (2010) that so-called "complex responsive processes", or what we would describe more broadly as complex systems, should be integrated with systems thinking, not seen as a rival theory. Complex systems are broader than complex responsive processes, and this term applies to a wide range of systems, some deterministic and some social. These systems are *complex* in that they are made up of individual parts and essentially the interactions between these individual parts.

Agents within the system interact with each other but *also with the system itself.* We will show, through introducing a range of agent-based models, that by looking at the system from the bottom up, we can *generate* systems behavior, which in turn can be sensed by the individual actors (with appropriate levels of systems intelligence), who can adapt their behavior not only to the local interaction but also to the system itself.

There are three levels of interaction that we can explore within these complex systems of interacting agents: behavioral interactions between agents, behavioral interactions between agents and the environment, and interactions between model users and the model itself.

## 7.2.2 Agent-Based Modeling

Agent-Based Modeling is a relatively recent approach to modeling systems of interacting individuals. Originally called Individual-Based Modeling (Hiebeler 1994; Grimm and Railsbark 1997), these models concentrate on the behavior of the components of the system rather than on the system itself. The system behavior results from the micro-level interactions among the agents, and while a central policy maker is not required, policy-like, or *emergent,* behaviors of the system can result from the interactions between individuals.

Agent-based models are typically conceived using simple behaviors of individual agents (which can be made more complicated or refined as the model is developed). These behaviors are boundedly rational and are based on the agent's own perception of its environment—perspectives that can differ between different agents. Typically, heuristics or simple rules are used to model behavior. But there is nothing in the philosophy of Agent-Based Modeling that requires simplicity of behavior: intricate decision rules can easily be modelled and studied. The advantage of agent-based approaches is that complexity of behavior can be increased, by sequentially turning on more and more complicated behavioral rules, in order to determine what behavioral characteristics are required for a system to change state.

Agents within an agent-based model are autonomous, in that the agents are individually modelled as different objects within the simulation. Each time interval, step or "tick" of the model results in agents' observing their environment (including interactions with other agents), in their undertaking an action or movement based on decision rules or heuristics and in the system's being updated as a result of all the individual movements of the agents.

It is worth noting that agent-based approaches are flourishing in behavioral finance (*Economist* 2010; Farmer and Foley 2009) and in behavioral economics (Tesfatsion 2002, 2006). We introduce below several models that focus on the interactions between agents.

Figure 7.1 shows how traditional models can be "agentized" in order to include behavioral effects that may be ignored or averaged out in traditional, analytical models and how some agent-based models have no equivalent in system-level models (shown by the question mark).

Agent-Based Modeling can be differentiated from System Dynamics modeling and discrete event simulation (Borshchev and Filippov 2004; Robinson 2014). System Dynamics modeling focuses on stocks and flows, concentrating on feedback loops and time delays that link these stocks. These feedback loops may compound or retard each other, in that they may be "reinforcing" or "balancing". System Dynamics models abstract away the individual entities that flow within the system, preferring to quantify these as a level of flow: individual entities are quantified rather than being modelled explicitly. A side effect of this is that the entities that compose the stocks and flows are treated as being *fungible*—their individuality is abstracted away. The interactions among stocks, flows, and delays can be shown on a System Dynamics diagram, which is a way of visually representing the differential equations that fully describe the model. While System Dynamics models are continuous, in that they evolve over time by means of differential equations, discrete event simulation models are discrete. *Discrete-Event Simulation* relies on modeling the flow of entities through a system from one "activity" to another, for example passengers flowing through an airport. As the activities (checkin, security etc.) do not clear at the same rate as the arrival of entities into the system, queues form and are studied. Changes can be made to the configuration of activities and the way that entities are allowed to travel through the system, and these configurations can be compared. Discrete event simulation, in contrast with System Dynamics models, can be modelled stochastically, in that events can occur randomly. *Agent-Based Modeling* can deal with both stochastic events and heterogeneity of entities, or, at the opposite extreme, we can use it to model deterministic events with a homogeneous population of agents. Potentially, agent-based models can deal with more specific

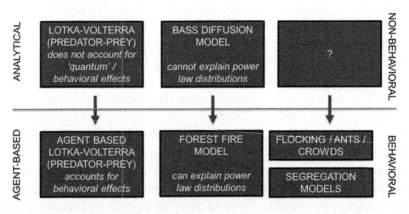

**Fig. 7.1** Agent-based vs. analytical modeling approaches

and idiosyncratic behaviors than Discrete-Event Simulation or System Dynamics can.

## 7.3    Introducing Behavior to Existing Modeling Techniques

We will introduce three ways that Agent-Based Modeling can incorporate behavioral aspects into the modeling repertoire. We shall see that even with homogeneous agents, behavior within the system produces interesting social- or system-level behavior. By opening up the ability to model interacting individuals, we open up a plethora of possibilities for explicitly studying how the behavior of individual agents changes the system as a whole.

The models are presented in order of increasing heterogeneity (and therefore number of behavioral characteristics) of the agents. Each model is spatial in that it locates agents with a set of coordinates in a space.

- In the first model, the Segregation model, agents are homogeneous in that they each have the same model-level parameter, that being the proportion of their neighbors of a different type (e.g. color, shape).
- The second model, the Predator–Prey model, introduces energy levels to the agents—when agents' energy is exhausted, they die.
- The third model, the Forest Fire model, has individuals in one of two states, activated (on fire) or prone to activation.

These models introduce the ability of agent-based models to incorporate the behaviors of individual actors.

The actors within the models as initially presented are not nuanced individuals exhibiting sophisticated behaviors (these are "white" or "grey" people; wolves or sheep; and, perhaps most esoterically, trees!), these are merely the building blocks *from which* sophisticated behavioral models can be created. If we do not understand the behaviors of models with simple rules, the complex interactions of more sophisticated models may confound our results. It is therefore important to start with the *simplest* model that exhibits interesting behavior (tipping points, power laws, quantization) and not to start from the most complicated system that we can imagine. The following are all dynamic models where behavioral interactions, either between individuals or between individuals and the environment, are critical in constructing the system, rather than in modeling the macro-level system itself.

## 7.3.1 Tipping Points from Individual Behavior: Segregation Models

Schelling's (1969, 1971) model of segregation was one of the first models to approach a modeling question not by looking at the macro-level dynamics of the system itself but rather by modeling the behavior of individual actors and, from those micro-level interactions, aggregating their behavior into the macro-level properties of the system.

The model is simple: individuals possess only one characteristic of interest—their happiness, which is derived from their type/color and the type/color of those around them. An agent's happiness level is generated by simply dividing the number of neighbors of the same type/color as themselves by the total number of neighbors. So, if a white agent is surrounded by 2 whites and 3 greys, their happiness level would be $2/5 = 0.4$. If the agent's happiness level is below a system-level tolerance parameter, the agent is unhappy; if the agent's happiness level is equal to or greater than the tolerance parameter, the agent is happy. While agents are homogeneous in the sense that they all have identical tolerance parameters, it is trivial to extend this to individual agents having heterogeneous tolerances. (Agents can possess other characteristics, such as shape, which can be used to extend the model.)

The model is constructed as follows (Fig. 7.2):

- $N$ agents are situated on a grid. $N/2$ are colored white, and $N/2$ are colored grey
- Each agent decides whether they are happy based on whether the percentage similar in their neighborhood is greater than or equal to the model-level tolerance parameter

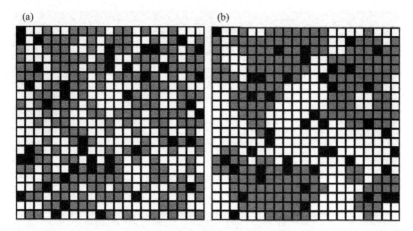

**Fig. 7.2** (a) Initial conditions (b) Equilibrium conditions showing segregation produced by agent-level behavior, not by the system itself

- Unhappy agents move to an unoccupied space
- The system updates until each agent is happy

The striking thing about this model is not that it explains segregation by individuals' being overtly intolerant but that it shows that preferences of having only around 30 % of neighbors of the same type/color as the focal agent (meaning that they are happy in a 2:1 minority) results in segregation, as seen in Fig. 7.3.

It is interesting to note that the system behavior, that of segregation, comes not from a policy of separating types/colors within a population but from the emergent interactions among agents.

Agents in the segregation model do not need to be heterogeneous, in that each member of the population need not have the same, system-defined parameter of the proportion of agents of the same type/color, that they wish to have in their neighborhood. Of course, the model can easily be extended to give each agent specific behavior rules based on their own color, the behavior of neighboring agents and so on, but this is not required to produce the interesting behavior exhibited by the model.

**Fig. 7.3** Agent-based operationalization of the Lotka–Volterra systems model

## 7.3.2 Individualizing Systems Models: Predator–Prey Models

System Dynamics models by definition examine the state of and changes to a system. Yet this system comprises interacting agents whose individual behavior aggregates to the behavior of the system.

The Lotka–Volterra population dynamics equations (Lotka 1920, 1925; Volterra 1926) are as follows:

$$\frac{dx}{dt} = \alpha x - \beta xy \tag{7.1}$$

$$\frac{dy}{dt} = -\gamma y + \delta xy \tag{7.2}$$

where $x$ and $y$ are the population of prey and predators, respectively, and $\alpha$, $\beta$, $\gamma$ and $\delta$ are parameters of the system representing the interaction of predators and prey.

The Lotka–Volterra model has been used widely within management science for modeling human systems as diverse as economic cycles (Goodwin 1967), stock markets (Lee et al. 2005) and the battle between old and new technologies, such as the fountain pen and the ballpoint pen (Modis 2003). All of these systems comprise interacting agents, yet these individual interactions are aggregated in the Lotka–Volterra population model into system-level dynamics.

While the differential equations linking the populations of prey and predator are undoubtedly elegant, they overlook an important aspect of the system: the fact that the total number of prey and predators is not a continuous variable; the values of $x$ and $y$ are in fact discrete. This matters where the number of individuals that have the potential to interact is low: there is no such thing as part of a predator or a prey interacting; either one predator interacts or no predators interact.

In order to convert the system-level model into a model where the interactions are of critical importance, we can personalize, or agentize, the model—in other words, each of the integer $x$'s and $y$'s (the quantities of prey and predators) are modelled as individual, autonomous agents.

This can be thought of as being analogous to a Kuhnian transition (Kuhn 1962) from viewing a physical system through the models of Newtonian mechanics to viewing it through alternative modeling techniques such as statistical mechanics or quantum mechanics. It is precisely this transition from treating the system as one entity to treating the system as comprising interacting agents that behavioral operational research is now facing: system-level approaches are appropriate only for a certain class of problems at a certain scale. To use a physical analogy, individual components of the system, for example atoms within a lump of uranium, can be averaged out and the macroscopic entity can be considered as one unit: if we throw a piece of uranium ore, we do not require any knowledge of quantum mechanics to predict its path. However, in order to understand the same uranium's behavior at a micro scale, we will need to view each atom separately using a different approach—that of quantum mechanics. Or indeed, if we are examining multiple interacting objects, such as atoms within a gas, we can move to system-level characteristics of statistical mechanics, where we ignore each individual atom and study the system as a whole. And we must note that where Behavioral

Operational Research can contribute most is not in the regime of order (where there is correlation in behaviors of individuals and traditional methodologies work best) nor in the chaotic regime (where the system is so complicated that we have no hope of understanding all behavioral interactions). Behavioral Operational Research can yield the most in this middle ground, that of complexity, where individual interactions are critical in determining how the system will behave.

Behavioral systems of interacting people *can* be modelled on the macro level by systems approaches, but this neglects potentially critical interactions between the actors that may be of vital importance. On one level, this may not matter, but on another, it may. A challenge for the field is to determine when individual behavioral interactions matter and when they can be averaged out and essentially ignored.

Order parameters (for a review see Sethna 2006) are a potential solution to determine when a system is in the state where behavioral interactions can be ignored and when it is in the state where behavioral interactions cannot be ignored and where the symmetry and homogeneity of individuals can no longer be assumed.

By instead modeling individual behavior within the model (Fig. 7.3), we can identify individuals within the system—in this case, we are calling them wolves and sheep (predators and prey), but they could as easily be individuals who are using old and new technologies.

The rules/heuristics for agentizing the Lotka–Volterra model are relatively simple:

- Populate the space with $x$ predators and $y$ prey. Give each agent (predator or prey) a random quantity of energy. Note that $x$ and $y$ are integers, as the number of agents is quantized: each predator contributes exactly 1 to the value of $x$; each prey contributes exactly 1 to the value of $y$.
- Allow the agents to move, predate, die, and reproduce.
- Movement—movement is undertaken by both predator and prey by taking a step of a random walk (in any direction) each time period. Movement is costly for predators, so they lose a unit of energy every time they move.

- Predation—if predators find themselves co-located with a prey, they will eat the prey; this adds an amount of energy to the individual predator's energy level.
- Death—each predator or prey whose energy level has been reduced to (or below) zero is removed.
- Reproduction—predators reproduce with a fixed probability; prey reproduce with a fixed probability. The energy level of the parent is divided equally between the parent and the offspring.

When the agent-based model and the System Dynamics models are run side-by-side (Wilensky 2005), we can see that the qualitative behavior of both systems (the System Dynamics model being the system itself and the agent-based model being the aggregate behavior of the individual agents) is remarkably similar (see Fig. 7.4). This process, called *docking*, is the alignment of different computational models (Axtell et al. 1996).

Averaging out individual behavior in the System Dynamics model, and thereby assuming homogeneous agents, produces an inferior model at the scale/order where individual behavior matters. It is in effect assuming statistical mechanics where the system reaches a thermodynamic limit (Hill 1994).

Averaging out of individual behavior to produce a statistic of representative agent behavior below this thermodynamic—or order parameter—limit is not required and, if done can produce an inferior model.

## 7.3.3   Power Laws: Forest Fire Models

The Forest Fire model (Bak et al. 1990; Drossel and Schwabl 1992) is a simple model of the interaction between agents. It is an interesting example of how the natural sciences make use of *toy models,* where the phenomenon of interest (percolation) is studied by abstracting away behavior. As we shall see, we can think of the Forest Fire model as a social network model.

Power laws and Zipf laws (1935, 1949) can be seen in the distribution of firm sizes (Axtell 2001) and were indeed studied by Herbert Simon (1955). It is also interesting to note that they were also studied by Lotka

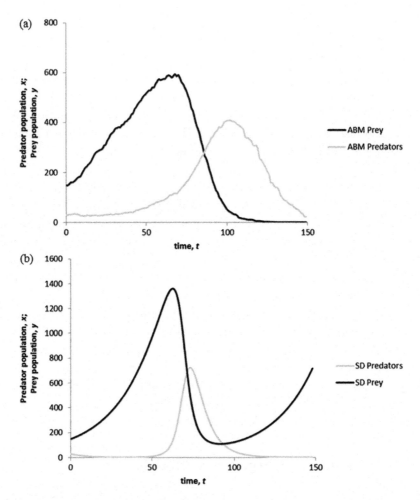

**Fig. 7.4** Population comparisons between (**a**) the Agent-based model (ABM) implementation and (**b**) the original System Dynamics (SD) Lotka–Volterra Model

(1926) (of the Lotka–Volterra equations, shown in our second agent-based model, above) in relation to scientific productions.

The Forest Fire model is based on a simple grid of interacting agents, in this case trees within a forest. The cells within the grid can be in any of three states: empty, occupied by a tree, or occupied by a tree that is on fire (see Fig. 7.5).

The rules of the Forest Fire model are as follows:

- An empty cell will turn into a tree with probability $p$
- A tree will catch fire with probability $f$: this is akin to lightning strikes within the forest
- A tree will also catch fire if at least one of its neighbors is on fire
- A burning tree will turn into an empty space

Even though the Forest Fire model is one of a fire spreading through the forest, it can also be thought of as the basis for diffusion of ideas by word-of-mouth interactions. It can also be thought of as a constrained social network model where an individual can have up to four or eight neighbors (depending on whether a Von Neumann or a Moore neighborhood is used). This can easily be extended to diffusion not on a grid but within a social network. Even though agents are represented on our grid, we can trivially transform this into a social network representation (see Fig. 7.6).

When the Forest Fire model is run, a lightning strike (with probability set by parameter $f$) causes the spread of the fire to contiguous areas

**Fig. 7.5**  The Drossel and Schwabl (1992) Forest Fire Model (Operationalized in Watts and Gilbert 2014) showing blank cells (*black*) and the spread of fire (*grey*) through trees (*white*)

(a)                                        (b)

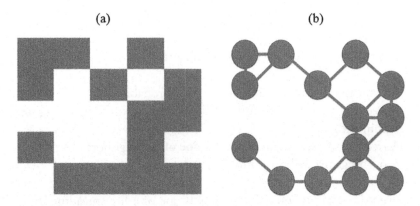

**Fig. 7.6** (a) Cellular and (b) Social network representations

of trees throughout the forest. The distribution of size of these fires in the Drossel and Schwabl (1992) model follows a power law distribution, meaning that large, catastrophic fires occur much less frequently than small fires. In the interpersonal world, this behavior has been found in distributions of sizes of riots. The Forest Fire model has also been used to augment the Bass (1969) diffusion model (Goldenberg et al. 2001).

The Forest Fire model is interesting from a behavioral operational research point of view, as it models the spread of an idea at a micro level. The system effect that is observed is the size of the outbreak—which is a power law distribution (see Fig. 7.7). This output cannot easily be modelled by conventional techniques.

The model also introduces the concept of a critical parameter—in the Forest Fire model, this is order $p/f$, where the behavior of the system changes from no outbreak to outbreak.

Schelling's Segregation model, Lotka–Volterra's Predator–Prey model, and Drossel–Schwabl's Forest Fire model are examples of how models from other disciplines can be used to create models that use individual characteristics other than ethnicity (in the Segregation model), individuals rather than animals (in the Predator–Prey model) and trees (in the Forest Fire model) to inform and create new models of behavioral operational research. A rich research agenda is opening up, which is outlined below.

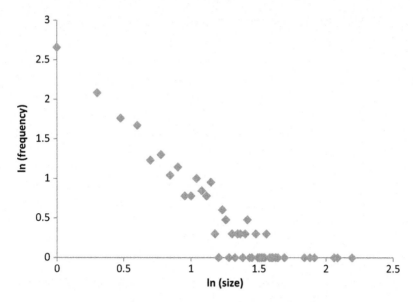

**Fig. 7.7** Sample power law of distribution of fire size

## 7.4 A Research Agenda for Agent-Based Behavioral Operational Research

We have reviewed several approaches where Agent-Based Modeling can be used to augment, and in certain circumstances improve, traditional system-level models.

Agent-based models, however, are not a panacea; still, there are circumstances where they undoubtedly unlock understanding of a system that would not be understood without them, for example when systems tip from one state to another.

It is important to note that we have introduced very simple models in this paper. This is deliberate. We are looking to introduce to the reader the simplest behavioral models that produce interesting results. Each of these models can be extended trivially to include more agent-specific parameters or behavioral assumptions. And this leads us to our first agenda item.

## 7.4.1 Which Behavioral Characteristics Matter?

A temptation of agent-based models as a modeling approach is to include every possible trait of behavior into the model. Sterman (1989) and Morecroft (1983, 1985) emphasize the effects of boundedly rational individual agents, yet they analyze the system *at* the system level. Agent-based models allow us to start our models with the simplest agent behavior that produces interesting results. However, in this modeling process (which may be facilitated as discussed below), an agent-based model allows us to include variables, parameters, and behaviors that can be switched on or off as part of the modeling process. In this way, we can extend the model; this can be a particularly fruitful area of future research as part of facilitated model building (see below).

## 7.4.2 Defining Order Parameters for Systems Where Intra-Model Behavior is Important

While model–individual interactions will always be important, we can also define regimes where behavioral interactions *within* the model are important. We want to be able to restrict our behavioral work to where behavioral interactions are actually important and change the model itself. We want to ignore regimes where systems are in a stable state and traditional models can be used; similarly, we want to avoid studying the behavioral implications of systems that are chaotic. We can define order parameters, for example the level of intolerance in the Schelling segregation model, which determine on the level of individual interaction where the system transitions from one state to another. The middle, complex regime is where we should concentrate our attention in Behavioral Operational Research.

## 7.4.3 Quantized/Individual Behavior Is Important: "Agentization" of Models

System Dynamics models ignore individuals and hence ignore individual behavior. The Lotka–Volterra model, when "agentized", produces qualitatively similar results but differs in that the system collapses in the agent-based model when the last agent is removed from the system. In a System Dynamics model, numbers of individuals below one can exist even if this has no parallel in reality. Behavioral effects exist on the individual level and not on the system level. Studying existing models and moving them to individual-based models rather than system models is a rich avenue for future research.

### 7.4.4 Toy Models for Behavioral Operational Research: Agent-Based Facilitation

We can learn from the natural sciences in creating simplified models of interaction that can be used to understand a *different but similar system*. We can then alter the agents within the model, using feedback from psychological understanding of individuals or feedback obtained by participants in the modeling process. In this way, we can experiment very quickly and efficiently with different behavioral heuristics.

Agent-Based Modeling has a clear opportunity to act as a part of facilitated model building (Franco and Montibeller 2010; Franco and Rouwette 2011; Rouwette et al. 2011) where participants are able to interact with, construct, and adapt models. Recent advances in Agent-Based Modeling software facilitates this, with newer software packages such as *NetLogo* creating huge opportunities to develop models on the fly rather than writing low-level code to manipulate agents in first-generation Agent-Based Modeling software such as *Swarm* and *RePast* (Robertson 2005).

Agent-based models such as the ones introduced in this paper, when presented to audiences, inevitably result in contributions from the audience suggesting ways of making more detailed behavioral rules for participants. In short, we can use agent-based models rather than System Dynamics (as discussed in Rouwette et al. 2002) or discrete event models to facilitate the process. Model building, facilitated or otherwise, using agent-based models, offers rich opportunities for model development and fertile ground for further research.

# References

Ackoff, R.L. 2006. Why few organizations adopt systems thinking. *Systems Research and Behavioral Science* 23: 705–708.

Axtell, R.L. 2001. Zipf distribution of U.S. firm sizes. *Science* 293: 1818–1820.

Axtell, R., R. Axelrod, J. Epstein, and M. Cohen. 1996. Aligning simulation models: A case study and results. *Computational and Mathematical Organization Theory* 1: 123–141.

Bak, P., K. Chen, and C. Tang. 1990. A forest-fire model and some thoughts on turbulence. *Physics Letters A* 147: 297–300.

Bass, F.M. 1969. A new product growth model for consumer durables. *Management Science* 15: 215–227.

Borshchev, A., and A. Filippov. 2004. From system dynamics and discrete event to practical agent based modeling: Reasons, techniques, tools. In: *Proceedings of the 22nd international conference of the System Dynamics Society (Vol. 22)*.

Coleman, J.S. 1987. Psychological structure and social structure in economic models. In *Rational choice: The contrast between economics and psychology*, ed. R. Hogarth and M. Reder. Chicago: University of Chicago Press.

Cronin, M.A., C. Gonzalez, and J.D. Sterman. 2009. Why don't well-educated adults understand accumulation? A challenge to researchers, educators, and citizens. *Organizational Behavior and Human Decision Processes* 108: 116–130.

Drossel, B., and F. Schwabl. 1992. Self-organized critical forest-fire model. *Physical Review Letters* 69: 1629–1632.

*Economist.* (2010). Agents of change. *Economist,* July 22.

Farmer, J.D., and D. Foley. 2009. The economy needs agent-based modeling. *Nature* 460: 685–686.

Forrester, J.W. 1961. *Industrial dynamics*. Cambridge, MA: MIT Press.

Franco, L.A., and G. Montibeller. 2010. Facilitated modeling in operational research. *European Journal of Operational Research* 205: 489–500.

Franco, L.A., and E.A.J.A. Rouwette. 2011. Decision development in facilitated modeling workshops. *European Journal of Operational Research* 212: 164–178.

Goldenberg, L., B. Libai, and E. Muller. 2001. Using complex systems analysis to advance marketing theory development: Modeling heterogeneity effects on new product growth through stochastic cellular automata. *Academy of Marketing Science Review* 9: 1–18.

Goldstein, J. 1999. Emergence as a construct: History and issues. *Emergence: Complexity and Organization* 1: 49–72.

Goodwin, R. 1967. A growth cycle. In *Socialism, capitalism, and economic growth*, ed. C.H. Feinstein. Cambridge: Cambridge University Press.

Grimm, V., and S.F. Railsbark. 1997. *Agent-based and individual-based modeling*. Princeton: Princeton University Press.

Hämäläinen, R.P., and E. Saarinen. 2006. Systems intelligence: A key competence for organizational life. *Reflections: The SoL Journal* 7: 191–201.

Hämäläinen, R.P., and E. Saarinen. 2008. Systems intelligence—The way forward? A note on Ackoff's 'Why few organizations adopt systems thinking'. *Systems Research and Behanvioral Science* 25: 821–825.

Hämäläinen, R.P., J. Luoma, and E. Saarinen. 2013. On the importance of behavioral operational research: The case of understanding and communicating about dynamic systems. *European Journal of Operational Research* 228: 623–634.

Hiebeler, D.E. 1994. *The Swarm simulation system and individual-based modeling*. Working paper series, 1994-11-065. Santa Fe: Santa Fe Institute

Hill, T.L. 1994. *Thermodynamics of small systems*. New York: Dover.

Johnson, N. 2009. Two's company, three is complexity. In *Simply complexity: A clear guide to complexity theory*, ed. N. Johnson. London: Oneworld.

Kuhn, T.S. 1962. *The structure of scientific revolutions*. Chicago: University of Chicago Press.

Lee, S.-J., D.-J. Lee, and H.-S. Oh. 2005. Technological forecasting at the Korean stock market: A dynamic competition analysis using Lotka–Volterra model. *Technological Forecasting and Social Change* 72: 1044–1057.

Lotka, A.J. 1920. Analytical note on certain rhythmic relations in organic systems. *Proceedings of the National Academy of Sciences of the United States of America* 6: 410–415.

Lotka, A.J. 1925. *Elements of physical biology*. Baltimore: Williams & Wilkins.

Lotka, A.J. 1926. The frequency distribution of scientific production. *Journal of the Washington Academy of Sciences* 16: 317–323.

Luoma, J., R.P. Hämäläinen, and E. Saarinen. 2010. Acting with systems intelligence: Integrating complex responsive processes with the systems perspective. *Journal of the Operational Research Society* 62: 3–11.

Modis, T. 2003. A scientific approach to modeling competition. *Industrial Physicist* 9: 25–27.

Morecroft, J. 1983. System dynamics: Portraying bounded rationality. *Omega* 11: 131–142.

Morecroft, J. 1985. Rationality in the analysis of behavioral simulation models. *Management Science* 31: 900–916.

Robertson, D.A. 2005. Agent-based modeling toolkits: NetLogo, RePast, and Swarm. *Academy of Management Learning and Education* 4: 524–527.

Robinson, S. 2014. *Simulation: The practice of model development and use*, 2nd ed. Basingstoke/New York: Palgrave Macmillan.

Rouwette, E.A.J.A., J.A.M. Vennix, and T. van Mullekom. 2002. Group model building effectiveness: A review of assessment studies. *System Dynamics Review* 18: 5–45.

Rouwette, E.A.J.A., J.A.M. Vennix, H. Korzilius, and E. Jacobs. 2011. Modeling as persuasion: The impact of group model building on attitudes and behavior. *System Dynamics Review* 27: 1–21.

Saarinen, E., and R.P. Hämäläinen. 2007. Systems intelligence: Connecting engineering thinking with human sensitivity. In *Systems intelligence in leadership and everyday life*, ed. R.P. Hämäläinen and E. Saarinen. Helsinki: University of Technology Helsinki.

Schelling, T.C. 1969. Models of segregation. *American Economic Review* 59: 488–493.

Schelling, T.C. 1971. Dynamic models of segregation. *Journal of Mathematical Sociology* 1: 143–186.

Schelling, T.C. 1978. *Micromotives and macrobehavior*. New York: Norton.

Sethna, J. 2006. *Statistical mechanics: Entropy, order parameters and complexity*. Oxford: Oxford University Press.

Simon, H. 1955. On a class of skew distribution functions. *Biometrika* 42: 425–440.

Simon, H. 1957. A behavioral model of rational choice. In *Models of man, social and rational: Mathematical essays on rational human behavior in a social setting*, ed. H. Simon. New York: Wiley.

Sterman, J.D. 1989. Modeling managerial behavior: Misperceptions of feedback in a dynamic decision making process. *Management Science* 35: 321–339.

Tesfatsion, L. 2002. Agent-based computational economics: Growing economies from the bottom up. *Artificial Life* 8: 55–82.

Tesfatsion, L. 2006. Agent-based computational economics: A constructive approach to economic theory. *Handbook of Computational Economics* 2: 831–880.

Volterra, V. 1926. Variazioni e Fluttuazioni del Numero d'Individui in Specie Animali Conviventi. *Mem. Acad Lincei Roma* 2: 31–113.

Watts, C., and N. Gilbert. 2014. *Simulating innovation: Computer-based tools for rethinking innovation*. Chichester: Edward Elgar.

Wilensky, U. 2005. *NetLogo Wolf Sheep Predation (docked) model*. Evanston: Center for Connected Learning and Computer-Based Modeling,

Northwestern University. http://ccl.northwestern.edu/netlogo/models/Wolf SheepPredation(docked)

Zipf, G.K. 1935. *The psychobiology of language: An introduction to dynamic philology*. Cambridge, MA: MIT Press.

Zipf, G.K. 1949. *Human behavior and the principle of least effort: An introduction to human ecology*. Cambridge, MA: Addison-Wesley Press.

# 8

# Modeling Behavioral Decision Making: Creation and Representation of Judgment

Martin Kunc

## 8.1 Introduction

There are different perspectives in the field of judgment and decision making. For example, Gigerenzer (2004, p. 62) suggests, "If you open a book on judgment and decision making, chances are that you will stumble over the following moral: good reasoning must adhere to the laws of logic, the calculus of probability, or the maximization of expected utility; if not there must be a cognitive or motivational flaw."

The processes of judgment and choice, which are the core of behavioral decision making, are interconnected, but they have been researched separately by different groups of psychologists (Goldstein and Hogarth 1997). On the one hand, studies on preferential choice assume it is rational to maximize expected utility, so evaluating deviations from expected utility theory is at the center of this research (Goldstein 2004). This line

M.H. Kunc (✉)
Warwick Business School, University of Warwick, Scarman Road,
Coventry CV4 7AL, UK

© The Editor(s) (if applicable) and The Author(s) 2016
M. Kunc et al. (eds.), *Behavioral Operational Research*,
DOI 10.1057/978-1-137-53551-1_8

of research, which includes deviances from Bayes' theorem, evolved into the heuristics-and-biases approach informed by Tversky and Kahneman's research (Goldstein 2004). On the other hand, studies on judgment have focused on accuracy rather than rationality, evaluating accuracy of judgment, e.g. individual intuitive predictions, with respect to simple statistical models (Goldstein 2004; Goldstein and Gigerenzer 2009). This area is called *Brunswikian*[1] research on judgment (Goldstein 2004). Basically, it suggests people infer or construct a percept from a collection of sensory cues that deliver incomplete and imperfect information (Goldstein 2004).

This chapter presents a model which uses Brunswikian principles to represent human behavior. The model reflects behavior classified as *fast and frugal heuristics* (Goldstein and Gigerenzer 2009) or *simple rules* (Sull and Eisenhardt 2012).

## 8.2   Research on Judgment: Brunswikian Principles

Goldstein and Hogarth (1997) suggest three basic principles of Brunswikian research. First, humans function in an environment they need to understand even though it is ambiguous and uncertain. Thus, adaptation to the environment can be described using deterministic models. Second, the human perceptual system combines information from different cues in order to generate a perception of the environment. However, this process is not perfect, and it needs to learn the correct interconnections between, or weights of, the cues. The process is interactive and uncertain over time, which may make it look incoherent to an outsider, as well as highly contextual. Third, it is important to study tasks and behavior in their natural environment. Thus, the manipulation of experimental factors deliberately destroying the interconnections established from learning processes can result in either misperception of the experimental stimuli or disoriented behavior. Brunswikian principles (Goldstein and Hogarth 1997) can provide a better approach to understanding and modeling behavioral deci-

---

[1] The term comes from the psychologist Ergon Brunswik. His main work is related to the area of perception and functionalization in the psychology field. A key article is "Representative Design and probabilistic Thoery in a functional psychology" published in 1955 by Psychological Review 62 (193–217).

sion making than preference choice when behavioral decision making needs to be embedded in OR models.

## 8.2.1 Considerations on Behavioral Experiments from a Brunswikian Perspective

The research on preference choices, heuristics-and-biases research is based on experiments consisting of an activity performed in highly elaborated situations; for an example see Tversky and Kahneman (1974). One-time activity implies an important restriction: participants cannot identify clear causality from their judgment. Learned causality originates only from multiple interactions, i.e. learning processes, which makes the results obtained from behavioral experiments potentially not realistic. The basic arguments supporting a learned-causality perspective are:

(i) Human beings, like any organisms, are adaptive systems whose behavior is a result of a process of evolution affected by social, educational and genetic factors. Consequently, their behavior has to be observed considering long-time horizons rather than hypothetical, snapshot situations.

(ii) Heuristics and biases are behavioral rules which originate from a process of evolution. Consequently, the origins of these heuristics and biases are related to a broader context, paying special attention to the relationship between heuristics and biases within the context where people use them.

(iii) Humans are controlled by goal-seeking feedback processes. The goals reflect the information necessary to balance our internal processes with the external environment. *Satisficing* (Winter 2000) rather than *maximizing* reflects the behavioral processes of goal attainment in an optimal way because it describes humans as minimizing the levels of energy employed to achieve their goals. Thus, the goal attainment process, as the selection of the first alternative encountered that meets minimal criteria for acceptability, cannot be considered non-optimal in this prespective. However, for an external observer this behavior may be considered non-rational, since it does not pursue the best alternative, and biased; but it may be an effective way to filter the environmental information necessary to reach the goals in an efficient manner.

(iv) Every organism including humans, tries to maintain a balance between internal processes and environment by adapting to changes. Therefore, the process always starts from a previous balanced situation—which is the existing anchor—and moves toward attaining the new goal defined by the environment—the adjustment behavior. Consequently, the main driver of behavior is a process of anchor-and-adjustment which can be observed only from the behavior and their components—heuristics and biases—within a specific context and over time.

## 8.3    Modeling Behavioral Decision Making

The behavioral decision making model presented here is based on Brunswikian concepts, which are integrated in a model called "Brunswick's lens model" (Goldstein 2004). Brunswik is considered a *functionalist* because he suggested the goal of psychology was to explain how humans managed to function in their environments (Goldstein 2004). Thus, Brunswik proposed that people face complex environments (focal object) which they perceive through sensory activities (cues). The percept (perception of the object) must be accurate enough (judgmental accuracy) to let them perform related activities and ensure their survival and well-being. Survival and well-being depend on the abilities to bring (i) perceptions into line with focal objects and (ii) focal objects into line with their desires (Goldstein 2004). However, the degree of correspondence between the focal object and its perception is mediated by proximal events and processes (means) (Goldstein 2004). The mediation process is encompassed under the concept of *vicarious functioning*, which refers to the multiplicity, flexibility and intersubstitutability of ways of using cues and means (Goldstein 2004). In Fig. 8.1, the process of selecting the cues to recombine into the perception of the focal object is captured by the weights for each cue $(r_n)$. Over time the selection of cues and means may vary so the resulting perception is stable only after a large number of trials (Goldstein 2004). Judgmental accuracy can be measured by the correlation between the characteristics of the focal object and the judgment (perception of the object). One of the key issues in this model is how to understand the complexity of the environment (focal object), which determines the identity of the

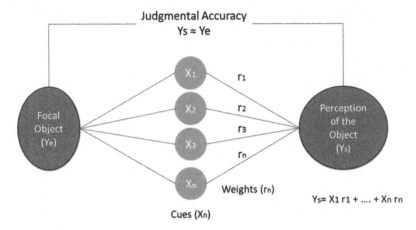

**Fig. 8.1** Brunswick's lens model

features that define the object, the strength in the descriptions between the features and the cues, and the interrelationships (weights) in the descriptors between the cues (Goldstein 2004). The research employing this model has demonstrated people's sensitivity to task environments and the process of learning as a way of adaptation to new environments (Goldstein 2004).

The model starts describing the process from basic learning about cues until it reaches more complex functionality yielded by a heuristics-and-biases approach.

### 8.3.1   Basic Process of Knowledge Creation

Consider for a moment the task of a manager who is controlling the level of inventory. The manager does not have any idea about the inventory level, so their knowledge (the perception) about the inventory is updated as they receive information over time (cues and weights). A first model describes the basic process of learning that controls the degree of knowledge (inventory level) as Fig. 8.2 presents. The variable *perceived inventory level* represents the subjective representation (the manager's knowledge about the level of inventory) of the environment (the real level of the inventory). The representation is increased by new information (daily readings of the inven-

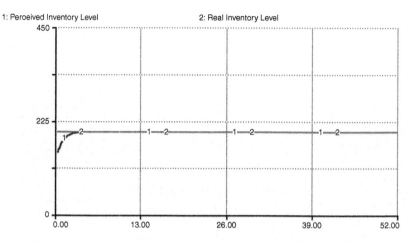

**Fig. 8.2** Matching real with perceived inventory after updating information

tory), which is incorporated if it implies a change on the level of knowledge stored. Otherwise, the updating adjustment rate is zero (see Fig. 8.2).

Basically, the level of knowledge (perceived inventory) is represented as a stock or accumulation that can be observed over time. The process for knowledge updating is an inflow, which provides the information to update the level of accumulated knowledge. In this simple situation, the perceived inventory level increases over time until it reaches the true state of the environment, the real inventory level. The equations of this model are presented below.

```
Perceived__Inventory_Level(t) = Perceived__Inventory_Level(t- dt) + (Updating) * dt

INIT Perceived__Inventory_Level = 150

INFLOWS:

Updating = Updating_Adjustment

Real_Inventory_Level_ = 200

Updating_Adjustment = Real_Inventory_Level_-Perceived__Inventory_Level
```

**Proposition 1** In order to investigate and model decision making processes, a processual approach is required. The approach involves matching the level of knowledge of the person with respect to the task or the focus of the decision. Therefore, there are two important conditions to consider: how fast the person builds their knowledge and their initial level of knowledge.

## 8.3.2 Information Selection and Its Influence on Decision Making

The model is now expanded to capture the knowledge creation process based on the subjective interpretation process of the environmental information. The model keeps the basic functionality described in the previous section, but it is expanded to reflect two issues: (i) updating of accumulated knowledge becomes an external process and (ii) the subjective interpretation of the information is subject to internal feedback that represents the level of dissatisfaction between the internal knowledge level and the environment, i.e. judgmental accuracy.

The updating process captures information from the environment, which is decoded into three possible interrelated cues. The person (manager) selects the weight for each cue (different sources for the daily readings of the inventory) that fits best with respect to the environment (real inventory level). The process of anchor-and-adjustment (Tversky and Kahneman 1974) starts with a certain level of knowledge (the variable *perceived inventory level*), which adjusts toward the environment (the variable *real inventory level*). People as adaptive systems are dominated by goal-seeking feedback processes. Thus, the determination of the adjustment to each cue is based on the level of dissatisfaction that the person has with their level of knowledge. Consequently, a *balancing feedback loop* exists between the level of accumulated knowledge and the weight of the cues employed to capture the environment, which is controlled by the level of satisfaction. (In this case, the aim is to reduce monthly dissatisfaction to zero.) This balancing feedback loop is also known as the *satisficing principle* (Simon 1979; Winter 2000). In other words, the model reflects the principles that people do not optimize but adapt their behavior within the limits of their rationality (bounded rationality) until they reach a satisfactory outcome (Simon 1979).

In this version of the model, the balancing process between knowledge and environment is exogenous, as the model is built as a game simulator and the person using the simulator must enter the weights for each cue. Figure 8.3 shows a stock-and-flow diagram where the broken line reflects the intervention of the person to update the weights.

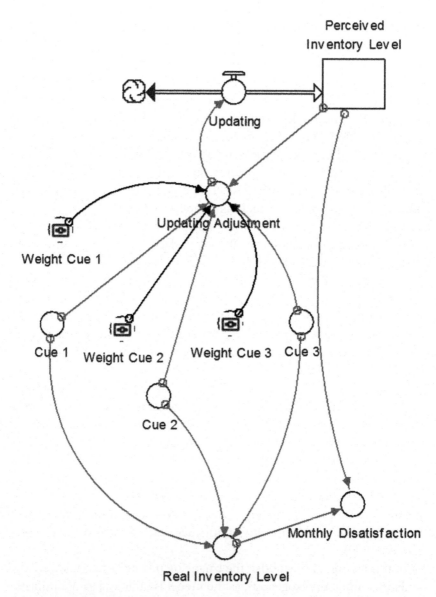

**Fig. 8.3** Stock and flow diagram showing the Brunswikian principle on decision making

The equations for the model are presented below.

```
Perceived__Inventory_Level(t) = Perceived__Inventory_Level(t - dt) + (Updating) * dt

INIT Perceived__Inventory_Level = 200

INFLOWS:

Updating = Updating_Adjustment

Updating_Adjustment = (Cue_1*Weight_Cue_1+Cue_2*Weight_Cue_2+Cue_3*Weight_Cue_3) -Perceived__Inventory_Level

Real_Inventory_Level_ =

a.   100*0.20+ 200*0.5+ SINWAVE(100,12.5)*0.3  →  A cyclical inventory

b.   100*0.20+ 200*0.5+ 100*0.3  →  A fixed inventory

c.   RANDOM(90,110)*0.20+ 200*0.5+ 100*0.3  →  A random inventory

d.   RANDOM(90,110)*0.20+ 200*0.5+ 100*0.3  →  A random inventory

Weight_Cue_1 = 0 (for scenarios b and c) and 0.20 (for scenarios a and d)

Weight_Cue_2 = 0.5

Weight_Cue_3 = 0.3
```

As Fig. 8.4 depicts, the process of knowledge (perceived inventory level) and environment (real inventory level) matching is not instantaneous because it involves a process of adjustment between the original level of

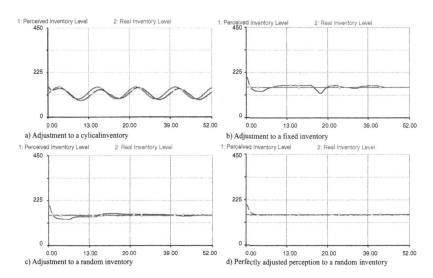

**Fig. 8.4**  Matching real with perceived inventory in diverse situations after updating information

knowledge (anchor) and the requirements from the environment. Fig 8.4. and 8.5 contain the four behaviors described in the equations of the model under the variable "Real Invertory level" and listed as a, b, c and d.

The level of knowledge adjustment involves a certain level of dissatisfaction as the person finds the correct weights (interconnections between different cues to create an image of the environment). Even finding the right weighting also takes time; because it is impossible to observe the future, updating processes are backward looking rather than forward looking (Gavetti and Levinthal 2000). Figure 8.5 displays this process.

**Proposition 2** Behavioral decision making must consider the physical impossibility of updating knowledge before evidence is presented. Subjective perceptions are updated as evidence comes. Thus, decision making accuracy (as well as heuristics, like overconfidence or preference reversals) is improved over time once the subject is able to interpret the evidence presented.

A person who selects the correct initial combination (see Fig. 8.5d) between all the possible cues and achieves a perfect match between

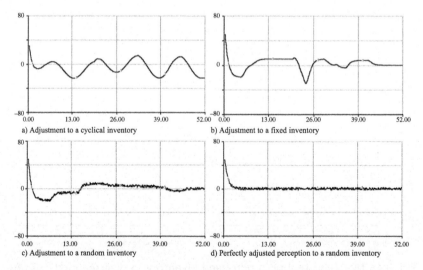

**Fig. 8.5** Dissatisfaction during adjustment processes in diverse situations

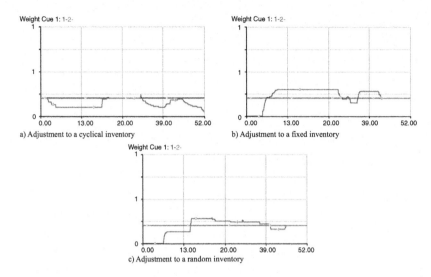

**Fig. 8.6** Cue adjustment processes in diverse situations

knowledge and environment has to be considered lucky. The person also needs to be patient, because they have to wait until the initial gap between perceived and real knowledge declines over time, which may create anxiety, leading to changes in the cues and weights. After reaching a satisfactory level, a person stops updating his/her knowledge and his/her performance can be considered *rational* (as well as *functional*) in the sense that is perfectly adapted to the requirements of the environment.

The behavior depicted in Fig. 8.6 reflects the process of cues (weights) adjustment through oscillations, which is a common goal-seeking feedback process with delay, until the person reaches a satisfactory situation.

This process of gradual adjustment in the coding of environmental information is generated because a natural process of action-result-reaction occurs. However, this process may work fine for some individuals but not for others. Thus, changes in internal adjustment processes influence the subjective perception of the environment. From this consideration, we suggest the next proposition:

**Proposition 3** Behavioral modeling of decision making must consider the diversity in environmental perception processes among subjects. Subjective perceptions of the same event may be completely different due to structural differences.

### 8.3.3   Environmental Influence on the Process of Information Selection and Its Consequence on Decision Making

To capture the effects of more complex and dynamic environments, the environment is changed to cyclical (scenario a) and random situations (scenarios c and d) to compare with & fixed invertory situation (scenario b). One of the main arguments against anchoring-and-adjustment processes is that the adjustment is insufficient (Tversky and Kahneman 1974). The model used in the previous simulations showed that this argument is erroneous if the person's percept is well calibrated (the cue's weights are correct) and the environment is stable. However, if the environment is dynamically complex, the anchoring-and-adjustment process will clearly be insufficient. One of the reasons is that people require more time to understand and learn the signals from a changing environment: the *calibration process*. A second reason is the nature of the updating process: it usually is backward oriented and has delays. Thus, dissatisfaction oscillates, as can be observed in Fig. 8.5a, following changes in the environment, because the existence of a delay between the reception of the information from the environment and the adjustment in the knowledge.

**Proposition 4** Anchoring-and-adjustment processes are powerful heuristics, which may seem to represent basic decision making processes. However, anchoring-and-adjustment is affected, like any heuristic, by the level of complexity of the environment. Modeling of decision making may need to consider complexity as well as ambiguity in the environment. Subjective perceptions of events take time to calibrate and obtain a reasonable image of the environment.

## 8.4 Final Considerations

The Brunswik model has been a cornerstone in *social judgment theory* and functionalism models (Goldstein 2004). Indirectly, functionalism has illuminated many areas of research in behavioral OR. For example, it demonstrated that learning from outcome feedback is slow and limited, leading to the development of the concept of *cognitive feedback* (Todd and Hammond 1965), which is at the core of behavioral experimentation related to misperceptions of feedback processes (Kunc 2012) and implies the importance of providing task information to subjects in experiments rather than simply informing them of the outcomes from trials. Another important finding is that the root of interpersonal conflicts may be cognitive, as people have shared goals but differ in their assessment of the situation (diverse cues and weights) and of the action consequently required to remediate it (perception) (Goldstein 2004). An example of this finding can be observed in Chap. 17, by Huh and Kunc (2016). A key contribution is to the area of heuristics in terms of computational speed (fast) and information requirements (frugal), in which Gigerenzer and colleagues evaluated the accuracy of judgment based on simple heuristics and their appropriateness in diverse environments (Goldstein 2004). Gigerenzer and colleagues propose that heuristics are tools employed by our minds to take advantage of the structure of the information existing in the environment to arrive at reasonable decisions, rather than unreliable aids limiting decision making performance (Gigerenzer and Todd 1999).

The Brunswik model can also illuminate future research in behavioral OR. For example, it shows that experimentation should follow representative design rather than systematic design[2] (Goldstein 2004). Representative design implies that the design of experiments should reflect the natural environment (stimuli and conditions) of the subjects in the experiments to reveal issues in judgment accuracy, known as ecological validity (Goldstein 2004). In other words, experiments using OR models need to be consistent with the potential use and users of the models, e.g. experimenting with optimization models dealing with issues

---

[2] Systematic design refers to the design of experiments where investigators define different stimuli to generate uncorrelated independent variables to test hypotheses about behavior.

in a supply chain should include subjects who are experienced in supply chain management and more importantly on the issue the optimization model is meant to solve. Behavioral OR without ecological validity may be useless. However, if the intention of the experimentation is to observe adaptation, then the manipulation of the environment and observation of learning will be a valid design (Goldstein 2004). This is one of the suggestions in Gary et al. (2008) regarding the use of System Dynamics in behavioral strategy. Another example is the Multi-Criteria Decision Analysis (MCDA) process (Figueira et al. 2005), which encompasses some of the tasks described in the Brunswick model: identifying cues and weights. Researchers in MCDA can employ the research techniques from functionalist psychology to evaluate the effectiveness of the method and uncover behavioral factors affecting the outcomes.

Finally, the following phrase summarizes the main distinction between functionalism and heuristics-and-biases research, with profound implications for behavioral OR practitioners:

*"One can be accurate without being rational (e.g. "right for the wrong reason") and one can be rational without being accurate (e.g. holding a coherent world-view that is out of touch of reality)".*

Goldstein 2004, p. 55

# References

Figueira, J., S. Greco, and M. Ehrgott. 2005. *Multiple criteria decision analysis: State of the art surveys* (Vol. 78). Springer Science & Business Media: New york.

Gary, S., M. Kunc, J. Morecroft, and S. Rockart. 2008. System dynamics and strategy. *System Dynamics Review* 24: 407–430.

Gavetti, G., and D.A. Levinthal. 2000. Looking forward and looking backward: Cognitive and experiential search. *Administrative Science Quarterly* 45: 113–137.

Gigerenzer, G., D.J. Koehler, and N. Heroes. 2004. Fast and frugal heuristics: The tools of bounded rationality. In *Blackwell handbook of judgment and decision-making*, 62–88. Chichester: Wiley.

Gigerenzer, G., and P.M. Todd. 1999. Fast and frugal heuristics: The adaptive toolbox. In *Simple heuristics that make us smart*, ed. G. Gigerenzer and P.M. Todd, 3–34. Oxford: Oxford University Press.

Goldstein, W.M. 2004. Social judgment theory: Applying and extending Brunswik's probabilistic functionalism. In *Blackwell handbook of judgment and decision-making*, ed. D.J. Koehler and N. Harvey, 37–61. Chichester: Wiley.

Goldstein, D.G., and G. Gigerenzer. 2009. Fast and frugal forecasting. *International Journal of Forecasting* 5: 760–772.

Goldstein, W.M., and R.M. Hogarth. 2004. Judgment and decision research: Some historical context. In *Research on judgment and decision making*, ed. W.M. Goldstein and R.M. Hogarth, 37–61. Cambridge: Cambridge University Press.

Huh, K., and M. Kunc. 2016. Supporting strategy: Behavioral influences on resource conceptualization processes. In *Behavioural operational research: Theory, methodology and practice*, ed. M. Kunc, J. Malpass, and L. White, 337–356. Basingstoke: Palgrave-Macmillan.

Kunc, M. 2012. Teaching strategic thinking using system dynamics: Lessons from a strategic development course. *System Dynamics Review* 28: 28–45.

Simon, H.A. 1979. *Models of thought*. New Haven: Yale University Press.

Sull, D., and K.M. Eisenhardt. 2012. Simple rules for a complex world. *Harvard Business Review* 90: 68–75.

Todd, F.J., and K.R. Hammond. 1965. Differential feedback in two multiple-cue probability learning tasks. *Behavioral Science* 10: 429–435.

Tversky, A., and D. Kahneman. 1974. Judgment under uncertainty: Heuristics and biases. *Science* 185: 1124–1131.

Winter, S.G. 2000. The satisficing principle in capability learning. *Strategic Management Journal* 21: 981–996.

# 9

# Big Data and Behavior in Operational Research: Towards a "SMART OR"

Leroy White, Katharina Burger and Mike Yearworth

## 9.1    Introduction

Recent decades have witnessed a new trend in Operational Research (OR) towards *Big Data* analytics (Davenport and Harris 2007; Davenport et al. 2010), with the number of empirical studies steadily growing (Sen 2013; Babai et al. 2012). By *Big Data* we mean proliferating and complex data sets that can be *open*, or shared online (McAfee and Brynjolfsson 2012). This trend complements traditional OR (Ranyard et al. 2015),

L. White (✉)
Warwick Business School, University of Warwick, Scarman Road, Coventry CV4 7AL, UK

K. Burger
Portsmouth Business School, University of Portsmouth, Portland Street, Portsmouth PO1 3DE, UK

M. Yearworth
Faculty of Engineering, University of Bristol, Queen's Building, University Walk, Clifton BS8 1TR, UK

© The Editor(s) (if applicable) and The Author(s) 2016      **177**
M. Kunc et al. (eds.), *Behavioral Operational Research*,
DOI 10.1057/978-1-137-53551-1_9

which is dominated by mathematical/analytical approaches (Liberatore and Luo 2010), and can help to address contemporary organisations/ organisational needs (Singhal and Singhal 2012). These needs are directly linked to new opportunities arising from the rapid development of digital technologies (e.g. the Internet and the Internet of things), which enable researchers to collect valuable data online (e.g. Google Analytics). Unfortunately, these data are not always well-structured. On the contrary, online data generated by the end consumer are often qualitative and highly unstructured. As a result, OR scholars are hardly able to apply traditional approaches to utilise them. In order to analyse data collected on the Internet, multiple methods are required which are able to explore the true value of online data.

At the same time, we see a potential paradigm shift in OR methods—and one that prompts new directions for research (Ranyard et al. 2015). The research contexts include human resources, managerial decision-making, consumer behavior, operational processes and policy interactions. However, there is also a need to see a change in our ability to leverage approaches to achieve control and precision in data use while maintaining realism in application and generality in theory development and practice. Thus: How can we take advantage of Big Data in OR? What new perspectives are needed? What will the new practices look like? What kinds of insights and value can they deliver in comparison to past developments? OR has broadened researchers' perspectives on social, organisational and policy systems by adopting models that combine social science, OR, computer science and network science. This involves interdisciplinary fields that leverage capabilities to collect and analyse data with an unprecedented breadth, depth and scale.

Behavior is now a key aspect in Big Data analytics. A growing number of specialist companies search, mine and analyse Big Data for descriptive, predictive and prescriptive behavioral insights. They employ a combination of hardware, software and services to support decision-makers through visualisation and interpretation of data. Overall, the challenges in understanding Big Data and using the insights derived to predict, prescribe or influence behavior suggest a need for co-design with groups of decision-makers that carefully weigh the opportunities and threats arising from the manifold and potential uses of Big Data technologies for organisational development and societal wellbeing.

In this chapter we wish to introduce the idea of SMART OR, which is *the creative use of Big Data and hard and soft OR to enhance collaborative behavior and positive results for decision-makers.* Thus, SMART OR should not only employ OR analysis techniques and/or the multiple methods of so called Big Data analysis but also combine them with techniques which are well-known for their end-consumer empirical, and sometimes qualitative, data analysis (Mingers and Rosenhead 2004), in particular those used in soft OR (Ranyard et al. 2015). Such multiple approaches will allow researchers not only to address the need to make use of online data but also to understand behavioral insights through incorporating interdisciplinary knowledge into OR Big Data analytics. Furthermore, the multiple approaches to Big Data analysis also allow researchers to respond to recent calls for data driven research in the social sciences disciplines (Simchi-Levi 2014). This chapter proposes a SMART OR approach for handling Big Data for exploring behavior in decision settings.

## 9.2   Big Data and Decision Analysis

There is increasing belief that Big Data can transform society. We take the view that Big Data can be the source of new energy for social transformation and decision-making, and for better private and public services (Schintler and Kulkani 2014). The emergence of the diversity of the types of data available across society offers new opportunities for organisations to show their worth. However, technical skills are needed to design and perform the complex analyses inherent in Big Data applications—but these skills alone will not unlock the full potential of Big Data. They need to be complemented with knowledge of the economic and social value of decision-making to translate the information into impact. However, the relation between value and impact must be viewed through the lens of effective data use for the empowerment of those marginalised from so called open data, i.e. recognising not everyone has the requisite access or the necessary processing resources (Gurstein 2011).

While there has been a growing interest in Big Data, interestingly, there are also countless organisations using and producing Big Data that are not just traditional information technology (IT) companies. Many different organisations are also increasingly generating large administrative data sets and social media platforms. The combination of these different data sources, and in particular the linkage together of different data sets, provides both great opportunities and challenges to organisations. For example, by collecting data by novel means to track sentiments and/or beliefs, Big Data can help to facilitate social and civic empowerment, and furthermore, to enhance and expand stakeholder participation in service development and delivery (Brabham 2009). However, some thought must be applied to the question of how social media enforce certain processes or patterns of usage on their users, thus colouring data. For example, current interest about the introduction of the "dislike" button in Facebook is prompting debate about the affordances offered by the social media platform and how the feature will be interpreted by its users. None-the-less, Big Data can be used to promote transparency and accountability, which in turn can engender trust between or within different stakeholder groups (Surowiecki 2004). Thus, Big Data will increasingly play an important part in shaping the landscape of decision-making. However, while there is increasing enthusiasm for exploiting Big Data and making better use of quantitative and qualitative data from a range of *open* and administrative sources, there is nonetheless a large gap between our understanding of Big Data and our decision-making. Briefly, the benefits of Big Data speak more to improving description and prediction than to strengthening the causal and explanatory knowledge that are crucial to decision analysis. Causal and explanatory knowledge are not obvious consequences of Big Data. But it is clear that Big Data can considerably thicken our description of service (for example, using Google Analytics). However, it is by no means certain that the most effective users of Big Data, in terms of their impact economically and socially, will be motivated to seek explanatory knowledge from their exploitation of Big Data. Such use at best might be thought of as mere atheoretical pragmatism, where the benefits to the interpreters of Big Data make them feel justified in their actions. However, and more seriously, this pragmatism may elide with the emergence of a new instrumentalism, exemplified by a return to old ideas in new guises, for example, Digital Taylorism (Brown and Lauder 2012).

At the same time, many organisations are organising their activities in a variety of novel ways and collecting data on their services and activities, through social media, machine log data, sensor data and other forms of data collection that are different from the more formalised approach, where the majority of data collection has been through offline resource projects, based on surveys and field studies. In the social sciences, the tradition is very different. Clearly, new technologies are providing the opportunity to collect large amounts of passive data about what's going on in a society as a whole. Thus, as more and more interaction of the services with the clients moves online, and organisations are collecting large amounts of *open* Big Data data as well as data from new sources (such as social media), the more there is a need to realise the potential in linking the novel forms of these data and outcomes. As Big Data become increasingly available and inexpensive, analytics will move from a field that relies predominantly on collection of small data to one focused both on Big Data collection—identifying and extracting relevant data from public sources and leveraging technology to capture Big Data from people in a free-living context—and on the development of new analytic methods to make sense of it all. However, Big Data from secondary sources are not likely to wholly replace new data collection.

There may also be some problems linking the data to decision-making. For some, Big Data sets seem to have limited use because of their irregularity and heterogeneity (Chen et al. 2012). The data tend to be inherently biased and lead to a conclusion that contemporary statistical analysis routines are inadequate to examine. But there are a number of things that offer hope. First, the type of information that may already be available could provide us with a large, diverse sample. Second, the data set is rich and anonymous; it may be possible to look at issues across a wide range of variables. The issue of statistical significance takes on new meaning when working with thousands of data points. Unlike smaller studies, where considerable effort is expended to gather an adequate sample size, any large data set will allow a researcher to find a *statistically significant* result. We will be able to measure more variables across time, space and policy domains, describing better contexts in which organisational decision-making and service delivery takes place. By way of a summary, these data types may include:

- Consumed data created as a by-product of digital services;
- Online data, e.g. social media, internet activity, web content, news feeds;
- Data from objects, e.g. satellites, machine logs, sensors;
- Actively supplied data, e.g. citizen reporting and crowdsourcing.

While the excitement of achieving new levels of statistical significance is enticing, suitable care must be taken with the techniques used to analyse such data. "Correlation is not causation" may be a tired mantra, but it does deserve further thought in an era where almost any data set can be analysed against any other. The "Spurious Correlation" web site[1] may be entertaining, but it makes a serious point. Without the intent to seek deeper explanatory models for data and with economic need driving pragmatic and purely instrumental approaches, knowledge is withheld from wider scrutiny, not maliciously but through lack of interest in discovering it, leaving the interpretation of "better" purely in the hands of those able to access and analyse the data.

## 9.3    Big Data Analytics

*Analytics* is defined as the process of transforming data into insight for making better decisions. Chen et al. (2012) and others proposed a classification of Big Data analytics into three main sub-types:

(i) *Descriptive analytics*: where analysis is made to describe a past situation in such a way that trends, patterns and exceptions become apparent. The first level of analytics explores what has occurred as a way to gain insight for better approaching the future, usually trying to answer the question of "what happened?" At one level there is *data mining*, which allows complex information to be obtained from

---

[1] http://www.tylervigen.com/spurious-correlations.

databases by aggregating multidimensional structures such as information cubes, where the data can be interrogated from different variables perspectives. At another there is *visualisation*, which represent data in visual form in order to enhance facts and patterns that may not be easy, or feasible at all, to identify in other formats.

(ii) *Predictive analytics*: where analyses focus on real time and historical data to make predictions in the form of probabilities of future events. They are based on the machine learning techniques and other computational algorithms of data mining. Tools include regression (linear and logistic), discriminant analysis, clustering and dimensionality reduction.

(iii) *Prescriptive analytics*: where analytics use predictions based on data to inform and suggest proposed sets of actions that can serve to take advantage of or to avoid a particular outcome. Prescriptive analytics are mainly associated with optimisation and simulation, and have special relevance in contexts of uncertainty relying on stochastic computational programming of random variables (e.g. Monte Carlo).

## 9.4    Big Data and Behavior

The challenges in interpreting large amounts of data in general may be distinguished from the challenges encountered in decisions regarding the use of behavioral Big Data to influence behavior. Behavioral OR has long been concerned with decision-makers' biases and limitations in dealing with ambiguity, information overload, pattern recognition and information relevance, to name but a few. Ongoing research in the fields of group decision-making and negotiation is thus relevant in the context of Big Data and behavioral OR. Furthermore, Ranyard et al. (2015) noted a lack of attention to soft OR and the Big Data analytics research. Soft OR offers methodological approaches of interest. Soft OR, with its demonstrated usefulness in facilitating group decision-making and development, may support decisions regarding the design of insight-generating behavioral experiments using Big Data platforms, such as social media, with the aim of understanding how collective behavior may be influenced.

To explore Big Data and behavioral OR, we first highlight the behavioral challenges that decision-makers face when confronted with large amounts of data and the role of behavioral OR in this context. Second, we discuss how behavioral insights from social media data may be used to *influence* collective behavior and how organisations may benefit from the use of soft OR approaches in related strategy development.

## 9.5    Behavior and Decision-Making with Large Amounts of Data

Simon's work on satisficing and bounded rationality (Simon 1955) has played a major role towards the development of behavioral OR. Simon's proposition was that people have a tendency towards satisficing rather than optimising when it comes to decision-making, whereby a decision is chosen which satisfies an individual's most important need, irrespective of whether the choice is ideal or desirable. Also, Simon contends that decision-makers' ability to act rationally is dependent on and bounded by the information they have access to and the computational capacity they possess. These factors time and time again lead the decision-maker to have biases towards certain types of actions or behaviors. By *biases* we mean a tendency towards a certain disposition. They are also referred to as *systematic errors in judgment* or *heuristics* (Kahneman and Tversky 1979; Kahneman et al. 1982; Gilovich et al. 2002). While there is a large stream of literature in this area, there is still a barrier to be overcome by decision-makers when faced with large amounts of data. This is because embracing data driven decision-making involves moving away from conventional decision-making processes. Concerns about cognitive limitations of decision-makers, and about interactive modeling with groups, seem to have driven attention to the creation of methods of elicitation that require only ordinal judgments as inputs. Even more, this explicit concern with methods that are cognitively sound have been the basis for the proposition that decision analysis take into account cognitive limitations of decision-makers in providing, processing and understanding information. With Big Data, we believe that there is scope for further discussion of these ideas. From a classical behavioral approach, the following would be the expectation in relation to decision-making and Big Data:

- *Information overload* is experienced at the point where decisions reflect a lesser utilisation of the available information (Schroder et al. 1967) or potentially useful information received becomes a hindrance rather than a help (Jacoby 1977). For example, there may be complications in distinguishing relevant information, difficulties in recognising correlation between details and overall perspective, lengthier decision times, a disregard for large amounts of information and inaccurate decisions (Eppler and Mengis 2004). It is not only the amount of information that determines information overload but also the specific characteristics of information, such as the level of uncertainty associated with the information and the level of ambiguity, complexity, etc. Information overload can also be due to the characteristics of the decision-maker (e.g. personal skills, experience, etc.). In order to deal with too much information, a decision-maker may stop searching once a satisfactory solution has been found; i.e. the satisficing heuristic (Buchanan and Kock 2001).
- *Information relevance* is where the unstructured nature of Big Data might potentially result in difficulty in choosing relevant data (see Davenport et al. 2010). There may be an exposure to excessive information that can lead to an inability to disregard irrelevant information. Excessive, hence irrelevant, information reduces decision-makers' ability to identify relevant information and consequently worsens decision-making performance. Finally, attention to irrelevant information has the potential to significantly limit the value that can be obtained from incorporating Big Data into the decision-making process.
- *Anchoring effect* is an often observed attitude that reflects a tendency to depend greatly on past performance and experience in decision-making (Kahneman et al. 1982). Anchoring, as a form of cognitive bias, may emanate from a common tendency to rely on prior information offered when making decisions. This may reflect an iner-

tia that avoids risk taking, and may be costly in the long-run, in that decision-makers may forgo emerging opportunities.

- *Pattern recognition* is where Big Data provides the decision-maker with the ability to search for patterns in a large population of data that would otherwise be undetectable in samples or even smaller data sets (Baron and Ensley 2006). Decision-makers can be vulnerable to various problems such as difficulty recognising patterns of evidence, applying prior knowledge to current judgment task (see anchoring), weighing evidence inappropriately and combining information into patterns. It is clear that providing decision-makers with more contextual knowledge will improve their ability to accurately recognise patterns (suggesting soft OR).

- *Ambiguity* may arise from variations in the amount and type of information available, differences in the source reliability and lack of causal knowledge of observed events (Frisch and Baron 1988). Unstructured data may be viewed as ambiguous and information ambiguity has been found to result in incorrect judgments. Individuals intolerant of ambiguity actively seek to reduce uncertainty by focusing on simple solutions and neglect additional information once a solution is identified (even one that is not optimal). Ambiguities that decision-makers encounter on stakeholder engagement affect their ability to accurately interpret evidence. In general, ambiguity-intolerant decision-makers have been found to be less confident about rendering opinions on decision statements. Decision-makers intolerant of ambiguity will likely be uncomfortable with the unstructured nature of Big Data and as a result may avoid or downplay ambiguous information which could result in less than optimal judgments, leading to decreased overall effectiveness (due to ignoring information cues). However, the use of soft analytic tools may help decision-makers overcome ambiguity-related cognitive limitations.

In sum, the above endeavour to catalogue these tendencies in decision-making is conducted against an objective ideal of rational decision-making. Each of these tendencies or bias, as it is discovered through laboratory experiment, leads to further questions as to its prevalence and relative importance as a member of an ever-growing list. The approach to investigation and discovery is aligned with a variance-oriented episte-mology (Van de Ven and Poole 2005) and is in effect following standard hypothetical-deductive method. The elimination, or mitigation, of these biases is then seen as the purpose of achieving appropriately detailed modeling (prediction) or experimental design (theory testing). However, the sheer quantity of biases discovered leads to enormous detail com-plexity in trying to eliminate them and thus raises the question as to the overall effectiveness of the approach. On the other hand, alignment with a process-oriented epistemology offers the opportunity to view collective decision-making from a perspective that

> …*may incorporate several different types of effects into their explanations, including critical events and turning points, contextual influence, formative patterns that give overall direction to the change, and causal factors that influ-ence the sequencing of events.* (Van de Ven and Poole 2005)

Here, the stages and/or types of decision-making can be investigated through a variety of approaches so long as the essential temporal nature of the process view is taken into account. The process ontology elides well with a focus on collective behavior (White 2016). Rather than the reductive and highly complex task of unpicking an exhaustive list of indi-vidual biases we can limit our investigations to accounts of what actually happens.

Big Data analytics providers have already developed sophisticated approaches for data capture, analysis and visualisation, employing hard OR techniques in the process. However, in all cases, a final step of human interpretation of data for specific problems, sectors and organisations remains. Specifically, challenges arising from Big Data for behavior in decision situations potentially aggravate the problem that already exists with traditional data, where decision-makers are challenged with the interpretation of exceptions and anomalies (Chen and Zhang 2014). Furthermore, while analytics applications may facilitate the identification of patterns, these still need to be made sense of in order to be *actionable patterns* (Hilbert 2012).

So far, the discussion has focused on facilitating the development of actionable patterns for organisational decision-makers using available

Big Data. However, the reciprocal interactions between the behavior of organisations that interpret Big Data and the behavior of users who generate it have not yet been sufficiently considered. Organisations increasingly go beyond an internally-focused response to insights from Big Data and aim to proactively *influence* collective behavior through the modification of the content that social media users are exposed to. The analysis of Big Data thus becomes a venture in nudging (or manipulating?) collective behavior.

## 9.6    Influencing Collective Behavior

Although many Big Data application areas involve predicting consumer behavior in response to past behavior and/or proposed interventions, relatively little attention has been paid to understanding the behavioral mechanisms at work. If, as suggested by Liberatore and Luo (2010) the analytics process is understood as consisting of a closed loop of data collection, analysis (predictive modeling and optimisation), insight generation and action/implementation, then the link between insight and action is, arguably, the least well-developed of the links for Big Data, at least in terms of formal modeling tools.

Bentley et al. (2014) provide an interesting account of the role of Big Data in the study of collective behavior. They offer an analysis of social media data, e.g. from social network sites such as Facebook and Twitter, to tell us about how information flows throughout the large and complex network of human interactions. At the same time, decision-making often involves gathering information to determine the consequences of possible actions (Simon 1955). Thus, we increasingly turn to search engines such as Google in particular, to provide information to support our everyday decisions.

Further studies have illustrated that online information gathering can also anticipate future collective behavior. For example, Goel et al. (2010) demonstrated that search query volume predicts the opening weekend box office revenue for films, first month sales of video games and chart rankings of songs. Aside from search data, other research has provided evidence that the massive data sets generated by our everyday actions in the real world can also support better forecasting of future behavior (King

2011). Big Data allow us to look for patterns in collective behavior which might recur in the future, similar to the way in which we as individuals rely on the statistical structure we have observed in the world when trying to forecast consequences of decisions (Giguère and Love 2013).

When considered at greater breadth, we argue in accordance with (Moat et al. 2014) that, in contrast to Bentley et al.'s conjecture, Big Data studies do far more than "allow us to see better how known behavioral patterns apply in novel contexts" (Bentley et al. 2014). Big Data offer us insight into information-gathering stages of real world decision-making processes that could not previously be observed, while large-scale records of real world activity enable us to better forecast future actions by allowing us to identify new patterns in our collective behavior (Moat et al. 2014). Such predictive power is not only of theoretical importance for behavioral science and operational research, but also of great practical consequence, as it opens up possibilities to reallocate resources to better support the wellbeing of society.

Another limitation of Bentley et al. (2014) proposed framework is the suggestion that decision-making can be understood along two dimensions. The first represents the degree to which an actor makes a decision independently versus one that is socially influenced. The second represents the degree of transparency in the payoffs and risks associated with the decisions actors make. In their response, Pfister and Böhm (2008) argue that "Independence is fictional, and social influences substantially permeate preference construction". They go on to state that "in a big-data era, it will become a critical issue for decision-makers to select the appropriate mode [...] from a dimension that runs from deliberate/emotionally complex to intuitive/emotionally simple".

Organisations are thus increasingly able to use the insights about behavioral dynamics in social media to influence collective behavior through targeted campaigns using social media. For example, Facebook's "Voter Megaphone" campaign,

>...which promotes voting by revealing the names and faces of friends who have already cast votes (and was portrayed to have increased voter turnout by some 340,000 in the 2010 US elections) has generated further controversy. While the promotion of voting appears to be a good use of social media, the fact that the

*Voter Megaphone project was also part of a study, and was thus only applied to certain users, raised ethical questions about the real world political impacts of this behavioral manipulation.*[2]

In the UK, Facebook's "I'm a Voter" button was introduced at the 2015 UK General Election. Similar campaigns have been conducted to increase registration as organ donors and to encourage tax paying. Overall, new ethical, political and regulatory questions arise as soon as the passive reception of unstructured social media data from an organisation's environment is turned into a pro-active strategy that aims to change (or nudge) the behavior of social media users by modifying the data they are exposed to.

This leads us to argue that the ability of decision-makers to extract maximum value from social media data that are imbued with behavioral insight is highly dependent on their ability to ask responsible questions for interventions in these media, questions that would allow them to study local, potentially organisation specific, assumptions and hypotheses about collective user/customer behavior in technology-rich societies. To facilitate the process of strategising for creative and ethical intervention in media that generate Big Data, SMART OR practitioners are ideally placed, as they can draw on rich sources, particularly when using soft OR methods that consider the field's critical dimensions (Ormerod and Ulrich 2013). Moreover, strategic systems thinking approaches, for example those that are intended to mitigate unintended consequences through the establishment of iterative collaborative learning systems, such as Soft Systems Methodology, complemented by simulation approaches (e.g. Discrete Event Simulation, Systems Dynamics, Agent-Based Modeling) may prove valuable in the design of interventions in big social media environments.

## 9.7    Conclusion

We thus suggest a research agenda for SMART OR, where *it is the creative use of Big Data and hard and soft OR to enhance collective behavior and positive results for decision-makers.* It is a multimethodology approach that

---

[2] https://changingbehaviours.wordpress.com/2015/02/18/behavioural-science-meets-data-science/.

seeks to facilitate the emergence of distributed agency towards a shared goal and which is appropriate in super-wicked problem contexts and that involves the creative use of different approaches for analysis. Since Soft OR, and its basis in collective decision-making, is essentially action oriented and located within a particular problem context and stakeholder grouping, we can tolerate these new biases—should they be observed by an external observer conducting an ethnography (say)—more as features of the subsequent process-oriented analysis, there being no objectively defined rational basis available to the group to eliminate them or regard them as deleterious to the decision-making process.

# References

Babai, M.Z., M.M. Ali, and K. Nikolopoulos. 2012. Impact of temporal aggregation on stock control performance of intermittent demand estimators: Empirical analysis. *Omega* 40: 713–721.

Baron, R.A., and M.D. Ensley. 2006. Opportunity recognition as the detection of meaningful patterns: Evidence from comparisons of novice and experienced entrepreneurs. *Management Science* 52: 1331–1344.

Bentley, R.A., M.J. O'Brien, and W.A. Brock. 2014. Mapping collective behaviour in the big-data era. *Behavioural and Brain Sciences* 37: 63–76.

Brabham, D.C. 2009. Crowdsourcing the public participation process for planning projects. *Planning Theory* 8: 242–262.

Brown, P., and H. Lauder. 2012. The great transformation in the global labour market. *Soundings* 51: 41–53.

Buchanan, J., & Kock, N. (2001). Information overload: A decision making perspective. In *Multiple Criteria Decision Making in the New Millennium* 51: (pp. 49-58). Springer Berlin Heidelberg.

Chen, C.P., and C.Y. Zhang. 2014. Data-intensive applications, challenges, techniques and technologies: A survey on big data. *Information Sciences* 275: 314–347.

Chen, H., R. Chiang, and V. Storey. 2012. Business intelligence and analytics: From big data to big impact. *MIS Quarterly* 36: 1165–88.

Davenport, T., and J. Harris. 2007. *Competing on analytics: The new science of winning*. Boston: Harvard Business School Press.

Davenport, T., J. Harris, and R. Morison. 2010. *Analytics at work: Smarter decisions better results*. Boston: Harvard Business School Press.

Eppler, M.J., and J. Mengis. 2004. The concept of information overload: A review of literature from organization science, accounting, marketing, MIS and related disciplines. *The Information Society* 20: 325–344.

Frisch, D., and J. Baron. 1988. Ambiguity and rationality. *Journal of Behavioral Decision Making* 1: 149–157.

Giguère, G., and B.C. Love. 2013. Limits in decision making arise from limits in memory retrieval. *Proceedings of the National Academy of Sciences USA* 110: 7613–7618.

Gilovich, T., D.W. Griffin, and D. Kahneman. 2002. *Heuristics and biases: The psychology of intuitive judgement.* Cambridge: Cambridge University Press.

Goel, S., J.M. Hofman, S. Lahaie, D.M. Pennock, and D.J. Watts. 2010. Predicting consumer behaviour with web search. *Proceedings of the National Academy of Sciences USA* 107: 17486–17490.

Gurstein, M.B. 2011. Open data: Empowering the empowered or effective data use for everyone? *First Monday* 16: 2–7.

Hilbert, M. 2012. Toward a synthesis of cognitive biases: How noisy information processing can bias human decision making. *Psychological Bulletin* 138: 211–237.

Jacoby, J. 1977. Information load and decision quality: Some contested issues. *Journal of Marketing Research* 14: 569–573.

Kahneman, D., and A. Tversky. 1979. Prospect theory: An analysis of decision under risk. *Econometrica: Journal of the Econometric Society* 47(2): 263291.

Kahneman, D., P. Slovic, and A. Tversky. 1982. *Judgment under uncertainty: Heuristics and biases.* Cambridge: Cambridge University Press.

King, G. 2011. Ensuring the data-rich future of the social sciences. *Science* 331: 719.

Liberatore, M., and W. Luo. 2010. The analytics movement: Implications for operations research. *Interfaces* 40: 313–336.

McAfee, A., and E. Brynjolfsson. 2012. Big data: The management revolution. *Harvard Business Review* 90: 60–68.

Mingers, J., and J. Rosenhead. 2004. Problem structuring methods in action. *European Journal of Operational Research* 152: 530–554.

Moat, H.S., C. Curme, H.E. Stanley, and T. Preis. 2014. Anticipating stock market movements with Google and Wikipedia. In *Nonlinear phenomena in complex systems: From nano to macro scale*, ed. D. Matrasulov and H.E. Stanley, 47–59. Netherlands: Springer.

Ormerod, R.J., and W. Ulrich. 2013. Operational research and ethics: A literature review. *European Journal of Operational Research* 228: 291–307.

Pfister, H.R., and G. Böhm. 2008. The multiplicity of emotions: A framework of emotional functions in decision making. *Judgment and Decision Making* 3: 5–17.

Ranyard, J.C., R. Fildes, and T.I. Hu. 2015. Reassessing the scope of OR practice: The influences of problem structuring methods and the analytics movement. *European Journal of Operational Research* 245: 1–13.

Schintler, L., and K. Kulkani. 2014. Big data for policy analysis: The good, the bad and the ugly. *Review of Policy Research* 31: 343–348.

Schroder, H.M., M.J. Driver, and S. Streufert. 1967. *Human information processing*. New York: Holt, Rinehart & Winston.

Sen, A. 2013. A comparison of mixed and dynamic pricing policies in revenue management. *Omega* 41: 586–597.

Simchi-Levi, D. 2014. OM forum-OM research: From problem-driven to data-driven research. *Manufacturing & Service Operations Management* 16: 210.

Simon, H.A. 1955. A behavioural model of rational choice. *Quarterly Journal of Economics* 69: 99–118.

Singhal, K., and J. Singhal. 2012. Imperatives of the science of operations and supply-chain management. *Journal of Operations Management* 30: 237–244.

Surowiecki, J. 2004. *The wisdom of crowds: Why the many are smarter than the few*. London: Little, Brown.

Van de Ven, A.H., and M.S. Poole. 2005. Alternative approaches for studying organizational change. *Organization Studies* 26: 1377–1404.

White, L. 2016. Behavioural operational research: Towards a framework for understanding behaviour in or interventions. *European Journal of Operational Research* 249: 827–841.

# 10

# Behavioral Issues in the Practical Application of Scenario Thinking: Cognitive Biases, Effective Group Facilitation and Overcoming Business-as-Usual Thinking

Stephanie Bryson, Megan Grime, Adarsh Murthy and George Wright

## 10.1 Introduction

Many companies typically tend to focus on their immediate business environment. They spend most of their energy and resources on their familiar set of products, customers, competitors, technologies and stakeholders. Psychological research has shown that such a focus risks missing key signals from the peripheral environment. A mind-set based on a false sense of business-as-usual can creep into organizations that are riding on the wave of a successful past. What is needed is not only to sense incipient change but also to anticipate change and to know where to look more carefully for clues. Seemingly random or disparate pieces of information—that at first appear to be background noise—need to be recognised as part of a larger pattern. The scenario thinking method focuses on enhancing a process of discussion and debate within a top management

S. Bryson (✉) • M. Grime • A. Murthy • G. Wright
Strathclyde Business School, University of Strathclyde, 199 Cathedral Street, Glasgow G4 0QU, UK

© The Editor(s) (if applicable) and The Author(s) 2016
M. Kunc et al. (eds.), *Behavioral Operational Research*,
DOI 10.1057/978-1-137-53551-1_10

team, in contrast to the traditional, more rationalistic approach involving the search for a single optimal strategy. As we shall show, scenario thinking allows managers to better recognise and interpret weak signals of change that are already emerging in the present. It facilitates a shift in managers' mental models and provides a challenge to counter business-as-usual thinking.

In the process of a scenario thinking intervention within an organization, team members must use their knowledge of past and current events within the market, firm, and customer-base to help anticipate the future. However, cognitive biases are thought to hinder the effectiveness and progression of scenario thinking. To date, a small number of researchers have published work analyzing the use of certain biases and heuristics within scenario thinking, which we further discuss in this chapter.

Within the group-based setting of a typical scenario workshop, a deliberate and high degree of *turbulence* is promoted in order to influence the process of surfacing codified and tacit knowledge with the subsequent aim of using this knowledge to enrich the group's framing of plausible futures. Given the complexity of scenario workshops, the many process steps involved and the aforementioned turbulence, an experienced facilitator is typically used to support and guide participants through the process. However, facilitation of scenario interventions is not without problems and issues. Indeed, Eden (1992) contended that learning within strategy development is a social process, with the power and politics inherent in this process. The role of facilitation in this social process is to achieve a negotiated conclusion to a scenario development process (Ackerman and Eden 2012).

## 10.2   The Prevalence of Business-as-Usual Thinking in Organizations

Companies typically tend to solve short-term problems in order to keep the business running. Psychological research has shown that a such a focus risks missing key signals from the periphery (Schoemaker et al. 2013). Also, organizations that have been successful in the past can fail to adapt and change as the external environment changes. In fact, when business conditions change, the most successful companies can be the slowest to adapt. It is ironic that many factors that led to a company's success in the first place—focus, confident leadership, corporate culture etc.—also are instrumental in the company's decline. The strategic frames, the processes, the relationships and values with which the managers operate lead to an organizational inertia that hinders sensing, digesting and acting in a dynamic environment that demands agile and decisive actions. A mind-set based on a false sense of business-as-usual creeps into organizations that are riding on the wave of a successful past. As Miller (1992) points out in his book, *The Icarus Paradox*, "Failure teaches leaders valuable lessons, but good results only re-inforce their preconceptions and tether them more firmly to their tried-and-true recipes" (Page 30). He continues, "stellar performers view the world through a narrowing telescope. One point of view takes over; one set of assumptions comes to dominate. The result is complacency and overconfidence" (Page 32). Moreover, one source of momentum is structural memory, which in essence relates to memory the organization builds up as a result of a perceived successful strategy; the more successful it is, the more it will be implemented routinely, automatically and unquestioningly. One underlying assumption inherent in such situations is that all other variables, most importantly those related to the external environment, have not changed.

A classic case-in-point is that of the company Kodak. Kodak was a market leader with tremendous market share and technology leadership in photography based on film. The camera/film industry was hit by a disruptive innovation (digital imaging) that destroyed the traditional business model based on film photography. Kodak was fully aware of the emergence of digital imaging, but it still struggled to respond effectively. Between 2003 and 2012, Kodak went through multiple restructuring and business model re-innovation efforts. Kodak finally filed for Chapter 11 bankruptcy in 2012, with enormous challenges and a bleak future ahead (Gaveti et al. 2004).

Another phenomenon, called hubris, is worth mentioning in this context. There is some evidence that hubris, defined as extreme pride or self-confidence, is salient with people in power, such as CEOs of companies. Petit and Bollaert (2012) have looked into the negative effects of CEO hubris on firm performance. Many top managers climb the ranks based on their past performance. Previous success leads them to strongly believe in their strategic intent thus far. Their confidence level increases with each step up the ladder. Overconfident people with power can be an extreme liability for a company. They tend to become overbearing (thinking, "I know better because I have succeeded in the past"), complacent (especially if they see no urgency to change; their experience and deep pockets will see them through) and blinkered (seeking information that supports their existing beliefs and ignore information that doesn't fit). Of course, not every successful manager is overbearing, complacent and blinkered. Rather, these are tendencies every manager should be aware of and guard against.

Regardless of past success, most companies limit their vision within the operating boundaries of their daily business. Few extend it to a peripheral vision involving remote markets, new competitors, emerging technologies and seemingly tangential information. What is needed is not only to sense incipient change,but also to anticipate change and to know where to look more carefully for clues. Companies that are able to anticipate market changes and quickly adapt their strategies are the ones with sustained success. These are companies that constantly try to integrate a wide range of market signals into their strategy making process and encourage a strategic conversation within the company. In his classic Harvard Business Review paper, De Geus (1997) analyzed organizations that successfully thrived over many years. He found high corporate "mortality rates"—for example, by 1983, one-third of the 1970 Fortune 500 companies had been acquired, broken into pieces or merged with other companies. One of the features common to some of the most resilient organizations is their sensitivity to the world around them. Given the extremely dynamic and complex environments that companies face, it is absolutely crucial that they install structures and processes that allow them to sense, recognize, react and adapt to their external context.

Scenario thinking, when practiced in a comprehensive and holistic manner, is a powerful method that can allow organizations not only to counter many of the perils described above but also to build sustained competitive advantage. Sull (2005) uses the term *fog of the future* to describe unpredictability. In an environment with deep uncertainties, the quest for the one perfect strategy can be a futile exercise. Instead, companies require structures and processes that allow them to be vigilant, open-minded and flexible enough to react fast. Ideally, mechanisms should be in place to counter biases in day-to-day decision making and to facilitate effective use of available information. The scenario thinking method provides such a process, in contrast to the traditional, more rationalistic approach involving the search for one optimal strategy.

## 10.2.1  Scenarios as an Antidote

The scenario thinking method can be used for various purposes. Van der Heijden et al. (2002) argued that it is very important to have clarity on the purpose of using this method. It can be permanently anchored in the regular strategic planning process or can be used to raise and/or answer specific strategy questions. The scenario thinking method provides a structure for understanding the business environment and challenges business-as-usual thinking. During a scenario workshop, managers are forced to think through their assumptions and thus can identify inconsistencies in their own thinking and in that of other participants. At the same time, scenario work necessitates undertaking a detailed analysis of the external world, challenges team members' perceptions, stretches their mental models and helps them develop a shared view of how the uncertainties and trends will develop and interact in the focal business context. Most managers use mental anchors from the recent past to future change. However, using past events can be highly misleading. Scenario thinking allows managers to better recognise and interpret weak signals. It facilitates a shift in mental models and systematically counters business-as-usual thinking. The process enables the organization to become what is known as a *learning organization*—one developing mechanisms to challenge its day-to-day decisions and developing structures to sense and anticipate external changes.

However, since scenario thinking is based on the judgments of participants in the process, what if those judgments are, in themselves, of poor quality? Perhaps judgmental flaws and biases at the level of the individual manager will be magnified rather than reduced with the group-based scenario workshop? It is to these issues that we turn next.

## 10.3  The Prevalence of Heuristics and Potential Biases within Scenario Thinking

In any scenario development process, team members must use their knowledge of past and current events to help anticipate the future (van der Heijden et al. 2002). The scenario method constructs a range of plausible futures to provide alternative frameworks by which an organization can gain early recognition of changes and facilitate strong organizational responses. In other words, the aim is to help management teams think more broadly, rather than to determine what they should think. The wider the range of plausible futures an organization can envision, the better position they will be in to anticipate the opportunities and threats that may emerge. With this focus in mind, biased thinking and misapplied heuristics can diminish the effectiveness and progression of scenario planning. As illustrated in the Icarus Paradox—and discussed in Sect. 10.2—a business-as-usual perspective can steer a firm into a narrow view of the future, resulting in a lack of ability to adjust to market and environmental changes.

In the 1970s, Kahneman and Tversky's work on cognitive biases and heuristics brought a new wave of insight into the field of judgment and decision making. They expanded on the perspective that cognitive experience is a dual system. System 1 constantly monitors the environment and makes basic assessments with little cognitive effort. System 2 directs attention and searches memory for answers. Thus, System 1 thinking is heuristic and can be biased, whereas System 2 thinking is engaged when complexity is consciously analysed—as in a scenario thinking intervention within an organization (Kahneman 2011).

To date, a small number of studies have empirically investigated the effects of cognitive heuristics—and potential resultant biases—in scenario thinking. Each study takes one of two perspectives, either how biases affect the scenario process or how the scenario process eliminates certain biases.

The most widely investigated bias in the literature is confidence. As Kahneman (2011, p. 17) stated, "We are prone to overestimate how much we understand about the world and to underestimate the role of chance in events." A variety of experimental methods have been employed to measure levels of confidence in forecasting efforts by people after partici-pating in scenario thinking exercises. Confidence—or *overconfidence,* as with Schoemaker (1993) and Bradfield (2008)—leads a group (or indi-vidual) to overvalue its own opinion on a subject, independent of the truth. This has the consequence of narrowing rather than broadening per-spectives during the scenario process. Schnaars and Topol (1987) found that reviewing scenarios increased individuals' confidence in their own generated forecasts compared to just reviewing graphical representations of past sales. Kuhn and Sniezek (1996) found similar results with their participants. Reviewing either single or multiple scenarios, regardless of message, increased confidence in participants' generated forecasts com-pared to those who reviewed no scenario. However, confidence in their forecasts decreased as the projected date moved farther into the future. That is, forecasting for 10 years in the future was given greater confidence ratings than forecasting for 20 years. Bradfield (2008) used observational measures to assess overconfidence in group work. Each group reflected on what was termed an "embedded cognitive script" (p. 209), in which scenarios appeared to come from a predetermined script including fac-tors with causal links among them that largely went unchanged even after suggestions of more extreme developments, more pressing factors and interventions by an expert facilitator, thus reflecting overconfidence and belief perseverance in their generated scenarios.

Schoemaker (1993), on the other hand, compared confidence ranges before and after participants generated their own scenarios, as opposed to reviewing them. Unlike the previous studies, Schoemaker's experiment showed that overconfidence decreased (i.e. confidence ranges increased) as an effect of scenario generation. The conscious exercise of thinking broadly about future possibilities helped counter the natural tendency to form a myopic view of the future (System 1 thinking). Sampling from experts in the field of U.S. freight transportation, Phandis et al. (2014) found results somewhat similar to Schoemaker's. Experts worked with a long-range planning horizon, generated a single scenario per group and then evaluated all scenarios from each group. Confidence levels in group forecasting did not increase after reviewing multiple scenarios. However, they did not decrease either. Furthermore, confidence levels were less likely to change after reviewing only a single scenario if prior assessments of the scenario already had the highest level of confidence.

It is clear that investigations into confidence and scenario planning yield varying, even opposing, results. This could be due to the different measurement tools, the different participant samplings (undergraduate and MBA students, CEOs, experts and colleagues), the difference between reviewing and generating scenarios or the specifics of the scenario topics. What is important to note is that confidence is an important element in the decision making process and, as such, requires our awareness of its effects and use. The more confident an individual is in his/her own judgment, the less likely he/she will be to willingly change his judgment. For scenario planning to be effective, both participants and practitioners must be open to differing views and opinions and allow malleability and novelty throughout the process.

A variety of other cognitive biases have also been explored in relation to scenario planning. Meissner and Wulf (2013) compared the effects of the full scenario process against a partial scenario process as well as a different traditional strategic planning exercise and their effects on framing bias and decision quality. When people's judgments are influenced by how information is presented to them, they are said to be working with a framing bias (Tversky and Kahneman 1981). An example of the framing bias can be seen when a firm is willing to adopt a business strategy that shows a 60 % success rate but is unwilling to adopt the exact same business strategy when it shows a 40 % failure rate. Results of the study revealed that a framing bias influenced the decision process in all groups except those that engaged in a full scenario or strategic planning process. However, participating in the full scenario process reduced the framing bias more than the comparable strategic planning tools, e.g. SWOT. Furthermore, decision quality was evaluated between the full scenario analysis group and the traditional strategic planning group. Meissner and Wulf's results demonstrated that participating in the full scenario process enhanced individual decision quality more than traditional strategic planning tools did.

Bradfield's (2008) experimental groups showed use of the availability heuristic by focusing their initial exploratory discussions toward more highly publicised and recent events, even when shown that some events were rarer and less threatening than other unconsidered events. The availability heuristic describes the tendency to overestimate the probability of events that are more easily remembered, i.e. more *available* to recall from memory (Tversky and Kahneman 1973). As a consequence, people tend to underestimate the probability of less easily remembered events. Schoemaker (1993), on the other hand, revealed that the scenario process could use one cognitive bias to counter a possibly more damaging bias. When participants were required to reflect on extreme scenarios—rare, yet plausible events—the belief bias appeared to counter the more commonly employed availability heuristic. Engagement in the scenario process prompts team members to devote attention to events that are less thought-about and lie beyond what is immediately recalled. By doing this, Schoemaker found that broadening one's focus to consider rare, yet plausible events allowed such events to be perceived as more believable than when normally evaluated. By increasing the believability of possible future events, the scenario thinking process guides team and individual problem solving toward a deeper understanding of the world in which the organization operates—beyond the readily available business-as-usual mind-set.

Tetlock (2006) found similar results with his study, but he expanded a bit more on the reasoning. Not only did engaging in a scenario process increase the imaginability of a variety of plausible outcomes, and thus the believability of those outcomes; he found the exercise has a countering effect on the hindsight bias as well. Also known as the *I-knew-it-all-along* effect, this is a failure of our autobiographical memory. In the face of new evidence, people have a tendency to misrepresent their original opinions when asked to reconstruct them, by showing a favoritism for the new evidence. However, through unpacking, reconstructing and focusing on alternatives throughout the scenario process, imaginability is extensively engaged. This leads to more accurate recall of previously offered factors. Tetlock holds that the hindsight bias limits our appreciation of our previously imagined possibilities. An important element to scenario planning is not to discredit too quickly previously offered forecasts and driving forces, because beliefs that were reasonable prior to new information can still offer beneficial support in other stages of the process by contoasting with new information.

We conclude that the analysis of complexity inherent in scenario thinking—i.e. System 2 thinking—can be helpful in overcoming bias in judgments/assessments derived by the unconscious use of System 1 mechanisms but can also be informed by the same mechanisms. At the same time, bias may be a by-product that is magnified by use of the scenario development process. As such, the facilitator of any scenario exercise must be alert to the potential issues that may arise, which we have documented and discussed. Success is found in the right balance of theory and imagination driven thinking. Developing this theme of bias and remedies, we next turn to the scenario intervention process itself. How can a management team best be facilitated to think deeply about the future?

## 10.4 Facilitating Scenario Interventions within Organizations

Within the group-based setting of a typical scenario workshop, a deliberate and high degree of turbulence is promoted in order to influence the process of surfacing codified and tacit knowledge (van der Heijden et al. 2002), with the aim of subsequently using this knowledge to enrich the group's framing of plausible futures. Turbulence can perhaps be equated to *equivocality*—described by Ackerman and Eden (2012, p. 24) as a fuzziness within which negotiations can be more effective, as this fuzziness provides participants with the opportunity to change their minds, essentially saving face. Given the complexity of scenario workshops, the many process steps involved and the aforementioned turbulence, an experienced facilitator is typically used to support and guide participants through the process. However, facilitation of scenario interventions is not without problems and issues. Van der Heijden et al. (2002) argued that a facilitator from within a host organization—but one who has no direct expertise in the substantive scenario issue—may not command the necessary authority with the participants to play the facilitator role effectively. This can be detrimental to perceived success of the intervention. In a study of MBA students within a teaching-based scenario intervention,

Bradfield (2008) found that although the student facilitator highlighted problematic issues in surfacing driving forces and causality, the group did not act on these alerts and continued to develop their own initial ideas. Members of this facilitated group concluded that the facilitator's interventions were passive and ineffective.

Indeed, Grinyer (2000) asserts that an external facilitator is more likely to be accepted as an objective party, can remain impartial throughout the proceedings and is therefore suitably positioned to challenge established views held by senior management without fear of reprisal. To be effective in the role, the facilitator requires skill in promotion of the sharing of divergent views within a scenario workshop—encouraging debate and open conversation. Ackerman and Eden (2012, p. 25) suggest that a facilitator who is liberal in praising group members for contributions (especially in the early stages of the workshop) will provide members with the incentive to defend their contributions; thus the possibility of changing opinion may be inhibited. Allocating praise and credit is perhaps more beneficial in the later stages of the workshop, when the group members are in the process of reaching agreement. Within the scenario workshop setting, the facilitator should not contribute to the content of the group's discussion; rather, the facilitator attends to member-provided content— given the interaction of content and process (Eden and Radford 1990). If the group members were to view the facilitator as an expert in content, then this, coupled with his/her facilitator status, may adversely impact group members' ability to call upon their own expertise. Furthermore, Phillips and Phillips (1993) contend that explicit contributions by the facilitator will reduce his/her ability to observe and intervene in the ongoing group process.

In a parallel literature, Schweiger and Sandberg (1986) found that where devils' advocacy is adopted in a strategic decision making context—to stimulate challenge and disagreement—the decisions taken are of higher quality in comparison to those taken by teams who did not adopt that approach. Fostering an environment where diverse views can be openly shared and contested thus creates the conditions whereby business-as-usual thinking can be challenged. Similarly, Amason and Schweiger (1994) contend that cognitive conflict—termed *task conflict* by De Dreu (2006), where there exist differences in judgments regarding a decision or choices of alternatives—is valuable. However, a scenario workshop facilitator needs to be sensitive to the fact that cognitive conflict may lead to relationship conflict, which can adversely impact group work—since any criticism received may be viewed as personal criticism.

To ensure the engagement of all participants in any group-based activity, Korsgaard et al. (1995) emphasised the importance of using processes designed to create perceived procedural justice—where everyone's input is considered and valued. The facilitator, aware of the importance of eliciting views from all group members, and in attempts to minimise participants' periodically disengaging from the process, should stimulate the expression of varied interpretations and reduce the dominance of powerful stakeholders in any conversation—for example, those who may consistently and excessively consume air-time when asserting an opinion, at the expense of others. Indeed, in the context of scenario planning, Hodgkinson and Wright (2002) highlighted how the dominating personality of a CEO adversely impacted a scenario intervention—even though the rules of procedural justice had been agreed with the CEO before the scenario intervention was initiated. Indeed, Ackerman and Eden (2012) contend that the strategy making process should encourage diversity of views in order to open up the strategic conversation, prior to seeking a convergence of views. The use of "transitional objects" (De Geus 1988) such as causality maps, which are continuously updated to capture the views of all participants, can influence shifts in thinking, since these tools encourage participants to consider alternative perspectives (Ackerman and Eden 2012). Furthermore, Ackerman and Eden (2012, p. 25) contend that their "approach to the design of the facilitated support must recognise the role of some degree of anonymity in the causal maps used to record and encourage effective conversation".

Within the scenario planning workshop, the facilitator must also be acutely aware of the importance of group composition and its effect, given the need to focus on the generation of uncertainties and on the assessment and consideration of causality, impacts and the development of scenario stories. Schwartz (2011) argued that within a scenario workshop, views that are not sufficiently diverse can influence the development of a rather restricted range of scenarios. Hodgkinson and Healey (2008) asserted that to augment group information processing capability, the composition of the scenario team should be heterogeneous in terms of background, roles, experiences, etc. Van der Heijden et al. (2002, p. 167) also recommend that the composition of the scenario team should be somewhat heterogeneous—since this will enhance the expression and generation of new information and perhaps trigger new thoughts on the inter-relationships between components of the scenarios that are in development. Moyer (1996), in a scenario planning intervention at British Airways, observed that group cohesion prevented the verbalisation of challenge within the groups of members' implicit assumptions. The balance between the expression of divergent views and group cohesion is, in our view, a crucial one—since artificial consensus will lead to the development of simplistic scenarios. Additionally, early convergence of views will not provide sufficient opportunities for group members to alter their thinking.

Hodgkinson and Healey (2008) and Franco et al. (2013) contend that the membership composition of a scenario team will influence the effectiveness of the scenario planning intervention. Furthermore, powerful stakeholders who are scenario team members can also adversely impact the scenario intervention (Cairns et al. 2006). Also, the cognitive styles of the participants engaged in the workshop activities should be considered by the facilitator in terms of their impacts on the scenario development activity. For example, based on the Jungian model (Jung 1923), Franco et al. (2013) proposed that the presence of combinations of the four styles of information gathering and evaluation should be evaluated within the group-based membership. For example, any scenario group membership characterised solely by intuition thinking (NT) and intuition feeling (NF) members, i.e. a homogenous intuitive group, will be more effective—by optimistically engaging in social–emotional and task processes—thus experiencing high levels of commitment and satisfaction. In such predictions of the success of group-based activity, it must be noted that the homogeneity of the group members relates to the cognitive styles of group members rather than to similarities/differences in social background, age, role, education, etc.

Hodgkinson and Clarke (2007) argued that individuals who are analytically inclined may, in a scenario planning exercise, slow the proceedings, given their inclination to approach the scenario development process in a rational argument–based, step by step manner,.whereas individuals who are intuitively orientated, in the sense that they prefer to gain an overview of issues rather than analyse details, will proceed more speedily through the scenario development process.

Indeed, the effectiveness of scenario interventions can also be impacted by an assertive-facilitator bias, namely the *facilitator effect,* where, as asserted by Franco and Meadows (2007), a facilitator identifies with participants of a similar cognitive type and consequently ends up disregarding the views/inputs from participants of different cognitive styles. Given the facilitator is actively engaged in the scenario process, it can be difficult to disassociate him/herself from the group, and consequently the facilitator may then unintentionally associate with the individuals who display cognitive characteristics similar to his/her own, discounting views that are perhaps different. Franco and Meadows (2007) suggested that in order to eradicate such potential bias, the facilitator should, a priori, be aware of the participants' cognitive styles as well as his/her own. Furthermore, the facilitator should be capable, through experience, of identifying when such a biasing situation is unfolding and take the necessary action to address the situation, perhaps by even-handedly restating alternative views and by summarising different positions neither positively or negatively, Grinyer (2000).

## 10.5 Conclusions

In summary, we have documented that scenario thinking interventions within organizations can provide a challenge to business-as-usual thinking. Such a challenge is non-adversarial and can be introduced as standard way that organizations are facilitated to think more broadly and deeply about their business environment. However, the scenario development process can have pitfalls and problems. Scenario thinking is based on judgments—and judgments are often produced by heuristic processes that may result in bias. These biases may be magnified rather than attenuated within the scenario development process. Additionally, the act of facilitating a group of individual managers to think about the future is problematic. The views of some group members may achieve, or be given, more influence on the in-development scenarios than the views of other participants. Clearly, the scenario workshop facilitator must be sensitive to both the individual cognitions and styles of each group member and to the on-going group-based processes and interactions.

In our analysis, the content of in-development scenarios can be improved, although indirectly, by the quality of the facilitation. The facilitator must be skilled in his/her ability to identify the on-going group dynamics and also possess the skills to successfully intervene when behaviors such as group-think are adversely impacting the search for information, the expression of divergent views or the consideration of alternatives—all of which contribute to subsequent shifts in group-based thinking and can overcome initial inherent bias. Effective intervention techniques such as "handing back in changed form" (Phillips and Phillips 1993) can provide the participants with a different meaning regarding the focal situation; here the facilitator presents an analysis of a situation from a different perspective or frame, which assists the group in assigning new significance to the situation, overcoming the initial overconfidence inherent in a singular framing. The facilitator must also be mindful of non-verbal cues and thus be able to quickly deduce their impacts to then effectively address the situation to ensure that all participants are allowed equal air-time and that their contributions are accurately reflected in subsequent documentation. As Ackerman and Eden (2012, p. 282) noted, "good facilitators will seek to record what was meant rather than precisely what was said."

# References

Ackerman, F., and C. Eden. 2012. *Making strategy, mapping out strategic success.* London: Sage.

Amason, A.C., and D.M. Schwieger. 1994. Resolving the paradox of conflict, strategic decision making and organisational performance. *International Journal of Conflict Management* 5: 236–253.

Bradfield, R. 2008. Cognitive barriers in the scenario development process. *Advances in Developing Human Resources* 10: 198–215.

Cairns, G., G. Wright, K. Van der Heijden, R. Bradfield, and G. Burt. 2006. Enhancing foresight between multiple agencies: Issues in the use of scenario thinking to overcome fragmentation. *Futures* 38: 1010–1025.

De Dreu, C. 2006. When too little or too much hurts: Evidence for a curvilinear relationship between task conflict and innovation in teams. *Journal of Management* 32: 83–107.

De Geus, A. 1988. Planning and learning. *Harvard Business Review*, March–April: 70–74.

De Geus, A. 1997. The living company. *Harvard Business Review (Harvard Business Publishing)* Reprint 97203: 51–59.

Eden, C. 1992. Strategic management as a social process. *Journal of Management Studies* 29: 799–811.

Eden, C., and J. Radford. 1990. *Tackling strategic problems: The role of group decisions support*. London: Sage.

Franco, A.L., and M. Meadows. 2007. Exploring new directions for research in problem structuring method: On role of cognitive style. *Journal of Operational Research Society* 58: 1621–1629.

Franco, A.L., M. Meadows, and S.J. Armstrong. 2013. Exploring individual differences in scenario planning workshops: A cognitive style framework. *Technological Forecasting & Social Change* 80: 723–734.

Gavetti, G.M., R. Henderson, and S. Giorgi. 2004. Kodak and the digital revolution (A). *Harvard Business School Case Collection 705–448*. (Revised November 2005)

Grinyer, P.H. 2000. A cognitive approach to group strategic decision taking: A discussion of evolved practice in the light of received results. *Journal of Operational Research Society* 51: 21–35.

Hodgkinson, G.P., and I. Clarke. 2007. Exploring the cognitive significance of organizational strategizing. *Human Relations* 60: 243–255.

Hodgkinson, G.P., and M.P. Healey. 2008. Toward a (pragmatic) science of strategic intervention: Design propositions for scenario planning. *Organization Studies* 29: 435–457.

Hodgkinson, G.P., and G. Wright. 2002. Confronting strategic inertia in a top management team: Learning from failure. *Organizational Studies* 23: 949–977.

Jung, C. 1923. *Psychological types*. London: Pantheon.

Kahneman, D. 2011. *Thinking fast and slow*. London: Penguin.

Korsgaard, M.A., D.M. Schweiger, and H.J. Sapienza. 1995. Building commitment, attachment and trust in strategic decision making teams: The role of procedural justice. *Academy of Management Journal* 38: 60–84.

Kuhn, K.M., and J.A. Sniezek. 1996. Confidence and uncertainty in judgmental forecasting: Differential effects of scenario presentation. *Journal of Behavioral Decision Making* 9: 231–247.

Meissner, P., and T. Wulf. 2013. Cognitive benefits of scenario planning: Its impact on biases and decision quality. *Technological Forecasting and Social Change* 80(4): 801–814.

Miller, D. 1992. The Icarus paradox: How exceptional companies bring about their own downfall. *Business Horizons* 35(1): 24–36.

Moyer, K. 1996. Scenario planning at British Airways. *Long Range Planning* 29(2): 172–181.

Petit, V., and H. Bollaert. 2012. Flying too close to the sun? Hubris among CEOs and how to prevent it. *Journal of Business Ethics* 108: 265–283.

Phandis, S., C. Caplice, Y. Sheffi, and M. Singh. 2014. Effect of scenario planning on field experts' judgment of long-range investment decisions. *Strategic Management Journal* 36: 1401–1411.

Phillips, L.D., and M.C. Phillips. 1993. Facilitated work groups: Theory and practice. *The Journal of Operational Research Society* 4: 533–549.

Schnaars, S.P., and M.T. Topol. 1987. The use of multiple scenarios in sales forecasting: An empirical test. *International Journal of Forecasting* 3: 405–419.

Schoemaker, P. 1993. Multiple scenario development: Its conceptual and behavioral foundation. *Strategic Management Journal* 14: 193–213.

Schoemaker, P.J.H., G.S. Day, and S.A. Snyder. 2013. Integrating organizational networks, weak signals, strategic radars and scenario planning. *Technological Forecasting & Social Change* 80: 815–824.

Schwartz, P. 2011. *Learnings from the long view*. San Francisco: Global Business Network.

Schweiger, D.M., and W.R. Sandberg. 1986. Group approaches for improving strategic decision making: A comparative analysis of dialectical enquiry, devils advocacy and consensus. *Academy of Management Journal* 29: 51–71.

Sull, D. N. 2005. Strategy as active waiting. *Harvard Business Review (Harvard Business Publishing)*. Reprint R0509G: 1–11.

Tetlock, P.E. 2006. *Expert political judgment: How good is it? How can we know?* Princeton: Princeton University Press.

Tversky, A., and D. Kahneman. 1973. Availability: A heuristic for judging frequency and probability. *Cognitive Psychology* 5(2): 207–232.

Tversky, A., and D. Kahneman. 1981. The framing of decisions and the psychology of choice. *Science* 211(4481): 453–458.

Van Der Heijden, K., R. Bradfield, G. Cairns, and G. Wright. 2002. *The sixth sense, accelerating organizational learning with scenarios.* Chichester: Wiley.

# 11

# The Impact of Group Model Building on Behavior

Etiënne A.J.A. Rouwette

## 11.1 Introduction

The first wave of group model building research consisted of over 130 studies describing single applications, brought together and analysed in two review papers. Research on exploring the underlying mechanism can broadly be placed into three groups: studies focusing on participants as recipients of information, those focusing on participants as sources of information, and those focusing on participants looking at the interaction between receiving and contributing information. The second wave of studies uses theories from social psychology to explain how modeling impacts knowledge and behavior. In modeling sessions, participants receive information, which might persuade them to change their evaluation of the issue at hand. Changes in evaluations in turn lead to changes in intentions and actions. While these studies focus on receiving informa-

Etiënne A.J.A. Rouwette (✉)
Radboud University, Thomas van Aquinostraat 1.1.31, P.O. Box 9108, 6500 HK Nijmegen, The Netherlands

© The Editor(s) (if applicable) and The Author(s) 2016    **213**
M. Kunc et al. (eds.), *Behavioral Operational Research*,
DOI 10.1057/978-1-137-53551-1_11

tion, the third wave of studies looks at participants as actively constructing information. A model helps to bring pieces of information together, but a necessary precondition is that information is brought out into the open. As each individual participant knows only a fragment of the total set of information, pieces of the puzzle need to be brought together to get an overview. This means that their decision to share information is crucial to the modeling effort. Research shows that members of freely interacting groups often do not share essential information, resulting in suboptimal decisions. Interaction in modeling groups is less free in the sense that participants are led through a series of steps designed to elicit and combine relevant information. It seems logical to expect that compared to freely interacting groups, modeling groups exchange more information and come to better decisions. Finally, a fourth wave of studies looks at the interaction between receiving and contributing information. How does the gradual emergence of model structure influence communication between participants? Do participants share information with all others equally, or are participants higher in the hierarchy more likely to send and receive?

This chapter starts by explaining the practice of group model building in more depth. The main part describes the four waves in turn. Ideas for further research are formulated at the end.

## 11.2  Group Model Building in Practice

An example may serve to show how group model building is used in practice. In 2012 a company active in the part-time labour market feared that the economic downturn that had started in 2008 would eventually impact their organisation (Bachurina 2012). The strategy of the company in essence came down to bringing together two types of clients: temporary workers looking for a job and company clients looking to fill temporary positions. In a growing economy, temporary workers would visit the company offices in increasing numbers. Companies often could not find new recruits fast enough and therefore hired the part-time labour organisation to find temporary workers. Some managers were worried that while this mechanism increased revenues in a growing economy, it would also lead to increasing losses in a downturn. A group model building project typically starts with a conversation between a contact client and a modeler. The client relates how he or she sees the problematic situation and the desired outcomes of a potential project. If facilitated System Dynamics modeling is found to be a suitable approach, a topic area is chosen and potential participants are invited to a series of sessions. A rule of thumb is to invite participants from all areas of expertise that bear on the topic, in addition to people who have a role in the implementation of conclusions.

In the first session, the aim of the project is introduced to the participants. Participants are invited to narrow down the issue that the modeling project will focus on. In System Dynamics, a problem is expressed in the form of a reference mode: the behavior of a performance measure over time. This reference mode may take the form of a drawing by participants or be constructed on the basis of data from information systems. The left hand side of Fig. 11.1 shows profit as the central reference mode in this case.

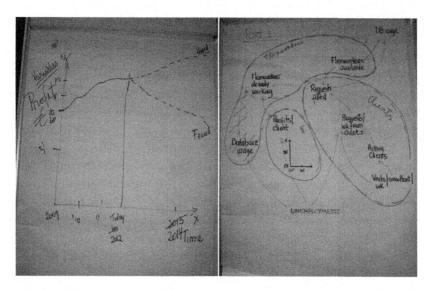

**Fig. 11.1** Reference mode of behavior (*left*) and causal diagram at end of first session

Expressing the central issue of interest in the form of a reference mode of behavior sets the stage for the rest of the modeling effort. In essence, participants are asked to identify how this behavior came about, by jointly building the model structure that is responsible for the problem. In this sense, system dynamicists strongly believe in operational thinking: those factors that are connected to the problem should be identified and related to one another. An example by Richmond (1993) may clarify what is meant by operational thinking. An economic journal published a study on a sophisticated econometric model designed to predict milk production in the United States. The model included a large set of variables linked together in complex equations, but the number of cows was not included in the model. "If one asks how milk is actually generated, one discovers that cows are absolutely essential to the process" (Richmond 1993, p. 128). The focus on operational thinking is different from other (facilitated) operational research modeling approaches that focus on mapping, for instance, ideal systems or personal beliefs on means–ends relations. Models that are created in group model building have a dual identity (Zagonel 2004). On the one hand, they can be seen as tools that align views of stakeholders (the boundary object view). On the other hand, models may be said to represent reality (the micro world view). Which of the two views is emphasised depends, among other things, on the aim of the modeling project.

In group model building, as in other facilitated modeling approaches, the person guiding the group through the steps of modeling remains neutral with regard to content. The facilitator helps the group to articulate their ideas and relate these to each other in a series of steps. Participants are asked to individually note down variables that relate to the issue of interest. These are collected and noted down on a whiteboard or computer screen. Next, the central variable, in this case the company's profit, is placed in the middle of the board or screen. The facilitator then asks the group members to suggest a variable that impacts the central variable. When one participant suggests a variable and its relation to the central variable, the facilitator notes this down on the screen and then asks the rest of the group if they agree. Other group members may suggest changes and additional variables, but the ground rule is that a relation is drawn only if all participants agree. In this way, a model is incrementally built and the list of unconnected variables grows smaller. The model at any time captures what has been discussed and agreed upon so far. The right hand side of Fig. 11.1 shows a causal loop diagram that emerged over the course of one session.

In follow-up sessions, the model may be expanded until the point where the group has sufficient confidence that the structure that has been built can explain the observed behavior. Analysis of the model concentrates on feedback loops. At the end of a group model building project, a model typically consists of multiple interacting feedback loops. When participants have adequate confidence in the model structure, policies to change the situation in a desired direction can be added to the model and their effects analysed. Projects may stop short of formal modeling when the client's goal of increased understanding has been reached. Nevertheless, most system dynamicists would agree that formal modeling, even without extensive reference data, will always contribute to the consistency of the model and improve understanding. Formalising the model comes down to expressing each relation in mathematical form and assigning parameter values.

Figure 11.2 shows a stock and flow diagram, which is used to visualise formal models. Formal models may be simulated over time, so that model behavior can be compared to the reference mode. This comparison is one of several validation tests that need to be passed if a model is to

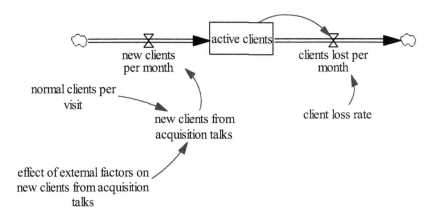

**Fig. 11.2**  Stock and flow diagram on client acquisition

be used as a micro world. Still, a formal model can operate as a boundary object. Vennix, one of the founders of group model building, once explained the benefits of a formal model to clients as follows: "What it brings to the process is one additional participant. This participant is rather dumb, as he only knows what you have told him. But he is also very consistent: he can tell you exactly what the consequences of your assumptions are." In the case of the temporary work organisation, the initial causal loop diagram was translated into a formal model. Data from the internal ERP system was used to populate the model with data. Testing ideas against data revealed several inconsistencies in the participants' reasoning. Different scenarios of economic growth were simulated and compared to the business-as-usual scenario. Contrary to expectations, the scenarios did not show large differences in number of clients or resulting profits. Consultant visits to prospective client organisations turned out to have a larger impact than initially assumed.

This example illustrates both one particular approach to working with participants and some of the core ideas of System Dynamics. System dynamicists assume that feedback loops are important elements of a system's structure and responsible for its unexpected behavior. As human beings lack the ability to predict how a system consisting of multiple interacting feedback loops will behave, mathematical models are necessary to infer behavior from structure. If the role of mathematical models is emphasised, it may seem a straightforward conclusion that the most important information on messy problems consists of precise, numerical data. We need numbers in order to build a mathematical model. What is far more important, however, is qualitative information on how decisions by actors in the system are made. To a large extent, this information cannot be found in information systems or databases but is part of stakeholders' mental data. "Searching questions, asked at points throughout the organisation under study by one skilled in knowing what is critical in System Dynamics, can divulge far more useful information than is apt to exist in recorded data" (Forrester 1961, p. 58). In other words, the idea that stakeholders are important sources of information has been around from the start of the System Dynamics field. Another role of stakeholders is in receiving and accepting model results and is closely related to implementation. Roberts (1973) highlighted the importance of choosing a problem that is relevant to a decision maker, otherwise he or she will not bother with the modeling process or the resulting recommendations. Apart from showing how the core assumptions of System Dynamics play out in practice, the example also shows one particular process of involving clients in System Dynamics modeling. A wide range of approaches to working with clients, from generic approaches to quite specific elements of modeling sessions, is reported in the literature. While participation in building System Dynamics models has been around since the start of the field in the 1950s, the term *group model building* was first used in a paper by Richardson and Andersen in 1995. *Group model building* now serves as a generic label for at least six distinct facilitated modeling formats, which are described in more depth by Andersen et al. (2007). Recently the focus of discussion has shifted to fine-grained analysis of short pieces of interaction. Andersen and Richardson (1997) introduced the idea of so-called scripts: precise descriptions of a specific phase in a modeling session of 20 min or less. Scripts have an aim, a step-by-step outline of what to say and do with clients and a specified product. By combining scripts, the agenda for a single session or project can be developed. Hovmand and colleagues (2012) have compiled a list of scripts and advice on how to use them, and made all material freely available via Wikibooks.[1]

## 11.3  First Wave: Reviews of Assessment Studies

The previous section indicated that although group model building applications have a set of core ideas in common, a wide variety of ways to involve clients may be used in practice. At least six different approaches have emerged, and a facilitator can choose from a list of scripts when designing a session or project. It is not surprising that the first wave of group model building evaluation has focused on bringing together different group model building applications and comparing them with regard to process and outcomes. Two reviews are available: Rouwette et al. (2002) gather group model building studies published up until

---

[1] https://en.wikibooks.org/wiki/Scriptapedia.

1999; Scott et al. (2015) look at studies published between 2001 and 2014.

Studies were included if they described a System Dynamics modeling project involving a client team in at least the stage of conceptualisation, and empirical results on its effectiveness were described. Rouwette et al. find a total of 107 studies, which in the main (84) address organisational problems, and strive for implementation of results. Those for which no implementation is expected are usually training or demonstration sessions, often with student participants. Studies also differ with regard to research design:

- 88 studies are qualitative case studies gathering data through observation (all 88), individual assessment interviews (six) and group interviews (two);
- 19 studies use a quantitative estimation of results, through a posttest survey (14) or through questionnaires employed at two points in time (five).

Before addressing the results of the review, four issues are important to address. First, it is likely that studies are biased towards successful interventions. Second, it is important to note that the majority of these studies depend on participants' self-assessment of results after the intervention. This is problematic, as people are poor judges of both the extent and the causes of learning (Nisbett and Wilson 1977). Only five studies collect data before and after the project. Third, group model building is not a uniform intervention but, as described in the previous section, uses a range of processes and scripts. Each of the applications addresses a particular problem and works with a particular group of participants, and the temporary workers case reported above offers one example. The range of available scripts and ways to design the process are reflected in the cases. About one in four starts from a preliminary model, the others from a blank sheet of paper. A total of 22 studies result in qualitative models; 85 result in a quantitative model of which 56 involve the client in the formalisation phase. About one half of the projects are completed within three months, and two out of three in six months. Fourth, studies look at a range of group model building outcomes, but no single study addresses the full set of outcomes. Given the variety in context and process of modeling interventions, outcomes are remarkably similar. These are some of the key outcomes reported in the review:

- Communication: measured in 40 studies, of which 39 indicate a positive effect
- Learning: 96 of 101 indicate a positive effect
- Consensus: 49 of 53 indicate a positive effect
- Commitment: 31 of 35 report a positive effect
- Changes in behavior: 29 of 30 report a positive effect
- Implementation of results: 42 of 84 report a positive effect

There are few differences in outcomes among types of studies. Qualitative models seem to be less likely to lead to commitment, consensus or system changes than (small or large) quantitative models. The context in which qualitative models are built is different and time investment is lower than for full quantification. Differences between types of modeling interventions may therefore also be due to differences in context or the time participants spent in sessions. On other outcome measures there are no differences. A recent review (Scott et al. 2015) looks at quantitative assessment studies published from 2001 to 2014. A total of 26 studies are found. Where studies in the previous review are to a large extent based on self-assessment of results after the intervention, 15 studies in this review use measurements at two points in time. Results are in line with the previous review, in that Scott and colleagues also find that group model building achieves a range of outcomes such as communication, learning, consensus, behavioral change and implementation. Four studies in the review compare the approach to "normal meetings" and find that group model building is more effective. No studies were found that compare effectiveness of group model building to other modeling interventions.

Several studies that are included in these reviews attempt to explain why outcomes were created. One causal mechanism, formulated at a quite generic level, is the following. Ultimately, the aim of facilitated System Dynamics is to change the problematic situation for the better. In order for *system improvement* to materialise, someone will have to imple-

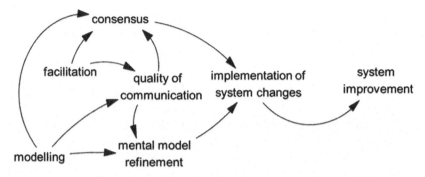

**Fig. 11.3** A possible causal mechanism relating the group model building process

ment system changes. These may be in line with recommendations from the modeling project or may come down to (conscious or unconscious) changes in individual behavior. Implementation of system changes is more likely if insight into the problem of interest has shifted (or in other words, if learning has occurred). Another influence on implementation may be the group consensus that has developed over the course of the modeling project. Consensus and insight may develop on the basis of the communication process between participants, which is supported by both the model and facilitation (Fig. 11.3).

In the next wave of evaluations several authors zoom in on particular elements of this causal chain, compare elements and relations to existing theories and test to what extent these explain group model building results.

## 11.4   Second Wave: Participants as Recipients of Information

The second wave of evaluation studies brings together those contributions that look at how people's opinions change due to the information they receive in the modeling engagement. Here the focus is still on participant behavior after the project, but an explanation is sought in the information that is exchanged during modeling. Two theories have been proposed. The first centres on the concept of mental models. This is a central concept in System Dynamics, as many in the field assume that lasting improvement in decision making can follow only from a significant change in decision makers' mental models (e.g. Doyle and Ford 1999; Geurts and Vennix 1989). Doyle and Ford (1999, p. 414) consider a number of different interpretations of the term used in System Dynamics publications and beyond, and ultimately arrive at the following definition: "A mental model of a dynamic system is a relatively enduring and accessible, but limited, internal conceptual representation of an external system (historical, existing or projected) whose structure is analogous to the perceived structure of that system." Richardson et al. (1994) specify in more detail which elements a mental model contains. They separate mental models into means, ends and means–ends models. Goals are stored in the ends model, while strategies, tactics and policy levers are part of the means model. The means–ends model connects these two and consists of detailed causal relations (design logic) as well as more simple if–then statements (operator logic). In driving a car, design logic refers, for instance, to the inner workings of the engine. An example of operator logic would be that if you brake hard on a wet road, your car is likely to skid. Andersen et al.'s (1994) preliminary conclusion is that providing operator logic is necessary for improving decisions in complex situations. This is surprising, as many system dynamicists would assume that making participants familiar with detailed model structure and its corresponding behavior is the key to increasing insight and changing behavior. In terms of Andersen and colleagues, this constitutes design logic and is not likely to be effective.

A second theory also focuses on how information changes participants' minds but, in addition, makes the link from changes in insights to changes in behavior explicit. This line of study (Rouwette et al. 2011; Rouwette et al. 2009) looks at the relation between attitudes and behavior and the impact of persuasion on attitude change. The impact of attitudes on behavior is shown in the right hand side of Fig. 11.4 below. In Ajzen's theory of planned behavior, (Ajzen 1991; Fishbein and Ajzen 2011) intentions are the immediate antecedent of behavior. Intentions

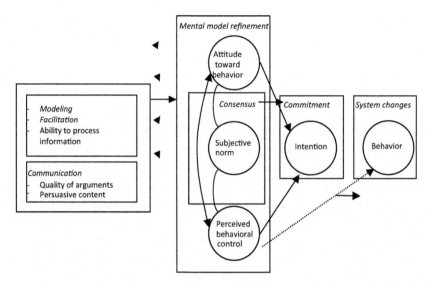

**Fig. 11.4** The impact of group model building on persuasion, attitudes and behavior (based on Rouwette 2003, p. 116)

are in turn explained by attitude toward behavior, subjective norm and perceived behavioral control.

Let's take a manager of the part-time labour company described in the example above as an example. Ajzen's theory addresses particular behaviors. Imagine the manager is considering hiring more personnel. The theory then assumes that her intention to hire personnel becomes stronger if:

- attitude toward behavior, or the evaluation of the outcomes of this action, becomes more positive; for instance, when he or she expects more personnel to be able to attract more company clients and eventually lead to more turnover;
- subjective norm, or the degree to which he or she expects significant others to think he or she should engage in this behavior, grows stronger; for instance, when he or she realises senior management is more positive about hiring than he or she expected;

- perceived behavioral control, or the evaluation of control over the behavior, increases; for instance, when he or she realises that employees can be hired faster than initially predicted.

Ajzen's theory is probably one of the most widely used in social psychology and has been tested in a multitude of studies. In addition to its conceptual structure, it also comes with recommendations on empirical testing. An example is Fishbein and Ajzen's (1975) emphasis on compatibility of measures in order to ensure a substantial correlation. They suggest that general attitudes with respect to organisations, institutions, groups, individuals or ideas are good predictors of general behavioral categories summed over multiple behaviors. In contrast, specific attitudes will be good predictors of specific actions.

Intentions, attitudes, norms and control can be related to the group model building outcomes discussed earlier. Intention is similar to commitment in that both capture the effort a person wants to exert in order to reach a goal. Attitude toward behavior is closely related to the ends model described before. The subjective norm and consensus are similar in their emphasis on the subjective or personal definition of a situation. Perceived behavioral control seems related to the means model mentioned earlier.

The left hand side of Fig. 11.4 shows how modeling and facilitation are related to changes in attitude, norm and control. Theories on persuasion (Chaiken et al. 1996; Petty and Cacioppo 1986; Petty and Wegener 1998) specify two routes through which attitudes can be changed: the central and the peripheral route. The central route consists of understanding and evaluation of arguments. A persuasive message is received; arguments in the message are identified, contrasted with existing knowledge and judged on their validity. Quality of arguments and their persuasiveness have an influence only when taking this first route. Following the peripheral route, evaluations are changed on the basis of simple decision rules, or heuristics. An example of a heuristic is: "if a large number of studies support these conclusions, I accept them as valid". The decision on which route will be used depends on the person's motivation and ability to process information. If both motivation and ability are high, the central route will be more effective in changing attitudes. Motivation is high when, for example, the situation is high in personal relevance.

Ability to process is high when a person can understand the message, deduce arguments and compare these to her own ideas. Rouwette (2003) assumes that ability to process information is where group model building makes an essential contribution, as it helps participants to integrate and structure available information about a problem.

What evidence has been found that group model building effects actually materialise along these lines? Rouwette (2003) uses the concepts described above to assess the effectiveness of modeling in five applied cases. A total of 29 participants and 86 behavioral options are included in the analysis. In line with expectations, participants perceive a high ability to process information and exchange of arguments. Attitudes and subjective norm change in line with project recommendations; perceived behavioral control does not change. Rouwette et al. (2011) test relations in the model proposed above in seven modeling cases (five from Rouwette's study and two additional cases), with a total of 42 participants and 124 behavioral options. As expected, participants are motivated and able to process information exchanged in the sessions. Information contained persuasive arguments. Ability to process information, however, impacts only one of the three variables, as expected. A structural equations analysis shows that ability has only a weak relation to attitude and no relation to subjective norm or perceived behavioral control. Both studies conclude that control does not change, and several reasons for this lack of impact come to mind. It may be that participants who before the modeling engagement see only a limited part of the issue, over the course of the project learn about other aspects and come to realise that the problem is even more complex than they initially thought. However, even if this is the case in qualitative projects, one would expect that the simulation of policies helps participants to identify levers for change and therefore increases their sense of control. Both qualitative and quantitative projects may suffer from an emphasis on design logic at the cost of operator logic and therefore may not give participants concrete guidelines to improve their situation (Andersen et al. 1994). With regard to attitudes, Rouwette (2003) does see a change in line with recommendations. But Rouwette et al. (2011) find that attitudes are only weakly related to ability to process and in addition are negatively impacted by argument quality. At first sight this result is difficult to understand: if there are better arguments for a proposed action, participants' support declines? One explanation may be the compatibility of measurements. Fishbein and Ajzen's (1975) recommendations on compatibility were followed with regard to all variables in Ajzen's theory except for communication. The measurement of ability to process is generic, but actions and corresponding intentions, attitudes, norms and control were formulated at a much more specific level. It may thus be the case that some participants felt that communication in general was quite open but that with regard to the particular action they were interested in, they did not hear anything that was both new and relevant.

The second wave of evaluation leaves us with a better understanding of what kind of information is particularly likely to change the opinion of participants in a modeling session. It also specifies the path from opinion to behavior after the modeling intervention. The causal mechanisms have been tested in a limited number of studies, yielding limited support but also pointing to measurement problems and possibly to unexpected impacts of modeling. It is also clear that the causal mechanisms presented here tell only part of the story. In particular, they give us little to go on when trying to pinpoint exactly which piece of modeling output is likely to sway participants. The general idea is that information needs to be relevant and novel to someone if it is to impact his opinion and may be more effective when formulated as operator logic. But in order to be persuasive, information apparently needs to be tailored to the person and even to the particular actions that person is considering. This means that a piece of information may change one person's opinion but not another's, or may change one type of behavior but not a slightly different type. Researchers in facilitated modeling may be most interested in a more generic question: in comparison to unsupported decision making, such as a free discussion, why does modeling seem to work better? In terms of the concepts introduced in this section, how does modeling help to identify effective arguments?

## 11.5 Third Wave: Participants as Sources of Information

Where the previous wave of studies tried to discover the causes of changes in behavior after sessions, studies in this third group focus squarely on behavior during sessions—in particular communicative behavior. The temporary workers case described at the beginning of this chapter showed how participants over the course of the project jointly construct a model of their situation of interest. The facilitator designs a process, typically with the help of scripts, which invites participants to identify relevant information and share it with others. Information is confronted and combined, and aspects that participants all agree to end up in the model. Participant opinions may also be compared against available data, contributing to further refinement of the model. Since the facilitator is neutral with regard to content and moreover does not have the detailed content knowledge that participants have, relevant variables, relations and loops will have to be suggested by participants. If a piece of information is not mentioned and not revealed by other data later, it will not be part of the model. At any moment during the modeling process, a participant has to decide if her personal expertise and opinion is relevant to the topic that is being discussed and, if so, formulate it in terms of the model. Fig. 11.2 shows a particular part of the temporary workers model: the part related to client acquisition. If the model is to represent client acquisition in a valid manner, participants with information on this topic will need to speak up so that their suggestions can be incorporated into the model. As participants come from different departments or organisations, it is not a given that they immediately see how their personal opinions and expertise are relevant to a particular topic.

This situation is similar to a line of research known as *hidden profile studies*. Stasser and Titus (1985, 2003) set out to study information sharing in groups. They provided group members with pieces of information, some of them known to one individual only and others known to more group members or to all of them. For instance, let's imagine there is a group of three people that want to choose between options A and B. There are four pieces of information in favour of option A. This information is shared, meaning that it is known to all three of the members. There are seven pieces of information in favour of option B. Only one of these is shared, and in addition each group member has two pieces that are only known to him or her. This is the unique information. If group members share all of their information, they will realise that there is more information in favour of B than of A (seven against four). However, before the discussion starts, each member has four pieces in favour of A and three in favour of B (one shared and two unique). Initially, he or she will think A is the best alternative. A hidden profile is created when each group member has unique information and the best alternative is hidden from members. They will have to pool their information in order to identify the best alternative. Typically, group members discuss shared information and only a minority of groups (around one in five) choose the best option. These findings have been supported by a series of studies (Stasser and Titus 2003). Some of these studies focused on ways to increase information exchange and prevent groups from falling into the hidden profile trap. Factors such as facilitation, assignment of expert roles, process accountability, a shared task representation, critical thinking norms and counterfactual thinking have been explored (McCardle-Keurentjes et al. 2008).

Many of these factors seem an inherent part of a facilitated modeling process. As a consequence, it does not seem too far-fetched to assume that participants in group model building are more likely than unsupported groups to exchange information and identify the best solution. McCardle-Keurentjes (2015; McCardle-Keurentjes et al. 2008) has tested this assumption in two group level[2] and one individual[3] experiments.

---

[2] In his master's thesis, Ansems (2010) uses part of the dataset of McCardle-Keurentjes (2015) to test the difference between two group model building meetings and two meetings as usual, with regard to critical events and decision development.

[3] The focus here is on modeling in groups, but several studies in addition to McCardle-Keurentjes's (2015) work offer relevant insights on the use of models in individual settings. Hodgkinson et al. (1999) conclude that cognitive mapping may be an effective means to limit effects of the framing bias; Wright and Goodwin (2002) offer a critique. Pala (2008) finds that causal loop diagrams can decrease escalation of commitment and selective exposure to information.

Participants in her study construct causal loop diagrams. Two outcomes in particular are relevant here: coverage of information (the extent to which task information is mentioned at least once) and focus of discussion (which part of the discussion focused on a particular type of information, for instance, unique or shared information). As the latter also includes mentioning a particular piece of information more than once, this outcome also fits into the next wave of studies, which addresses interaction between sending and receiving information. Contrary to expectations, model building groups had no better coverage of unique information and neither did they focus more of their discussion on unique information. Modeling groups also did not make decisions of higher quality than unsupported groups. Modeling groups did spend more time on long term information and less time on discussing solutions. The main outcomes expected of the individual experiment are likewise not found. McCardle-Keurentjes suggests several possible reasons for the lack of differences between modeling and unsupported groups. The participants in her controlled experiments were students, with no stake nor substantial experience in the problem to be discussed. The time for discussion and model construction was limited to one hour.

The third wave of evaluation leaves us with somewhat of a puzzle. As McCardle-Keurentjes (2015) notes, testing whether unique information would be exchanged more in group model building than in unsupported meetings would seem to constitute an easy test. However, the intervention failed that test. Part of the explanation may indeed be that in her experiment time was limited (one hour versus a minimum of two times three hours for qualitative modeling in real-life settings). But why facilitated System Dynamics did not contribute to better *coverage* of unique information, even if in only one hour, is unclear. The next wave again evaluates modeling in applied settings, looking at how contribution and reception of information interact.

## 11.6 Fourth Wave: Interaction Between Contributing and Receiving of Information

The description of the second wave of studies ended with the question of how group model building helps to identify arguments. From the third wave no definite conclusion could be drawn: facilitated modeling does not seem to make it more likely that unique information is identified. Which other explanations for the effects of modeling on insight, attitudes and behavior were suggested? Three ideas are put forward in the literature.[4] Black and Andersen (2012) propose that models can function as boundary objects. De Gooyert (2016) understands the modeling process as the construction of a shared frame of reference. Van Nistelrooij et al. (2012) turn to social exchange theory to better understand the role of power distance in communication.

According to Black and Andersen (2012), the importance of boundary objects follows from their use as a tangible representation of dependencies across disciplinary, organisational, social or cultural lines that can be transformed by all discussion participants. A representation functions as a boundary object if it is a tangible two- or three-dimensional shared object; depicts dependencies among participants' objectives, expertise, resources and actions; and—importantly—can be changed by all involved. Black and Andersen describe how a boundary object is incrementally built, using examples of modeling groups struggling with conflict. "The visible script products, wielded as boundary objects, provide early and growing evidence that participants are being heard by facilitators and by one another. This evidence builds trust and at least a limited sense of psychological safety [...]" (Black and Andersen 2012, p. 203). The first stage of building the boundary object is to generate tangible

---

[4] Two master's thesis studies using a limited set of groups are also relevant to the interaction between sending and receiving information. Van Kessel (2012) looks at the difference between five group model building meetings and five meetings as usual with regard to decision process (equality of interactions and perceived procedural justice) and outcomes (outcome satisfaction, decision scheme satisfaction, consensus and commitment). Participants are students. Adriaans (2014) analyses two group model building sessions with medical specialists with regard to information elaboration and asking questions.

ideas for the group to consider. In the second stage, group members identify interdependencies between ideas and perspectives, showing consequences of the ideas identified so far. Black and Andersen describe how two groups with opposing points of view managed to work together in listing their ideas and identifying interdependencies, using a computer system that allowed ideas to be represented anonymously. By uncoupling ideas from people, the group managed to build on each other's contributions. The third stage is a discussion that transforms some of the ideas, by modifying what was gathered so far on the basis of the group's shared input. The emerging diagram helps to depersonalise conflict and in one case ran directly counter to the ideas of a powerful executive in the meeting, without challenging him directly. Finally, in the fourth stage the group uses the transformed ideas and prioritisation to identify ways forward. In a session with representatives of different agencies, the first three stages had been completed and a shared representation built, to some extent bridging the differences in goals, areas of expertise and actions of participants. When the close of the session drew near, the commissioner who had convened the meeting decided to bypass the shared visual representation and unilaterally proposed a list of eight actions to take the results further. The participants never followed up on the discussion, and the actions were not implemented. Black and Andersen assume that the commissioner's unilateral proposal took away the opportunity for the participants to transform the shared representation and that therefore the fourth stage, identifying actions together, was never completed. By laying out four stages of information exchange in modeling sessions, each stage building on the former and all four necessary if the group wants to identify joint actions, Black and Andersen (2012) enrich our understanding of how group model building helps to identify arguments. In effect, when information shared by participants is solidified in the form of a visual representation, this establishes a level of trust. Trust in turn allows the group to move on to exchanging another kind of information, in turn enriching the diagram, and so on.

De Gooyert (2016) draws on the framing literature to conceptualise what is going on in modeling sessions (e.g. Kaplan 2008; Snow et al. 1986). He analyses eight sessions with a total of 96 participants. Each session lasted about five hours and brought together 8–15 participants from a range of organisations in the energy sector. On the basis of video recordings and transcriptions of the conversations in the workshops, De Gooyert analyses how participants engage in frame building and frame relating. Frame building comes down to identifying important cues and expressing the meaning attached to these cues, justifying ideas using analogies, metaphors or other sources of authority. Interestingly, listening plays an important role in frame building, as it helps to confirm and amplify suggested frames. As soon as a frame is relatively stable, participants start to connect it to other frames. De Gooyert finds several frame relating strategies: translating, extending, dissecting, appealing and merging, thereby refining the work of Snow et al. (1986). Strategies for frame building and relating explain why some workshops result in more shared cognitions and others fail to achieve convergence.

Van Nistelrooij et al. (2012) offer another perspective on how sending and receiving of information interact. They build on social exchange theory (Lawler et al. 2008; Lawler and Yoon 1998), which looks at how social exchanges take place in a network. For each interacting dyad in the network, the difference in power between the partners in the dyad shapes their exchange relation. A higher power difference will lead to a lower number of exchanges. Successful exchanges will in turn lead both partners in the dyad to attach more positive emotions to the relation. This in turn fosters commitment to the relation and a feeling of cohesion. In a pilot study, Van Nistelrooij et al. compare meetings in a Dutch government organisation with a total of 11 participants. Participants met once in a regular meeting and once in a group model building meeting. The first half hour of each meeting was transcribed, coded by a single coder and analysed with regard to interactions. Power was measured by asking organisation members to indicate the perceived power of each meeting participant. Employees of the focus organisation were presented with a matrix of 16 members of their organisation. People were presented in pairs, and for each pair the employees were asked which one was higher in authority. As expected, in the regular meeting the interaction between partners in a dyad dropped off fast with increasing power distance. In the group model building session, the decline was much less prominent. These results provide some evidence for the idea that in facilitated modeling participants interact on a more equal level than in a meeting as usual. However, the content of the exchanges was not yet analysed, so it remained to be seen how important or relevant the information exchanged in dyads was. Ideally, one would like to see that a participant who is perceived to be in a lower power position reveals crucial information that makes the model more relevant to the problem at stake.

The fourth wave of studies offers three pathways in which contributing and receiving of information interact. Four incremental stages of constructing shared visual representations help participants to build trust and joint understanding. Frame building and relating help to achieve convergence in opinions. There is some indication that facilitation and modeling neutralise the effect of power differences: even partners in a dyad that are very different in power exchange information in modeling sessions, but less so in meetings as usual.

## 11.7  Conclusion

In this contribution I reviewed studies on the impact of facilitated System Dynamics modeling, with a particular emphasis on behavior. Behavior has been studied from two perspectives. On the one hand, System Dynamics modeling aims to change a problematic situation for the better, which necessitates implementation of results. Implementation assumes that at least some stakeholders in the situation at hand change their behavior. On the other hand, a facilitated approach also encourages particular behavior of participants in sessions while discouraging other types of behavior. For instance, information sharing and equal participation are supported, high levels of cognitive conflict and politicking are avoided. Early evaluation studies of group model building concentrated on implementation, or behavior after the sessions. To explain (lack of) implementation, researchers and practitioners frequently referred to the interaction between participants, the problem and the model, much of which can be observed during modeling sessions. To check assumptions on effective ingredients, most early studies relied on opinions of participants assessed in interviews or questionnaires after the sessions. Only recently have studies tried to open the black box by capturing and analysing what goes on

**Table 11.1** Main topics in four phases of group model building evaluation and selected references

| | |
|---|---|
| *Reviews of assessment studies* | |
| A review of 107 studies shows the effect of modeling on communication, learning, consensus, commitment, behavior and implementation | Rouwette et al. (2002) |
| A review of 26 quantitative assessments shows similar outcomes | Scott et al. (2015) |
| *Receiver perspective* | |
| Mental models consist of means, ends and means–ends models; operator logic may be more effective in changing mental models than design logic | Richardson et al. (1994), Andersen et al. (1994) |
| The impact of modeling may be understood in terms of persuasion and the impact of attitudes, subjective norms and perceived control on behavior | Rouwette (2003) |
| *Sender perspective* | |
| Participants in modeling sessions may have unique information that needs to be shared before the best solution can be identified (hidden profile condition) | McCardle-Keurentjes (2015) |
| *Interaction of sending and receiving information* | |
| Models operate as boundary objects and are constructed in four iterative phases | Black and Andersen (2012) |
| Participants in modeling sessions build and relate frames | De Gooyert (2016) |
| Perceived power of participants does not impact information sharing in modeling sessions | Van Nistelrooij et al. (2012) |

in model-supported meetings. This contribution described four phases of evaluation of group model building: reviews of assessment studies, the receiver perspective, the sender perspective, and interaction of sending and receiving information. Table 11.1 presents the key topics.

The picture that emerges after describing these four phases of evaluation is more consistent than perhaps expected. Theories and studies, some of them preliminary, seem to build on each other and fill in each other's blind spots. In broad lines, and with some ideas more supported by evidence than others, the impact of group model building on behavior seems to materialise along the following lines: A group of participants is brought together because of their knowledge, power and/or interest in a dynamic problem. There may be a degree of conflict between participants, but all commit to spending a limited time on trying to better understand the problem. A facilitator guides them through a process of building a model that attempts to explain the problematic behavior over time. Participants share their ideas on the problem, first drawing up a list and then relating ideas. The resulting diagram is modified on the basis of the group discussion, may be compared to available data, and ultimately points to actions that may improve the situation. Each phase that is completed successfully creates trust and lays the groundwork for the next stage. In the process, participants build a joint understanding by constructing and relating frames. Facilitation and modeling help participants, despite their differences in power, to bring relevant information out into the open. Unique information is shared, but not more than in regular meetings. So far, behavior in meetings was discussed. Because participants receive new and relevant information that may lead them to reconsider some of their opinions, behavior outside of sessions is also impacted. Participants change their ideas on desirable ends and about how means and ends relate. This is closely related to changes in attitudes and subjective norm. If the information in the session represents not only design logic but also operator logic, perceptions of means and of behavioral control may also change. Opinions on ends (attitudes), means (perceived control) and means–ends relations converge and create a strong subjective norm. All of these contribute to changed intentions and ultimately changed behavior. Provided that the quality of the model is sufficient, implementation of proposed recommendations will help to change the situation for the better.

There are several spots in which details are missing from this picture. Possibly, on closer inspection, inconsistencies or impossibilities will emerge, as in the works of Escher and Magritte. It is likely to be too much too hope for that facilitated modeling turns out to be a purely democratic process in which the truth is jointly discovered and recommendations are implemented. What sounds more realistic is that group model building helps to counter some biases in human decision making, by exploiting others. This is similar to Schoemaker's (1993) discovery that the use of multiple scenarios reduces overconfidence by reinforcing the conjunction fallacy.

Several limitations, puzzles and avenues for further research stand out. McCardle-Keurentjes (2015) arrives at the surprising conclusion that students participating in group model building do not exchange more unique information than students participating in meetings as usual. In addition, many of the positive results of the reviews (Rouwette et al. 2002; Scott et al. 2015) follow from participants' self-assessment of results after the intervention, while we know that people are poor judges of learning (Nisbett and Wilson 1977). De Gooyert (2016) points out that System Dynamics seems to have a blind spot in the sense that it does not address the political dimension of the policy process. Alternative paths through which group model building influences participants' behavior inside and outside of sessions can be identified. The fact that participants in System Dynamics modeling are asked a descriptive or explanatory question may be important: How are decisions made in this part of the problem? How can we explain the observed data? This is different from asking how future goals may be achieved, or who was involved in/is responsible for the problem or any number of other questions. Another factor may be the level of formality of the models used: formal enough to provide some structure to the conversation, but not so formal as to stifle discussion (Andersen et al. 2007). Finally, a lot can be learned from a comparison between group model building and other facilitated modeling approaches. For instance, Tavella and Franco (2015) also look at micro level interactions between participants, and between participants and the model. Franco, Rouwette and Korzilius (2015) use interaction analysis to understand how consensus develops in modeling groups.

An earlier study (Rouwette and Vennix 2006) concluded by saying that the most promising path forward was to determine the "differences that matter", between problems, between client groups and between modeling interventions. Ten years later there is more clarity on possible causal paths, starting from behavior in modeling sessions, via opinions and attitudes of participants, to behavior in and effects on the problem of interest. Maybe, in addition to conducting more fine-grained empirical studies, we also need further development in terms of conceptual understanding. Perhaps it is time to turn our sketch of causal mechanisms into a simulation model and to test its dynamic implications.

# References

Adriaans, J. (2014). *The black box of interaction processes. Underlying causes of team performance in group model building meetings: Information elaboration and asking questions.* Masters thesis, Radboud University, Nijmegen.

Ajzen, I. 1991. The theory of planned behavior. *Organizational Behavior and Human Decision Processes* 50: 179–211.

Andersen, D.F., and G. Richardson. 1997. Scripts for group model building. *System Dynamics Review* 13: 107–129.

Andersen D.F., T.A. Maxwell, G.P. Richardson, and T.R. Stewart. 1994. *Mental models and dynamic decision making in a simulation of welfare reform.* Paper presented at the international system dynamics conference: Social and public policy, Stirling.

Andersen, D.F., J.A.M. Vennix, G.P. Richardson, and E.A.J.A. Rouwette. 2007. Group model building: Problem structuring, policy simulation and decision support. *Journal of the Operational Research Society* 58: 691–694.

Ansems, R. 2010. *The effectiveness of group model building, linking facilitated modelling with critical events and group decision development.* Masters thesis, Radboud University, Nijmegen.

Bachurina, A. 2012. *Creating synergies among data sources: An analysis of methodologies for eliciting participant knowledge and mining client data during the model development process.* Masters thesis, Radboud University, Nijmegen.

Black, L., and D. Andersen. 2012. Using visual representations as boundary objects to resolve conflict in collaborative model-building approaches. *Systems Research and Behavioral Science* 29: 194–208.

Chaiken, S., R. Giner-Sorolla, and S. Chen. 1996. Beyond accuracy: Defense and impression motives in heuristic and systematic information processing. In: *The psychology of action: Linking cognition and motivation to action,* eds. P. Gollwitzer and J.A. Bargh, 553–578. New York: Guilford.

De Gooyert, V. 2016. *Stakeholder dynamics in the Dutch energy transition: Towards a shared frame of reference.* PhD, Radboud University, Nijmegen.

Doyle, J., and D. Ford. 1999. Mental models concepts revisited: Some clarifications and a reply to Lane. *System Dynamics Review* 15: 411–415.

Fishbein, M., and I. Ajzen. 1975. *Belief, attitude, intention and behavior. An introduction to theory and research.* Reading: Addison-Wesley.

Fishbein, M., and I. Ajzen. 2011. *Predicting and changing behavior: The reasoned action approach.* New York: Taylor and Francis.

Forrester, J.W. 1961. *Industrial dynamics.* Williston, VT: Pegasus Communications.

Franco, L.A., E.A.J.A. Rouwette, and H. Korzilius. 2015. Different paths to consensus? The impact of need for closure on model-supported group conflict management. *European European Journal of Operational Research.* doi:10.1016/j.ejor.2015.06.056.

Geurts, J., and J.A.M. Vennix. 1989. *Verkenningen in Beleidsanalyse. Theorie en Praktijk van Modelbouw en Simulatie (Explorations in policy analysis. Theory and practice of modelling and simulation).* Zeist: Kerckebosch.

Hodgkinson, G.P., N.J. Bown, A.J. Maule, K.W. Glaister, and A.D. Pearman. 1999. Breaking the frame: An analysis of strategic cognition and decision making under uncertainty. *Strategic Management Journal* 20: 977–985.

Hovmand, P.S., D.F. Andersen, E.A.J.A. Rouwette, G.P. Richardson, K. Rux, and A. Calhoun. 2012. Group model-building 'Scripts' as a collaborative planning tool. *Systems Research and Behavioral Science* 29: 179–193.

Kaplan, S. 2008. Framing contests: Strategy making under uncertainty. *Organization Science* 19: 729–752.

Lawler, E.J., and J. Yoon. 1998. Network structure and emotions in exchange relations. *American Sociological Review* 63: 871–894.

Lawler, E.J., S.R. Thye, and J. Yoon. 2008. Social exchange and micro social order. *American Sociological Review* 73: 519–542.

McCardle-Keurentjes, M.H.F. 2015. *Facilitated modelling and hidden profiles. An experimental evaluation of group model building.* PhD, Radboud University, Nijmegen.

McCardle-Keurentjes, M.H.F., E.A.J.A. Rouwette, and J.A.M. Vennix. 2008. *Effectiveness of group model building in discovering hidden profiles in strategic decision-making.* Paper presented at the system dynamics conference, Athens. http://www.systemdynamics.org/conferences/2008/proceed/papers/MCCAR357.pdf

Nisbett, R., and T. Wilson. 1977. Telling more than we can know: Verbal reports on mental processes. *Psychological Review* 84: 231–259.

Pala, O. 2008. *Selective exposure to information in the context of escalation of commitment.* PhD thesis, Radboud University, Nijmegen.

Petty, R., and J. Cacioppo. 1986. The elaboration likelihood model of persuasion. *Advances in Experimental Social Psychology* 19: 123–205.

Petty, R., and D. Wegener. 1998. Attitude change. Multiple roles for persuasion variables. In: *The handbook of social psychology*, eds. D. Gilbert, S. Fiske and G. Lindzey (Vol. 1, 4th ed., 323–390). Boston: McGraw-Hill.

Richardson, G.P., and D.F. Andersen. 1995. Teamwork in group model building. *System Dynamics Review* 11: 113–137.

Richardson, G.P., D.F. Andersen, T.A. Maxwell, and T.R. Stewart. 1994. *Foundations of mental model research*. Paper presented at the ISDC 1994, Stirling.

Richmond, B. 1993. Systems thinking: Critical thinking skills for the 1990s and beyond. *System Dynamics Review* 9: 113–133.

Roberts, E. 1973. Strategies for effective implementation of complex corporate models. *TIMS-ORSA Interfaces* 8(part 1): 26–33.

Rouwette, E.A.J.A. 2003. *Group model building as mutual persuasion*. Nijmegen: Wolf Legal.

Rouwette, E.A.J.A., and J.A.M. Vennix. 2006. System dynamics and organizational interventions. *Systems Research and Behavioral Science* 23: 451–466.

Rouwette, E.A.J.A., J.A.M. Vennix, and T. Van Mullekom. 2002. Group model building effectiveness. A review of assessment studies. *System Dynamics Review* 18: 5–45.

Rouwette, E.A.J.A., J.A.M. Vennix, and A.J.A. Felling. 2009. On evaluating the performance of problem structuring methods: An attempt at formulating a conceptual model. *Group Decision and Negotiation* 18: 567–587.

Rouwette, E.A.J.A., H. Korzilius, J.A.M. Vennix, and E. Jacobs. 2011. Modeling as persuasion: The impact of group model building on attitudes and behavior. *System Dynamics Review* 27: 1–21.

Schoemaker, P.J.H. 1993. Multiple scenario development: Its conceptual and behavioral foundation. *Strategic Management Journal* 14: 193–213.

Scott, R.J., R.Y. Cavana, and D. Cameron. 2016. Recent evidence on the effectiveness of group model building. *European Journal of Operational Research* 249(3), 908–918.

Snow, D.A., E.B. Rochford Jr., S.K. Worden, and R.D. Benford. 1986. Frame alignment processes, micromobilization, and movement participation. *American Sociological Review* 51: 464–481.

Stasser, G., and W. Titus. 1985. Pooling of unshared information in group decision making: Biased information sampling during discussion. *Journal of Personality and Social Psychology* 48: 1467–1478.

Stasser, G., and W. Titus. 2003. Hidden profiles: A brief history. *Psychological Inquiry* 14: 304–313.

Tavella, E., and L.A. Franco. 2015. Dynamics of group knowledge production in facilitated modelling workshops: An exploratory study. *Group Decision and Negotiation* 24: 451–475.

Van Kessel, H. 2012. *The effectiveness of group model building and group decision making. An experimental comparison of the interactions and the outcomes of a group model building session with a meeting as usual.* Masters thesis, Radboud University, Nijmegen.

Van Nistelrooij, L., E. Rouwette, I. Verstijnen, and J. Vennix. 2012. *Power-levelling as an effect of group model building.* Paper presented at the proceedings of the 2012 international system dynamics conference.

Wright, G., and P. Goodwin. 2002. Eliminating a framing bias by using simple instructions to 'think harder' and respondents with managerial experience: Comment on 'breaking the frame'. *Strategic Management Journal* 23: 1059–1067.

Zagonel, A. 2004. *Reflecting on group model building used to support welfare reform in New York state.* Doctoral, SUNY, Albany.

# Part III

Practice

# 12

# Overview: Behavioral Operational Research in Practice

## Katharina Burger and Jonathan Malpass

## 12.1 Introduction

One of the purposes of this book is to understand the application of Behavioral Operational Research (BOR) in Practice. Thus far, the book has addressed theoretical and methodological issues of BOR. For the practitioner, the question remains: what does BOR in Practice look like? What methods have been used, and therefore, what do I need to do for it to be BOR?

It can be argued that all practical applications of operational research are, in fact, *behavioral* OR, as the user of a model or the customer requesting a model will interpret the results, which will have some influence on

K. Burger (✉)
Portsmouth Business School, University of Portsmouth, Portland Street, Portsmouth PO1 3DE, UK

J. Malpass
Research and Innovation, BT Technology, Services and Operations, Adastral Park, Martlesham Heath IP5 3RE, UK

© The Editor(s) (if applicable) and The Author(s) 2016                    **245**
M. Kunc et al. (eds.), *Behavioral Operational Research*,
DOI 10.1057/978-1-137-53551-1_12

their behavior. For example, a very mathematical (NP-hard) approach can be used to determine the optimal stacking formation of containers on a cargo ship (Wei-ying et al. 2005), but what happens when one of the customers of the cargo company wants to pay a premium so that their container is unloaded within the first hour after docking?

This being the case, given that behavioral aspects of OR can be considered in almost any application area, a comprehensive review of the practice of BOR is an elusive venture. Thus, to delineate the scope of this chapter, we begin by adopting the definition of BOR that was discussed elsewhere in this book: BOR is the subject that covers (*i*) the incorporation of behavioral factors in models, (*ii*) modeling of behavior and (*iii*) understanding how behavior is influenced by models. By focusing on the practical applications of BOR rather than on theoretical and philosophical debates, this chapter seeks to study how the definition applies to *behavioral operational research in practice* (BOR in Practice).

This chapter traces the historical background of BOR in Practice, from journal papers in the 1950s through to the most recent conference presentations at EURO 2015, highlighting the growth of the subject area in recent years and the breadth of approaches that fall under the BOR umbrella. BOR in Practice is shown to be a multi-disciplinary endeavor, incorporating studies concerned with the reduction of biases and errors as well as those on the opposite side of the spectrum, studying ecological rationality, all of which are conducted with a view to supporting decision making in the widest sense.

## 12.2 History and Developments

In order to understand the history of BOR in Practice, a—necessarily selective—search for journal publications in two digital libraries (JSTOR [Journal Storage] and Business Source Complete) was conducted and a review of recent conference proceedings was undertaken (Notes 1, 2 and 3).

In a first step, a search for the keywords "behavioral" and "operational research" and "practice" in journals in the disciplines of business, management and organizational behavior was conducted in JSTOR. In a second step, a search in Business Source Complete was carried out, using the query "behavioral" and "operational research" in all fields. Subsequently, the keyword "practice" was used to narrow the results to 47 papers. A process of qualitative coding of the papers' abstracts was undertaken to organize the results into the categories of Behavior in Models (15 articles), Modeling of Behavior (5) and Behavior influenced by Models (13). This led to a categorization of 70% of the search results. The remaining results did not fit into any of the three specified categories, for example because the article mainly addressed philosophical issues or reviewed OR as a field rather than specifically focusing on BOR in practice. The top 5 articles by relevance scores are presented in this section (Sect. 12.2), and more information about the remaining papers is given in Sect. 12.3.

The search results suggest that a recognition of the importance of behavior in and for the practice of OR dates back more than 50 years, but when did behavioral OR become a more popular area of study?

In terms of publication frequency, the results suggest that there were only a few publications per year between 1956 and 1970, which increased slightly between 1970 and 2000. However, since the turn of the century, the number of relevant papers per year appears to have increased (see Fig. 12.1).

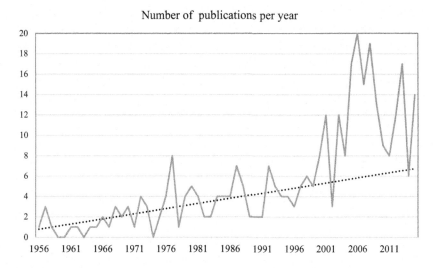

Number of publications per year

**Fig. 12.1** Trend line showing the number of behavioral OR publications since 1956. Trend line calculated using 1956–1999 data only

## 12.2.1 Making the Case for BOR

In 1964, Dutton and Walton argued in "Operational Research and the Behavioral Sciences" that the low behavioral science content in OR interferes with the achievement of operational researchers' own chosen aims but that steps could be taken to integrate behavioral science concepts into work in OR. Similarly, in "Operational Research in Business", Moore (1967) discussed the behavioral sciences as a promising area for the development of the field of OR. Moore (1967) reviewed different application areas of OR, considering the discipline's background; identified some classical lines of study; discussed applications to quantitative methods in business; and highlighted some challenges associated with an integration of research findings from the behavioral sciences into the practice of OR.

## 12.2.2 Education for BOR

Around the same time, Cook (1966) offered a practitioner's viewpoint on "Education for Operational Research" and discussed how education for OR could be advanced through university–industry collaboration as well as over the career-span of an OR expert. Relatedly, in "Teaching Operational Research Technique", Tate (1977) suggested that OR technique extends beyond quantitative modeling skills and argued that teamwork should be included in university training courses, as OR practitioners need to support the different phases of "maintaining client relations, generating many alternatives, conducting approximate appraisals, modeling rigorously, managing effectively" (Tate 1977).

## 12.2.3 BOR and Strategy Support

The final paper in the top five is the more recent discussion of "Strategy, Performance and Operational Research", by Dyson (2000), which was part of a Special Issue on "OR and Strategy" in the *Journal of the Operational Research Society*. In this paper, Dyson argued that OR is well fitted to handle strategic issues, since the modeling approach of OR facilitates understanding, learning and the evaluation of strategies prior to action.

Overall, a review of the top 5 search results suggests that BOR in Practice is concerned with the integration of insights about human behavior into the enactment of facilitated decision making processes. Similarly, the remaining search results suggest that—as a multi-methodological endeavor—BOR in Practice maintains a wide empirical research program.

The following section presents the search results, categorized by their contributions to the incorporation of behavioral factors in models, to the modeling of behavior or to the study of behavior influenced by models.

## 12.3  BOR in Practice

Many of the retrieved articles sought to make contributions to the practice of BOR by developing new ways of incorporating behavioral factors into models and studied—at times conceptually—how interactions with models occur in practice. Only a few of the identified studies developed models of behavior with explicit applications to practice, suggesting that this might be an area for further development.

In the following sub-sections, the approaches and areas of application of the categorized articles are presented.

### 12.3.1 The Incorporation of Behavioral Factors in Models

The search results covered a wide range of applications to business operations, including contractual coordination mechanisms, financial and budgetary decision making practices, information systems development and innovation process management.

Studying behavior in multi-organizational relationships, Katok et al. (2008) investigated the effect of review periods on Inventory Service-Level Agreements as coordination mechanisms and concluded that, in practice, longer review periods might be more effective than shorter ones for inducing service improvements. Related to operations management, de Brito and van der Laan (2009) showed that in the case of imperfect information, the most informed method does not necessarily lead to the best performance, which has implications for investments in product return information systems. Researching the influence of cost and quality priorities on the propensity to outsource production, Gray et al. (2009) concluded that the competitive priority placed on cost played an integral role in sourcing decisions, while, surprisingly, conformance quality priorities did not. In their study of decision making in financial and budgetary management, Lima Filho and Bruni (2013) confirmed the use of heuristics by individuals who are involved in budgeting practices. Lastly, with applications to innovation processes, Froehle and Roth (2007) developed a resource-process framework of new service development to guide and organize future research on new service development.

In addition to specific application areas in business operations, a number of search results related to wider research on human decision making behavior. One of the earliest search results was Arrow and Hurwicz's (1957) contribution to decision theory and operational research, which identified problems that frequently arise in many practices without diminishing returns to scale. Adopting a simulation approach, Stewart (2005) studied the impact of biases due to anchoring and adjustment and avoidance of sure loss in decision making on model performance. Taking a more holistic view, Luoma et al. (2011) developed a framework that integrates systems thinking and complex responsive processes into a model of systems intelligence.

Finally, a number of search results were specific to a particular sector or infrastructure, for example, to healthcare and transport.

In the area of healthcare, Brailsford et al. (2012) incorporated human behavior in simulation of breast cancer screening programs and concluded that increasing attendance at screenings through education or publicity campaigns can be as effective as decreasing the intervals between screenings. Vasilakis et al. (2007) developed a simulation model involving the scheduling of clinic appointments in surgical care, leading to a better understanding of differential impacts on different segments of patient flow and across surgical priority groups.

In the area of transport system management, Tzeng, Chen and Wang (1998) argued that, from a behavioral perspective, traditional weighting methods account for too few factors to deal with decisions properly. Based on mode-choice behavior data from motorcycle users, they proposed a weight-assessing method with habitual domains and discussed its significant application potential in practice. Similarly, in the transport sector, seeking to improve the relevance of existing models, Clark and Watling (2006) developed a sensitivity analysis for a type of decision support model which is widely used by traffic practitioners concerning the operation and management of traffic networks.

Overall, BOR in Practice appears to utilize theories from multiple disciplinary backgrounds, so that research contributes to the understanding of interactions between individuals, groups and their environment, which is also a characteristic of search results that fell in the category of Modeling of Behavior.

## 12.3.2 Modeling of Behavior

BOR requires a more complex approach to understanding traditional OR settings by demanding that attention be paid to interactions with models in problem contexts. As such, a number of search results were concerned with understanding the affordances of scaffolded shared learning processes for the emergence of collective behaviors.

Developing a conceptualization of *knowledge behavior*, Swart and Powell (2012) proposed an analytical theory of knowledge behavior in networks to understand the interplay between the connective topology of the network, the characteristics of knowers, and the behavioral characteristics of knowledge itself.

Regarding theory for practice developments, White (2008) suggested that an understanding of network learning in inter-organizational partnerships should include Social Network Analysis and Soft Operational Research in order to provide greater insight into the systems level phenomenon of collaboration.

Concerned with the theory–practice gap, Lane (2006) critically commented on prior research which provided theoretical analysis of the social dimension of System Dynamics. With regard to the suggestion that System Dynamics models can represent agency–structure interaction consequences in social systems, he asked: "It works in practice but does it work in theory?"

Lastly, concerned with modeling behavior in work environments, Sawhney (2013) studied how process-focused training, job-rotation training and positive reward structures impact acquired labor flexibility. Studying difficulties associated with behavioral change, Tully (1968) concluded that relevance of resources and goals, together with group norms, influences the likelihood of the application of a problem solution.

Overall, the retrieved search results suggest that notions of predictability need to be reconciled with the understanding that affective, emotional, value-based behaviors influence OR modeling processes and cannot be rationalized away through more OR technology, but rather that they need to be understood as constituting activity. Hence, the interest turns to understanding dynamics of group behavior in interaction with models.[1]

## 12.3.3 Behavior Influenced by Models

A number of search results were concerned with understanding behavior with models, including case studies, experiments and conceptual developments.

Grinyer (2000) discussed a cognitive approach to group strategic decision making, which was used by an international energy company, and reflected on the conceptual foundations of the process and its inter-relationships. Relatedly, Nutt (1977) undertook an experimental comparison of the effectiveness of three planning methods, based on systems ideas, behavioral science concepts and heuristics. The results of the experiment indicated that the systems approach produced better-quality plans, while the behavioral approach produced more new ideas.

---

[1] The definition of 'models' adopted in the coding process includes cognitive maps, mental maps, cultural schemata, norms and values, as well as management processes, scripted guidelines and management decision support models, i.e. all types of conceptual and materialised models that mediate behavior and the exploration (models as tools for thinking) of problem situations.

Similarly, exploring model-mediated decision making, Morton and Fasolo studied processes of structuring, value elicitation and weighting to understand behavior with multi-criteria decision analysis (Morton and Fasolo 2009).

A related group of studies explore the ways in which models of management systems and processes influence behavior. For example, De Leeuw and van den Berg (2011) contribute to a better understanding of the ways in which performance management practices influence behavior of individuals. A similar aim was pursued by Samson and Terziovski (1999) who studied behavior with Total Quality Management (TQM) practices and its relationship to organizational performance. The question of how to implement abstract models was considered by Schultz (1980), who studied the theory–practice gap through a case study with students in an MBA program, leading to a reflection on the design of OR education programs and specifically on the implementation of models.

Finally, a number of studies are concerned with the ways in which models influence behavior, specifically considering the socio-cultural context of modeling in OR practice.

In "Problem Construction and the Influence of O.R.", Eden (1982) discussed the social context of undertaking OR projects in organizations, leading to recommendations to provide OR practitioners with techniques to manage problems in teams in a multi-methodological endeavor "without recourse to backroom wizardry" (Eden 1982).

White (2006) explored the concept of aesthetics in relation to systems and OR processes and presented "Critical Imagination" as a model for understanding systems and OR practice. Through the perspective of Critical Systems Thinking, Ulrich (2001) sought to promote reflective approaches in the pursuit of competence in systemic research and practice.

Cultural influences in relation to OR models and modeling approaches were studied by Paucar-Caceres (2009), who suggested that the increasing number of soft OR approaches developed in the UK is a direct consequence of the pragmatism in management education and management practice in Britain. Strümpfer and Ryan (2000) reflected on the role of Russell Ackoff in introducing systems theory in South Africa, and in

"Model World: Have Model, Will Travel" Gass (1990) suggested that the success of management science and OR rests on the cultural, ethical, behavioral and bureaucratic structures that influence a country's and a person's approach to decision making.

In sum, the brief review of the search results suggest that Behavioral OR in Practice has long been a concern in the OR community and that a more comprehensive study of the diversity of approaches may be fruitful to develop richer picture of its character to date.

**Table 12.1** A selection of BOR in practice areas

| | |
|---|---|
| Sectors and industries | Advertising; agriculture; airlines; automotive industry; chemical industry; crime; economics; education; energy; finance; health (incl. Medical services); housing; law; local government; manufacturing; marketing; military; retail; pharmaceuticals; public sector/government; shipping; sports; telecommunications; tourism; transport; utilities |
| Areas and disciplines | Auctions (incl. e-auctions); call centers; disaster management & recovery; e-commerce; e-government; evacuation; in-store design; knowledge management; on-line services; project management; risk management; supply chain management (incl. Inventory management and inventory control); technology adoption; traffic management; workforce management & planning |
| Processes of concern | Customer attitudes; citizen engagement; facilitation, collaboration and negotiation; network design; participatory decision making; planning, incl. capacity planning and demand planning; portfolio selection; revenue management, dynamic pricing, pricing strategy; routing; scheduling |
| Theories and approaches | Analytics (incl. big data, pattern recognition, measuring the effect of interventions, statistical methods); markov (and hidden markov) models; Game Theory (incl. competitions, bargaining, negotiations and the moral hazard problem); forecasting; network flow models and location models; optimization methods (incl. Fuzzy optimization); process mining; queuing theory; studies of biases and bounded rationality; heuristics and metaheuristics; human choice modeling and random utility theory; analytical hierarchy/network process; problem structuring methods, Soft Systems Methodology and rich pictures; multi-criteria decision modeling, Data Envelopment Analysis and analytics; simulation (incl. Discrete-Event Simulation, System Dynamics and agent-based simulation); social networks analysis; and others |

### 12.3.4 An Outlook

Finally, with the aim of highlighting recent developments in BOR in Practice, a review of the technical programs of three international OR conferences was undertaken (Note 3). The review shows that there is a very active BOR community covering a wide range of OR methods in many sectors (Table 12.1).

The overview of practice areas suggests that traditional OR methods, such as mathematical programming, together with more recent developments, such as social simulation models, be brought to bear on various problems within organizational and business environments and beyond.

One of the recurrent themes at the conferences is the practice of the design of OR learning environments, considering processes of human–environment/technology interaction. Moreover, given the relevance of mediated human behavior in OR processes, it is not surprising that complex application areas of OR related to societal problems, sustainable living and development, common pool resource management and smart city operations are increasingly considered through the lens of BOR.

It could be argued that it is through its traditional pragmatist focus on interventions in problem situations, rather than the aspiration to develop grand theories, that BOR in Practice shows great potential for developing novel multi, multi-discipline approaches to analyze and support decision making in and beyond organizations.

At IFORS 2014, Stewart Robinson, president of the OR Society, asked, "Have I been doing BOR for the past 20 years?" (Robinson 2014). The presentation was a testament to the multiple definitions of behavioral OR and the increasing interest in discussing its character in the OR community. So what have we learned from this review about BOR in, and for, Practice?

## 12.4 Conclusion

The review has highlighted the multi-disciplinary background of BOR methodologies in practice. The breadth of application areas that were identified supports the view that OR is defined more by its methodologies than by its specific application areas.

A distinctive characteristic of BOR in Practice appears to be that it further develops an empirically informed understanding of the socio-technical interactions between practitioners and models in their organizational environments. As such, a concern is evident for the reflexive treatment of cultural, social and historical influences on the behavior of those building and interacting with models. For practitioners, this interest in understanding how models mediate behavior calls for thinking beyond methods, to consider how thinking and acting are shaped, enabled and constrained by the use of (B)OR methods.

At the core of BOR in practice appears to be the study of dynamics in and beyond organizational contexts, with the aim of understanding how behaviors are related to sustainable value creation. The increasing accessibility of computational simulation technology and the availability of big behavioral data sets are two related developments that support the growth of BOR in and for practice. Designing behavioral OR interventions is likely going to require multi-skilled practitioners or multi-disciplinary teamwork, including approaches from cognitive and social psychology, theories of group dynamics and programming skills for simulation models. Collaborative work in both the practitioner and the academic communities, working towards empirically informed BOR methodologies, seems desirable.

This section of the book includes five examples of BOR in Practice, covering a variety of methods and sectors. In Chap. 13, "Healthcare: Including Human Behavior in Simulation Models", Brailsford addresses how to incorporate behavioral factors into OR methods. Next, Malpass shows how the success of transformation projects in British Telecommunications (BT) was enhanced by understanding behavior in Chap. 14, "Service Operations: Behavioral Operational Research in BT." This is followed by "Smart Cities: Big Data and Behavior in OR" (Chap. 15), where White, Burger and Yearworth present a discussion of the ways in which behavioral OR and big data offer new opportunities in and for OR practice. In Chap. 16, "Mergers and Acquisitions: Decision Making in Integration Projects", Atkinson and Gary discuss the application of a soft OR technique. In the final chapter in this section (Chap. 17), Huh and Kunc analyze how *behavioral group dynamics* impact the effectiveness of the strategic conversation and the understanding of the contribution of strategic resources to firm performance in "Supporting Strategy: Behavioral Influences on Resource Conceptualization Processes". Overall, the contributions demonstrate the creative methodological innovations in the growing field of BOR and yet, they still only touch on the numerous areas in which BOR can be—and is being—used *in practice*.

## 12.4.1 Notes

### Note 1

When changing the JSTOR search query to the US spelling "behavioral" and the more common term "Operational Research", the search results are substantially different. For example, by relevance, the top 5 journal publications would be:

| Citation | Key point |
|---|---|
| Dorfman R (1960). Operational Research. *The American Economic Review* **50**: 575–623 | Suggests that *"we must recognize the firm for what operational research has disclosed it to be: often fumbling, sluggish, timid, uncertain, and perplexed by unsolvable problems"* |
| R. L. A. (1956). Operations-Research Services. *Operational Research* **4**: 599–608 | In the 'Management's Corner' of the Journal; presents six self-portraits of industrial operations-research service providers |
| Liberatore M J and Luo W (2010). The Analytics Movement: Implications for Operational Research. *Interfaces* **40**: 313–324 | Discusses the drivers of the analytics movement and the opportunities and implications for OR |
| Bonder S (1979). Changing the Future of Operational Research. *Operational Research* **27**:209–224 | Suggests that *"it is time to stop the continual controversy between OR practitioners and mathematical theorists regarding the nature of OR, since neither activity by itself is sufficient"* |
| Churchman C W (1970). Operational Research as a Profession, *Management Science* **17**: B37-B53 | Encourages the OR profession to embrace its *"mysteries"* and *"irrational side"* |

Overall, these results support the suggestion that a consideration of behavior in the practice of operational research has been a concern—in both the British and the American OR communities for more than 50 years. For a more considered discussion of the more-than-linguistic differences in the development of these communities over time, see Paucar-Caceres (2011).

## Note 2

The search, conducted on 24 July 2015, returned 335 results in 87 different journals. However, this journal list of 87 journals includes only 10 journals (15%) from the COPIOR (Committee of Professors in OR) journal list and only 10 journals (16%) from the list of Operational Research and Management Science journals in the 2015 ABS journal guide. Duplicates having been eliminated, 89 OR/MS journals remain on the combined COPIOR/ABS list that do not appear in the search results. An indicative search query in one of the journals that is included on the combined list, the *System Dynamics Review,* for the keywords "behavioral 'operational research' practice" returns 88 results on the publisher's website. The same search query (behavioral AND "operational research" AND practice AND "System Dynamics Review" (SO Publication Name)) in Business Source Complete returns 0 results. It is thus likely that a comprehensive search combining results from the individual journals obtained through the journal publishers' search engines would return a much broader set of potentially relevant articles.

The Top 10 Journals for BOR publications, according to the Business Source Complete data set, are:

| Journal | Number |
| --- | --- |
| *European Journal of Operational Research* | 89 |
| *Systems Research and Behavioral Science* | 29 |
| *Journal of the Operational Research Society* | 26 |
| *Journal of Operations Management* | 17 |
| *Management Services* | 15 |
| *Interfaces* | 12 |
| *Journal of Behavioral Decision Making* | 10 |
| *Operational Research* | 9 |
| *Manufacturing & Service Operations Management* | 5 |
| *International Journal of Operations & Production Management* | 4 |

## Note 3

The reviewed conferences were: EURO26: 26th European Conference on Operational Research, Rome, 2013; IFORS20: 20th Conference of the International Federation of Operational Research Societies, Barcelona, 2014; EURO27, 27th European Conference on Operational Research,

Glasgow, 2014. For the review, a keyword search for (behavior/behavior/behavioral/behavioral, practice, human, people, consumer) was conducted. Abstracts with either keyword were retained. Excluded were results such as the behavior of algorithms, stochastic behavior, nonlinear behavior, behavior of neural networks, behavior of supply chains or transport systems (without consideration of human factors), behaviors of cars and busses, algorithm behavior, search behavior, firm behavior, behavior of macroscopic densities, behavior of charged particles in an electrical field, etc.

# References

Arrow, K., and L. Hurwicz. 1957. Gradient methods for constrained maxima. *Operations Research* 5: 258–265.

Bonder, S. 1979. Changing the future of operations research. *Operations Research* 27: 209–224.

Brailsford, S.C., P.R. Harper, and J. Sykes. 2012. Incorporating human behaviour in simulation models of screening for breast cancer. *European Journal of Operational Research* 219: 491–507.

Churchman, C.W. 1970. Operations research as a profession. *Management Science* 17: B37–B53.

Clark, S.D., and D.P. Watling. 2006. Applications of sensitivity analysis for probit stochastic network equilibrium. *European Journal of Operational Research* 175: 894–911.

Cook, S.L. 1966. Education for operational research. *Operational Research Quarterly* 17: 95–98.

de Brito, M.P., and E.A. van der Laan. 2009. Inventory control with product returns: The impact of imperfect information. *European Journal of Operational Research* 194: 85–101.

de Leeuw, S., and J.P. van den Berg. 2011. Improving operational performance by influencing shopfloor behavior via performance management practices. *Journal of Operations Management* 29: 224–235.

Dorfman, R. 1960. Operations research. *The American Economic Review* 50: 575–623.

Dutton, J.M., and R.E. Walton. 1964. Operational research and the behavioural sciences. *Operational Research Quarterly* 15: 207–217.

Dyson, R. 2000. Strategy, performance and operational research. *Journal of the Operational Research Society* 51: 5–11.

Eden, C. 1982. Problem construction and the influence of O.R. *Interfaces* 12: 50–60.

Froehle, C.M., and A.V. Roth. 2007. A resource-process framework of new service development. *Production and Operations Management* 16: 169–188.

Gass, S.I. 1990. Model world: Have model, will travel. *Interfaces* 20: 67–71.

Gray, J.V., A.V. Roth, and B. Tomlin. 2009. The influence of cost and quality priorities on the propensity to outsource production. *Decision Sciences* 40: 697–726.

Grinyer, P.H. 2000. A cognitive approach to group strategic decision taking: A discussion of evolved practice in the light of received research results. *Journal of the Operational Research Society* 51: 21–35.

Katok, E., D. Thomas, and A. Davis. 2008. Inventory service-level agreements as coordination mechanisms: The effect of review periods. *Manufacturing and Service Operations Management* 10: 609–624.

Lane, D.C. 2006. It works in practice but does it work in theory? *Systems Research and Behavioral Science* 23: 565–570.

Liberatore, M.J., and W. Luo. 2010. The analytics movement: Implications for operations research. *Interfaces* 40: 313–324.

Lima Filho, R.N., and A.L. Bruni. 2013. The more I do, the more I commit errors? An analysis of the presence of cognitive bias in judgments about the budget. *Base* 10: 224–239.

Luoma, J., R.P. Hämäläinen, and E. Saarinen. 2011. Acting with systems intelligence: Integrating complex responsive processes with the systems perspective. *Journal of the Operational Research Society* 62: 3–11.

Moore, P.G. 1967. Operational research in business. *Journal of the Institute of Actuaries (1886–1994)* 93: 323–385.

Morton, A., and B. Fasolo. 2009. Behavioural decision theory for multi-criteria decision analysis: A guided tour. *Journal of the Operational Research Society* 60: 268–275.

Nutt, P.C. 1977. An experimental comparison of the effectiveness of three planning methods. *Management Science* 23: 499–511.

Paucar-Caceres, A. 2009. Pragmatism and rationalism in the development of management science methodologies in the UK and France. *Systems Research and Behavioral Science* 26: 429–444.

Paucar-Caceres, A. 2011. The development of management sciences/operational research discourses: Surveying the trends in the US and the UK. *Journal of the Operational Research Society* 62: 1452–1470.

R L A. 1956. Operations-research services. *Operations Research* 4: 599–608.

Robinson, S. 2014. Have I been doing BOR for the past 20 years? 20th conference of the International Federation of Operational Research Societies.

Samson, D., and M. Terziovski. 1999. The relationship between total quality management practices and operational performance. *Journal of Operations Management* 17: 393–409.

Sawhney, R. 2013. Implementing labor flexibility: A missing link between acquired labor flexibility and plant performance. *Journal of Operations Management* 31: 98–108.

Schultz, H. 1980. Practice what you teach. *Interfaces* 10: 34–39.

Stewart, T.J. 2005. Goal programming and cognitive biases in decision-making. *Journal of the Operational Research Society* 56: 1166–1175.

Strümpfer, J., and T. Ryan. 2000. The development of systems thinking in Southern Africa: A contribution. *Systems Research and Behavioral Science* 17: 325.

Swart, J., and J. Powell. 2012. An analytical theory of knowledge behaviour in networks. *European Journal of Operational Research* 223: 807–817.

Tate, T.B. 1977. Teaching operational research technique. *Journal of the Operational Research Society* 28: 765–779.

Tully, J. 1968. Farmers' problems of behavioural change. *Human Relations* 21: 373–382.

Tzeng, G.H., T.Y. Chen and J.C. Wang. 1998. A weight-assessing method with havitual domains. *European Journal of Operational Research* 110(2): 342–367.

Ulrich, W. 2001. The quest for competence in systemic research and practice. *Systems Research and Behavioral Science* 18: 3–28.

Vasilakis, C., B.G. Sobolev, L. Kuramoto, and A.R. Levy. 2007. A simulation study of scheduling clinic appointments in surgical care: Individual surgeon versus pooled lists. *Journal of the Operational Research Society* 58: 202–211.

Wei-ying, Z., L. Yan, and J. Zhuo-shang. 2005. Model and algorithm for container ship stowage planning based on bin-packing problem. *Journal of Marine Science and Application* 4: 30–36.

White, L. 2006. Aesthetics in OR/systems practice: Towards a concept of critical imagination as a challenge to systems thinking. *Systems Research and Behavioral Science* 23: 779–791.

White, L. 2008. Connecting organizations: Developing the idea of network learning in inter-organizational settings. *Systems Research and Behavioral Science* 25: 701–716.

# 13

# Healthcare: Human Behavior in Simulation Models

Sally C. Brailsford

## 13.1 Introduction

### 13.1.1 Context

There can be little doubt that healthcare is a hugely popular application area for Operational Research (OR) approaches and in particular simulation modeling. Literature surveys over the decades report many examples (Tunnicliffe Wilson 1981; Jun, Jacobson and Swisher 1999; Fone et al. 2003). Recent reviews (Katsaliaki and Mustafee 2011; Hulshof et al. 2012) show an increasing trend, with a wider use of System Dynamics and agent-based simulation. However, one common feature of all these reviews and survey papers is the lack of reported implementation of model findings and recommendations. This raises an interesting question: is healthcare special, or different in some way, from other application areas?

S.C. Brailsford (✉)
Southampton Business School, University of Southampton, Building 2, Southampton SO17 1TR, UK

This question has been widely addressed (Tako and Robinson 2015). The RIGHT study (Brailsford et al. 2009) certainly suggests that healthcare models are implemented less frequently than models for manufacturing systems or defense applications.

Of course, more fundamentally, before we start worrying about whether healthcare is special we could ask whether the same is actually true of other application domains. Do academic papers systematically fail to report implementation of OR models? If so, is this because the models (or more precisely their results) are genuinely not implemented, or is it simply due to the fact that academics need to "publish or perish" before any potential users have had time to implement anything and see the outcome? If the former is true, then could this be because human behavior is not adequately taken account of, either within the design of the actual model or in the way the model is used? Do such models assume that all decision-makers are rational and utilitarian? Do models ignore, or oversimplify, the differing perspectives of different stakeholders? These are profound issues, addressed elsewhere in this book. This chapter focuses specifically on one particular aspect of behavioral OR, namely whether it is desirable (and possible) to incorporate human behavior within the conceptual design of a simulation model.

## 13.1.2 Personal Perspective

My own scientific background, while possibly somewhat unusual, is certainly not in the *behavioral sciences*. Having obtained a Bachelor's degree in mathematics, I then spent a number of years working in the UK National Health Service (NHS) as a nurse, before embarking on an academic career in Operational Research in the late 1980s. For the first ten years I was firmly based in the quantitative OR tradition and mainly used Discrete-Event Simulation (DES) for classical resource allocation type problems. For example, my PhD involved developing a DES model for hospital capacity planning for the AIDS epidemic in the UK. This model was a standard process-flow queuing model whose novelty lay in the fact that patients simultaneously progressed through disease stages and capacity-limited hospital processes. Nevertheless, the patients in the model were just entities, essentially widgets on a production line, which I felt slightly uncomfortable about given my nursing background. I can still vividly remember a visit to a pediatric hospital, where a few patients with hemophilia had unwittingly been given HIV-infected Factor 8, the blood clotting factor genetically missing in hemophilia. This had of course happened in the early 1980s before HIV was identified: transfusion-infected patients provided much useful data at the time since the exact date of infection was known. I remember being intensely moved by the sight of several small boys who did not only have hemophilia, bad enough on its own, but also HIV, a death sentence at the time. These young children, the same age as my own sons, were the objects inside my computer program.

However it was only in the mid-1990s, when I worked on a research project about screening for diabetic retinopathy, when I really began to think seriously about the implications of models that contained human beings. The hemophiliac children provided a salutary reminder of the context of my AIDS model, but to address the model's purpose the model did not need to reflect these children's behavior, let alone my emotional response to them. On the other hand, the diabetic retinopathy screening model definitely did need to include some aspects of patient behavior in order to address its purpose. This NHS-funded project concerned the evaluation of different screening policies for an eye condition which is the leading cause of preventable blindness in developed countries. Clinicians agreed that patients with diabetes should be routinely screened for the early signs of retinopathy, which can then be successfully treated by laser, but there was no consensus about the optimal policy in terms of which medical staff did the screening, how frequently, with what technology and where. We developed a DES model to test a wide variety of policies and compared them all in terms of cost per sight-year saved (Davies et al. 2000).

## 13.1.3 The Need to Model Human Behavior

One of the most interesting findings from the diabetic retinopathy work was that the parameter to which the model was most sensitive was a behavioral one, namely the probability of a patient attending for screening. Compared with this, it made relatively little difference what test was used, whether it was performed by a family practitioner, an optometrist or a consultant ophthalmologist, or whether the test was done six-monthly, annually or every two years. However, it made an enormous difference how many people actually showed up for screening. Moreover, clinicians told us that patients who did not attend for screening were often poorly compliant with other important aspects of treatment such as following dietary advice. As a consequence, their diabetes was less well controlled and they were actually *more* likely to have retinopathy.

This sparked my interest in modeling human behavior. What was the point of making massive efforts to calculate age-specific and ethnicity-specific disease transition probabilities, and to scour the literature for randomized control studies to obtain the accuracy of the different screening tests, when the most important parameter, the probability of attendance, was represented by one single number? Moreover, it seemed obvious to me that patient behavior can influence health outcomes. Adherence to medication, i.e. taking a drug correctly (or even taking it at all) can be surprisingly low, even among people with life-threatening conditions such as diabetes. A systematic review by McNabb (1997), which studied the attitudes of patients with diabetes to all aspects of their treatment, found that adherence to insulin injections and other medication varied enormously, from as low as 20 % in one study to 80 % in another. Any model which ignored these behavioral factors would surely give unreliable results.

## 13.1.4 Focus of This Chapter

This chapter focuses specifically on simulation models for healthcare applications in which the simulated objects (entities) are human beings. Therefore, we shall not consider pharmacological or bio-informatics models, where the simulated objects are molecules, and we also exclude probabilistic Markovian decision tree models as used by health economists, although some of the following discussion is relevant for these approaches. However, we do consider microsimulation, more common in epidemiology and demography than in OR. From an OR perspective the three most widely used simulation paradigms applied in healthcare are Discrete-Event Simulation (DES), System Dynamics (SD) and, more recently, Agent-Based Modeling (ABM). It could be argued that DES lends itself least well to modeling human behavior, although I have suggested, in a paper entitled "Discrete Event Simulation is Alive and Kicking!" (Brailsford 2013), that many of the vaunted benefits of ABM can be achieved using traditional DES.

## 13.2 Simulation in Health

### 13.2.1 Discrete-Event Simulation

DES is used to model stochastic queuing systems. The objects that queue are called entities, and the *services* they queue for are called activities. Activities can be resource-constrained and are stochastic in nature: their durations are drawn from probability distributions. Entities can be given attributes or characteristics that determine their routing round the system, and/or the resources they require, and/or the duration of the activity. Resources such as medical staff can also be modeled as *co-operating* entities if we want to do more than just count the number of busy servers. Clearly, DES lends itself very well to modeling patient flows in healthcare systems (Davies and Davies 1994): anyone who has ever been a patient in any healthcare system will inevitably have experienced either a virtual or a physical wait at some point.

One obvious way of modeling human behavior in a DES is to give the entities attributes which correspond to relevant types of behavior. For example, nurse entities in an Emergency Department (ED) simulation may be junior or senior, and this may affect the time they take to perform certain tasks or their confidence to perform these tasks correctly. A patient entity may become more anxious as their waiting time increases, and this may affect their health status. Of course, this begs the question about exactly how such effects are quantified, since they need to be expressed in some kind of algebraic form when encoded in the model. The same issue arises in System Dynamics, when qualitative effects in a causal loop diagram need to be *translated* into a quantitative stock-flow model.

In our ED example, the doctors may say that if a senior nurse makes the initial assessment of a patient's severity (triage) then the process is quicker and more accurate than if a junior nurse does it, since junior nurses may be over-cautious as well as more painstaking. Having established that nurse seniority is an important factor, it is then necessary to quantify its effect on both the duration and the outcome of the triage activity by collecting data and fitting probability distributions for both types of nurse: a time-consuming activity!

## 13.2.2 System Dynamics

Proponents of this approach would argue that SD is all about behavior. SD has qualitative and quantitative aspects, and both are very useful in healthcare modeling. Many, if not all, healthcare systems are complex and interconnected and it is difficult to draw boundaries around one particular part of the system. System Dynamics is discussed at length elsewhere in this book.

## 13.2.3 Agent-Based Modeling

ABM is also discussed in detail elsewhere in this book. Like SD, its proponents argue that it is the ideal vehicle for modeling human behavior since agents are autonomous beings who can learn, communicate and make decisions. ABM in the social sciences has been popular since the 1990s (Gilbert and Troitzch 1999), and models been used to investigate how individual characteristics affect emergent behavior of the whole population, and to better understand interactions between individuals. Within the mainstream OR health modeling community it is still a relatively new approach and while there are now many academic papers using ABM for healthcare applications, it is still much less widely used for practical applications than either SD or DES. However, the availability and increasing user-friendliness of off-the-shelf software tools like Anylogic (2015) has helped ABM to gain popularity rapidly in recent years.

## 13.2.4 Microsimulation

This approach is akin to Monte Carlo simulation in that it uses random sampling to obtain numerical estimates for quantities which cannot be derived analytically. It is also similar to a DES in which the entities pass through the system one at a time rather than all at once and the activities are unconstrained, i.e. there are no resources and no queues. In demography, a microsimulation model might take a cohort of people one by one through their life course, where the dwelling time in each stage (e.g. single, married, divorced and widowed) for each person is sampled from an appropriate probability distribution. In a healthcare context, such a model might take a cohort of patients one by one through the stages of a disease. This is the modeling approach used in the case study in Sect. 13.5, screening for breast cancer.

# 13.3  Models from Health Psychology

Conner and Norman (1995, 2005) provide an excellent overview of the main models in the psychology literature for predicting health-related behavior. We focus on two which could potentially be incorporated in DES models.

## 13.3.1 The Health Belief Model

One of the oldest and most widely used models is Rosenstock and Becker's Health Belief Model (1974, 1996), shown in Fig. 13.1. Its main virtue is its simplicity: the elements in the boxes are lay terms and can be easily understood. The Health Belief Model (HBM) holds that four basic things affect the likelihood of a person performing some health-related action, in this case attendance for screening:

(i)   Perceived susceptibility (*How likely am I personally to go blind?*)
(ii)  Perceived severity (*How bad do I think it would be to be blind?*)
(iii) Perceived benefits (*Do I think screening could stop me going blind?*)
(iv)  Perceived barriers (*What might make it difficult for me to attend?*)

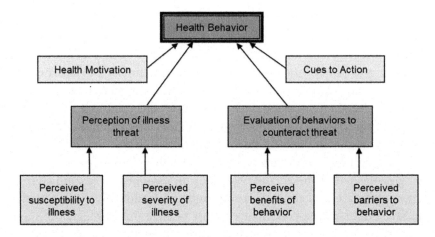

**Fig. 13.1**    The Health Belief Model (Rosenstock 1996 and Becker 1974)

In addition, the HBM says that attendance for screening can be affected by a person's general interest in their own health (motivation), and other external trigger events or *cues to action*, e.g. I have a friend with diabetes who has just gone blind.

One disadvantage of the HBM for modeling is the fact that there is no obvious formal mathematical relationship between the model elements. Furthermore, the variables are highly subjective (how bad do I think it would be to be blind) and difficult to quantify. Moreover, the HBM does not include other variables which psychologists have been found in practice to be important, such as a person's intentions to perform some action and social pressures.

## 13.3.2 The Theory of Planned Behavior

A psychological model, which at first glance seemed to be more promising, was Ajzen's (Ajzen 1988, 1991). This is an extension of the Theory of Reasoned Action (Fishbein and Ajzen 1975), developed specifically for health behavior. Fishbein and Ajzen do not, of course, suggest that people consciously perform these calculations, but rather, the equations represent the effects of learning. The model structure is shown in Fig. 13.2.

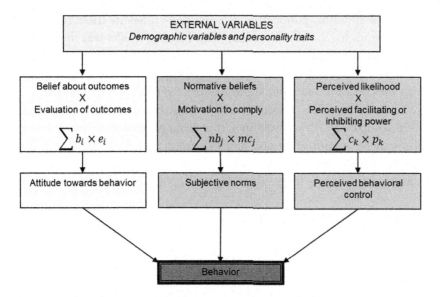

**Fig. 13.2** The Theory of Planned Behavior (Ajzen 1988)

The Theory of Planned Behavior (TPB) appears to have the greatest potential to be modelled mathematically. According to this model, motivation to behave in a particular way is determined by the extent to which people believe the behavior will lead to outcomes which they value (*attitude*), that other people whose opinions they value want them to do it (*subjective norms*) and they believe they have the necessary resources and opportunities to do it (*perceived behavioral control*). The model has been widely tested and successfully applied (Conner and Norman 1995). It incorporates many important cognitive variables: intentions, outcome expectancies and perceived behavioral control. It also incorporates social pressures and makes clear causal links between variables and behavior.

## 13.4 Case Study 1: Screening for Diabetic Retinopathy

This model is described in detail in Brailsford and Schmidt (2003). In the original DES model (Davies et al. 2000), patients with diabetes progressed through a number of disease stages corresponding to the natural (untreated) history of diabetic retinopathy. The dwelling times in these stages were derived from the medical literature. This baseline model was then used to test the outcomes of different screening strategies, where the probabilities of correctly detecting disease were also derived from clinical studies, along with the effects of treatment and the associated costs of both screening and treatment. The main outcome measure was the total cost per sight-year saved compared with the baseline, for a given population. The probability of a patient attending on any given occasion was 85%, based again on the medical literature: patients who did not attend would be invited again (once) with the same probability of attending the second time.

## 13.4.1 The HBM-PECS Model

The new behavioral model used a combination of the HBM and an agent-based architecture developed by Schmidt called PECS (Schmidt 2000). PECS stands for Physis, Emotion, Cognition and Status, and represents the *forces* acting on a person which determine their behavior. Figure 13.3 shows how the PECS elements (shown in green) influence the HBM

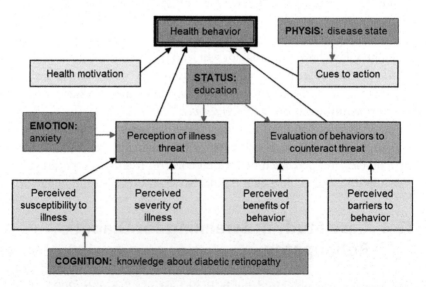

**Fig. 13.3** The HBM combined with the PECS constructs for diabetic retinopathy

constructs. The assumptions underlying the selection of the PECS components were as follows:

- *Physis*: the stage of retinopathy may affect attendance; we assumed that this might act as a trigger.
- *Emotion*: anxiety and individual perceptions of the overall threat of blindness will, together, influence a person's perceived susceptibility to becoming blind themselves. We assumed that highly anxious people are more likely to attend.
- *Cognition*: knowledge and understanding about diabetic retinopathy will influence a person's perceptions about the severity of the disease and their evaluation of the benefits of screening.
- *Status*: educational level is likely to determine ability to evaluate behaviors to counteract the threat of blindness, and also perceptions of the threat itself.

## 13.4.2 Calculating the Probability of Attendance

Empirical research shows that the number of previous attendances for screening is a key factor in predicting future attendance (Weinberg et al. 1997). This was also included in our model. Each time an individual was invited for screening their probability of compliance was calculated as

$$\text{compliance} = v \times m \times p \tag{13.1}$$

where $m$ is the motivation to comply, randomly sampled as either low (0.6), medium (0.9) or high (1.0), $v$ is the compliance history defined by the equation

$$v = 1 - (0.1)^{\text{no. of previous visits}} \tag{13.2}$$

and $p$ is the output of the PECS model, calculated in a highly simplistic way. Every person was assigned a value of 1, 2 or 3 for each of the four PECS components, representing a score of low, medium or high on that factor. The average of these PECS values was used to calculate $p$ and finally the (normalized) value of $v \times m \times p$ was used to give a probability of attendance for each patient.

### 13.4.3 Reflections

Like the original model, this model was coded in Pascal (Borland Delphi), using Davies' Patient-Oriented Simulation Technique (Davies and Davies 1994). The equations and relationships used in the HBM/PECS model were chosen arbitrarily (albeit based on the commonsense assumptions listed above) and the model was more of a proof-of-concept than a validated model to depict attendance behavior. The model results demonstrated variability in years of sight saved when compared with the widely used fixed percentage attendance assumption. The work presented in the following section represents the next step in developing a more realistic model of attendance behavior.

## 13.5 Case Study 2: Screening for Breast Cancer

This model is described in detail in Brailsford et al. (2012). Breast cancer is a major cause of death in women, but in most cases early detection and treatment greatly increase the probability of survival. In developed countries, routine X-ray screening for breast cancer (mammography) is typically offered to women approximately between the ages of 50 and 65, in order to detect very small tumors of which the woman herself is unaware. The model evaluated five different screening policies, varying the frequency of screening and the age limits.

### 13.5.1 The Mammography Model

The model was a microsimulation built in Microsoft Visual Basic for Applications. Each woman is taken through time from birth until death. During the course of her simulated life she may (or may not) develop breast cancer, be invited for screening, or attend a screening session. If breast cancer develops then it could be detected either by mammography, or by self-detection through breast self-examination, or through the development of clinical symptoms. Detected cancers are treated and the patient's survival probability recalculated. Like the diabetic retinopathy model, a vast amount of data derived from the medical literature was required to parameterize the model. The model results include the number of screen-detected cancers, life years saved and attendance for screening.

The model contains four options for modeling attendance: "local" or "global" percentage attendance, the Theory of Planned Behavior and a compliance model developed by Baker and Atherill (2002). Local percentage attendance means that every woman attends a fixed proportion $p\%$ of screening sessions. Global percentage attendance means that $p\%$ of women attend every screen and $1-p\%$ of women are never screened. These two methods only require one fixed parameter $p$, which was set at 84.7%, the average attendance rate for our data using the TPB.

## 13.5.2 The TPB Model

In the TPB the three predictor variables—attitude, perceived behavioral control (PBC) and subjective norms—are combined using linear regression to predict intention to attend. Intention to attend and PBC are then used to predict the behavior itself, again using linear regression. We required estimates of the distributions and correlations between these three TPB constructs. We were very fortunate to have access to an outstanding dataset kindly provided by Derek Rutter, who used the TPB in a study to predict attendance at breast cancer screening (Rutter 2000). His questionnaire comprised 106 demographic and socio-economic variables, as well as recognized measures for the qualitative constructs in the TPB. The dataset contained 1846 cases, 1586 of whom subsequently attended for screening, and 283 who did not. Each simulated woman was given three TPB parameter values corresponding to a case from the original dataset, selected at random.

### 13.5.3 Baker and Atherill's Method

This model is based on an empirical dataset containing 17,709 patients' attendance histories for up to five consecutive screens. Like Weinberg et al. (1997), these data suggested that a patient's previous attendance pattern is a strong predictor of their future attendance. The full mathematical details of this model can be found in Baker and Atherill (2002) but, in a nutshell, the model calculates the log probability of attendance, assigning greater weight to the first attendance (or non-attendance) and further attendances are weighted geometrically. Age is also included as a covariate.

### 13.5.4 Results

Overall, the different options for modeling attendance produced similar results regarding the ranking of the five screening policies. However, the choice of behavioral model affected the outcome when deciding whether to extend the current UK screening policy (baseline scenario, 3-yearly from age 50 to 65), either by screening the same ages bi-annually (scenario A), or extending the lower age limit to 45 (scenario B). If Baker and Atherill's method or the global percentage option were used, no significant differences were observed between the three scenarios. However, if either the local percentage or the TPB approach were used then scenario A would be preferred. Overall, the global percentage option (arguably the least realistic) produced lower proportions of screen detected cancers than those observed in both the local percentage and the TPB.

### 13.5.5 Sensitivity Analysis of the TPB Variables

Our results showed that PBC had the greatest effect, followed by subjective norms and lastly attitude which had little effect by itself. Increasing PBC by 10 % resulted in a 2 % increase in life years saved. Increasing all constructs by 10 % produced a significant 4 % increase in both the number of screen detected breast tumors, a 1 % decrease in the average tumor size at detection and a 4% increase in the total number of life years saved. This is approximately equivalent to the increase in life years saved by increasing the maximum age of screening from 64 to 69, screening every three years in both scenarios. Whilst earlier results suggested that the UK would see approximately 15% more screen detected tumors if the lower age for screening was reduced to age 45, the sensitivity analysis reveals that a 4% increase can be achieved simply by increasing the TPB values of the population by 10% and not altering the current screening regime at all.

### 13.5.6 Reflections

This model shows that the simplistic approaches of local and global percentage attendance typically used in the screening modeling literature can undoubtedly be improved upon, and that the insights offered by more detailed models of human behavior offer exciting potential to the users of such models. More research is required to understand the causality between behavioral interventions and their impact in practice. The model did not consider the relative costs of interventions, but the results do suggest that *nudge*-type interventions aimed at modifying behavioral factors could potentially be very cost-effective.

## 13.6 Conclusion

Without doubt, modeling behavioral factors at this level of detail adds greatly to the data requirements of any DES model. Such models are already "data hungry" in the sense that they require a lot of individual-level data in order to fit activity distributions and estimate transition and branching probabilities. In the case of the PECS model, which was essentially a proof-of-concept, we largely used hypothetical data for the behavioral parameters, albeit based wherever possible on common sense or expert judgment. Clearly, nobody would base a real-world policy decision about retinopathy screening on the output of such a model. On the other hand, in the case of the breast cancer model, we were very fortunate to have access to a large secondary dataset on which to estimate the behavioral parameters. If we had had to collect these data ourselves, the model would almost certainly never have been built.

The seventeenth century French philosopher and mathematician Blaise Pascal (after whom the programming language in which I wrote the model described in Sect. 13.1.2 was named) clearly did not believe human behavior was sufficiently predictable to be modeled:

> *What a chimera the human being is! What a novelty, what a monster, what a chaos, what a contradiction, what a prodigy! Judge of all things, powerless earthworm, dark room of uncertainty, the glory and the shame of the universe. When he praises himself, I will humble him; when he humbles himself, I will praise him; and I will go on contradicting him until he comprehends that he is incomprehensible.* (Pascal, Pensées, 1671)

Therefore, the question remains: is it worth the effort to try to include behavioral factors in healthcare models? Furthermore, what is so special about healthcare that means that we particularly need to include human behavior in healthcare models? In the military domain, *human factors* have long been recognized as important and included in simulation models. It is difficult to think of many totally automated systems where there is no interaction whatsoever with human operators, users or decision-makers. Surely, when we are modeling any system which involves human beings, we need to take into account their behavior?

**Acknowledgements** We are grateful to Professor Derek Rutter in the Department of Psychology, University of Kent, UK, for the provision of behavioral data and specialist advice.

# References

Ajzen, A. 1988. *Attitudes personality and behaviour.* Milton Keynes: Open University Press.

Ajzen, A. 1991. The theory of planned behaviour. *Organizational Behaviour and Human Decision Processes* 50: 179–211.

Anylogic. 2015. http://www.anylogic.com/. Accessed 07 Sept 2015.

Baker, R. D., & Atherill, P. L. (2002). Improving appointment scheduling for medical screening. *IMA Journal of Management Mathematics*, *13*(4), 225-243.

Becker, M.H. 1974. The Health Belief Model and sick role behavior. *Health Education Monographs* 2: 409–419.

Brailsford, S.C. 2013. Discrete-event simulation is alive and kicking. *Journal of Simulation* 8: 1–13.

Brailsford, S.C., and B. Schmidt. 2003. Towards incorporating human behaviour in models of health care systems: An approach using discrete event simulation. *European Journal of Operational Research* 150: 19–31.

Brailsford, S.C., P.R. Harper, B. Patel, and M. Pitt. 2009. An analysis of the academic literature on simulation and modelling in healthcare. *Journal of Simulation* 3: 130–140.

Brailsford, S.C., P.R. Harper, and J. Sykes. 2012. Incorporating human behaviour in simulation models of screening for breast cancer. *European Journal of Operational Research* 219: 491–507.

Conner, M., and P. Norman. 1995, 2005. *Predicting health behaviour: Research and practice with social cognition models.* Buckingham: Open University Press.

Davies, R., and H. Davies. 1994. Modelling patient flows and resource provision in health systems. *Omega* 22: 123–131.

Davies, R.M., S.C. Brailsford, P.J. Roderick, C.R. Canning, and D.N. Crabbe. 2000. Using simulation modelling for evaluating screening services for diabetic retinopathy. *Journal of the Operational Research Society* 51: 476–484.

Fishbein, M., and A. Ajzen. 1975. *Belief, attitude intention and behaviour.* New York: Wiley.

Fone, D., S. Hollinghurst, M. Temple, A. Round, N. Lester, A. Weightman, K. Roberts, E. Coyle, G. Bevan, and S. Palmer. 2003. Systematic review of the use and value of computer simulation modelling in population health and healthcare delivery. *Journal of Public Health Medicine* 25: 325–335.

Gilbert, N., and K.G. Troitzch. 1999. *Simulation for the social scientist.* Buckingham: Open University Press.

Hulshof, P.J.H., N. Kortbeek, R.J. Boucherie, E.W. Hans, and P.J.M. Bakker. 2012. Taxonomic classification of planning decisions in health care: A structured review of the state of the art in OR/MS. *Health Systems* 1: 129–175.

Jun, J.B., S.H. Jacobson, and J.R. Swisher. 1999. Application of discrete-event simulation in health care clinics: A survey. *Journal of the Operational Research Society* 50: 109–123.

Katsaliaki, K., and N. Mustafee. 2011. Applications of simulation within the healthcare context. *Journal of the Operational Research Society* 62: 1431–1451.

McNabb, W.L. 1997. Adherence in diabetes: Can we define it and can we measure it. *Diabetes Care* 20: 215–219.

Pascal, B. 1671. Pensées sur la Religion et sur quelques autres Sujets. http://www.gutenberg.org/files/18269/18269-0.txt. Accessed 15 July 2015.

Rosenstock, I.M. 1996. Why people use health services. *Millbank Memorial Fund Quarterly* 44: 94–124.

Rutter, D.R. 2000. Attendance and re-attendance for breast cancer screening: A prospective 3 year test of the theory of planned behaviour. *British Journal of Health Psychology* 5: 1–13.

Schmidt, B. 2000. How to give agents a personality. http://schmidt-bernd.eu/modelle/HowtogiveAgents.pdf. Accessed 03 May 2015.

Tako, A.A., and S. Robinson. 2015. Is simulation in health different? *Journal of the Operational Research Society* 66: 602–614.

Tunnicliffe Wilson, J.C. 1981. Implementation of computer simulation projects in health care. *Journal of the Operational Research Society* 32: 825–832.

Weinberg, A.D., H.P. Cooper, M. Lane, and S. Kripalani. 1997. Screening behaviors and long-term compliance with mammography guidelines in a breast cancer screening program. *American Journal of Preventive Medicine* 13: 29–35.

# 14

# Service Operations: Behavioral Operational Research in British Telecommunications

## Jonathan Malpass

## 14.1 Introduction

Service organizations rely on the ability to change on a regular basis in order to meet the myriad drivers that underpin a successful business. High levels of customer service are central to retaining customers and growing revenues, but managing costs, improving efficiency and maintaining existing products whilst introducing new innovations and ensuring an engaged and motivated workforce are also key business imperatives. Service transformation can be achieved via process and decision-making automation (Owusu and O'Brien 2013), but human behavior does not always conform to the rationality of an algorithm (Kahneman 2011), and so intervention in models and deviation from expectations need to be understood for transformation activities to be effective. This chapter offers an account of the transformation of service operations in the telecommunications industry, focusing on the case of British Telecommunications (BT).

J. Malpass (✉)
Research & Innovation, BT Technology, Services and Operations,
Adastral Park, Martlesham Heath, Ipswich IP5 3RE, UK

© The Editor(s) (if applicable) and The Author(s) 2016
M. Kunc et al. (eds.), *Behavioral Operational Research*,
DOI 10.1057/978-1-137-53551-1_14

**281**

## 14.1.1 OR in the Telecoms Industry

The use of operational research methods is as essential to business improvement in the telecommunications sector as it is to any industry. The focus of the industry tends to be on delivering service rather than manufactured products (Johnston and Morris 1985; Duclos, Siha and Lummus 1995); optimal network design is a key aspect of service operations and also subject to intensive research from OR scholars from different parts of the world: USA, UK and Europe (Roy et al. 2010; Campbell and O'Kelly 2012).

Whilst a full literature review of the OR in telecommunications would deserve a chapter in itself, a brief search reveals a wide variety of applications and Management Science practice. For example, Tsang and Voudouris (1997) applied fast local search and guided local search algorithms to workforce scheduling and demonstrated their superior performance over other methods, including simulated annealing and genetic algorithms. Other optimization techniques, such as linear programming (Mitchell, Farwell and Ramsden 2006), non-linear programming (Migdalas 2006), metaheuristics (Martins and Ribeiro 2006) and integer programming (Lee and Lewis 2006), form part of a handbook dedicated to optimization in telecommunications.

Queueing theory has been applied in general, e.g. using single server queues (Addie and Zuckerman 1994), and has been applied specifically to call centers (Koole and Mandelbaum 2002). Simulation has been used in business scenarios in an attempt to improve business transformation activities (Dennis et al. 2000), and its application within the telecoms sector was the subject of the paper that won the 1992 Franz Edelman Award (Brigandi et al. 1994).

Decision support systems research has been used to assist with project selection (Tian et al. 2005) and with organization-wide issues (Kim et al. 1997). Other methods applied to the telecoms industry include Data Envelopment Analysis (Kim, Park and Park 1999) and situation-actor-process–learning-action-performance (SAP-LAP) model (Pramod and Banwet 2010) as well as statistical analysis (Tang et al. 2008). In fact, modern analytical techniques have been at the forefront of OR in general but also in telecoms (Spott et al. 2013).

Forecasting and supply chain are subject to much research, and the service supply chain is no exception. Akkermans and Vos (2003) investigated the bullwhip effect on supply chains within telecoms, and Lamothe, Mahmoudi and Thierry (2007) studied the impact of co-operation in forecasting on the supply chain.

Data from telecoms companies have been used to investigate social networks (Pandit et al. 2008), which in turn can be helpful in inferring trends and patterns. With the growth of Big Data, telecoms companies are looking to extract greater information from the vast warehouses of data (Ratti et al. 2010).

Finally (at least in this brief overview), Management Science has been used across the sector to study a variety of subjects, including: manufacturing flexibility (Gerwin 1993), the philosophy of Management Science (Pilkington and Liston-Heyes 1999), outsourcing (Berggren and Bengtsson 2004) and information technology (IT) operations management (Yong and Yuan 2009).

## 14.1.2 A Brief History of BT

BT has been constantly evolving since its first incarnation, the Electric Telegraph Company, was established in 1846 (BT 2015). For most of its history the organization held a virtual monopoly of UK telecommunications, which ended in 1982. Since privatization in 1984, BT Group plc has continued to change and now has some 90,000 employees serving customers in 170 countries. Recent changes, such as the rise of mobile and data communications, have meant even greater competition to BT's traditional services. BT's recent move into media and content delivery is representative of BT's continuous evolution.

The success of the business has been built on key technological innovations, such as digital communication networks (British Telecom 1982), blown fiber optic cables (Cockrill et al. 1997) and superfast broadband (Payne and Davey 2002). However, it has been the ability to transform how the many tens of thousands of employees' work has enabled BT to deliver the requisite service levels; the use of operational research techniques has been fundamental to this transformation (Voudouris et al. 2008; Owusu et al. 2013).

### 14.1.3 Behavioral OR in BT

Until recently, the use of behavior in models and the understanding of how models and methods impact behavior have not been seriously addressed. Failing to consider behavior has the potential to render very complex models virtually useless or to make the outcome of transformation activities completely different to that expected. However, transformational projects have a greater chance of success and in turn deliver benefits to the business by ensuring that user and staff behavior is understood and accounted for.

This chapter describes a number of case studies relating how behavioral OR (BOR) has been used in BT and the lessons that have been learned, which, in turn, have meant that OR-driven business transformation activities are achieving greater success.

## 14.2 Methodology for Behavioral Studies

Understanding behavior, whether determining modeling parameters or comprehending how people interact with systems or are influenced by results of models, is difficult. When the behavior being studied is that of people going about their jobs, it is also unrealistic to conduct laboratory-style experiments. The approach adopted within BT follows a framework comprising four steps: (i) OR Project, (ii) Behavioral Study, (iii) Quantitative Analysis and (iv) Report (see Fig. 14.1). In practice, these steps rarely happen in a linear fashion. For example, whilst the OR project is the core step, the behavioral study can precede it, run concur-

**Fig. 14.1** Framework for Behavioral Operational Research study

rently or be conducted after implementation. A quantitative analysis is conducted to understand the impact of the OR project and may be run at various times to capture the relevant information. Reporting progress and results to key stakeholders is also essential so that appropriate decisions can be made.

Given the wide variety of situations that BOR may be applied to, there is no one technique to study behavior, so the approach is to use a number of methods and apply the one that is most appropriate to the particular study. Table 14.1 summarizes the methods used and their advantages and disadvantages.

The next sections provide an overview of different projects where the framework for behavioral operational research has been employed.

**Table 14.1** Summary of behavioral research methods used in BT

| Method | What/when | Advantages | Disadvantages |
|---|---|---|---|
| Day-in-the-Life-of (DILO) | • Whole day spent job-shadowing subject to capture the various behaviors that occur over time;<br>• Informal questioning and conversation provide supplementary data;<br>• Used with mobile employees or when observing workplaces | • Able to capture a wide variety of behaviors and information;<br>• Able to observe what subject actually does, rather than relying on what they say they do;<br>• Longer periods of time allow workers to relax, rapport to be established and informal conversation can elicit extra information;<br>• Enables a real deep dive into the detail of enquiry rather than a superficial overview;<br>• Little/zero impact on daily working operations | • Time-consuming;<br>• Difficult to record, although video can be used;<br>• Very small sample size, so may not be good representation of population;<br>• Day may be atypical;<br>• Researcher can introduce bias |
| Face-to-face interviews | • Researcher conducts semi-structured interviews with set questions and time to allow interviewee to talk about related issues;<br>• Used with co-located employees | • Recordable;<br>• Easier to establish rapport with subject;<br>• Able to monitor subject's behavior;<br>• Allows interviewee to answer sensitive questions in confidence;<br>• Many interviews in one day;<br>• Transcriptions from interviews enable detailed analysis, e.g. grounded theory (Martin and Turner 1986) | • May impact on operational rotas as employees need to be taken off line/off rotas;<br>• Researcher can introduce bias |

**Table 14.1**   (continued)

| Method | What/when | Advantages | Disadvantages |
|---|---|---|---|
| Telephone interviews | • Researcher conducts semi-structured interviews with set questions and time to allow interviewee to talk about related issues;<br>• Used with geographically dispersed employees | • Recordable;<br>• Aallows interviewee to answer sensitive questions in confidence;<br>• Many interviews in short space of time;<br>• Transcriptions from interviews enable detailed analysis (e.g. grounded theory) | • May impact on operational rotas as employees need to be taken off line/off rotas;<br>• Not able to monitor subject's behavior;<br>• Difficult to establish whether interviewees are able to answer freely;<br>• Researcher can introduce bias |
| Focus groups | • Researcher facilitates discussion about set of questions;<br>• Used with co-located subjects where group interactions are useful | • Recordable;<br>• Several subjects at a time;<br>• Can monitor subjects' behavior and reactions | • May impacts on operational rotas as numerous employees need to be taken off line/off rotas at the same time.<br>• One or two subjects can dominate;<br>• Large groups means sensitive issues are inappropriate;<br>• Researcher can inject bias |
| Surveys | • Researcher conducts on-line surveys of multiple subjects | • Potential to collect a lot of data from a lot of subjects;<br>• Easy to analyze;<br>• Rapid turnaround compared to interviews and other methods | • Survey development can be time-consuming;<br>• Risk of non-completion;<br>• Risk of misinterpretation of the questions;<br>• Removes the ability to observe/record behavioral traits |

# 14.3  Behavioral OR in BT

## 14.3.1 Managing the Workforce

Arguably, the biggest single OR project in BT is the management of field operations, which since the late 1980s has become increasingly automated. Perhaps the most fundamental change in how the field engineering workforce operated came with BT's own Big Bang moment: in the early 1990s, the traditional allocation of paper-based *job packs* was replaced by an automated work allocation system known as Work Manager (Garwood 1996). When this system was first developed, BT employed about 50,000 field engineers across the UK to maintain networks, repair faults and provide service to customers. Work Manager was designed to "get the right person, in the right place, at the right time."

The algorithm which underpinned the system was a real-time algorithm (RTA) that determined the next task for an engineer in a reactive way (Laithwaite 1995). A further improvement was made by introducing a *Dynamic Scheduler* into Work Manager (Lesaint et al. 1998). One aspect of this development was to address some of the behavioral issues that had become apparent since the initial deployment of Work Manager, namely:

- Customers who request, cancel or amend jobs unpredictably,
- Engineers whose availability is subject to last-minute changes and whose task completion times vary,
- Resource managers who may modify provisional schedules and review business objectives at any time.

The Dynamic Scheduler comprised the reactive component of Work Manager and a predictive scheduling element, based on a combination of heuristic search and constraint-based reasoning, which was a variant of the Vehicle Routing Problem (Laporte and Osman 1995).

The new system automated work management and field communications and was used by both field engineers and office-based work allocators whose job had previously been to issue paper-based *job packs* to engineers. The introduction of Work Manager saw a number of unanticipated behaviors that, left unchecked, could threaten the success of the deployment. The most problematic of these behaviors was the practice of *hard-pinning*, i.e. intervening in the system and manually assigning an engineer to a task.

The allocators were used to being in control of the work and were reluctant to believe that an automated system could produce an outcome as effectively as their own approach. Work Manager automatically identified the engineer who was both skilled and available for the task, yet the allocators had an understanding of *softer* factors, such as an engineer who knew the area or the customer, and felt that they could make better decisions than the system.

In theory, the occasional hard-pinning of tasks would not unduly affect the effectiveness of the dynamic scheduler; however, as allocators were used to dividing tasks amongst a team of engineers, their desire to continue doing so saw levels of manual intervention rise to between 40 % and 50 %. This not only could damage the performance of the system but was time consuming to the allocation teams, who then had insufficient time to carry out other duties.

Two schools of thought arose over the ideal level of hard-pinning. Experiments were carried out where the dynamic scheduler was first switched off and allocators required to assign all tasks; the experiment was then reversed and the system was allowed to run without any intervention. Eventually, the results proved that some intervention was useful, for instance where an engineer had to revisit a locale or a customer within a few days. The experiments also allowed the allocators to understand that Work Manager would deliver an optimal solution and that their *control* of the whole issue of work allocation needed to be relaxed. The current approach is to allow for a small amount of tasks to be hard-pinned—ideally no more than 10 %.

In this study, the BOR study framework outlined in Sect. 14.2 was only loosely followed. The OR project was developed without any behavioral considerations; however, once behavior was recognized as essential to the success of the project, the behavioral study and quantitative analysis were conducted and changes to the project adopted as a result of the findings.

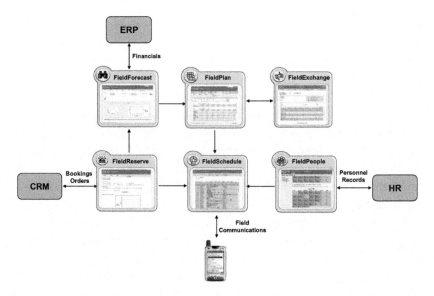

**Fig. 14.2**  Schematic view of the Field Optimization Suite

## 14.3.2 Workforce Optimization

The next phase of OR-driven operational transformation within BT came through the development of a single, end-to-end resource management tool, Field Optimization Suite (FOS). With a focus on effective planning of resources, the tool combines demand forecasting, resource planning, reservations and scheduling (Voudouris et al. 2006; Owusu et al. 2006) (see Fig. 14.2).

FOS was developed from two earlier projects aimed at automating the resource management processes in BT. The traditional approach was analogous to the work allocation transformation in Sect. 14.1.3. Teams of planners were responsible for their own areas, and each went through the same basic process: derive a demand forecast (mainly based on their experience and intuition) and develop a plan based on the local resources, the expected productivity for the workforce and some additional factors.

One approach investigated the use of software agents to enhance workflow between planning teams (Shepherdson, Thompson and Odgers 1999). Advantages of using agents centered on the use of a common approach and language, auditable processes and workflows, and specialist *broker* agents to communicate between teams.

The second approach was a combination of artificial intelligence (AI) and OR techniques (Owusu et al. 2003). The Automated Resource Management System (ARMS) used a variety of time series forecasting techniques and a dynamic planner which applied constructive search and local search methods to optimize resources.

FOS has since been deployed in a number of BT's operational teams. In conjunction with the deployment of the system, the impact on the teams who use FOS has also been studied. The next four sections address issues within some of the components of FOS: forecasting, planning, scheduling and rostering.

This optimization project adopted a loose interpretation of the BOR study framework: understanding and modeling behavior were a fundamental driver of the whole project and preceded the full deployment of the OR project: the quantitative analysis which followed demonstrated the success of the project.

### 14.3.3 Issues in Forecasting

In a study of one of the first teams to use FOS, it was found that the forecast function was not used at all (Malpass 2009). It was found that users had no confidence in the forecast and said it was because it "doesn't reflect reality". A bigger problem was that there was some reluctance to use it. Not only was it something new, but it was also seen as a *black box*, and the users did not understand how the forecasts were derived. This prompted a revision of both the algorithms and the interface so that users had greater understanding of the forecasting approach. Since then, the tool has become the planning tool throughout the organization and, whilst willingness to use the tool is no longer an issue, some aspects of behavior that the tool causes have an impact on day-to-day operations.

One particularly long-running issue concerns managers' repeatedly asking for improvements in forecast accuracy, which has in the past caused frustration amongst the people responsible for producing the forecasts. Managers' desires to have more accurate forecasts is often misplaced, resulting either in wasted effort trying to find improved models, when in fact they succeed only in temporarily modeling noise, or in failure to manage the inherent variation in the data (Malpass 2013a). Further work demonstrated that there is a limit to forecast accuracy; communicating that the level of noise in the data directly affects accuracy has meant that other mechanisms have been introduced to manage variation.

In this study, the OR Project was designed and deployed without consideration of user behavior. As a result of the users' reluctance to use the forecast tool, the behavioral study was undertaken and the project revised. It was as a result of this study that behavior became an integral part of further OR projects.

## 14.3.4 Issues in Planning

System Dynamics (SD) has been used to model the service performance of a BT line of business based on strategic planning decisions (Jensen, Lyons and Buckhurst 2013). The approach has incorporated some behavioral aspects, and it draws attention to the fact that tension is created between parts of the process or actors in the organization as different demands are required.

In a study (Malpass 2015) of how the planning teams make decisions and the impact that those decisions have on others, a system thinking (Senge 1990) approach was taken to capture the behavior. In interviews, various stakeholders were asked how they made decisions, over what factors they had control and by whom they were influenced. Various scenarios unfolded; by way of example, one such scenario is described in Fig. 14.3.

The planning team are responsible for taking the demand forecast and determining the appropriate resources to meet that expected demand. The plan for the week ahead is agreed at the end of the current week, and thence only minor changes to the next day's plan are permitted. The planners aim to hit a target workstack that ensures that there is sufficient work for field engineers to perform. Too little work and the engineers will be under-utilized—and fail their productivity target. Too much work and there will be too few engineers to carry out all the work required and the

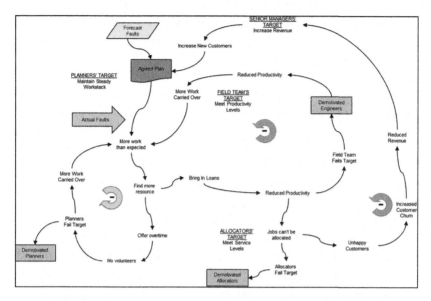

**Fig. 14.3** Visualization of behavior in planning, field and allocation teams

allocators—who are targeted on meeting service levels—will struggle to issue all the tasks on time, which in turn impacts customer satisfaction.

In this scenario, the senior manager has imposed a target to increase the number of new customers and a resource plan has been agreed to meet this demand. However, a higher than expected volume of faults occurred, which has increased the workstack beyond acceptable levels. The planning team's first step is to offer overtime to engineers in a bid to complete the necessary tasks on time. However, in this instance, there was no take up of the offer, and so tasks failed and were carried over to the next day—so the planners missed their target.

To compensate, engineers from a neighboring team are brought in to assist; unfortunately, these engineers are less familiar with the geography and the local network, and so their productivity is reduced, meaning that the field team miss their target, which in turn has an impact on their morale, and so their productivity is further reduced (Hardy, Alcock and Malpass, 2015). Consequently, more jobs are carried over and the workstack increases.

The allocators, meanwhile, struggle to issue tasks in time to meet service levels. Not only do they miss their targets and become demotivated, but because appointments are missed, customers become unhappy, which potentially increases customer churn, which has a negative effect on revenue—one of the main targets of the senior manager.

This is just one scenario, but the behavior of one group of people—in this instance, the engineers who refuse the offer of overtime—has a huge impact on all the stakeholders in the process, the customer and ultimately the bottom line. In reality, the planners have a number of different levers they can use to try to maintain the balance, but it is a delicate operation and can quickly become chaotic.

This study has been conducted over a number of years, and as a result the OR project and behavioral study have been developing over time, running sometimes separately and sometimes in parallel. Again, this project highlights that the framework can be interpreted in a number of ways and needs to be adapted according to the specific project.

## 14.3.5 Issues in Scheduling

In a recent transformational activity, one engineering organization sought to enact a fundamental change to the way that engineers were allocated work, predicated on an ability of engineers to carry out work that they would not previously have been able to perform. In this organization, engineers belonged to one of four skill groups, each requiring specialist skills. The process for allocating work to engineers using Work Manager (outlined in Sect. 14.1.3) prioritizes jobs based on location and skill-set and consequently will not issue a job belonging to one skill-set to an engineer from another skill-set. As a result, this particular group of engineers regularly travelled long distances to carry out basic tasks, many of which could be performed by colleagues with another skill-set.

The transformational activity was to provide all the engineers from an area with visibility of all the work in that area and empower them to decide which jobs they would carry out. Some level of *control* was retained by the work allocators, who monitored the workstack to ensure that service levels were met and major problems were averted.

By way of example, two scenarios occurred during a series of Day-in-the-Life-of studies (Malpass 2013b). The first saw one engineer spend a total of more than two hours travelling between his four jobs, but these included two tasks in locations where colleagues had previously visited—tasks which, in theory, they could have performed. The second saw another engineer leave a location and travel for more than forty minutes before being asked to return to the same location to carry out a non-urgent task rather than complete an additional service-affecting task in his new location.

These issues highlight the conflicting interests that impact scheduling. The behavioral study highlighted that engineers were focused on their own work-type and productivity, not the overall workstack or the number of issues with the network. In order to deliver the transformational change, not only did the scheduling algorithm need to be altered and engineers be empowered to select appropriate tasks but the measures and objectives of the engineers, allocators and managers needed to be changed. Instead of a focus on a single aspect, global views were required.

Consequently, engineers, concerned that they would not have time to do anything other than their own work, and allocators, concerned that they would not be able to meet service levels, were encouraged look at the total workstack, the general health of the network and other measures, such as total travel time, rather than individual productivity.

The framework for this project followed a different pattern. After a request for a new OR solution, the behavioral study was undertaken in order to identify issues that might arise in the deployment of the scheduling solution. As a result, the OR project was not radically altered but the manner of its deployment was carefully managed; the quantitative analysis was robust, proving benefits to both engineers and managers.

## 14.3.6 Issues in Rostering

The development of appropriate roster patterns is essential to provide the highest levels of customer service. Understanding demand is part of the forecasting element of FOS, but patterns in the data can be useful, especially if the resource can be matched accordingly. There are two very distinct patterns in demand for BT's services: first, there are peaks in demand at the start of the working day and again in the early afternoon, and second, there is a higher level of demand for services on Mondays and Fridays.

Understanding the customer has helped with resourcing to meet this demand. The peaks during the day reflect customers' wishes to have appointments either first thing in the morning or straight after lunch. Higher demand on Mondays is driven by an increase in faults being reported after the weekend and on Fridays by its being a more traditional day for new installations (e.g. more people moving house).

However, despite understanding customer behavior, it is not always possible to meet the demand with the available resources. To try to overcome this, dynamic pricing has been used to investigate whether there would be any benefit in trying to change customer behavior by offering incentives in return for appointments at times that are less convenient to the customer but that enable the business to be more efficient (Rana and Oliveria 2015). In principle, the concept of dynamic pricing and reinforcement learning has its merits; its application in BT is still being investigated.

This particular rostering example illustrates how the OR project and an understanding of behavior can be studied at the same time in order to provide an understanding of whether deploying the OR solution may be of benefit. The quantitative analysis is essential, but the decision is dependent on the success of the research.

## 14.3.7 Understanding Customer Behavior

The use of behavioral factors in OR models is, arguably, the most difficult of the three aspects of BOR to perform, as capturing behavior has been time-consuming and costly. However, with technological developments, describing behavior—particularly customer behavior—has become more prevalent. Three particular projects have sought to identify customer habits and how they relate to customer churn, i.e. customers choosing to switch to another service provider, in the attempt to reduce the number of customers who leave.

Data mining and machine learning techniques, allied to traditional statistical techniques, have been used to predict customer events and, by doing so, to proactively manage the customer journey and thus reduce churn. One such project identified the number of times a customer contacts BT as a key driver of churn (Nauck 2011); consequently, a customer identified as making a number of calls in a short space of time is now directed to a team of contact center agents who take personal responsibility for resolving the customer problem.

A similar analysis has been undertaken to understand one of BT's newer services—TV. Analysis of customer behaviors, such as the frequency of instances that customer watches TV and the total time spent watching TV in a given period, has been used to develop understanding of how likely customers who call to complain about the service they receive are to switch to another provider. Using this information has led to enhancements in the service and an improvement in customer service levels.

Another application of using customer behavior has been to identify customers who call frequently but who do not have service issues. One category of these customers are the *non-payers,* who tend to call repeatedly until they speak to an agent that will grant them extra time before they must pay the bill; by understanding this behavior, the queuing system has been modified to direct the customer to a single co-located, specially trained team which is then able to monitor demand and use traditional queuing theory approaches to ensure that the staffing levels are sufficient to meet demand (Hardy, Alcock and Malpass, 2013).

## 14.4 Conclusions

At first glance, Behavioral Operational Research may appear to be a new discipline that has yet to gain serious traction in business. However, as this chapter has discussed, there have been many instances of the use of OR methods in transformation projects in BT. A framework for BOR studies has been presented, and the various examples have demonstrated that a flexible approach needs to be adopted during service transformation projects. Regardless of when the behavioral study is conducted, it is clear that understanding behavior has enhanced the success of that transformation.

Furthermore, this chapter has described how each of the three aspects of BOR has been used: *behavior in models* is arguably the most difficult to carry out, but with the recent developments in analytics and big data, gaining insight into the vast quantities of customer data that a business such as BT has is becoming easier to achieve; *behavior with models* is the area in which most practice has occurred in BT, and understanding how people interact with models and systems has led to both further improvements to the system and increased benefits as users and managers understand the effectiveness of the OR model; *behavior beyond models* and influencing the decision-maker is also of great importance to businesses, and the OR practitioner must pay as much attention to aspect of BOR as to the others, as it is the decision-maker who can fundamentally transform the business, be it at an operational or a strategic level.

# References

Addie, R.G., and M. Zuckerman. 1994. An approximation for performance evaluation of stationary single server queues. *IEE Transactions on Communications* 42: 3150–3160.

Akkermans, H., and B. Vos. 2003. Amplification in service supply chains: An exploratory case study from the telecom industry. *Production and Operations Management* 12: 204–223.

Berggren, C., and L. Bengtsson. 2004. Rethinking outsourcing in manufacturing: A tale of two telecom firms. *European Management Journal* 22: 211–223.

Brigandi, A.J., D.R. Dargon, M.J. Sheehan, and T. Spencer. 1994. AT&T's call processing simulator (CAPS) operational design for inbound call centers. *Interfaces* 24: 6–28.

British Telecom. 1982. *System X: The way ahead.* http://www.samhallas.co.uk/repository/po_docs/system_x.pdf. Accessed 03 May 2016.

BT. 2015. Our history. http://btplc.com/thegroup/btshistory/index.htm. Accessed 26 Jan 2015.

Campbell, J.F., and M.E. O'Kelly. 2012. Twenty-five years of hub location research. *Transportation Science* 46: 153–169.

Cockrill, K., J. Nixey, R. Studd, M. Davies, and R. Sutehall. 1997. Blown fibre – A reference test blowing route. *International wire & cable symposium proceedings*.

Dennis, S., B. King, M. Hind, and S. Robinson. 2000. Applications of business process simulation and lean techniques in British Telecommunications Plc. *Proceedings of the 2000 winter simulation conference*, pp. 2015–2021.

Duclos, L.K., S.M. Siha, and R.R. Lummus. 1995. JIT in services: A review of current practices and future directions for research. *International Journal of Service Industry Management* 6: 36–52.

Garwood, G.J. 1996. Work manager. *BT Technology Journal* 14: 58–68.

Gerwin, D. 1993. Manufacturing flexibility: A strategic perspective. *Management Science* 39: 395–410.

Hardy, B., T. Alcock, and J. Malpass. 2013. *Morale within six BT retail consumer contact centres*. BT internal report.

Hardy, B., T. Alcock, and J. Malpass. 2015. Morale: Unravelling its components and testing its impact within contact centres. In *Winning Ideas: The Management Articles of the Year*, 7–13. Chartered Management Institute.

Jensen, K., M. Lyons, and N. Buckhurst. 2013. System dynamics models of field force operations. In *Transforming field and service operations*, ed. O. Owusu, P. O'Brien, J. McCall, and N.F. Doherty, 47–69. Heidelberg: Springer.

Johnston, R., and B. Morris. 1985. Monitoring and control in service operations. *International Journal of Operations & Production Management* 5: 32–38.

Kahneman, D. 2011. *Thinking, fast and slow*. London: Penguin.

Kim, Y.-G., H.-W. Kim, J.-W. Yoon, and H.-S. Ryu. 1997. Building an organizational decision support system for Korea Telecom: A process redesign approach. *Decision Support Systems* 19: 255–269.

Kim, S.-H., C.-G. Park, and K.-S. Park. 1999. An application of data envelopment analysis in telephone offices evaluation with partial data. *Computers & Operations Research* 26: 59–72.

Koole, G., and A. Mandelbaum. 2002. Queueing models of call centers: An introduction. *Annals of Operations Research* 113: 41–59.

Laithwaite, R. 1995. Work allocation challenges and solutions in a large-scale work management environment. *BT Technology Journal* 13: 46–54.

Lamothe, J., J. Mahmoudi, and C. Thierry. 2007. Cooperation to reduce risk in a telecom supply chain. *Supply Chain Forum: An International Journal* 8: 36–52.

Laporte, G., and I.H. Osman. 1995. Routing problems: A bibliography. *Annals of Operations Research* 61: 227–262.

Lee, E.K., and D.P. Lewis. 2006. Integer programming for telecommunications. In *Handbook of optimization in telecommunications*, ed. M.G.C. Resende and P. Pardalos, 67–102. New York: Springer.

Lesaint, D., N. Azarmi, R. Laithwaite, and P. Walker. 1998. Engineering dynamic scheduler for work manager. *BT Technology Journal* 16: 16–29.

Malpass, J. 2009. *Openreach FOS audit*. BT internal report.

Malpass, J. 2013a. Understanding the risks of forecasting. In *Transforming field and service operations*, ed. O. Owusu, P. O'Brien, J. McCall, and N.F. Doherty, 70–83. Heidelberg: Springer.

Malpass, J. 2013b. *IXD: Voice of the engineer/FLM*. BT internal report.

Malpass, J. 2015. *A study of behavior in planning teams*. BT internal report.

Martin, P.Y., and B.A. Turner. 1986. Grounded theory and organizational research. *Journal of Applied Behavioral Science* 22: 141–157.

Martins, S.L., and C.C. Ribeiro. 2006. Metaheuristics and applications to optimization problems in telecommunications. In *Handbook of optimization in telecommunications*, ed. M.G.C. Resende and P. Pardalos, 103–128. New York: Springer.

Migdalas, A. 2006. Non-linear programming in telecommunications. In *Handbook of optimization in telecommunications*, ed. M.G.C. Resende and P. Pardalos, 27–66. New York: Springer.

Mitchell, J.E., K. Farwell, and D. Ramsden. 2006. Interior point methods for large-scale linear programming. In *Handbook of optimization in telecommunications*, ed. M.G.C. Resende and P. Pardalos, 3–25. New York: Springer.

Nauck, D. 2011. *ECLIPSE OCR analysis (repeat calls)*. BT internal report.

Owusu, O., and P. O'Brien. 2013. Transforming field and service operations with automation. In *Transforming field and service operations*, ed. O. Owusu, P. O'Brien, J. McCall, and N.F. Doherty, 15–28. Heidelberg: Springer.

Owusu, O., C. Voudouris, R. Dorne, C. Ladde, G. Anim-Ansah, K. Gasson, and G. Connolly. 2003. ARMS—Application of AI and OR methods to resource management. *BT Technology Journal* 21: 27–31.

Owusu, O., C. Voudouris, M. Kern, A. Garyfalos, G. Anim-Ansah, and B. Virginas. 2006. On optimising resource planning in BT plc with FOS. *IEEE: International conference on services systems and services management*, IEEE/SSSM06.

Owusu, O., P. O'Brien, J. McCall, and N.F. Doherty. 2013. *Transforming field and service operations*. Heidelberg: Springer.

Pandit. V., N. Modani, S. Mukherjea, A.A. Nanavati, S. Roy, and A. Agarwal. 2008. Extracting dense communities from telecom call graphs. *Communication systems software and middleware and workshops, 2008. COMSWARE 2008. 3rd international conference on communication.* IEEE, pp. 82–89.

Payne, D.B., and R.P. Davey. 2002. The future of fiber access systems. *BT Technology Journal* 20: 104–114.

Pilkington, A., and C. Liston-Heyes. 1999. Is production and operations management a discipline? A citation/co-citation study. *International Journal of Operations & Production Management* 19: 7–20.

Pramod, V.R., and D.K. Banwet. 2010. System modelling of telecom service sector supply chain: A SAP-LAP analysis. *International Journal of Business Excellence* 3: 38–64.

Rana, R., and F. Oliveria. 2015. Dynamic pricing of perishable products under incomplete information using reinforcement learning. *Expert Systems with Applications* 42: 426–436.

Ratti, C., S. Sobolevsky, F. Calabrese, C. Andris, J. Reades, M. Martino, R. Claxton, and S.H. Strogatz. 2010. Redrawing the map of Great Britain from a network of human interactions. *PLoS ONE* 5, e14248.

Roy, R., A. Nag, and B. Mukherjee. 2010. Telecom mesh network upgrade to manage traffic growth. *Journal of Optical Communications and Networking* 2: 256–265.

Senge, P.M. 1990. *The fifth discipline.* New York: Doubleday/Currency.

Shepherdson, J., S. Thompson, and B. Odgers. 1999. *Cross organisational workflow co-ordinated by software agents.* BT internal report.

Spott, M., D. Nauck, and P. Taylor. 2013. Modern analytics in field and service operations. In *Transforming field and service operations,* ed. O. Owusu, P. O'Brien, J. McCall, and N.F. Doherty, 85–99. Heidelberg: Springer.

Tang, J., R. Li, Y. Shi, and C. Fan. 2008. Application of principal component analysis to performance evaluation of telecom enterprises. *Journal of Northeastern University (Natural Science)* 29: 488.

Tian, Q., J. Ma, J. Liang, R.C.W. Kwok, and O. Liu. 2005. An organizational decision support system for effective R&D project selection. *Decision Support Systems* 39: 403–413.

Tsang, E., and C. Voudouris. 1997. Fast local search and guided local search and their application to British Telecom's workforce scheduling problem. *Operations Research Letters* 20: 119–127.

Voudouris, C., O. Owusu, R. Dorne, and A. McCormick. 2006. FOS: An advanced planning and scheduling suite for service operations. *IEEE:*

*International conference on services systems and services management*, IEEE/ SSSM06.

Voudouris, C., O. Owusu, R. Dorne, and D. Lesaint. 2008. *Service chain management*. Berlin: Springer.

Yong, D., and Z. Yuan. 2009. Research on the business service management in the IT operation management of China Telecom. *Telecommunications Science* 9: 017.

# 15

# SMART Cities: Big Data and Behavioral Operational Research

Leroy White, Katharina Burger and Mike Yearworth

## 15.1 Introduction

We define SMART OR as *the creative use of Big Data with Hard and Soft OR to enhance behavior and positive results for decision makers*. It is a multi-methodology approach (Mingers and Brocklesby 1997) that seeks to bring about the emergence of distributed agency towards a shared goal, which is appropriate in super-wicked (Lazarus 2009) problem contexts and that involves the creative use of different approaches for analysis.

L. White (✉)
Warwick Business School, University of Warwick, Coventry CV4 7AL, UK

K. Burger
Portsmouth Business School, University of Portsmouth, Portland Street, Portsmouth PO1 3DE, UK

M. Yearworth
Faculty of Engineering, University of Bristol, Queen's Building, University Walk, Clifton, Bristol BS8 1TR, UK

© The Editor(s) (if applicable) and The Author(s) 2016　　**303**
M. Kunc et al. (eds.), *Behavioral Operational Research*,
DOI 10.1057/978-1-137-53551-1_15

It is essentially action oriented and located within a particular problem context and stakeholder grouping and can take into account a number of biases—should they be observed by an external observer. In the following sections we describe three case studies and derive five perspectives that contextualize SMART OR: the implications of super-wicked problems, the encouragement of wider participation in the implementation of collaborative stakeholder engagement platforms, the synthesis of methods and data to support group decision making, the enhanced collaboratory and the notion of the Living Lab. We then outline how these strands come together in our conceptualization of SMART OR.

## 15.2  Context for SMART OR

### 15.2.1 CASE 1: The STEEP Project

The European Union (EU)-funded SMART Cities project Systems Thinking for Energy Efficient Planning (STEEP) uses a systemic Problem Structuring Method (PSM) based on Checkland's Soft Systems Methodology (SSM) (Checkland and Scholes 1999) to support group decision making for energy planning in three urban regeneration districts in Bristol, San Sebastián and Florence. Similar applications of PSMs in this context have been reported and provided supporting justification for their relevance in this multi-agency setting (Coelho, Antunes and Martins 2010; Franco 2008; Neves et al. 2004). Whilst it was not originally conceived as a big data project, some of the developments in the project since starting in 2013 have contributed directly to our thinking about SMART OR. These specific developments have occurred in response to (i) the need to make the STEEP methodology "open source" to satisfy an EU funding requirement, (ii) awareness of the implications of "super-wicked" problems (Lazarus 2009), especially with respect to timescales for decision making (Levin et al. 2007) and (iii) developments in the project to widen stakeholder participation through the use of a collaborative stakeholder engagement platform. In the following sections we outline how these three strands have come together in the STEEP project to contribute to our conceptualization of SMART OR.

The concept of the STEEP methodology's being *open source* was meant to convey to interested parties, primarily but not exclusively in the SMART Cities domain, that comprehensive information about how to apply the methodology and the necessary tool support would be freely available. At the design phase of the STEEP project, this was conceived as being delivered by a set of videos and slides of a training workshop that was principally used to train the project participants in the methodology. This complete documentation of the methodology is available online.[1] Furthermore, all of the project deliverables, which include (i) in-depth description of the methodology, (ii) reflections on its scalability and (iii) detailed internal evaluation, was made publicly available on project completion in late 2015. As the project developed through the experience of running group model building workshops in the three cities, refinements to the methodology were conceived to address some of the weaknesses that were apparent. The majority of these developments were concerned with the (i) the co-dependence of stakeholder group formation and gaining agreement over a suitable transformational goal and (ii) understanding the decision making "architecture" of a complex multi-agency setting in order to be effective.

The Hierarchical Process Modeling (HPM) approach (Davis et al. 2010) used in the STEEP methodology is perfectly capable of expressing the STEEP methodology itself. Inspired by Checkland's expression of SSM using a Purposeful Activity System Model (Checkland 1981) and also by work on the difference between SSM *content* (SSM$_c$) and SSM *process* (SSM$_p$) (Checkland and Winter 2006), we decided to express the *enhanced* STEEP methodology in HPM form too, in effect to turn the methodology into a self-describing form that could be built into a collaborative platform. We return to this development later, when we discuss the process of widening participation through the use of a collaborative stakeholder engagement platform.

**The first perspective relevant to our concept of SMART OR is the *implications of Super-Wicked Problems.*** The case for and the use of OR processes are frequently made in response to the challenge of interventions in wicked and messy problem contexts (Ackoff 1981;

---

[1] See http://smartsteep.eu/resources.

Mingers 2011; Rittel and Webber 1973; Rosenhead 1992). Energy planning efforts are a class of problems that could be described as "wicked" or "messy" in that they are problems that are difficult or impossible to solve because of incomplete, contradictory and changing requirements that are often difficult to reconcile (Rittel and Webber 1973). In terms of an energy planning context, there are problems whose solution requires a great number of people to change their mindsets and behavior; thus it is a situation that is more than likely to be a wicked problem (Lazarus 2009; Yearworth 2015).

Extending the arguments about problems as "wicked" or "messy" would mean addressing uncertainty and risk more explicitly (Horlick-Jones et al. 2001). The embedding of risk issues in which there are sectional interests and hidden agendas that permeate and obscure uncertainty and risk presents a serious challenge to policy decisions. Horn and Weber (2007) claim that these are a "social mess" in that they are characterized as a set of inter-related problems and other messes: a complexity—or systems of systems—which is amongst the factors that make social messes so resistant to analysis and, more importantly, to resolution. A further extension is that exacerbating the effects of risk and uncertainty ensures that the problem situation is a super-wicked problem (Lazarus 2009). Here, if the challenges of wicked, messy, swampy problems are not enough, the emergence of the concept of *super-wicked* problems layers an extra burden of urgency and self-cause onto the structuring of problems and the design of interventions (Lazarus 2009). Lazarus describes four additions to the original Rittel and Webber definitions. These are: (i) time is running out, (ii) there is an absence of a single controlling authority, (iii) *we* caused the problem in the first place and (iv) behavioral research suggests that we use *hyperbolic* (Laibson 1997) or psychological accounting (Tversky and Kahneman 1992) rather than rational discounting of future cash flows in our decision making.

Focusing on the first of Lazarus' proposed additions, we have taken the view that if time is indeed running out for decision makers then (OR) interventions should in themselves be timely. One obvious place to look for time saving is in the cumbersome and difficult process of the group model building workshops. Would it be possible to use big data and OR processes to implement and host a number of tools that together could be used to replace the workshop? Morton, Ackermann and Belton (2007) have already made a contribution to answering this question. The timely, workshop-less intervention is returned to in the discussion.

**The second perspective relevant to our development of SMART OR concerns encouraging *wider participation in the implementation of a collaborative stakeholder engagement platform.*** The original purpose was to provide a collaborative environment in which stakeholders could share geo-located data typically associated with the use of Geographical Information Systems (GISs). The domain of energy planning readily embraces use of geo-located data to present information about power-grids, heat maps etc. In keeping with the open source methodology concept of the project, the GIS capability of the STEEP collaborative stakeholder engagement platform was embedded into a wiki to provide a readily available environment where energy-planning documents can be constructed easily. Geo-data can be literally dragged and dropped into the platform and the data rendered as a map with all of the normal GIS capabilities available. Having been constructed, this GIS/wiki combination was further enhanced by the capability to collaboratively develop HPMs of the sort described in the STEEP methodology. With this in place, it was considered that the STEEP collaborative stakeholder engagement platform now offered the necessary capability for workshop-less group model building workshops to take place. The extensibility of the platform means that almost any sort of data analysis capability can be added as required; for example a relatively late extension in the project was the addition of the R software for statistical computing and graphics.

**The third perspective relevant to our concept of SMART OR is the *synthesis of methods and data to support group decision making.*** The STEEP collaborative stakeholder engagement, with native GIS and HPM capability, provides the nexus where data, big or otherwise, can be integrated with PSM to enable timely and informed decision making by groups of stakeholders. However, the availability of data and an open source methodology do not per se lead to problem structuring. A collaborative platform is collaborative only in the presence of some agency that motivates or animates the methodology into purposeful action. For SMART OR to be realized, this question must be addressed. Here the solution is suggested by a number of researchers (Ackermann et al. 2005; Bana e Costa et al. 2014; Bryson et al. 2004; Franco 2007, 2009).

## 15.2.2 CASE 2: The Future City Demonstrator: Big Open Data in the SMART City Ecosystem

The availability of big data is often seen as an enabler of more effective and efficient management of public services and infrastructures, benefitting citizens who create (actively or passively) much of the data that is used. Big data arise in a variety of socio-technical systems through social media, smart phone apps, smart utility meters, card payments and infrastructure sensors. In a "co-incidence between what are now being called SMART cities and big data" (Batty 2013), increasingly, in SMART cities, traditional data sets and sensor-generated data are augmented by crowd-sourced data. But how can cities realize the promises of smarter city living with big data?

In 2012, the Technology Strategy Board (a UK governmental body) launched the Future City Demonstrator competition for a £25 million award to advance SMART city living through the creation of a scaled-up testbed. A consortium of partners, led by ARUP and including IBM, the University of Bristol, Knowle West Media Centre, Hewlett-Packard, Toshiba and Advancing Sustainability LLP, was involved in the development of Bristol City Council's feasibility study (Bristol City Council 2012). Bristol won a runner-up award of £3 million, and the University of Bristol, together with ARUP, facilitated the development of a business development plan for Bristol Futures. One of the key questions that the collaborative approach to the Future City Demonstrator aimed to answer was: how can the value creation opportunities arising from big open data be realized in Bristol?

In workshops with a wide range of stakeholders from the public, private and third sectors, a SMART OR approach to big data management was developed, which involves the integration of information technology and citizen skill development to use big data productively. The approach combines hard integration through the City Operating Platform and soft integration through engagement with citizens and other local stakeholders in the Living Lab. The metaphor of an ecosystem was used to illustrate the need to integrate different types of data from different sources and the need to create the necessary infrastructure (the operating platform) together with a user group (Living Lab) directed towards focus areas (mobility, workplace, health and governance) that emerged from the workshops. Understanding "how all these dimensions are coalescing, merging, complementing, and substituting for one another [...] has never been more urgent [...] and constitutes a major challenge for planning and design in the near future." (Batty 2012). In the context of SMART OR, soft OR methods can thus be usefully employed to identify key areas of focus in city data repositories and hard OR approaches may be particularly useful during the planning of hardware and software solutions for platform design. This information can then be brought together in workshops, thus constituting a creative SMART OR approach aimed at understanding the interaction between data and sensemaking. We consider this to be an enhancement to the idea of a collaboratory (Williamson 2014), where (i) Soft OR provides explicit process methodology embodied in way in which the platform works and (ii) ideas of widening participation and implicit inclusion of non-expert stakeholders in the process, thus moving towards Callon's model of knowledge co-production (Callon 1999). We consider both of these to be essential additions to the current definitions of a collaboratory.

Thus, **our fourth perspective relevant to our concept of SMART OR is the *enhanced collaboratory*.** In our case, the Bristol City Operating Platform (B-COP) provides an integration of a wide range of sources in Bristol, including public sector data, sensor data from across the city and user-generated social media data. In this scenario, the City Council acts as the platform operator and then provides access to data sets. The platform users, including citizens, developers, businesses and City Council departments, are then able use the data to create information products. Under the title, Open Data Bristol (Bristol City Council 2014), Bristol City Council now develops an open data store and facilitates access through applications development. The platform offers public access to static and streaming real-time open data related to government, communities, education, energy, finance, mobility, environment, land use, health, safety and the Internet of Things, amongst others.

Long-term viability of open data platforms depends on the users to engage with the data and exploit the associated opportunities for collective behavior. This hard system approach is thus embedded in the SMART city ecosystem, which also considers making the data useable in daily life to a wide range of citizens. Soft OR interventions in the context of the commissioned follow-up study for Bristol City Council, ARUP and University of Bristol facilitated the exploration of business models that might be suitable for SMART city governance in the big data era. The recommendation included a systems model, which identified potential links amongst idea generators, projects, data results and revenue streams. It suggested a role of the Future City Team and partners as incubator, facilitator and coordinator interacting with research institutes and universities, software developers and private companies and small and medium enterprises (SME), and most importantly with the city's Living Lab in order to create value for users and citizens. One emergent outcome from the ecosystem is a joint venture between Bristol City Council and the University of Bristol, called Bristol Is Open,[2] explicitly designed to provide a "city operating system".

In sum, SMART OR, the *creative use of big data with Hard and Soft OR*, in the SMART city ecosystem, may scaffold the ability of multi-organizational stakeholders to exploit the value co-creation opportunities arising from big open data. Developing a creative mix of scaffolds by combining hard OR approaches for city analytics with Soft OR approaches may help with the development of a situated, reflexive and contextually nuanced epistemology for public value generation from big open data.

### 15.2.3 CASE 3: The City Dashboard: Co-creating Visual Interfaces

Big open data in a city's infosphere offers new opportunities for collaboration in the improvement of communities. This may include new approaches to governance, transport, waste management, energy generation and air quality, i.e. new approaches to governing the commons.

However, one of the most significant challenges on the way to enabling citizen-led approaches to city problems that big open data affords is the facilitation of meaningful engagement with the processes for accessing, analyzing and sharing information.

---

[2] http://www.bristolisopen.com.

The urban digital narrative (Srivastava and Vakali 2012) emerges at the intersection between individual stories of citizens and the sensor-generated data about systems and behaviors. The challenge is to learn to listen to the urban digital narrative, or in other words, to *feel the urban pulse* by understanding what the different forms of data narrate about the people in context, i.e. the collective behavior of citizens.

The Bristol Futures Directorate, a directorate within Bristol City Council, was established to enable the productive use of green and digital technologies. As such,

> One of our goals in Bristol is to recognize that the relationship between the council and citizens is changing. Councils need to move towards becoming 'lead citizens'. We need to share the information we have and listen to our citizens, making sure they are empowered to make decisions with us. (Kevin O'Malley, Bristol City Council, cited in Local Government Association 2011, p. 4)

The context for such collaborative citizenship development with regard to big data can be established through Living Labs. Living Labs facilitate the learning of multiple organizations about the ways in which citizens interact with technology and thus provide an ideal context to explore how the data they generate may be made accessible for community development and local public value. Bristol City Council funded the development of a city dashboard prototype in Knowle West's Media Centre, the City's Living Lab. The dashboard

> is an online place where citizens can see how well the city is performing and view visual representations of open data gathered across the city's neighborhoods, such as health statistics, house prices, crime level and traffic flow. Having this useful data at their fingertips will inspire Bristolians to take an active part in their city, from trying something new in their lives to actively seeking to make differences in their areas. (KWMC 2015)

In the development of the dashboard, participants interacted with *traditional* media such as flipcharts, complemented by digital interfaces such as laptops and interactive whiteboards. From a SMART OR point of view, recent streams of OR research on model mediated learning in context (White, Burger and Yearworth 2016; Franco 2013) are particularly relevant.

The example of the dashboard shows the intertwined nature of hard-soft OR and material-social decision supports and thus demonstrates the need to creatively combine OR methods to facilitate sensemaking and mangling in SMART city environments (Pickering (1995) White et al. 2016). Soft OR methods influence the design of the people side, through engagement workshops and joint planning approaches, giving focus to the types of services that should be improved. Furthermore, they inform the design of the visual interfaces, such as the dashboard, so that concerns of the community are reflected. This first step of guiding the focus of the data exploration is thus amenable to Soft OR approaches in Living Labs.

Thus, **our fifth perspective relevant to our concept of SMART OR is the *notion of the Living Lab.*** Here, OR/analytics approaches may inform the platform design and data processing, and visualizations may be developed jointly with users, bringing data to life. In the SMART city context, SMART OR may be frequently used in Living Lab situations where the creative potential of multi-methodology comes to life in the co-creation of digital interfaces that facilitate the emergence of goal-directed collective behavior and *positive results for decision makers.*

The case study has addressed the challenge of realizing the public value of an information marketplace through SMART OR. Given the strong focus on visual dynamics and Soft OR's traditional focus on facilitated modeling, the case study has sought to show that OR is extremely well positioned to respond to the challenge of understanding the increased digitalization of representations in the SMART city environment. As the case study sought to show, particularly in the context of facilitating skills development in the design and exploration of the opportunities associated with technologies for big data capture, analysis and interpretation, the use of Soft OR methods may provide suitable scaffolds.

## 15.3 Discussion and Conclusion

SMART OR is proposed as a set of processes that aim to support analytics-informed strategic changes in the behavior of groups through collaborative questioning of big data and the joint interpretation of visualized analytics.

SMART OR, which includes problem structuring, might help in the process of translating data analytics into actionable insight and behavior by facilitating the process of visualized data interpretation, which is variable and dependent on the perception and actualization of affordances in the analytics reports and applications. Problem structuring interventions have been shown to provide a number of *sensemaking affordances* to groups of decision makers, which suggests that the interpretation of big data analytics may benefit from facilitated group-based problem structuring (Paroutis, Franco and Papadopoulos 2015; Tavella and Franco 2015; Greiffenhagen 2013). At a meta-reflexive level, based on the group interventions, SMART OR may help the development of an understanding of the (local) strategies that individuals use in analyzing and evaluating large quantities of information. For example, think-aloud verbal protocols to gather evidence about the decision makers' reasoning and judgment process in the interpretation of analytics, outliers and anomalies can be used during SMART OR interventions.

Furthermore, SMART OR has particular value in supporting the process of co-designing visual interfaces and analytics reporting tools that decision makers may use effectively for decision support. The visualization of big data is by no means a guarantor for its *correct* or efficacious interpretation or translation into meaningful action. SMART OR studies, combining PSMs to prompt critical (disruptive) learning moments, for example with videotaped episodes and participant interaction data logging to provide a mirror of behavior during the interpretation process (Engeström et al. 1996; White et al. 2016), thus appear supportive of bridging processes amongst data, insight and action.

Especially in the context of big data analytics for societal benefit, SMART OR thus has clear implications for the scaffolding of the user-friendly design of digital/visual big social data interfaces. When data visualization platforms are developed jointly with users and decision makers, through SMART OR interventions, the *relevant information* is decided upon collaboratively by determining the questions to be asked and areas to be monitored, thereby alleviating the problem of *information overload*. Rather than black boxing the process of *pattern recognition*, it can be made transparent, by jointly developing targeted questions which are to be asked of the social media users, driven by stakeholders' concerns. Lastly, *ambiguity*, resulting from contradictory views or multiple priority areas for development that may be mentioned in the data, becomes a matter of debate, thereby re-connecting big data with existing forms of deliberative decision making, such as community fora, local government committees and/or committee meetings in organizations. SMART OR thus recognizes the importance of these debating stages in developing *actionable patterns* from big data, as it is likely that any of the problems identified on the basis of data will require involvement of multiple stakeholders for their resolution.

Moreover, SMART OR may be beneficial in facilitating the development of information marketplaces. In these contexts, the questions of *information overload and information relevance* are not seen as individual biases to be mitigated but as concepts that can be understood only in retrospect and over time, by studying the collective behavior of local digital entrepreneurs who use the big data sets made accessible to them for the creation of value with new products and services, such as city and community apps. *Pattern recognition and ambiguity* are thus seen as potential sources of entrepreneurial creativity in the exploitation of big data. In this context, SMART OR is less focused on structuring the exploitation of big data—which is seen as an entrepreneurial achievement—but it is called upon in the facilitation of the design of such information marketplaces through the support of the planning process for the provision of big data sets as a raw material for new venture creation. Local governments may thus employ Soft OR methods to understand how open data platforms may be developed and sustained. This may involve the facilitation of cross-city learning, employing PSMs, as well as scaffolds for ongoing learning and review processes within local governments. Given the interdisciplinary nature of big social data, Soft OR approaches may be particularly useful in facilitating communication across different local government departments who have stakes in the collection and sharing of data. Furthermore, in facilitating big open data entrepreneurs, attention is drawn to skills development, which may take the forms of hackathons, idea labs and open data competitions that—in their format as interventions—may all benefit from SMART OR support, drawing on successful strategies from strategic systems thinking to assist entrepreneurial decision makers and event planners in the integration of big data in decision making processes.

Overall, SMART OR views big data as a resource for examination and suggests that Soft OR processes may provide the procedural scaffolds to guide the data exploration, whereby changes in strategic collective behavior are informed by insights obtained through joint, technology-supported questioning and interpretation processes. In the context of real-time data collection and geographically dispersed modes of working, the principles of collaborative sensemaking from Soft OR approaches increasingly need to be applied outside of one-off workshop settings and instead need to become shared and integrated practices for the exchange of viewpoints, the joint interpretation of data and the shared development of relevant questions to ask of the data so that behavioral adaptations can be agreed. In super-wicked problem situations, the ability to assemble multiple knowledges in technology-supported collaborative stakeholder platforms, based on the principles of Soft OR interventions, may offer a more responsive process of collectively structuring problematic situations. To gain insight into changing ways of living with big data, SMART OR processes embedded in Living Labs may support theory development. In the context of smarter cities, learning in Living Labs may inform the emerging shape of SMART OR interventions for the co-design of meaningful visualizations of community-relevant data to develop new insights into ways to improve decision making through locally relevant data.

# References

Ackermann, F., L.A. Franco, B. Gallupe, and M. Parent. 2005. GSS for multi-organizational collaboration: Reflections on process and content. *Group Decision and Negotiation* 14: 307–331.

Ackoff, R.L. 1981. The art and science of mess management. *Interfaces* 11: 20–26.

Bana e Costa, C.A., J.C. Lourenço, M.D. Oliveira, and J.C. Bana e Costa. 2014. A socio-technical approach for group decision support in public strategic planning: The Pernambuco PPA case. *Group Decision and Negotiation* 23: 5–29.

Batty, M. 2012. Smart cities, big data. *Environment and Planning-Part B* 39: 191.

Batty, M. 2013. Big data, smart cities and city planning. *Dialogues in Human Geography* 3: 274–279.

Bristol City Council. 2012. Connect Bristol feasibility study. https://connect. innovateuk.org/documents/3130726/3794125/Feasibility%20Study%20 -%20Bristol%20City%20Council.pdf. Accessed 15 Nov 2015.

Bristol City Council. 2014. Bristol City Council | Open Data Bristol. https:// opendata.bristol.gov.uk/. Accessed 15 Nov 2015.

Bryson, J.M., F. Ackermann, C. Eden, and C.B. Finn. 2004. *Visible thinking: Unlocking causal mapping for practical business results.* New York: Wiley.

Callon, M. 1999. The role of lay people in the production and dissemination of scientific knowledge. *Science, Technology & Society* 4: 81–94.

Checkland, P. 1981. *Systems thinking, systems practice.* Chichester: Wiley.

Checkland, P., and J. Scholes. 1999. *Soft systems methodology in action.* Chichester: Wiley.

Checkland, P., and M. Winter. 2006. Process and content: Two ways of using SSM. *Journal of the Operational Research Society* 57: 1435–1441.

Coelho, D., C.H. Antunes, and A.G. Martins. 2010. Using SSM for structuring decision support in urban energy planning. *Technological and Economic Development of Economy* 16: 641–653.

Davis, J., A. MacDonald, and L. White. 2010. Problem-structuring methods and project management: An example of stakeholder involvement using hierarchical process modelling methodology. *Journal of the Operational Research Society* 61: 893–904.

Engeström, Y., J. Virkkunen, M. Helle, J. Pihlaja, and R. Poikela. 1996. The change laboratory as a tool for transforming work. *Lifelong Learning in Europe* 1: 10–17.

Franco, L.A. 2007. Assessing the impact of problem structuring methods in multi-organizational settings: An empirical investigation. *Journal of the Operational Research Society* 58: 760–768.

Franco, L.A. 2008. Facilitating collaboration with problem structuring methods: A case study of an inter-organisational construction partnership. *Group Decision and Negotiation* 17: 267–286.

Franco, L.A. 2009. Problem structuring methods as intervention tools: Reflections from their use with multi-organisational teams. *Omega* 37: 193–203.

Franco, L.A. 2013. Rethinking soft OR interventions: Models as boundary objects. *European Journal of Operational Research* 231: 720–733.

Greiffenhagen, C. 2013. Visual grammar in practice: Negotiating the arrangement of speech bubbles in storyboards. *Semiotica* 195: 127–167.

Horlick-Jones, T., J. Rosenhead, I. Georgiou, J. Ravetzd, and R. Löfstedte. 2001. Decision support for organisational risk management by problem structuring. *Health, Risk & Society* 3: 141–165.

Horn, R.E., and R.P. Weber. 2007. *New tools for resolving wicked problems: Mess mapping and resolution mapping processes*. Watertown: Strategy Kinetics LLC.

KWMC. 2015. City dashboard – How's Bristol doing? http://kwmc.org.uk/ projects/citydashboard. Accessed 15 Nov 2015.

Laibson, D. 1997. Golden eggs and hyperbolic discounting. *The Quarterly Journal of Economics* 112: 443–477.

Lazarus, R.J. 2009. Super wicked problems and climate change: Restraining the present to liberate the future. *Cornell Law Review* 94: 1153–1234.

Levin, K., B. Cashore, S. Bernstein, and G. Auld. 2007. Playing it forward: Path dependency, progressive incrementalism, and the 'super wicked' problem of global climate change. *International studies association 48th annual convention*, 28 Feb.

Local Government Association. 2011. *Case study. Bristol City Council: Bringing open data to life*. http://www.local.gov.uk/documents/10180/11643/Bristol+ City+Council_+Bringing+open+data+to+life.pdf/ed8db46c-e3e3-427c-b33b-c1aa4bd72e4f. Accessed 15 Nov 2015

Mingers, J. 2011. Soft OR comes of age – But not everywhere! *Omega* 39: 729–741.

Mingers, J., and J. Brocklesby. 1997. Multimethodology: Towards a framework for mixing methodologies. *Omega* 25: 489–509.

Morton, A., F. Ackermann, and V. Belton. 2007. Problem structuring without workshops? Experiences with distributed interaction within a PSM process. *Journal of the Operational Research Society* 58: 547–556.

Neves, L.M.P., A.G. Martins, C.H. Antunes, and L.C. Dias. 2004. Using SSM to rethink the analysis of energy efficiency initiatives. *Journal of the Operational Research Society* 55: 968–975.

Paroutis, S., L.A. Franco, and T. Papadopoulos. 2015. Visual interactions with strategy tools: Producing strategic knowledge in workshops. *British Journal of Management* 26: S48–S66.

Pickering, A. 1995. *The mangle of practice: Time, agency, and science*. Chicago and London: University of Chicago Press.

Rittel, H.W., and M.M. Webber. 1973. Dilemmas in a general theory of planning. *Policy sciences* 4: 155–169.

Rosenhead, J. 1992. Into the swamp: The analysis of social issues. *Journal of the Operational Research Society* 43: 293–305.

Srivastava, L., and A. Vakali. 2012. *Towards a narrative-aware design framework for smart urban environments The Future Internet*, 166–177. Berlin/Heidelberg: Springer.

Tavella, E., and L.A. Franco. 2015. Dynamics of group knowledge production in facilitated modelling workshops: An exploratory study. *Group Decision and Negotiation* 24: 451–475.

Tversky, A., and D. Kahneman. 1992. Advances in prospect theory: Cumulative representation of uncertainty. *Journal of Risk and Uncertainty* 5: 297–323.

Van de Ven, A.H., and M.S. Poole. 2005. Alternative approaches for studying organizational change. *Organization Studies* 26: 1377–1404.

White, L., K. Burger, and M. Yearworth. 2016. Understanding behaviour in problem structuring methods interventions with activity theory. *European Journal of Operational Research* 249: 983–1004.

Williamson, A. 2014. *The collaboratory: A co-creative stakeholder engagement process for solving complex problems*, ed. K. Muff. Sheffield: Greenleaf.

Yearworth, M. 2015. Sustainability as a "super wicked" problem: Opportunities and limits for engineering methodology. *Intelligent Buildings International* 8: 37–47.

# 16

# Mergers and Acquisitions: Modeling Decision Making in Integration Projects

Shanie Atkinson and Michael Shayne Gary

## 16.1 Introduction

Models that include behavioral components have a long history in Operational Research and related disciplines (Cyert and March 1963; Forrester 1961; Simon 1955). However, the last decade has seen a burgeoning of interest in incorporating realistic, behavioral aspects of human reasoning, problem solving and decision making in models (Bendoly et al. 2010; Gino and Pisano 2008). This chapter explores how to model behavior and also how models behave. These topics are explored using an example model of a merger and acquisition integration project.

To provide the foundations for our example model, we start by discussing some of the different ways behavior has been modeled and how model behavior has been analysed. Behavioral models have emerged in

S. Atkinson (✉) • M.S. Gary
School of Management, UNSW Australia Business School,
The University of New South Wales, 1029 High Street, Kensington,
Sydney, NSW 2033, Australia

© The Editor(s) (if applicable) and The Author(s) 2016          **319**
M. Kunc et al. (eds.), *Behavioral Operational Research*,
DOI 10.1057/978-1-137-53551-1_16

order to cope with the ill-structured, complex and dynamic problems that do not lend themselves to optimal analytical solutions. In 1958, Simon and Newell posited that "... we now have the elements of a theory of heuristic (as contrasted with algorithmic) problem solving, and we can use this theory both to understand human heuristic processes and to simulate such processes with digital computers." Much progress has been made since that optimistic statement was published, and the diversity of research streams has led to an abundant variety of different ways behavior has been modelled and how model behavior has been analyzed.

Behavioral assumptions have been incorporated into a range of different types of models, including (not an exhaustive list): agent based models, discrete event models, System Dynamics models, NK models, stochastic models, lattice models, behavioral Game Theory models, neural network models, probabilistic decision making models and also multi-method models that draw on two or more approaches. There are many different types of computer simulation approaches, and usage of the term "computer simulation" encompasses virtually any computer-based representation.

In addition, a range of different aspects of behavior has been incorporated into models. This includes (again, not an exhaustive list): cognitive biases, heuristics, decision rules, policies, routines, perceptions, search rules, misperceptions of feedback, social interaction rules, emotions and learning.

The next section discusses an example model of a merger and acquisition (M&A) integration project to illustrate how this model incorporates realistic assumptions about human behavior. This is a dynamic, complex phenomenon for which new insights are sorely needed. The value of worldwide M&A investments totalled US$3.5 trillion during 2014. Research shows, however, that a large percentage of M&A investments destroy economic value (for a review, see Haleblian et al. 2009; for the latest meta analysis, see King et al. 2004). Industry studies estimate that between 70 % and 90 % of M&A's fail to deliver the benefits that initially motivated the deal (Christensen et al. 2011). Research has not converged on a set of factors that consistently predict post-acquisition performance (Cartwright and Schoenberg 2006; King et al. 2004). There are critical gaps in existing theory and empirical findings. This dynamic, complex problem is one for which behavioral modeling is well-suited to generate new insights (Gary et al. 2008)

## 16.2 How to Model Behavior: Illustrative Model of an M&A Integration Project

A System Dynamics model of an M&A integration project is presented in this section. The information feedback structure of the model emerged from multiple data sources, including interviews with expert informants, focus group workshops and industry expert reports and studies.

We conducted individual interviews with 21 post-acquisition integration professionals, who collectively had been directly involved in over 200 post-acquisition integrations. Causal diagrams were constructed iteratively throughout the period of data collection. Each causal link was reviewed as it emerged, to assess whether the relationship was consistent with multiple data sources and whether it was supported by prior studies. Behavioral components in the model included a number of managerial policies typically used in an M&A integration.

Following the conclusion of the individual interviews, two workshops were held to discuss the findings from the individual interviews, including the longitudinal performance patterns and the causal diagrams. There were four participants in the first workshop and seven participants in the second. The workshop groups were asked to evaluate the preliminary findings and to elaborate, refine and correct the performance patterns and causal diagrams. Overall, the individual interviews and workshops involved 26 people. The outcomes from the group workshops included broad agreement about the preliminary findings and extensions to the causal diagram.

### 16.2.1 Typical Patterns of Behavior

Our interviews with experts identified four commonly observed performance outcomes in post-acquisition integration. These performance outcome scenarios are: (i) Fulfilled or Exceeded Expectations, (ii) Below

Forecast, (iii) Synergy Creep and (iv) Death Spiral. The performance outcome measure adopted is Realized Synergies—these are the financial synergies realized as a result of the integration work. Descriptions of all four patterns are provided below.

In the Fulfilled or Exceeded Expectations scenario, the integration rolls out as planned and the target synergies are achieved as forecast. Expectations are exceeded when the realized synergies are higher and achieved earlier than expected. This may occur due to strong management involvement in pre-deal planning, adoption of effective governance processes throughout the integration, communicating effectively about the integration throughout the process, adopting appropriate synergy targets, allocating adequate resources to the integration projects, maintaining high employee morale and commitment, and retaining talented employees. Effective management of all of these aspects of the integration drives realized synergies to achieve or exceed the initial forecast. As one expert explained:

> *The best run processes feel very simple ... it is about having people on the hook all the way through ... the people who are ultimately responsible for doing the integration.*

Interviews believed the Synergy Creep scenario occurs to some extent in the majority of post-acquisition integrations. Under the Creep scenario, synergies are initially achieved as planned, but then the energy and enthusiasm for synergy initiatives wane as the perceived date for the end of the integration approaches, management are distracted finding and starting new projects or roles and management focus moves away. As a result, synergy monitoring and tracking decline or stop.

Once integration synergy tracking declines or stops, there is a claw back of cost savings or loss of revenue enhancement gains. This claw back was referred to by interviewees as *creep*. For example, employees that were made redundant as part of the cost saving plans are re-employed as contractors. One expert explained:

> *So often you'll see synergies probably not tracked with the right amount of rigour. And I'll give you a classic example ... we think we can reduce costs by about 2 million bucks by making a whole bunch of redundancies in our finance depart-*

*ment. But then you find that six months down the line all of a sudden you've got rid of your fifteen or twenty people but suddenly you've got seven or eight new contractors working, providing services because you got rid of all these people, and now you've got contractors. Ultimately the actual impact to the P&L is potentially increased costs or costs haven't gone down by the amount that you initially thought. They did go down initially but it's crept back into the business.*

The Below Forecast scenario occurs when outcomes are consistently below forecast. Some synergies are realized from the integration, but not all of the synergies are achievable or there are substantial delays. As a result, the total Realized synergies end up lower than forecast. Fatigue occurs where the integration project continues for longer than initially expected. Integration fatigue decreases commitment to the integration as enthusiasm wanes. Both integration fatigue and declining commitment decrease the pace and the quality of work on the integration initiatives, resulting in a lowered rate of synergy realisation and amount of potential synergies captured. An expert explained that the Below Forecast scenario is initially the outcome of the difference between forecast synergies and actual synergies Realized over time as a result of low quality assessment of synergies in the due diligence phase of the project (pre-integration):

> *"… if the synergies that you came up with up front aren't right, if your assumptions were bad, you need to go out and find some more synergies, because we still need to realise that. People actually get fatigued and tired of continually trying to find and chase synergies."*

The fourth scenario, the Death Spiral pattern, occurs when the pressures of the integration are not well managed and they *break the business.* There may be numerous initial causes for pressure to occur, but poor management decisions and processes create the downward spiral. Initial pressures may be the result of unachievable synergy targets. Poor assessment of synergies may drive up levels of fatigue and drive down management commitment, especially when management is "given a KPI that is something he doesn't believe in." Both reduce the rate of synergy realisation and the amount of potential synergies achieved.

When pressure to achieve new synergies is poorly managed then, rising levels of uncertainty lead to higher levels of voluntary turnover and in turn to further escalation of uncertainty, triggering numerous feedback effects that drive the deterioration in performance outcomes. Rising fatigue leads to further declines in commitment, which in turn undermine productivity and quality. These feedback effects are exacerbated by a declining level of experience in the organization as a result of unintended employee departures. Also, these feedbacks add costs and delays to the integration process that have flow-on effects to the broader business. Once activated, these feedbacks can cause a downward spiral in the post-acquisition integration. One expert consultant explains the Death Spiral effect:

> *it is a cancer … it is debilitating … it creates a negative vibe that impacts value and performance … it is a distraction to everything and people do not want to be there and it is usually your star performers that leave … it is like a death spiral effect and it is hard to get momentum around the business to drive the integration program … and people talk to their customers about it.*

## 16.2.2 Feedback Structure

A causal diagram was developed throughout the data collection process and portrays a post-acquisition integration from the date of initiation of the integration project through to the end of the integration. After the interviews and group workshops, the causal loop diagram was converted into a simulation model of a post-acquisition integration project. The model sector diagram, provided in Fig. 16.1, shows the final simulation model consisting of four sectors. There are numerous behavioral assumptions embedded in the model, including assumptions about the how managers and employees respond to different environmental cues. We provide an overview of the sectors and the feedbacks between them below.

Starting at the top of Fig. 16.1, the Cost and Revenue Synergies sector includes the level of financial synergies sought from the integration project that motivated the transaction. The goal of achieving the Target Synergies drives the integration process and is in units of $million/Year annual, on-going financial synergies (e.g. $150M/Year). This is a prominent behavioral component of the model and represents management's goal-setting process for the overall integration project.

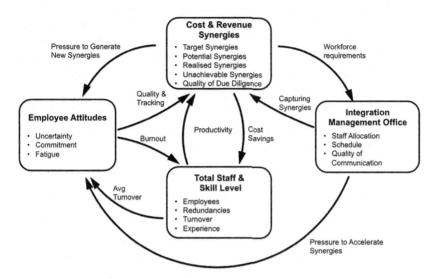

**Fig. 16.1**  Sector diagram of an M&A integration project

Synergies Underway are the cost savings and revenue synergies that are currently in progress and that could potentially be realized from the integration process. Realized Synergies are the actual amount realized through completing synergy initiatives.

Unachievable Synergies are the synergies underway that are not actually achievable and are influenced by the accuracy of the due diligence work to identify and estimate the potential synergies in the pre-integration phase of the transaction. The level of Unachievable Synergies is also influenced by the quality of work during the integration, which is in turn influenced by constructs in the Employee Attitudes sector. Whenever there are Unachievable Synergies, the gap between Target Synergies and Realized Synergies creates management pressure for the employees to generate new synergies. The Pressure to Generate New Synergies impacts the Employee Attitudes sector.

Finally, the amount of financial synergies that still need to be realized to achieve the Target Synergies determines the remaining Workforce Requirements for the integration project that are an input for the Integration Management Office (IMO) sector. The IMO sector includes the allocation and management of resources to implement the integration initiatives and realize synergies on schedule. The IMO sector includes policies for staff allocation to the integration project, the overall schedule for the integration, and also the amount and quality of communication to employees about the integration. In addition, the IMO includes a management policy for the pressure exerted on employees to increase the pace of synergy realization, and this Pressure to Accelerate Synergies impacts the Employee Attitudes sector.

The Employee Attitudes sector includes Employee Uncertainty, Commitment and Fatigue as a result of the integration process. These behavioral components have a large effect on the dynamics of the integration project. As one example, the evolution of these factors over time determines the quality and tracking of synergies that are inputs to the Cost & Revenue Synergies sector. Uncertainty can occur when there are unexpected changes during the integration. Uncertainty is associated with decreased security, influence and control and is related to increased employee turnover (Bastien 1987).

Commitment includes the level of employee engagement with and dedication to the organizational goals. Employee engagement is defined as "involvement and satisfaction with as well as enthusiasm for the work" (Harter et al. 2002, p. 269). The level of fatigue affects commitment, including enthusiasm and energy directed towards achieving the integration project goals.

Integration fatigue occurs over time in the integration due to burnout and the introduction of cynicism toward the integration work and involves decreasing energy and enthusiasm for the integration work. As explained by one expert: who refers to intergration fatigue as synergy fatigue.

*Synergy fatigue, if they're still chasing synergies, often comes in. So if people who've been on the program since the beginning start to get tired, they lose their energy and enthusiasm.*

The onset of integration fatigue is described by another expert:

*People continually get asked … to go out and find some more synergies, because we still need to realise that [the forecast synergies]. And people actually get fatigued and tired of continually trying to find and chase synergies … 'Synergy fatigue', which literally [is] where people are just 'I can't handle this anymore', 'I can't find any more synergies'.*

Levels of Uncertainty, Commitment and Fatigue included in the Employee Attitudes sector will affect the choice of employees to remain with the organization or seek employment elsewhere (increasing Turnover). This relationship is included as a link from the Employee Attitudes to the Total Staff and Skill Level sectors, labeled Burnout.

The Total Staff and Skill level sector includes the number of employees retained in the broader organization and their average skill level. Some cost synergies may come from staff redundancies, and this relationship is included in the link from the Synergy Tracking sector to the Total Staff and Skill Level sector. The sector also includes Employee Redundancies and Voluntary Turnover together, along with the effects on the average level of Skill and Experience retained in the organization. The level of Skill and Experience will affect the productivity of employees and the rate of synergy realization. This relationship is captured in the link from the Total Staff and Skill Level sector to the Cost and Revenue Synergies sector and is labeled Productivity.

The level of Redundancies and Turnover in the organization has a strong influence on employee uncertainty in the Employee Attitudes sector. This relationship is captured in the link from the Total Staff and Skill level sector to the Employee Attitudes sector and is labeled Average Turnover.

With this overview of the model sectors, Fig. 16.2 shows the full causal diagram, operationalizing the feedback loops described above. Below we discuss some of the model equations.

Target Synergies are formulated as an exogenous input to the model from the due diligence phase. Target Synergies may be realized through revenue uplift or through cost savings delivered by the integration of the businesses. As an illustrative example, target synergies may be forecast to total $150 million per annum, with management expecting that this total value can be realized over a three-year period.

The stock (or state variable) of Potential Synergies Underway includes the synergies associated with integration initiatives currently in progress

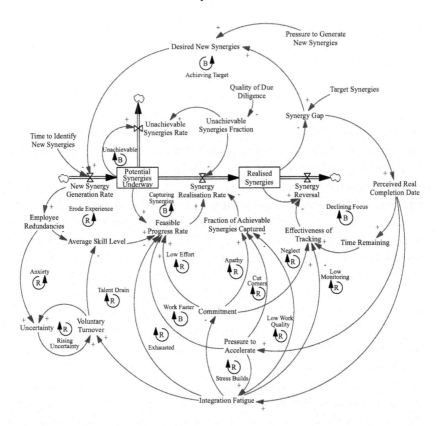

**Fig. 16.2** Causal diagram of feedback structure driving M&A integration performance

and yet to be delivered. The initial value includes the total value of the Target Synergies the integration is expected to deliver plus a margin that includes the estimate of unachievable synergies. This behavioral assumption in the model captures the idea that management will estimate that some fraction of the target synergies identified in due diligence will not be achievable and that therefore the project needs to begin with synergy initiatives underway that account for these unachievable synergies. As defined in Eq. 16.1, Potential Synergies Underway are either realized at the Synergy Realization Rate or discovered to be unachievable at the

Unachievable Synergies Rate. Equation 16.2 provides the initial value for this state variable and includes an estimation of the amount of synergies identified in due diligence that are not achievable.

$$\frac{d\left(\text{Potential Synergies Underway}\right)}{dt}$$
$$= \text{New Synergy Generation Rate} - \text{Synergy Realization Rate}$$
$$- \text{Unachievable Synergies Rate} \qquad (16.1)$$

$$\text{Initial Synergies Underway} = \text{Target Synergies} *$$
$$\left( \begin{array}{l} 1 + \text{Initial Estimate of Unachievale} \\ \text{Synergies Work \%} \end{array} \right) \qquad (16.2)$$

As the integration project synergy initiatives advance, Potential Synergies Underway are captured at the Synergy Realization Rate shown in the Capturing Synergies balancing feedback loop in Fig. 16.2. The Synergy Realization rate is determined by the Feasible Progress Rate, the Fraction of Achievable Synergies Captured and the Unachievable Synergies Fraction.

Despite efforts to validate the existence of synergies during the due diligence evaluation phase, some synergies initially believed to be achievable may not be achievable. For example, experts we interviewed highlighted that often the cost to shut down a legacy IT system outweighs the economic benefits and that as a result the legacy system is not ultimately shut down. In this case, cost saving synergies expected from the shut-down and the headcount reduction expected due to redundancy following the shut-down of the system are classified as Unachievable Synergies and the initiatives associated with these synergies are stopped together with the associated synergies removed from the stock of Potential Synergies Underway. Another example is where planned rationalization of office space requires breaking a lease that involves penalties, resulting in the plan becoming declared uneconomical and not plausible in the short to medium term. Synergies may be unachievable due to poor assessment in the pre-integration, due diligence work or as a result of poor integration work quality. Poor quality work results in a lower fraction of expected synergies being achieved and may result from fatigue and low levels of commitment to the process. For example, a lack of attention to servicing customers may result in the loss of potential revenue synergies from cross-selling products.

It takes time to discover the synergies are unachievable, but as work on the integration progresses, this comes to light. The discovery of Unachievable Synergies forms a second balancing loop, labelled Unachievable in Fig. 16.2.

Management continuously compares the total Realized Synergies and Potential Synergies Underway to the Target Synergies to monitor whether there is a Synergy Gap: a difference between the target and already realized synergies plus the synergies still underway or in progress. The Synergy Gap is defined as given in Eq. 16.3.

$$\text{Synergy Gap} = \text{Target Synergies} - \text{Potential Synergies Underway} - \text{Realized Synergies} \quad (16.3)$$

When there is a Synergy Gap, management may choose to exert pressure to search for, identify and generate new synergies to close this gap. The Desired New Synergies are defined as the Synergy Gap multiplied by the Pressure to Generate New Synergies. The management pressure to generate new synergies to replace unachievable synergies can range from 0 pressure to 100 % pressure, and the assumption for this behavioral component of the model—provided in Eq. 16.5—is 100 % pressure to always fully close the synergy gap and achieve target synergies. The New Synergy Generation Rate is defined as the Desired New Synergies divided by the Time to Identify New Synergies. The balancing feedback loop capturing new synergy generation is labeled Achieving Target.

$$\text{Desired New Synergies} = \text{Synergy Gap} * \text{Pressure to Generate New Synergies} \quad (16.4)$$

$$\text{Pressure to Generate New Synergies} = 1 \quad (16.5)$$

$$\text{New Synergy Generation Rate} = \frac{\text{Desired New Synergies}}{\text{Time to Identify New Synergies}} \quad (16.6)$$

Now that we have discussed some of the equations for three of the feedback loops in the model to illustrate how to model behavior, we now turn to the simulation experiments to illustrate how models behave.

## 16.3 How Models Behave: Simulation Experiments

The simulation model was developed from the causal diagram that emerged from the interviews and workshops. The simulation model enables us to test whether the feedback structure in the causal diagram is capable of generating the patterns of behavior identified in our interviews. We extensively tested each model sector as the full model was being constructed and then performed comprehensive sensitivity tests of the full model. Based on our interviews, a 60-month (five-year) period was considered to be an appropriate time horizon to capture the performance effects of a typical, large-scale integration. The Death Spiral scenario is discussed below to illustrate how the model behaves.

Figure 16.3 shows the simulation experiment with the model parameterised for the Death Spiral scenario. In this scenario, management implementation decisions in the integration project trigger a series of vicious reinforcing feedback loops that lead to a downward spiral in performance. Line 1 of the Top Panel of Fig. 16.3 shows that Realized Synergies initially increase early in the integration but peak in month 18 of an integration project that is originally scheduled for completion in 36 months. After month 18, the Realized Synergies decline as fast as they were captured until almost all of the Realized Synergies have been lost.

An integration project that ends up in the Death Spiral scenario starts off with initial Target Synergies that are overestimated, and consequently a large Synergy Gap emerges relatively quickly in the integration project. In response, management exerts Pressure to Generate New Synergies to replace unachievable synergies as they are discovered. This pressure increases the search for and identification of new synergies. For example, this pressure to find new synergies may increase employee redundancies to achieve additional cost savings. Increasing employee redundancies

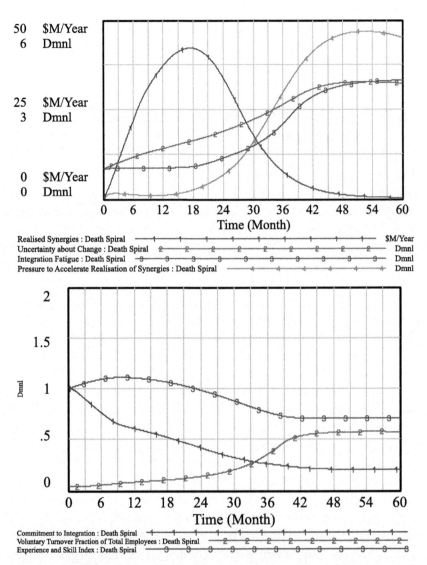

**Fig. 16.3** *Top Panel*: Realized synergies, uncertainty about change, integration fatigue, and pressure to accelerate realisation of synergies in death spiral scenario. *Bottom Panel*: Commitment to integration, voluntary turnover fraction of total employees, and experience and skill level index in the death spiral scenario

increases the level of employee uncertainty about the changes associated with the integration, as shown in Line 2 of the Top Panel of Fig. 16.3. The pressure to generate more synergies also leads to increasing integration fatigue, as shown in Line 3 of the Top Panel of Fig. 16.3.

Increasing fatigue reduces the feasible progress rate as employees' work productivity declines. In addition, the quality of work completed by fatigued employees reduces the fraction of achievable synergies captured. As a result, the Synergy Gap continues to increase as the project falls further behind and management updates the Perceived Real Completion Date. In response to an increasing Perceived Completion Date, management apply Pressure to Accelerate the realisation of synergies in an attempt to realise synergies more rapidly and get the integration back on track by closing the Synergy Gap. Line 4 of the top panel of Fig. 16.3 shows that Pressure to Accelerate rises over time in the Death Spiral scenario.

Rising Pressure to Accelerate synergies does increase the Feasible Progress Rate, thereby increasing the Synergy Realisation Rate in the Work Faster balancing loop in Fig. 16.2. However, rising Pressure to Accelerate synergies also decreases work quality as the error rate increases with faster work in the Cut Corners reinforcing loop. In addition, rising Pressure to Accelerate the realisation of synergies increases the level of fatigue in employees as staff work harder or longer in the Stress Builds reinforcing loop.

Over time, increasing Integration Fatigue also leads to falling employee commitment to achieve the integration outcomes. Line 1 of the bottom panel of Fig. 16.3 shows how employee commitment deteriorates over time in the Death Spiral scenario.

Rising Integration Fatigue also leads to increasing Voluntary Turnover of staff as fatigued employees choose to exit the organisation and take up employment elsewhere (Lyneis and Ford 2007). The high levels of voluntary turnover in the Death Spiral scenario are shown in the simulation outcomes as Line 2 in the bottom panel of Fig. 16.3. In the interviews, experts commented that it was usually the most experienced people who left first, as they were able to more easily find work elsewhere. Oliva, Sterman and Giese (2003) also discussed how sustained long weeks of work increase turnover. It is common in integration projects to work long hours over a sustained period of time when under pressure. Increasing

Voluntary Turnover further increases Uncertainty and also undermines Average Skill Level of employees in the Talent Drain reinforcing loop.

The high level of voluntary turnover, in addition to employee redundancies, causes the level of experience and skill retained in the organisation to decline. Line 3 of the bottom panel of Fig. 16.3 shows the simulation outcomes for the average experience and skill level retained in the organisation as an index of the initial experience and skill level. In the Death Spiral scenario, the average experience and skill level declines dramatically over time. The lower level of skill undermines the rate of progress on integration initiatives by decreasing the Feasible Progress Rate in the Erode Experience reinforcing loop.

High rates of voluntary turnover also lead to increasing uncertainty as remaining employees see many of their friends and co-workers departing the organisation and roles are reallocated. Higher uncertainty leads to a further increase in Voluntary Turnover in the Rising Uncertainty reinforcing loop. In addition, increasing Voluntary Turnover further decreases the Average Skill Level in the organisation, creating the Anxiety reinforcing loop in Fig. 16.2.

This illustrative example shows how models behave, partly as a consequence of the behavioral assumptions embedded in the model. In the M&A Integration Project model, the simulation experiments demonstrate how Pressure to Generate New Synergies and Pressure to Accelerate synergies can activate multiple reinforcing feedback loops with the potential to *break the business.*

## 16.4 Discussion

This chapter has focused on how to model behavior and how models behave. These points were discussed by way of an illustrative example model of an M&A integration project. The model contains a wide range of behavioral assumptions formulated as decision policies based on information feedback control theory. These decision policies include selective filtering of information cues, biases, expectation formation, misperceptions of feedback, perception delays and implementation delays. In other words, decision policies can be formulated to incorporate all elements of bounded rationality.

To illustrate how to model behavior, we provided an overview of the model sectors and the feedbacks between the sectors. Subsequently, the more detailed feedback structure in the causal diagram was discussed, and then a small number of the model equations were explained.

To illustrate how models behave, we discussed the Death Spiral scenario and explained the dynamics over time for several model variables that contribute to the dynamic behavior for this scenario. Our simulation experiments show that poor management policies drive the Death Spiral performance pattern. When the integration project starts to go wrong, management pressure to generate new synergies and to accelerate synergies activate a large number of reinforcing feedback loops that lead to the Death Spiral. However, managerial decisions can prevent the vicious reinforcing feedback loops from dominating the process and the outcomes. Deciding when to apply pressure to generate new synergies and to accelerate synergy realisation to meet targets and how much pressure to apply are difficult challenges in a high-order, nonlinear system such as management of an M&A integration project.

Behavior models incorporating realistic assumptions about human cognition and emotions hold much promise for generating new insights about such complex, dynamic problems.

# References

Bastien, D.T. 1987. Common patterns of behavior and communication in corporate mergers and acquisitions. *Human Resource Management* 26: 17–33.

Bendoly, E., R. Croson, P. Goncalves, and K. Schultz. 2010. Bodies of knowledge for research in behavioral operations. *Production and Operations Management* 19: 434–452.

Cartwright, S., and R. Schoenberg. 2006. Thirty years of mergers and acquisitions research: Recent advances and future opportunities. *British Journal of Management* 17: S1–S5.

Christensen, C.M., R. Alton, C. Rising, and A. Waldeck. 2011. The Big idea: The new M&A playbook. *Harvard Business Review* 89: 48–57.

Cyert, R., and J. March. 1963. *A behavioral theory of the firm*. Cambridge, MA: Blackwell.

Forrester, J.W. 1961. *Industrial dynamics*. Cambridge, MA: MIT Press.

Gary, M.S., M. Kunc, J.D.W. Morecroft, and S.F. Rockart. 2008. System dynamics and strategy. *System Dynamics Review* 24: 407–429.

Gino, F., and G. Pisano. 2008. Toward a theory of behavioral operations. *Manufacturing & Service Operations Management* 10: 676–691.

Haleblian, J., C.E. Devers, G. McNamara, M.A. Carpenter, and R.B. Davison. 2009. Taking stock of what we know about mergers and acquisitions: A review and research agenda. *Journal of Management* 35: 469–502.

Harter, J.K., F.L. Schmidt, and T.L. Hayes. 2002. Business-unit-level relationship between employee satisfaction, employee engagement and business outcomes: A meta-analysis. *Journal of Applied Psychology* 87: 268–279.

King, D.R., D.R. Dalton, C.M. Daily, and J.G. Covin. 2004. Meta-analyses of post-acquisition performance: Indications of unidentified moderators. *Strategic Management Journal* 25: 187–200.

Lyneis, J.M., and D.N. Ford. 2007. System dynamics applied to project management: A survey, assessment and directions for future research. *System Dynamics Review* 23: 157–189.

Oliva, R., J.D. Sterman, and M. Giese. 2003. Limits to growth in the new economy: Exploring the 'get big fast' strategy in e-commerce. *System Dynamics Review* 19: 83–117.

Simon, H.A. 1955. A behavioral model of rational choice. *Quarterly Journal of Economics* 69: 99–118.

# 17

# Supporting Strategy: Behavioral Influences on Resource Conceptualization Processes

Kenneth Kyunghyun Huh and Martin Kunc

## 17.1 Introduction

In most organizations, strategy is developed by a group of managers through a series of meetings. Strategy, as an outcome of group decision processes, can be influenced by various substantive factors, such as managerial mental models (Kunc and Morecroft 2010), current firm resources and constraints (Barney 1991), past strategic decisions (Hutzschenreuter and Volberda 2007) and even luck (Mintzberg and Waters 1985). In addition to the previous factors, behavioral factors are considered to be equally influential in the process (Powell et al. 2011). For example, biases can be generated by the method employed to design the strategy (Podsakoff et al. 2003).

K. Huh (✉)
IMS Consulting Group, IMS Health, L12, Garden Square, 968 West Beijing Road, Shanghai, People's Republic of China

M. Kunc
Warwick Business School, University of Warwick, Scarman Road, Coventry CV4 7AL, UK

© The Editor(s) (if applicable) and The Author(s) 2016    **337**
M. Kunc et al. (eds.), *Behavioral Operational Research*,
DOI 10.1057/978-1-137-53551-1_17

In this chapter, we explore the impact of behavioral factors affecting a key activity in the development of strategies based on strategic resources: resource conceptualization (Kunc and Morecroft 2009; Kunc and Morecroft 2010). We performed an in-depth study of two groups of experienced managers who were designing resource-based strategies. We analyzed the data obtained from the groups' discussions both quantitatively and qualitatively (Jehn 1997) to identify the set of factors responsible for the behavior of the groups during the process.

The chapter is organized as follows: The first section discusses the role of group decision processes in resource conceptualization. The second section explains the overall research methodology. Then, results of the quantitative and qualitative analyses are displayed, followed by a discussion of the findings along with a consideration of the limitations of the study. The paper ends with implications for practitioners and researchers.

## 17.2    The Role of Group Decision Making Processes During the Development of Strategies Using Strategic Resources

For a firm, resources and products are two sides of the same coin (Wernerfelt 1984). Making products requires the employment of multiple resources, and diverse resources are used to produce different products. If managers define the product and its market, they will be able to infer the resource requirements. Conversely, if managers can clearly specify a resource profile, they will be able to define the set of products where the firm can compete efficiently (Barney 1991). Thus, the performance of firms is determined by strategic decisions responsible for developing the system of resources which supports the implementation of the strategy—a perspective known as the resource-based view (RBV) of the firm (Barney 1986, 1991; Foss 1997). System Dynamics scholars have developed a tool, called resource mapping, to support resource management (Kunc and Morecroft 2009). Resource management, which comprises managerial decisions to expand or reduce the amount of resources existing in a firm, is essentially a behavioral process strongly influenced by the cognition of managers, since "managers' mental models influence the resources that are acquired and developed, while a firm's current resources and capabilities shape those mental models and influence managerial perceptions" (Maritan and Peteraf 2011, p. 9).

Following the cognitive perspective of strategic management research (Walsh 1995), we suggest that the development of strategic resources, whether through identification (Barney 1986) or through accumulation (Dierickx and Cool 1989), are spawned from managerial strategic decisions influenced by managerial cognition (Walsh 1995). Research into the managerial process performed for resource building activities, such as conceptualization and development, is important as part of the role of Operational Research (OR) in supporting strategy for a number of reasons. Firstly, managers face uncertainties and complexity (Amit and Schoemaker 1993). Secondly, managers with limited cognitive abilities engage in simplifying heuristics (Zajac and Bazerman 1991) and cognitive biases (Barnes and James 1984; Das and Bing-Sheng 1999; Schwenk 1984, 1986). Thirdly, managers perceive and interpret particular information differently and have different strategic insights even using similar analytical frameworks (Gavetti and Levinthal 2004).

Resource conceptualization, as the first step in resource management, is a process occurring within a group of managers with heterogeneous perspectives about the strategic value of a resource. Group decision processes have been theorized and tested from various angles in the strategic management literature (Jarzabkowski et al. 2007). Among the different theoretical concepts for the analysis of group processes, the intrinsic characteristics of the resources and their interrelationships indicate three key behavioral factors which are related to the process of resource conceptualization: *deliberateness*, referring to the level of analysis employed in the resource conceptualization process; *overload*, indicating the level of stress generated by the amount of information processed to identify resources; and *intra-group conflict*, capturing the impact of conflicts on the selection of the resources deemed strategic. Each of these three factors is now explored in more detail:

- *Deliberateness.* The level of deliberateness represents the degree of behavioral rationality involved in the strategy process. More specifically, a deliberate strategy process typically is structured and analytical and follows a formal behavior (De Wit and Meyer 2004; Goold 1992; Mintzberg and Waters 1985). Deliberateness corresponds to the degree of systematic behavior engaged in by a group of managers during the selection of the set of strategic resources.

- *Overload.* Information overload (Speier et al. 1999) is prevalent in decision making processes when managers believe themselves to be dealing with an excessive amount of information. The role of overload has been studied and tested across various organizational decision making settings (Swain and Haka 2000), and overload has been found to be detrimental to decision quality. Thus, a group of managers may be overloaded with too much information regarding the right set of resources to develop, such as characteristics (e.g. value, rareness) or linkages, which leads them to employ behavioral biases.

- *Intra-group conflict.* Conflict is a common component of group behavioral processes that has a strong influence on the outcome of strategic decision processes. Conflict consists of two categories: functional task-related conflict (cognitive conflict) and dysfunctional emotion-related conflict (affective conflict) (Jehn 1995; Mooney et al. 2007). Task-related conflict stimulates the discussion among the decision makers, leading the group to evaluate issues from various angles and generating positive group dynamics (Amason 1996). However, cognitive conflict can develop into affective conflict when heated discussions during cognitive conflict lead to emotional clashes (Jehn 1997) and aggressive behavior. Since many resources are difficult to identify due to their characteristics and impact on performance, cognitive conflict can escalate into affective conflict, affecting the final selection of the resource.

## 17.3 Observational Study

We conducted an observational study (Henderson et al. 2006; Weingart et al. 2007) to understand the role of group dynamics within a resource conceptualization process. The groups employed resource mapping to facilitate this process. Resource mapping is an OR technique developed to support managers' visualization of the set of strategic resources based on stocks, flows and feedback processes, but the map is employed to facilitate the discussion about characteristics of and linkages between resources (Kunc and Morecroft 2009). The technique is based on the premise that firms are systems of interconnected resources that determine their performance over time (Miller and Shamsie 1996; Morecroft et al. 2002). A standard resource map represents the resources and their accumulation rates, as well as their linkages, using specific graphical notation (stocks, flows and feedback loops). Such a representation is used to elicit the managers' perspective about the resources that are strategically relevant and to facilitate group discussion about their relevance and development during strategy implementation processes (Kunc and Morecroft 2009). In other words, resource mapping is a problem structuring method employed to support resource-based strategies.

The study involved two groups of participants. Each group conceptualized the resources of a firm before suggesting strategies while the discussion was recorded by video camera (Haw and Hadfield 2011). Each group consisted of seven experienced managers, with an average age of 35. Group A was asked to develop a strategy for a low-cost airline company, whereas Group B was asked to develop a strategy for a computer devices manufacturing firm. The participants had learnt the use of resource mapping in a course before the study, and they used resource mapping alone in the study, which is a common process with strategy tools but uncommon with OR tools, which are usually facilitated by an expert (O'Brien and Dyson 2007).

## 17.3.1 Operationalization of the Group Behavioral Dynamic Process

Five measures were employed to study the behavioral components of the groups' dynamics. The first two measures described the outcome of the group process, and the next three measures described the behavior associated with the group dynamic process.

- *Resource map complexity.* We used resource map complexity as a measure of group outcome. This measure is based on Gary and Wood's (2011) measurement of mental model complexity, which computes the number of inferred causal linkages between the resources as an indication of resource map complexity. The complexity score could not serve as a definite measure of group effectiveness, so it was complemented with a qualitative analysis of the dynamics of resource conceptualization over time.

- *Satisfaction.* We used group members' perceived satisfaction with the process as another measure of group outcome. Intra-group conflicts were found to have a negative relationship with group members' satisfaction, but affective conflict in particular exhibited the strongest negative relationship (Jehn 1995; Jehn and Mannix 2001). Although past research indicates that group outcome and group satisfaction do not have any significant relationship (Schweiger et al. 1986), group satisfaction has been widely utilized to measure a group's perceived effectiveness indirectly (Amason 1996; Jehn 1995; Jehn et al. 2008).
- *Deliberateness.* Based on the review of the strategy process literature (De Wit and Meyer 2004; Goold 1992; Mintzberg and Waters 1985), we evaluated the level of structure, analytical focus and formality of the behavioral processes in the group.
- *Overload.* We followed the definition of *overload* as a situation where demand for cognitive process exceeds cognitive process capacity (Speier et al. 1999), leading to detrimental behavior. Three conditions can cause an overload: information over-supply, high demand for information, and high need for multi-tasking (Edmunds and Morris 2000; Eppler and Mengis 2004; Kirsh 2000; O'Reilly 1980).
- *Intra-group conflicts.* Based on the literature on intra-group conflicts (Jehn 1997; Jehn et al. 2008; Mooney et al. 2007), we captured the types of conflicts presented during the group discussions based on Jehn's (1994) questions.

## 17.4 Results

### 17.4.1 Quantitative Analysis of the Group Behavioral Dynamic Process

Based on the five dimensions discussed previously, we conducted a preliminary comparison between the two groups to have an insight into the differences between them. The data is presented in Table 17.1.

It is noticeable that each group had substantially different scores for most of the criteria. Group A scored higher in deliberateness and certainly had less overload and affective conflict than Group B. Although

**Table 17.1**  Result of quantitative analysis of the group behavioral dynamic process

| Construct | Average score | |
|---|---|---|
| | Group A | Group B |
| Mental model complexity | 23.0 | 17.0 |
| Satisfaction | 5.7 | 3.9 |
| Level of deliberateness | 4.6 | 2.4 |
| Overload | 2.7 | 6.1 |
| Cognitive conflict | 5.8 | 5.0 |
| Affective conflict | 2.4 | 4.7 |

there is a difference of 0.8 for the cognitive conflict measure, it is debatable whether Group A exhibited more cognitive conflict than Group B, since the difference is not large.

## 17.4.2 Qualitative Analysis of the Group Behavioral Dynamic Process

Below we describe the two groups' resource conceptualization processes in chronological order, along with appropriate quotations to illustrate their behavior. We divided the process into a number of phases to break down complex behavior into manageable pieces; the phases were distinguished when the nature of the task changed or a major breakdown occurred.

### 17.4.2.1  Group A: Incremental and Causal Linkage-Oriented Resource Conceptualization Process

Group A engaged in a well-organized rational-behavior group process and followed four major phases during their resource conceptualization. Figure 17.1 shows changes in number of resources and organizational components, along with the list of resources (in bold font) and organizational components at the end of each phase. The group finished their resource conceptualization in the first two phases and spent the next two phases refining and improving the resource map.

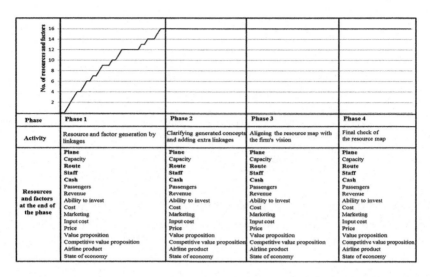

| Phase | Phase 1 | Phase 2 | Phase 3 | Phase 4 |
|---|---|---|---|---|
| Activity | Resource and factor generation by linkages | Clarifying generated concepts and adding extra linkages | Aligning the resource map with the firm's vision | Final check of the resource map |
| Resources and factors at the end of the phase | Plane<br>Capacity<br>Route<br>Staff<br>Cash<br>Passengers<br>Revenue<br>Ability to invest<br>Cost<br>Marketing<br>Input cost<br>Price<br>Value proposition<br>Competitive value proposition<br>Airline product<br>State of economy | Plane<br>Capacity<br>Route<br>Staff<br>Cash<br>Passengers<br>Revenue<br>Ability to invest<br>Cost<br>Marketing<br>Input cost<br>Price<br>Value proposition<br>Competitive value proposition<br>Airline product<br>State of economy | Plane<br>Capacity<br>Route<br>Staff<br>Cash<br>Passengers<br>Revenue<br>Ability to invest<br>Cost<br>Marketing<br>Input cost<br>Price<br>Value proposition<br>Competitive value proposition<br>Airline product<br>State of economy | Plane<br>Capacity<br>Route<br>Staff<br>Cash<br>Passengers<br>Revenue<br>Ability to invest<br>Cost<br>Marketing<br>Input cost<br>Price<br>Value proposition<br>Competitive value proposition<br>Airline product<br>State of economy |

**Fig. 17.1** Changes in Group A's number of resources/factors in chronological order

*Phase 1* The group started with *planes* as the first important resource and then developed the resource map based on the causal linkages from it. The group agreed that an increased number of planes led to an increase in routes, which in turn increased the number of staff. As can be seen from the following quotation, it was evident that the group paid an equal amount of attention to both resource conceptualization and the linkages between resources.

> *Speaker 1: "Well I guess you'd start…I would start [with ]planes."*
> *Speaker 1: "Planes. We should have capacity somewhere."*
> *Speaker 2: "But that means if you have more []planes, then more capacity."*
> *Speaker 1: "Yeah."*
> *Speaker 3: "We can have more planes, more routes."*
> *Speaker 2: "We have got more routes … then."*
> *Speaker 1: "We can have staff also."*
> *Speaker 1: "But staff also fall into … More capacity into staff."*

During the discussion, Group A experienced cognitive conflicts. However, the members systematically exchanged their opinions freely and could successfully disclose their differences without becoming disturbed. The group managed its conflict well and reached closure before developing affective conflicts. All resources and organizational factors developed during Phase 1, which resulted from rational discussions, remained in the final resource map.

*Phase 2* Once the group had conceptualized all resources, the group revisited the resource map to further understand the causal relationships between resources and factors. The group confirmed the existence of causal linkages between resources and organizational factors and then searched for further potential linkages between them. Through this process, the resources that were loosely related to each other were connected with extra linkages and intermediate concepts. This task facilitated the visualization of the influences between them. Furthermore, the group was able to build a mutual understanding of the resource map. In other words, each individual mental model depicting the strategic resources necessary for the strategy was successfully elicited for incorporation into the resource map.

*Phase 3* The group debated the contribution of the resources conceptualized in the resource map with the vision of the firm. Through this phase, the group was able to develop a better understanding of the relationship between the key resources and the vision.

*Phase 4* Finally, the group employed the resource map to develop a number of strategies.

### 17.4.2.2  Group B: Divergent and Individual Resources-Oriented Process

Group B spent the entire time conceptualizing individual resources. We have divided their process into five phases. Figure 17.2 shows the changes in number of resources and organizational factors chronologically, together with the list of resources and organizational factors at the end of each phase.

As can be seen from Fig. 17.2, Group B's resource conceptualization process was more complex than Group A's. Group B experienced three major breakdowns during resource conceptualization, which led them to discard the resources/factors and causal linkages identified in a previous stage.

*Phase 1* Group B conceptualized resources without considering potential linkages between them. Ignoring the linkages, Group B members listed concepts without any restriction. Any resource or organizational factor that a member mentioned was added directly onto the whiteboard where they were drawing their resource map. The situation rapidly resulted in chaotic behavior.

*Speaker 1: "So what resources are relevant to a company, then?"*
*Speaker 1: "Staff?"*
*Speaker 2: "Cash."*
*Speaker 3: "Yeah, everybody needs cash."*
*Speaker 4: "Product?"*
*Speaker 2: "Customer."*
*Speaker 3: "Premises?"*
*Speaker 1: "Equipment?"*

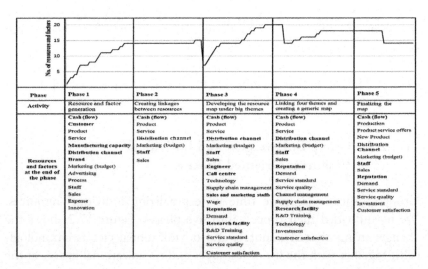

**Fig. 17.2** Changes in Group B's number of resources/factors in chronological order

*Phase 2* Group members had different ideas about how resources and factors were linked in the business and how they contributed to the performance of the business. Clearly, linking them was not a simple task. The problems seemed to be caused by two issues. Firstly, the relationships between resources were not one-to-one and direct. For example, one resource could affect various resources. Trying to understand multiple relationships between multiple resources/factors required group members to process a large volume of information leading to overload. Secondly, some resources were linked only indirectly, so a mediating resource or organizational factor intervened in the connection, as the following quote illustrates

> *Speaker 5: "Sales … Sales staffs generate cash flow."*
> *Speaker 3: "Well they generate … They take cash flow away, but they create sales, so they're creating cash."*
> *Speaker 3: "But [it's ]a negative, isn't it? Because it's a cost."*
> *Speaker 5: "But the sales team sells through the stores, and they—"*
> *Speaker 6: "—generate more revenue, and at the same time if you increase their sales through number, you bleed from wages, so …"*
> *Speaker 3: "Hmm …"*

As the group tried to find interrelationships, a series of heated discussions were triggered, because all members had different ideas. The discussions were not systematic, as they were often interrupted by other topics. Such interruptions were caused by the multiple tasks facing the group. The group was actually doing two tasks simultaneously: identifying causal relationships between existing resources and discovering the intermediate organizational factors and resources mediating between two resources. The anarchic group process unintentionally developed into affective conflicts.

*Phase 3* After the group agreed to change their approach, they decided to split the tasks into more manageable themes: resources related to specific areas of the business, e.g. marketing, and then linking together of the resources afterwards. The tasks were divided into key themes: marketing, production, R&D and supply chain. Group members formed subgroups, but there was no communication between the sub-groups during this phase, which led them to develop rather independent resource maps of the business units. Behavior continued to be chaotic.

*Phase 4* The group attempted to link the four themes once they were all developed, yet a second breakdown occurred. The group struggled to link the themes, e.g. linking production with marketing, because there were independent resource maps. The group was forced to eliminate contradicting and duplicated resources and factors. They decided to abandon their resource map for a second time. The group attempted to build the resource map as a single group and make it as simple as possible.

*Phase 5* The group finalized the resource map. The final resource map of the group was missing a number of well-developed firm-specific resources and factors that they had developed during earlier phases. Dissatisfaction among group members was inevitable.

> *Speaker 3:* "We made a quite generic map which can fit pretty much any company, not only our firm. It's pretty much an ordinary company's map we have here, isn't it?"
> *Speaker 7:* "I suppose so, but you know, I think we need to be more firm specific ... or ... I don't know, they are—"
> *Speaker 3:* "You are going to now? [looks at watch]"
> *Speaker 4:* "We do only have five minutes."
> *Speaker 3:* "We could have done ... I don't know ..."
> *Speaker 1:* "So this is our resource map ..."
> *Speaker 5:* "If I was the CEO, I would have said, 'So what, you need to tell me why, what's good about it.'"

## 17.5  Discussion

We identified three key behavioral differences during a resource conceptualization process.

(i) Group A appreciated the relationships between the resources and conceptualized the resources one by one in a causally oriented manner, whereas Group B conceptualized resources without any restriction and attempted to link the resources that had been generated. Group A engaged in a more structured and orderly process of resource conceptualization than Group B did.

(ii) Both Group A and Group B experienced disagreements among their members, which sometimes led to cognitive conflicts. However, Group A had positive cognitive conflict as the members did not interrupt or introduce other topics during a specific discussion. Group B, on the other hand, often endured disruption of discussions due to the issues with uncovering and agreeing the strategic resources. Moreover, this anarchic style of discussion triggered emotional tension among the members of Group B.

(iii) The orderly process adopted by Group A strictly restricted the members to discussing one strategic resource at a time, leading the group to enjoy a process free from breakdown. In contrast, Group B experienced a number of breakdowns, as they were not able to manage the excessive volume of information they were required to process.

In terms of the behavioral concepts defined in 17.3.1, we observed that:

## 17.5.1 Level of Deliberateness

Group A had a structured and formal process. Using various analytical frameworks, the group engaged in a comprehensive resource conceptualization process. This group followed a more systematic and analytical formation of strategy (Ansoff 1987; Ketokivi and Castañer 2004), leading to low ambiguity and more rational behavior.

Group B was rather unstructured, leading to a lack of clarity. This resulted in continuous discussions and distractions, ending in a rather general set of resources. The group failed to effectively manage the process and experienced severe breakdowns in their resource conceptualization process, resulting in chaotic behavior. The messy process affected the ability to manage and synthesize a large amount of information and to use analytical frameworks. The management team failed to cope with the challenge of managing complexity and thus ended with an unsatisfactory group decision outcome.

## 17.5.2 Information Overload Experienced in Group Behavior

The two groups had different levels of information overload. Group B, with its anarchic process, experienced a high level of overload, leading to high levels of ambiguity in their understanding of the strategic resources. Group B struggled to handle various resources simultaneously, overloading their capacity to process the complexity of a resource-based strategy. Furthermore, the group did not agree in which order they would investigate the resources and causal linkages, finishing with high levels of confusion and chaotic behavior. Lack of agreement caused additional burdens on their cognition and resulted in multiple conflicts. Group A did not experience these problems, as the group followed a well-structured group process, finishing with clear understanding of the resources and their interrelationships, so it did not suffer information overload in exploring all resources considered to be necessary for the strategy.

## 17.5.3 Intra-Group Conflicts

Cognitive conflicts were evident in both groups. Since individual managers have different insights into their firms' resource systems (Morecroft et al. 2002; Walsh 1995), it was natural for managers to disagree and experience conflict over defining the importance of a resource. Group A, with a highly structured conceptualization process, did not have to sacrifice their efficiency due to affective conflicts. Furthermore, they were able to maximize the effectiveness of cognitive conflicts, as the group was able to focus on the topic of the discussion during episodes of cognitive conflict. Chaotic Group B, on the other hand, had unclear and discontinuous episodes of cognitive conflicts, leading to behavioral biases, e.g. confirmation bias. As a result of this process, the group members were not able to take full advantage of cognitive conflicts to reduce confirmation bias, as they did not reach agreement on most of these conflicts.

Affective conflict was arguably more evident in the chaotic group, as this group experienced more tension between members, possibly triggered by unproductive cognitive conflicts, along with stress and frustration that were caused by lack of time and wasted effort. Affective conflicts hindered the resource conceptualization process with unnecessary emotional tension. Furthermore, the situation posed a potential threat to subsequent group and organizational processes, as the emotional tension could cause further affective conflicts in different contexts (Jehn 1997) and increase the communication barriers among the members of the group, leading to high levels of causal ambiguity.

Table 17.2 summarizes the differences in the group dynamic process and the behavioral factors considered.

## 17.6  Conclusion

Using a behavioral perspective, this study looked into the complex dynamics within group resource conceptualization processes using resource mapping, which is a problem structuring method for resource-based strategies. We suggest that group dynamic behavioral processes can affect the level of structure experienced during a group's resource conceptualization process. We expect that groups of managers who experience effective cognitive conflicts with low levels of overload and affective conflicts will be capable of conceptualizing systemically firm-specific and idiosyncratic resource systems with low levels of causal ambiguity, leading to positive organizational performance. In contrast, groups of managers under chaotic behavior are more likely to conceptualize a set of generic resources with loose linkages between them, leading to high levels of causal ambiguity, which can generate important biases in their decision making process and poor organizational performance.

In conclusion, we believe the study offers two major contributions to the field of behavioral OR and strategy. Firstly, the study has identified various method biases (Podsakoff et al. 2003) associated with the

**Table 17.2** Behavioral group dynamic processes in resource conceptualization

| Group dynamic process variables | Systemic process-based group (Group A) | Discrete process-based group (Group B) |
|---|---|---|
| Deliberateness of the resource conceptualization | Deliberate and well-structured resource conceptualization | Started with a comprehensive resource/factor identification but overall, experienced an anarchic and messy resource conceptualization process |
| Cognitive overload | Complex task of resource conceptualization was well managed with an orderly and well-structured conceptualization process | Complex task of resource conceptualization was not managed. Instead, an anarchic group process caused a high level of information demand and processing, which led to cognitive overload |
| Cognitive conflicts | Efficient and effective interactions between heterogeneous mental models regarding the resource system due to clear form of cognitive conflicts | Inefficient and ineffective interactions between heterogeneous mental models regarding the resource system due to unclear form of cognitive conflicts |
| Affective conflicts | The group was able to focus without a high level of tension/affective conflicts | The resource conceptualization process was hindered by a high level of tension/affective conflicts |
| Causal ambiguity | Low level of causal ambiguity and a unique bundle of resources | High level of causal ambiguity and a generic bundle of resources |

strategic decision process and the tool supporting the process, in this case: resource mapping. More studies should be conducted towards this direction to further identify factors which influence the decision making process. Secondly, the study has demonstrated the importance of having structured strategy decision making process to avoid future behavioral biases in decision making. Group dynamics can improve during the resource mapping process when a facilitated decision making process is used, which is an important thread in the OR literature (Rouwette

2011). In summary, we believe there is a high degree of synergy to be achieved by combining the academic research in the behavioral OR and strategy literature.

# References

Amason, A.C. 1996. Distinguishing the effects of functional and dysfunctional conflict on strategic decision making: Resolving a paradox for top management teams. *Academy of Management Journal* 39: 123–148.

Amit, R., and P.J.H. Schoemaker. 1993. Strategic assets and organizational rent. *Strategic Management Journal* 14: 33–33.

Ansoff, H.I. 1987. *Corporate strategy* (Rev. ed.). Penguin: London.

Barnes, J., and H. James. 1984. Cognitive biases and their impact on strategic planning. *Strategic Management Journal* 5: 129–137.

Barney, J.B. 1986. Strategic factor markets: Expectations, luck and business strategy. *Management Science* 32: 1231–1241.

Barney, J.B. 1991. Firm resources and sustained competitive advantage. *Journal of Management* 17: 99–120.

Das, T.K., and T. Bing-Sheng. 1999. Cognitive biases and strategic decision processes: An integrative perspective. *Journal of Management Studies* 36: 757–778.

De Wit, B., and R. Meyer. 2004. *Strategy: Process, content, context: An international perspective*, 3rd ed. London: Thomson Learning.

Dierickx, I., and K. Cool. 1989. Asset stock accumulation and sustainability of competitive advantage. *Management Science* 35: 1504–1511.

Edmunds, A., and A. Morris. 2000. The problem of information overload in business organisations: A review of the literature. *International Journal of Information Management* 20: 17–28.

Eppler, M.J., and J. Mengis. 2004. The concept of information overload: A review of literature from organization science, accounting, marketing, MIS and related disciplines. *The Information Society* 20: 325–344.

Foss, N. 1997. *Resources, firms, and strategies: A reader in the resource-based perspective*. Oxford: Oxford University Press.

Gary, M.S., and R.E. Wood. 2011. Mental models, decision rules and performance heterogeneity. *Strategic Management Journal* 32: 569–594.

Gavetti, G., and D.A. Levinthal. 2004. The strategy field from the perspective of management science: Divergent strands and possible integration. *Management Science* 50: 1309–1318.

Goold, M. 1992. Design, learning and planning: A further observation on the design school debate. *Strategic Management Journal* 13: 169–170.

Haw, K., and M. Hadfield. 2011. *Video in social science research: Functions and forms*. New York: Routledge.

Henderson, M.D., Y. Trope, and P.J. Carnevale. 2006. Negotiation from a near and distant time perspective. *Journal of Personality and Social Psychology* 91: 712–729.

Hutzschenreuter, T., and H.W. Volberda. 2007. The role of path dependency and managerial intentionality: A perspective on international business research. *Journal of International Business Studies* 38: 1055–1068.

Jarzabkowski, P., J. Balogun, and D. Seidl. 2007. Strategizing: The challenges of a practice perspective. *Human Relations* 60: 5–27.

Jehn, K. 1994. Enhancing effectiveness: An investigation of advantages and disadvantages of value-based intragroup conflict. *International Journal of Conflict Management* 5: 223–238.

Jehn, K. 1995. A multi-method examination of the benefits and detriments of intragroup conflict. *Administrative Science Quarterly* 40: 256–282.

Jehn, K. 1997. A qualitative analysis of conflict types and dimensions in organizational groups. *Administrative Science Quarterly* 42: 530–557.

Jehn, K., and E. Mannix. 2001. The dynamic nature of conflict: A longitudinal study of intragroup conflict and group performance. *Academy of Management Journal* 44: 238–251.

Jehn, K., L. Greer, S. Levine, and G. Szulanski. 2008. The effects of conflict types, dimensions, and emergent states on group outcomes. *Group Decision and Negotiation* 17: 465–495.

Ketokivi, M., and X. Castañer. 2004. Strategic planning as an integrative device. *Administrative Science Quarterly* 49: 337–365.

Kirsh, D. 2000. A few thoughts on cognitive overload. *Intellectica* 1: 19–51.

Kunc, M., and J. Morecroft. 2009. Resource-based strategies and problem structuring: Using resource maps to manage resource systems. *Journal of the Operational Research Society* 60: 191–199.

Kunc, M., and J. Morecroft. 2010. Managerial decision-making and firm performance under a resource-based paradigm. *Strategic Management Journal* 31: 1164–1182.

Maritan, C.A., and M.A. Peteraf. 2011. Building a bridge between resource acquisition and resource accumulation. *Journal of Management* 7: 1374–1389.

Miller, D., and J. Shamsie. 1996. The resource-based view of the firm in two environments: The Hollywood film studios from 1936 to 1965. *Academy of Management Journal* 39: 519–543.

Mintzberg, H., and J. Waters. 1985. Of strategies, deliberate and emergent. *Strategic Management Journal* 6: 257–272.

Mooney, A.C., P.J. Holahan, and A.C. Amason. 2007. Don't take it personally: Exploring cognitive conflict as a mediator of affective conflict. *Journal of Management Studies* 44: 733–758.

Morecroft, J.D.W., R. Sanchez, and A. Heene. 2002. *Systems perspectives on resources, capabilities and management processes.* Oxford: Elsevier Science.

O'Brien, F.A., and R.G. Dyson. 2007. *Supporting strategy: Frameworks, methods and models.* Chichester: Wiley.

O'Reilly III, C.A. 1980. Individuals and information overload in organizations: Is more necessarily better? *Academy of Management Journal* 23: 684–696.

Podsakoff, P.M., S.B. MacKenzie, J. Lee, and N.P. Podsakoff. 2003. Common method biases in behavioural research: A critical review of the literature and recommended remedies. *Journal of Applied Psychology* 88: 879–903.

Powell, T.C., D. Lovallo, and C.R. Fox. 2011. Behavioral strategy. *Strategic Management Journal* 32: 1369–1386.

Rouwette, E.A.J.A. 2011. Facilitated modelling in strategy development: Measuring the impact on communication, consensus and commitment. *Journal of the Operational Research Society* 62: 879–887.

Schweiger, D.M., W.R. Sandberg, and J.W. Ragan. 1986. Group approaches for improving strategic decision making: A comparative analysis of dialectical inquiry, devil's advocacy and consensus. *Academy of Management Journal* 29: 51–71.

Schwenk, C.R. 1984. Cognitive simplification processes in strategic decision-making. *Strategic Management Journal* 5: 111–128.

Schwenk, C.R. 1986. Information, cognitive biases and commitment to a course of action. *Academy of Management Review* 11: 298–310.

Speier, C., J.S. Valacich, and I. Vessey. 1999. The influence of task interruption on individual decision making: An information overload perspective. *Decision Sciences* 30: 337–360.

Swain, M.R., and S.F. Haka. 2000. Effects of information load on capital budgeting decisions. *Behavioral Research in Accounting* 12: 171–198.

Walsh, J.P. 1995. Managerial and organizational cognition: Notes from a trip down memory lane. *Organization Science* 6: 280–321.

Weingart, L.R., J.M. Brett, M. Olekalns, and P.L. Smith. 2007. Conflicting social motives in negotiating groups. *Journal of Personality and Social Psychology* 93: 994–1010.

Wernerfelt, B. 1984. A resource-based view of the firm. *Strategic Management Journal* 5: 171–180.

Zajac, E.J., and M.H. Bazerman. 1991. Blind spots in industry and competitor analysis: Implications of interfirm (mis)perceptions for strategic decisions. *Academy of Management Review* 16: 37–56.

# Part IV

**Future Directions**

# 18

# The Past, Present and Futures of Behavioral Operational Research

Geoff Royston

## 18.1 Introduction

What took us so long? Why, given the obvious importance of human perceptions, thought and behavior in most of the problems that Operational Research (OR) tackles, have we paid so much more attention to what could be called *decision physics*—scheduling, routing, allocation and so on—than to what might be termed *decision psychology*? Why, given our early-stated quest, as it used to appear in the OR Society journal, to address complex problems "arising in the direction and management of large systems of men, machines, materials and money", did we not consider the influence of the first element of that list as least as much as we considered the rest?

Maybe there were good reasons? Or maybe the charge is unfair: perhaps we have not been quite as neglectful in the past of human factors as

G. Royston (✉)
South View, Copgrove Road, Burton Leonard, Harrogate, North Yorkshire HG3 3SJ, UK

© The Editor(s) (if applicable) and The Author(s) 2016
M. Kunc et al. (eds.), *Behavioral Operational Research*,
DOI 10.1057/978-1-137-53551-1_18

it may seem? But why has there been such a rapid increase in interest in the last few years? And where might this lead?

This chapter will address all these issues (largely from a perspective of experience in the UK, with a nod towards developments in Europe and on the other side of the Atlantic), but it starts with a personal story. It concerns an experience back in the 1980s which brought home to me how *real world* operational research cannot just be about the logical structure and dynamics of inanimate entities but also has to allow for the thinking and behavior of human beings. It is a story about a birth.

## 18.1.1 An Alarming Tale

After going into labor with our first child and being admitted to hospital, my wife, as is common practice in maternity wards, was hooked up to an electronic fetal heart monitor. The idea of such monitoring is to detect early signs of any fetal distress and to thus assist timely intervention with any necessary remedial actions (see Fig. 18.1a).

The reality was rather different. The monitor alarm went off (much to the consternation of the parents-to-be); a nurse was called, who listened to the baby's heartbeat with a traditional stethoscope, fiddled with the monitor leads and announced, "Probably just a loose connection, it's always happening with the monitors". The alarm triggering was repeated several times during the labor, with decreasing attention being paid to what clearly were (correctly) regarded as false alarms. All eventually turned out well, with the delivery of a healthy baby boy (recently now himself a parent!).

Reflecting on the experience shortly afterwards, it became clear to me, as discussed in Royston (1982), that, seen as a whole system, the set-up was functioning not as in Fig. 18.1a but as in Fig. 18.1b. For a monitor, as indeed for any diagnostic test, clinical or otherwise, there is generally a trade-off between *sensitivity* (proportion of true problems it detects) and *specificity* (proportion of non-problems it correctly classifies as such), so higher sensitivity results in lower specificity and hence more false alarms as well as more *genuine ones* (we shall define the proportion of genuine cases as *problem prevalence*). But—and here is the crucial behavioral element—the higher the perceived false alarm rate, the less attention people will pay

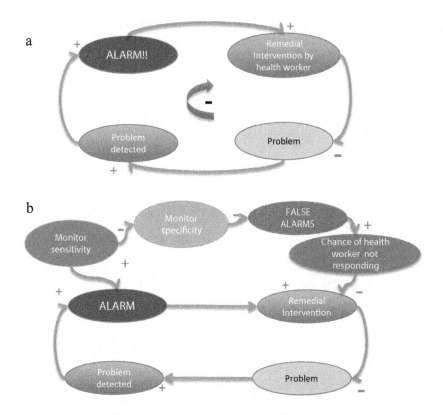

**Fig. 18.1** Human behavior forms a key component of an alarm system. **(a)** A very simple model of fetal heart monitoring. **(b)** False alarms lead to behavioral response, degrading the performance of the monitoring *system*

to the warning signal (think about car alarms)—exactly the situation with the fetal heart monitoring story. The danger, of course, is that amongst the false alarms there will be some genuine ones, and many of these also will be ignored (think about the boy who cried wolf).

Using Bayes' theorem and some approximate but not unrealistic parameter values allows a rough quantification of the above situation (see text box below). Despite using a *monitor* that will detect most problems, the *monitor-human system* is likely, once the behavioral response to false alarms is taken into account, to detect only a small fraction of them. (Perhaps it was just as well that the nurse was relying not on the *monitor-*

*human system* but on the *monitor-stethoscope-human system*, though this suggests that the traditional *stethoscope-human system* might have been a more cost-effective approach!)

---

**Illustrative Analysis of Impact of Behavioral Effects on Alarm Systems**

Suppose:

- **Sensitivity** ($p_a$) = 95% (i.e. the machine will correctly detect 95% of problems)
- **Specificity** ($p_b$) = 70% (i.e. the machine will incorrectly classify 30% of non-problems as problems)
- Problem **prevalence**($p_c$) = 5% (i.e. cases where there really is a problem)

*Then, using* **Bayes' formula:**
*the* **probability** *that an alarm will be* **genuine**
= $(p_c \times p_a)/[(p_c \times p_a) + (1 - p_c) \times (1 - p_b)]$
= **14%;** *so* **86% of alarms** *will be* **false**

- *The chance that a health care worker will* **respond** *to an alarm is a* **cognitive and behavioral factor.**
- *It will depend on their knowledge or perception of the false alarm rate:* *the* **higher the false alarm rate, the lower the human response.**
- *Suppose, say, their probability of responding to any given alarm is simply equal to the overall proportion of alarms that are not false.*

**The detection rate of the alarm system falls from a notional 95% to just 13%** (95% × 14%) **once the behavioral effect is taken into account.**

---

The message of this tale for OR seems clear. Human factors cannot be ignored; they can make an important difference to model realism, see e.g. Baines et al. (2004). Most of the situations we are called upon to investigate and improve comprise not only equipment, information, money and so on but also involve people. Analysis that fails to allow for, and modeling that fails to incorporate, human thought and behavior is likely to fall short.

## 18.2  Behavioral OR in the Past

### 18.2.1 The Early Years

Although the OR approach can be traced back to Babbage, or earlier (see e.g. Royston 2013a), its origin under the specific name of "operational research" was the work immediately before the Second World War on the effective integration of the then new technology of radar into Britain's air defence information system, work estimated by Goodeve (1948) to have *doubled* the efficacy of the UK fighter command in the Battle of Britain at a time when national survival hung in the balance.

Underlying wartime OR was a concern about the reliability of conventional military thinking and decision making; that relying on feelings, past practice, or "common sense" could lead to poor solutions, whereas rigorous analysis could reveal much better ones—hence the need to "avoid running the war by gusts of emotion" (Blackett 1962). OR wartime experience was to provide many examples of the benefits of the analytical approach, such as the counter-intuitive advantages of setting depth-charges to detonate at considerably shallower levels than where most of the submarines being attacked would be likely to be; of large convoys' being almost as hard to spot but easier to defend than small ones; or the benefits of painting the undersides of aircraft in a dark, seemingly more conspicuous, color (see especially Kirby 2003 and Budiansky 2013).

By and large, wartime OR appears to been able to focus on decision physics and avoid decision psychology through relying on the statistical *law of large numbers* that can smooth out the variability that the involvement of people can bring to situations, allowing underlying regularities to emerge. However, this early work did include some examination of human factors—for example, the work on radar included "highlighting significant differences in the skill of radar operators" and then recommending "improvements in training procedures" (Kirby 2003, p. 73). Further, the importance of human factors not only in the content but also in the conduct of analytical work was also well-recognized in wartime OR—"it must be stated once and for all that report writing is a very poor substitute for a senior officer [in the OR team] who can discuss the idea with his equals in Armies, Corps and Divisions" (Kirby 2003, p. 125).

## 18.2.2 The Post-war Period

As, after the war, OR spread from the military to the civil sphere and was faced with working in an environment where problems could be more complex and more multi-faceted and have less clear-cut objectives, the need to widen the OR armory beyond that supplied by the mathematical and physical sciences became more apparent.

In particular, there was a clear emerging need for social scientists and operational researchers to better understand each other's worlds and to explore opportunities for collaboration. That was the aim of the first international conference to be held by the Operational Research Society, in September 1964 at the University of Cambridge, on "Operational Research and the Social Sciences", from which the 48 papers and associated commentaries were later brought together in a book (Lawrence 1966). In his opening address to that conference, Sir Charles Goodeve (the first chair of the OR Club, founded in 1948, later to become the OR Society) set the scene by noting that "operational research people are very much concerned with change and can deal with the logic, including the economics, of it. But attitudes of people—managers, technicians, workpeople, salesmen, customers etc.—can throw the best of predictions into confusion". The conference was judged a success, though, its reporter observed, only up to a point; "The number of papers, either from the behavioral side carrying conviction as operational research studies, or from operational research convincingly modeling human behavior, was small, perhaps nil" (Lawrence 1966, p. 6), echoing a concern that had been raised earlier by Dutton and Walton (1964), who had argued that "in so far as Behavioral science is concerned, operational research has failed to be scientific enough".

Meantime, on the other side of the Atlantic, influential (later to be Nobel Prize–winning) work on human cognition and decision making behavior was being done by Herbert Simon at Carnegie Mellon University. Simon introduced the world to the concepts of *bounded rationality* and *satisficing*, which were developed from the understanding that in the real world, information relevant to decisions is generally partial and uncertain, with limited available time and capability to process it, and so methods are required to make the best one can of such situations—to reach not an *optimal* solution but one that is satisfactory or good enough. In Simon's (1969) seminal book "The Sciences of the Artificial" (which ran to three editions, the third in 1996), he contrasted (pp. 27–8) what he saw as the classical operational research approach of optimizing in a greatly simplified model of the real world, with what he saw as the artificial intelligence approach of satisficing in a nearly realistic model, noting that "sometimes one will be preferred, sometimes the other".

## 18.2.3 Heading for the Turn of the Century

One of the speakers at the 1964 conference was Russ Ackoff. At it he said, "In principle it [operational research] should involve behavioral science in all its efforts … [this] will succeed however, only if the operational researcher becomes more willing than he is now to face and deal with behavioral variables explicitly" (Lawrence 1966, pp. 437–38). Such thinking came to a head in his two iconoclastic papers (Ackoff 1979a, b), in which he warned that traditional techniques of analysis—techniques he himself had done much to promulgate—were insufficient for tackling important managerial and societal problems.

At about the same time, in his classic book "Management", Peter Drucker (1977) criticised management science as paying too little attention to issues of human behavior. He stated that it did not adequately reflect the fact that a business enterprise is made up of human beings and so its operations could not be regarded as a purely mechanistic process; its domain of study needed to include people's—especially managers'—assumptions, opinions and errors and thus that it did not sufficiently respect its subject matter—interestingly, much the same criticism that had been made over a decade earlier by Dutton and Walton (1964)—and a pretty damning charge for any discipline!

Such concerns were considered in influential books by thinkers like Donald Schön (1983) and Hilton Boothroyd (1978), who argued for expanding the role of the OR professional from that of technical expert with an emphasis on solving precise and sometimes unrealistic problems to that of reflective inquirer with an emphasis on helpful ways of framing and structuring problems of the real world.

The most prominent result of such critiques was the development of what came to be called soft *OR*, featuring *problem structuring* approaches pioneered by Peter Checkland, Colin Eden, John Friend and others and popularised by the book "Rational Analysis for a Problematic World", edited by Jonathan Rosenhead (1989). These approaches undoubtedly widened the vision of OR, at least in the UK, and did much to meet the criticisms of Ackoff and others. They showed that *soft* skills are not some sort of optional sugary coating for the crunchy kernel of *hard* OR but that problem solving is always embedded, albeit to varying depths, in problem setting and structuring.

In April 1989, 25 years after the first conference on "Operational Research and the Social Sciences", a second was held (also at Cambridge University). In its proceedings (Jackson, Keys and Cropper 1989), the preface notes that "mutual understanding had proved more difficult than many must have hoped for in 1964" and that "practitioners who have integrated traditional OR and social science are relatively few and far between", citing, as harsh evidence of this, "the loss in 1985 of the institutional embodiment of the theme of the 1964 conference, the Centre for Organisational and Operational Research based at the Tavistock Institute for Human Relations".[1] (One could add also that Ackoff had despaired of OR in the USA developing in the direction he had called for and had instead struck out on his own, founding a "Social Systems Sciences" programme at the University of Pennsylvania.)

However, the conference organizers also noted that there "remains a feeling that the full potential of bringing together the two sides to address current problems of organisations and society remains to be realised". It was observed that "Few these days regard OR as being simply applied mathematics … [there is] recognition that OR is process of intervention in organisational and human affairs". The development of soft OR in

---

[1] The Centre for Organisational and Operational Research was founded in 1963, as a joint commitment by the Councils of the OR Society and the Tavistock Institute to establish a new research centre to expand the scope of OR through close association with practicing social scientists. During its life of over two decades, it conducted pioneering projects in industry and civil government—"taking OR into a world characterised by complex webs of shared accountability"—and nurtured new methods, such as AIDA (Analysis of Interconnected Decision Areas) and the Strategic Choice approach. Its legacy can be seen in the continued use of such approaches, both in the UK and in other countries, and in developments in community OR and OR for international development.

the intervening 25 years was highlighted: "There has been a penetration and diffusion of ideas from the social sciences into OR, reflected most strongly in the body of writing about soft OR methods and soft systems thinking". And there was some helpful movement observed in the other direction too—the social science disciplines were now having to "become more pragmatic, providing more points of contact with operational researchers".

The conference proceedings include a plenary paper by John Burgoyne, "A Behavioral Science Perspective on Operational Research Practice". This notes that behavioral science can be seen at one level as a *tool* for OR—a *technical servant*—and at another as an overlapping discipline—an *intellectual partner* He also identifies a third level—*radical critic*—in which OR itself becomes the focus of social research, an interesting wider topic taken up by Abbott (1988). In Burgoynes' discussion of behavioral science as a tool for OT he points out that this tool can be of two types; the first being "contribution of concepts, models and measures" - particularly by including some behavioral variables in the *content* of OR models - and the second being "dealing with the client system" - assisting with the *process* of interaction with the client. And in discussing behavioral science as an overlapping discipline, he highlights decision making as a key research area of mutual interest, noting not only the rise of expert systems and artificial intelligence but also the deeper issues of choice, sense-making and agency. Another quarter-century on, these points are of continuing relevance, as can be seen clearly in this book, where there is wide coverage of topics ranging from the modeling of thought and behavior and the incorporation of behavioral factors in models to how people understand models and how thought and behavior is influenced by modeling work.

## 18.2.4 Two Areas of Behavioral Strength: Decision Analysis and System Dynamics

Although the development of *soft OR* came in part from criticisms of OR's focus on the logical aspects of situations and relative neglect of human factors (and, more generally, its emphasis on analysis and theoretical puzzle solving at the expense of synthesis and design for *real world* systems), its problem structuring methods—with the clear exception of cognitive mapping, (Eden 1988), which explicitly drew on *personal constructs* theory from psychology (Kelly 1955)—did not derive from or draw strongly upon the behavioral sciences.

The picture is rather different for another area, decision analysis, in which OR has long been involved—for example, in 1980, the USA's OR Society Institute for Operational Research and the Managment Sciences (INFORMS) (Operational Research Society of America (ORSA)), as it was then) set up a special interest group on decision analysis, which by 1996 had become a full-blown Decision Analysis Society (within the INFORMS umbrella). In its early days (see Howard 1966; Raiffa 1968), decision analysis, which could reasonably be argued to have had enough on its plate at the time, like proselytizing the use of tools such as decision trees and a Bayesian approach for decision making, was mainly logic-focused. However, as time went on it widened its perspective, tackling more complex issues involving multiple decision criteria, (e.g. Keeney and Raiffa 1976). This included starting to pay more attention to cognitive and behavioral factors, (e.g. Keeney 1992). By then some would be saying (Phillips 1989) that "decision theory has now evolved from a somewhat abstract mathematical discipline ... to a framework for thinking that enables different perspectives on a problem to be brought together".

If decision analysis merits mention as one area of OR in which cognitive and behavioral factors were increasingly well recognised, then another is System Dynamics. Created in the 1950s by Jay Forrester at MIT, initially with a focus on industrial problems (Forrester 1961) but expanding through the next two decades to address first the problems of cities (Forrester 1969) and then, in "Limits to Growth", those of the world (Meadows et al. 1972), System Dynamics proved a versatile approach. The ability of System Dynamics modeling to represent, at least at a fairly aggregate level, many of the characteristics of human thought and behavior (feedback, non-linearity and so on), its interest in modeling not only the systems about which decisions are to be made but also the decision making systems themselves and its capacity to model qualitative as well as quantitative variables all made this approach attractive where human behavior and thinking needed to be represented. It is therefore not surprising that System Dynamics has stood out as a modeling approach in the management sciences that has not fought shy of modeling behavior (e.g. Sastry and Sterman 1993).

Unfortunately—in part perhaps because of concerns by some that these very modeling characteristics were too far removed from mainstream OR modeling of the more tangible and mechanistic features of processes and systems—the System Dynamics and OR communities have not always been as close as they might be. However, by the turn of the century, as evidenced by the publication of a special issue of the *Journal of the Operational Research Society* on System Dynamics (Ranyard et al. 1999), any such gap looked to have considerably narrowed. And as more recent evidence of this, it is noteworthy that the OR Society's President's Medal for 2014 was awarded to David Lane for the application of systems modeling approaches in the Munro Review—a major review of child protection commissioned by the UK Government (Lane, Munro, and Husemann 2016).

## 18.3 Behavioral OR Today

As the contents of this book clearly demonstrate, there has recently been a dramatic upswing in OR's attention to human behavior. In the last two or three years we have been seeing a transforming picture on behavioral OR. Both the IFORS conference in 2014 and the EURO conference in 2015, for the first time, had streams on the topic; a special issue of the *European Journal of Operational Research* on behavioral OR was announced, attracting the submission of over 80 papers; and in 2014, following two workshops to consider the area, the OR Society set up a Special Interest Group on Behavioral OR.

Slightly preceding this flurry of interest has been an important vanguard of activity arguing for greater attention to be paid to cognitive and behavioral issues in the operations management area, as usefully reviewed by Loch and Wu (2007) and Gino and Pisano (2008). INFORMS has a section on behavioral operations management and has held an annual international conference on this topic since 2006. A comprehensive handbook on behavioral operations management has recently been published (Bendoly et al. 2015). Most, if not all, of this activity has quite directly read across to the area of behavioral operational research as a whole.

There are various reasons for this increased interest, of which I would suggest that the following three are of especial importance:

## 18.3.1 Developments in "Real World" Economics and Psychology

In a book somewhat provocatively titled *The Death of Economics* (Ormerod 1995), it was noted that economies are not precise, controllable machines but dynamic organisms not fully amenable to investigation by conventional analytical, overly mathematicised approaches. Related doubts about the real world relevance of traditional economic theory were also apparent from the rise of the field of experimental economics, testing how people made economic decisions in practice, and thus seeking to remedy how economics had paid too much attention to theories about how the world works and not enough to how people actually behave. Such developments were brought to the attention of a wider public in popular science books like *Freakonomics* (Levitt and Dubner 2005).

Two key figures in this development are the economist Richard Thaler, who co-wrote the best-seller *Nudge* (Thaler and Sunstein 2008), about using behavioral insights to get big effects from small changes, and the psychologist Daniel Kahneman, a leading candidate, and not only in also being a Nobel laureate, for the inheritance of Herbert Simon's cognitive and behavioral mantle. In his book *Thinking Fast and Slow*, Kahneman (2011) demonstrates how managers and others actually make decisions, particularly decisions under uncertainty. He explains how people have two decision making approaches: one rational and slow, the other intuitive and fast. Both have advantages and disadvantages, and much has been done to clarify these and to establish the situations in which each approach performs best.

A related strand of work is that on simple *fast and frugal* classification and decision heuristics, as researched by Gigerenzer and Goldstein (1996) and Gigerenzer and Selten (2001). These heuristics can be at least as powerful as more elaborate and data-hungry algorithms and are more likely to be used in the messy conditions of the real world. (This can be literally life-saving; a "fast and frugal" approach is used in checklists such as the famous Apgar test for determining if newborn babies are in serious distress.)

Richard Thaler has recently written an account (2015) of the development of the new field of behavioral economics, which he did so much to create. In his book, *Misbehaving: The Making of Behavioral Economics*, Thaler summarizes a key argument for behavioral economics thus: traditional economic theory assumes people choose by optimizing, that their choices are rational and unbiased—in short, that they are *Econs* (think *Star Trek*'s Mr Spock); the problem is that people are *Humans*, not *Econs*, and that makes traditional economics ("= optimization + equilibrium") flawed.

OR seems to have been slow (certainly compared to economics, which has come up from behind in this area) to take advantage of this burgeoning body of new knowledge about real world decision making, perhaps because, unlike economics, it has been less wedded to the use of theories whose limitations have been exposed by behavioral research. Of course, OR practitioners do not get far without being aware of the importance of behavior in the process of interaction with clients—the second of the behavioral elements requiring OR's attention mentioned at the 1989 conference by Burgoyne—and have long recognized this in their work (e.g. Abdel-Malek et al. 1999). But OR has been slow and patchy in developing the first area that Burgoyne (and Dutton before him) noted—drawing on scientific advances in understanding behavioral factors and building that into the content of our analysis and modeling. In some particular fields, notably defense, progress in this area is apparent and has been supported by deliberations at the national level, such as the seminal review *Behavioral Modeling and Simulation: From Individuals to Societies*, by the National Research Council in the USA (Zacharias et al. 2008). Marketing is another area in which behavioral factors are often built into the content of analysis and modeling (Steenkamp 2000). But so far, such an approach does not permeate management science as a whole, and as the behavioral sciences advance, this becomes a progressively riskier position. Clients also are aware of some of these advances, are concerned about failures of conventional analytical approaches (e.g. in financial crises) and are looking for better ones, so OR needs to up its game.

## 18.3.2 Emerging Insights about Complexity and Increasing Ability to Model It

The 1980s and 1990s saw the rise of what has been called *complexity science* (Érdi 2008; Mitchell 2009). Its domain comprises systems that are even more complex than those typically studied in System Dynamics: systems that adapt, are self-organizing or display emergent properties—what has been called *generative complexity*. To the insights about behavioral phenomena already gained from System Dynamics are now added those coming from the study of generative complexity. (Lord Robert May gave some vivid illustrations from finance, ecology and epidemiology (May et al. 2008) when he delivered the Operational Research Society's annual Blackett memorial lecture in 2010.)

A common feature of such complex adaptive systems is that they contain interacting agents (and, in biological and social systems, interacting sentient agents). Agent interaction is a key driver for many behavioral and social phenomena—for example, the spread of rumors and riots, runs on banks or segregation in cities. The growth in interest in complex adaptive systems involving behavior and social life has been synergistically associated with the increasing capacity to simulate them on computers, leading to a whole new field of agent based modeling (Miller and Page 2007). A nice example of how it is now feasible to extend modeling from decision physics to decision pyschology can be found in developments in the simulation of crowd behavior (important, for instance, in designing safe arrangements for large public gatherings or emergency evacuations), which typically used to be based on fluid dynamics models but can now, through agent based modeling, also incorporate individual decision making (Xiaoping et al. 2009).

Complementing this growth in computing power is a huge expansion of data available for studying complex phenomena in business and society—the rise of *Big Data*—opening up rich seams of data to be mined for behavioral insights and for behavioral modeling (e.g. papers in Chen et al. 2012)

### 18.3.3 Developments in Communicating with Clients

As has already been mentioned, behavioral OR embraces not only the incorporation of behavioral factors in analyses and models but also behavioral aspects of OR practice, such as how clients and indeed the public understand and use modeling concepts and results—see, for example, Sweeney and Sterman (2000) and Hämäläinen et al. (2013). Misperceptions are ubiquitous and can have serious, even global, consequences. For example, understanding of climate change appears to be distorted by lack of appreciation of the basic dynamics of the relationship between flows and stocks of atmospheric carbon dioxide (Sterman 2008). Another telling example, somewhat outside the world of OR but with lessons for us, comes from the *Challenger* space shuttle disaster, where misleading selection and presentation to senior managers of data in charts on rocket motor damage led to a go-ahead on a launch in very cold weather, with tragic results (Tufte 1997, pp. 39–49).

In part at least because of the rise of *big data analytics*, greater attention is now being paid to such matters as data visualization. This can help people understand analytical findings and avoid confusion—confusion which in some areas can be on matters of life and death, for example, avoiding serious misperceptions about health risks. Many people, including professionals such as clinicians, are confused by numerical descriptions of probability—and may consequently advise patients quite incorrectly about health risks—but understand much better when probabilities are expressed in simple visual formats (see, for example, work on risk communication by Calman and Royston 1997; Gigerenzer 2014).

## 18.4 Possible Futures for Behavioral OR

### 18.4.1 Where Now for Behavioral OR?

There is of course more than one future for behavioral OR. That future will depend both on the attitudes of the OR community and on external developments.

One possible future, in which behavioral OR would not feature strongly, would be one in which OR focuses sharply on its classical quantitative strengths and concentrates on exploiting new opportunities for deploying them, such as provided by the rise of big data and analytics, limiting its areas of interest mainly to what was referred to above as decision physics.

A very different, radical, scenario, one that perhaps was amongst the aspirations of some at the 1964 and 1989 conferences on OR and the social sciences, would be one where OR redoubles efforts to address social and political issues, pays vastly more attention to human behavior and becomes radically transformed into an applied social science focusing on tackling *messy* and *wicked* problems that arise in these domains.

I do not think either of these futures is likely to come about, although from past experience the first seems more probable than the second. Recklessly ignoring the hazards of crystal ball gazing, I will suggest what I think is most likely to happen and, abandoning impartiality, why I consider this would be a good thing.

The future for OR in general, and of behavioral OR in particular, will be continue to be a result of the interplay of the future demands of its clients and the future supply of the knowledge and skills of its practitioners. There seems likely to be increasing client demand for attention to behavioral aspects of situations, given the all-too-obvious results of ignoring these (e.g. bank failures). At the same time, there seems likely to be an increasing supply of analytical and modeling tools, drawing on a combination of steadily deepening insights from the cognitive and behavioral sciences, linked to insights from studies of complexity and networks and to the ever-expanding power of computing and availability of data, to enable much better analysis and modeling of human decisions and behavior, and driving a continuing rise in computational social science. This would not suggest a realization of either the "classical" or the "radical" scenario for OR outlined above but could lead to a future position somewhere between the two. (One reason that OR has fallen short of some of the grander hopes for its relationships with the social and political sciences may be that the gap between these and its home base in the physical and mathematical sciences was just too big to bridge—whereas a step to embrace the behavioral sciences looks much more manageable.)

Let me try to set this in a wider context, seen from the standpoint that OR has to draw its skills and knowledge from various disciplines (see e.g. Müller-Merbach 2009). I have previously suggested that if OR is to fulfill its mission as "the science of better", it needs to develop and proclaim a firmer intellectual and professional foundation as *system improvement science* for the real world and that this involves paying attention to all four panes of what I have described as the *Johari window for OR* (Royston 2013b, c)

## 18.4.2 The Johari Window of OR

The Johari window, as illustrated in Fig. 18.2a, was devised, back in the mid 1950s, by two US psychologists, Joseph Luft and Harrington Ingham (1955), to explore the fact that perception involves both the observed and the observer and that all of us have open and hidden parts.

The *open* window pane is the part of ourselves that both we and others see. The *hidden* window pane is our private space, which we know but others do not. The *blind* window pane is what others see but we are not aware of. The *unknown* is the part of us that is seen by neither ourselves nor others.

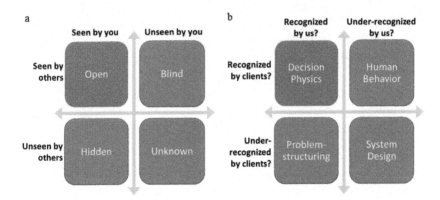

Fig. 18.2   The Johari window provides a wider view of OR. (a) The Johari window. (b) A Johari window for OR?

The Johari window was designed to illuminate interpersonal perception, but we can apply the idea to perceptions of OR (Royston 2013c). The *open* part would be the traditional part of OR—quantitative analysis in routing, scheduling, packing etc.—what I have called *decision physics*. The *hidden* part might be the *softer* parts of OR—clients often don't see that we can help with framing and structuring problems, not just with crunching numbers. The behavioral aspects of issues seem often to be our *blind* part—the aspects overlooked in OR's general focus on modeling the *physics* rather than the *psychology* of situations. Finally, a candidate for the *unknown* part might be our work on *system design*—a high proportion of OR is about this, but we often seem to give little recognition to or publicity for that work of synthesis compared to our analytical work on decision making, and so we run the risk of being unaware of relevant key concepts and skills and of our clients' overlooking or underestimating our contributions of this type.

The Johari window perspective suggests that OR needs to embody all four of these panes and to ensure they are in the visible *open* quadrant. Of the three panes that appear not to be fully positioned as they should be, the one on human behavior looks in most need of urgent attention. I suggest therefore that the development of behavioral OR is the most

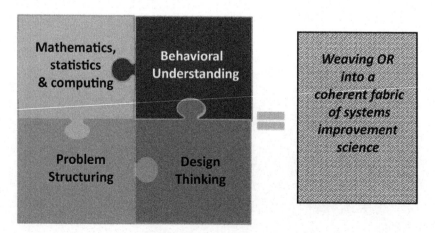

Fig. 18.3 Behavioral understanding is a key thread in a coherent fabric of OR

pressing and important element of building OR as a visibly coherent real world science of systems improvement (Fig. 18.3).

## 18.4.3 A Few Last Words

Such a development will of course not take place without a lot of thought and effort. In particular, it will require some major enhancements to education and training in OR which, with some exceptions where courses are offered on decision science, typically pay scant attention to areas such as cognitive or behavioral science. Some reframing of education and training in OR, so it first focuses on the problems of improving systems and only then addresses the tools most required for this, would do a lot to get things moving in the right direction, not least because it would indicate what elements of behavioral science should feature most prominently in an articulated "science of better".

It may be objected that there is insufficient room for this in a crowded academic syllabus. Less space may need to be allocated to some old favorites to make room for the new. So here is a suggested test for any candidate module, **new or old**: *"How much will this add to equipping a student of OR to fulfill our mission of improving complex systems in the 'real world'—systems which generally include sentient beings as well as inanimate objects?"*

There may be some qualms not just over the educational and training challenges of such change but also over the ethical ones. One of the participants at the 1989 conference on OR and the Social Sciences voiced concerns about behavioral science being "inherently manipulative on behalf of the dominant sections of society" (Rosenhead in Jackson et al. 1989, p. 92). Others may take a more positive view. However, it would seem wise to note the words written by Richard Thaler (2015) at the end of his book about behavioral economics:

*Whenever anyone asks me to sign a copy of* Nudge, *I always add the phrase "nudge for good". … Businesses or governments with bad intentions can use the findings of the behavioral sciences for self-serving purposes … Behavioral scientists have a lot of wisdom to offer to help make the world a better place. Let's use their wisdom by carefully selecting nudges based on science, and then subjecting these interventions to rigorous tests.*

"Behavioral OR for good" does not seem such a bad slogan!

Where might this all lead to in, say, the next decade or two? Paradoxically, success in this enterprise could mean that behavioral OR would eventually cease being seen as a separate branch of OR. Greater attention to and analysis of cognitive and behavioral factors in our work, and fuller incorporation of them in our models, may simply become part and parcel of how OR is done. I think that is how it should be. The legacy of behavioral OR will have been making a vital contribution to putting the "science of better" on a firmer, more coherent, conceptual and practical base and enhancing, maybe even transforming, the capability and reputation of operational research for improving the design, delivery and performance of systems and processes in the real world.

# References

Abbott, A. 1988. *The system of professions.* Chicago: University of Chicago Press.

Abdel-Malek, L., C. Wolf, F. Johnson, and T. Spencer III. 1999. OR practice: Survey results and reflections of practising INFORMS members. *Journal of the Operational Research Society* 50: 994–1003.

Ackoff, R.L. 1979a. The future of operational research is past. *Journal of the Operational Research Society* 30: 93–104.

Ackoff, R.L. 1979b. Resurrecting the future of operational research. *Journal of the Operational Research Society* 30: 189–199.

Baines, T., S. Mason, P.O. Siebers, and J. Ladbrook. 2004. Humans: The missing link in manufacturing simulation? *Simulation Modelling Practice and Theory* 12: 515–526.

Bendoly, E., W. Van Wezel, and D.G. Bachrach (eds.). 2015. *The handbook of behavioral operations management: Social and psychological dynamics in production and service settings.* New York: Oxford University Press.

Blackett, P.M.S. 1962. Scientists at the operational level (reprinted from 1941). In *Studies of war*, 171–176. Edinburgh: Oliver and Boyd.

Boothroyd, H. 1978. *Articulate intervention.* London: Taylor and Francis.

Budiansky, S. 2013. *Blackett's war.* New York: Knopf.

Calman, K., and G. Royston. 1997. Risk language and dialects. *British Medical Journal* 315: 939–942.

Chen, H., R.H.L. Chiang, C.H. Lindner, and V.C. Storey. 2012. Business intelligence and analytics: From big data to big impact. *MIS Quarterly Special Issue on Business Intelligence Research* 36: 1165–1188.

Drucker, P.F. 1977. *Management*. London: Pan.

Dutton, J.M., and R.E. Walton. 1964. Operational research and the behavioural sciences. *Operational Research Quarterly* 15: 207–217.

Eden, C. 1988. Cognitive mapping. *European Journal of Operational Research* 36: 1–13.

Erdi, P. 2008. Complexity of the brain: Structure, function and dynamics. *Complexity Explained* 237–303.

Forrester, J.W. 1961. *Industrial dynamics*. Cambridge, MA: Productivity Press.

Forrester, J.W. 1969. *Urban dynamics*. Cambridge, MA: Productivity Pres.

Gigerenzer, G. 2014. What doctors need to know. In *Risk savvy*. London: Allen Lane.

Gigerenzer, G., and D.G. Goldstein. 1996. Reasoning the fast and frugal way: Models of bounded rationality. *Psychological Review* 103: 650–669.

Gigerenzer, G., and R. Selten, eds. 2001. Why and when do simple heuristics work? In *Bounded rationality: The adaptive toolbox*. Cambridge, MA: MIT Press.

Gino, F., and G. Pisano. 2008. Toward a theory of behavioral operations. *Manufacturing and Service Operations Management* 10: 676–691.

Goodeve, C. 1948. Operational research. *Nature* 164: 377–384.

Hämäläinen, R.P., J. Luoma, and E. Saarinen. 2013. On the importance of behavioral operational research: The case of understanding and communicating about dynamic systems. *European Journal of Operational Research* 228: 623–634.

Howard, R.A. 1966. Decision analysis: Applied decision theory. *Proceedings of the fourth international conference on operational research*, 55–71. New York: Wiley-Interscience.

Jackson, M.C., P. Keys, and S.A. Cropper (eds.). 1989. *Operational research and the social sciences*. New York: Plenum Press.

Kahneman, D. 2011. *Thinking fast and slow*. London: Allen Lane.

Keeney, R.L. 1992. *Value focused thinking*. Cambridge, MA: Harvard University Press.

Keeney, R.L., and H. Raiffa. 1976. *Decisions with multiple objectives*. New York: Wiley.

Kelly, G.A. 1955. *The theory of personal constructs*. New York: Norton.

Kirby, M.W. 2003. *Operational research in war and peace: The British experience from the 1930s to 1970*. London: Imperial College Press.

Lane, C., E. Munro, and E. Husemann. 2016. Blending systems thinking approaches for organisational analysis: reviewing child protection in England. *European Journal of Operational Research 251*(2): 613–623.

Lawrence, J.L. (ed.). 1966. *Operational research and the social sciences*. London: Tavistock.

Levitt, S.D., and S.J. Dubner. 2005. *Freakonomics*. London: Allen Lane.

Loch, C.H., and Y. Wu. 2007. Behavioral operations management. *Foundations and Trends in Technology, Information and Operations Management* 1: 121–232.

Luft, J., and H. Ingham. 1955. The Johari window, a graphic model of interpersonal awareness. *Proceedings of the western training laboratory in group development*. University of California, Los Angeles.

May, R.M., S.A. Levin, and G. Sugihara. 2008. Ecology for bankers. *Nature* 451: 893–895.

Meadows, D.H., D.L. Meadows, J. Randers, and W.W. Behrens III. 1972. *The limits to growth*. New York: Universe Books.

Miller, J.H., and S.E. Page. 2007. *Complex adaptive systems: An introduction to computational models of social life*. Princeton, NJ: Princeton University Press.

Mitchell, M. 2009. *Complexity: A guided tour*. Oxford: Oxford University Press.

Müller-Merbach, H. 2009. The interdisciplinary generalist. *Omega* 37: 495–496.

Ormerod, P. 1995. *Death to economics*. New York: Wiley.

Phillips, L.D. 1989. Decision analysis in the 1990s. In *Tutorial papers in operational research*, ed. A. Shahini and R. Stainton. Birmingham: Operational Research Society.

Raiffa, H. 1968. *Decision analysis*. Reading, MA: Addison-Wesley.

Ranyard, J.C., R.G. Coyle, and J.D.W. Morecroft, eds. 1999. System dynamics for policy, strategy and management education. *Special Issue of the Journal of the Operational Research Society 50*(4): 291–449.

Rosenhead, J. (ed.). 1989. *Rational analysis for a problematic world*. Chichester/New York: Wiley.

Royston, G. 1982. Fetal heart monitoring: A systems view. *Lancet* 319: 861.

Royston, G. 2013a. Operational research for the real world. *Journal of the Operational Research Society* 64: 793–804.

Royston, G. 2013b. *Uncovering the hidden world of OR- the secret science of systems improvement*, conference presentation at EURO26, Rome, July 2013.

availableviawww.theorsociety.com/Pages/Networking/DocumentRepository. aspx

Royston, G. 2013c. A Johari window for OR? www.theorsociety.com/Pages/ Feature/Feature201309Johari.aspx

Sastry, A., and J. Sterman. 1993. Desert island dynamics: An annotated guide to the essential system dynamics literature. In *Proceedings of the 1993 international system dynamics society conference*, eds. E. Zepeda and J. Machuca. Albany: System Dynamics Society.

Schön, D.A. 1983. *The reflective practitioner*. New York: Basic Books.

Simon, H.A. 1969. *The sciences of the artificial*, 3rd ed. Cambridge, MA: MIT Press.

Steenkamp, J.-B.E.M. 2000. Introduction to the special issue on marketing modelling on the threshold of the 21st century (editorial). *International Journal of Research in Marketing* 17: 99–104.

Sterman, J.D. 2008. Risk communication on climate: Mental models and mass balance. *Science* 322(5901): 532–533.

Sweeney, L.B., and J.D. Sterman. 2000. Bathtub dynamics: Initial results of a systems thinking inventory. *System Dynamics Review* 16(4): 249–286.

Thaler, R.H. 2015. *Misbehaving: The making of behavioral economics*. New York: Penguin.

Thaler, R.H., and C.R. Sunstein. 2008. *Nudge*. New Haven: Yale University Press.

Tufte, E.R. 1997. *Visual explanations: Images and quantities, evidence and narrative*. Cheshire: Graphics Press.

Xiaoping, Z., Z. Tingkuan, and L. Mengting. 2009. Modeling crowd evacuation of a building based on seven methodological approaches. *Building and Environment* 44: 437–445.

Zacharias, G.L., J. MacMillan, and S.B. Van Hemel, eds. 2008. *Behavioral modelling and simulation: From individuals to societies*, Committee on organizational modelling from individuals to societies, National Research Council. Washington, DC: The National Academies Press.

# Index

© The Editor(s) (if applicable) and The Author(s) 2016
M. Kunc et al. (eds.), *Behavioral Operational Research*,
DOI 10.1057/978-1-137-53551-1

Printed by Printforce, the Netherlands